Praise for the fiction work of William Fredrick Cooper

For the award winning, *Essence* magazine bestselling novel
"There's Always a Reason" (2007)

"There's Always a Reason" is a good read for anyone looking into
the psyche of the sensitive African-American male."
—*Ebony* MAGAZINE (MARCH 2007)

"William McCall's unapologetic emotional vulnerability forms
the book's refreshing heart and through him, [William Fredrick]
Cooper conveys both an understanding of and a frustration with the
games men and women play."
—*Publishers Weekly* (JANUARY 2007)

"Bringing out so many deep-rooted feelings as I was reading it, I
was so overwhelmed with emotion that I could barely see…"
—ZANE, *New York Times* BESTSELLING AUTHOR OF *Love Is Never
Painless, Afterburn, Addicted, Skyscraper* AND *Nervous* (JANUARY 2007)

"William Fredrick Cooper strokes his paper with heat and passion!
Heartfelt and intense! Seldom does a male writer dive so deeply into
the well of human emotion."
—TRACY PRICE-THOMPSON, 2005 WINNER OF THE ZORA NEALE
HURSTON/RICHARD WRIGHT AWARD FOR CONTEMPORARY FICTION

ONE
SEASON
(IN PINSTRIPES)

A MEMOIR

ALSO BY WILLIAM FREDRICK COOPER
There's Always a Reason
Six Days in January

ONE SEASON
(IN PINSTRIPES)

A MEMOIR

WILLIAM FREDRICK COOPER

SBI

STREBOR BOOKS

NEW YORK LONDON TORONTO SYDNEY

Strebor Books
P.O. Box 6505
Largo, MD 20792
http://www.streborbooks.com

ISBN 978-1-59309-354-9
ISBN 978-1-4516-0801-4 (ebook)
LCCN 2010940492

First Strebor Books trade paperback edition March 2011

Cover design: www.mariondesigns.com

10 9 8 7 6 5 4 3 2 1

Manufactured in the United States of America

For information regarding special discounts for bulk purchases,
please contact Simon & Schuster Special Sales at 1-866-506-1949
or business@simonandschuster.com

The Simon & Schuster Speakers Bureau can bring authors to your live event.
For more information or to book an event, contact the Simon & Schuster Speakers
Bureau at 1-866-248-3049 or visit our website at www.simonspeakers.com.

To Renard Manley
(May 6, 1948 – October 8, 2010)
You were the most courageous and loving man I ever met.
I'll always remember you, brother.
See you again, when God calls me home.

PROLOGUE:
THE PLANS GOD HAS FOR YOU

Unlike many of the stories I have written in my past, this one starts with a real-life protagonist, William Fredrick Cooper, at church.

Cleaning a church.

Dreams that come true always start with obedience to the Most High, even when you don't realize it.

But as with everything we do in life, only God knows the plans He has for all of us.

We're the last to know, what He wants us to know, when He wants us to know.

Such was the case in December 2008, when I took on a temporary assignment as a sexton at my dwelling place, Harlem's First Corinthian Baptist Church. Like a desert needing a torrential rainstorm in the worst way, I was desperate for some sort of income; any income. Let go from an Assistant Managing Clerk position at a midtown law firm in March 2008, my nine months of unemployment took me to South Carolina and back, looking for something, anything to restore order to a world in disarray.

"I got your back," Cheryl Smith, my future fiancée, said after my return, then turned her words to action by splitting her salary into two as I continued searching for work.

Going from agency to agency, I was met with the aftershocks of a failed Bush administration: No one was hiring clerks in the legal profession; in fact, many law firms were in the process of offering buyout and layoff packages to long-tenured employees. Even returning to my occupational roots by becoming a foot messenger for a day, I was unceremoniously canned after one day, because I was overqualified.

Through it all, my better half remained steadfast in her encouragement. But even then the wells once plentiful in supply slowly diminished; the resourceful waters having been replaced by growing debt, tension and frustration. Though nary a discouraging word was spoken, the shine in her eyes, once sparkling like enthusiastic diamonds, was slowly fading. The glow having been replaced by sadness, the new story was now of a woman growing weary of carrying a burden alone.

When you reach the end of your rope, that is when God swoops in, for you cannot be a vessel He can use if you are filled with resistance; and more importantly, too much of yourself. My favorite scripture, 2 Corinthians 4: 7-9 speaks of being in troubled, trying times while living in perplexing uncertainty, but knowing God will direct our steps when we've thrown our hands up. I seriously doubted that portion of Paul's letter to the Corinthian congregation on December 8, 2008, when my senior pastor, Michael A. Walrond, Jr., gave me the responsibility of maintaining a 50,000-square-foot, ninety-five-year-old landmark building, with a three-tier balcony and 1,800-seating capacity.

Having no prior cleaning experience, save the childhood experience of weekly mopping and waxing floors, cleaning restrooms and washing walls in my mother's Staten Island apartment, all I could rely on was God's strength, and hoped that He was happy with my efforts. After all, He had shown me in my literary travels that with a mustard seed of faith, I could accomplish anything.

So for nine-to-twelve-hour days for three months, (two of which were spent substituting for the absent/injured custodians) the Trustees of the church and I maintained the landmark building to the best of our abilities. And what began for me as a humbling experience turned into one of transformation; a healing place for my soul.

And mind.

And body.

And spirit.

Something I had been running from for years.

Something God was now forcing me to do.

Like a river running in many directions except the right way, I was so consumed in my efforts at becoming "the next big thing" in African-American literature that I forgot who was in charge of my life. Slowly losing my virtues and character while becoming obsessed with this endeavor, my poor judgment in terms of associations often led to critical mistakes when pursuing my dreams.

That should have been a strong indicator that I had morphed into someone I didn't recognize.

More importantly, I wasn't paying homage to the source behind my writing gift. While the purpose behind my books, delivering messages to adults about men of color and their feelings concerning issues of the heart, was pure, that my teenage daughter was unable to read some of my compositions should have delivered the message that I was astray. Maybe the reason why my literary success was uneven—each triumph was met with an even greater personal setback—should have screamed volumes.

Refusing to heed all warning signals that things were awry, perhaps the brutal things said about my character by literary peers, family and friends—words like "weak," "selfish," "self-absorbed," "pretentious," and "phony" were bandied about—and vicious, hurtful rumors that were shooting distress flares into the night should have said something.

Those things combined with a fragile psyche feeling unworthy of God's blessings of greatness led to the most bittersweet moment of my life:

On March 20, 2008, exactly one year after the publication release of my second novel, *There's Always A Reason*—and the very same week it made the April 2008 *Essence* magazine bestsellers list—I checked myself into New York Presbyterian Hospital. Battling an emotional meltdown, for two nights my life played like an endless movie. Running the good, bad and ugly of the past year, the film always ended with a blank screen, like some purpose in my life remained inconclusive.

Emotionally drained, a painful truth had to be faced: It was obvious that God wasn't steering my vessel to abundance. While my intentions were noble, my passion, career and life were like the Titanic after it hit that iceberg: sinking fast. Discombobulated while dwelling in defeat, dejection and despondency, debris and darkness surrounding my depression, God intervened just before I reached the bottom of an ocean of wasted talent, where many lay after the Most High has taken back His gift.

Taking refuge in His comforting embrace, hour upon hour was spent with Him in His sanctuary. Whether I was cleaning the church interior, shoveling snow outside during Sunday service in tears, praying in worship, or giving praise alone at the altar after a long day, I begged for one last chance with the gifts of love, life and passion He had blessed me with.

More importantly, help me be a better man, I asked Him repeatedly during those ninety days. And like a recovering alcoholic taking one day at a time, I asked Him daily for my continued growth.

In some weird way, after my assignment ended at First Corinthian Baptist Church in early March 2009, I felt like a new door was about to open in my life, one that I would stroll through and enjoy what appeared on the other side. About a week later, I came across an advertisement in the *New York Post* concerning maintenance work at the newly constructed Citi Field ballpark.

The home of the New York Mets, I sighed.

Though I was a New York Yankees fan at heart, at that particular juncture I was more of a fan of having a job.

Having no other options to weigh, I took the #7 train to Flushing, completed the application, and Express-mailed it before I returned home.

With this move, I had taken my first baby step on the path God was constructing.

When you take one step toward Him…

God takes two to you.

How else could I explain the phone call I received from the Alliance/First Quality Maintenance Management Company while playing Scrabble one Saturday afternoon three weeks later, telling me to report to *the new Yankee Stadium*?

"It would be an honor to work there," was my instinctive response. While those words escaped me, the words "pride," "tradition" and "excellence" flowed through my mind. So many recollections of my youth flashed before me: early morning high school sports arguments in the cafeteria over breakfast; Phil Rizzuto birthday wishes to any and everyone over eighty during the WPIX-11 television broadcasts; trips to the old stadium by way of my *Staten Island Advance* newspaper route in the late 1970s; and how I baffled high school gym teachers and local sportswriters with my extensive knowledge of sports history along the way.

And with this job, I concluded, I would finally be able to contribute my small part to its storied history.

Arriving early at the new stadium on April 1st, I took a ten-minute walk around the place before entering. The stadium exterior, a sturdy combination of limestone, granite and concrete, featured the building's name above each gate entrance in bold V-cut and gold-leaf letters. One particular opening, the GATE 4 entrance, was more prominent than others. Accentuated by its concrete, dark gray background, the famous interlocking NY insignia appeared on the ground.

This must be for premium season-ticket holders, I deduced.

Completing my tour on River Avenue, I saw a blue "Housekeeping Entrance" sign and the long line of future colleagues. Eventually inside, the three hundred or so applicants that were chosen out of over five thousand were seated in right centerfield section 103 for orientation. Immediately noticing that the seat width and leg room was wider than at the *House That Ruth Built*, a three-minute scan of the surroundings told me that *Jeter's House* incorporated many of the elements that made the previous stadium so special.

Adorning the interior of the stadium were hundreds of photographs capturing the history of the Yankees. The grandstand seating, beautiful in its rich blue, stretched well beyond the left- and right-field foul poles.

In contrast from the original Yankee Stadium lay the seating tiers. Inversely opposed to the stacked appearance of yore, the Field, Main, Upper and Grandstand Levels spread outward like a rising bowl, placing the paying customers further back from the playing field, but *lower* to it. In sacrificing seats for better sightlines and more leg room (in 2008, the seating capacity at the Old Stadium was 57,936; the second coming seats an approximate total of 51,000), about two-thirds of the stadium seating looked to be in the Field and Main levels.

Peering upward in wide-eyed admiration, I gawked in awe at the re-created trademark that lined the roof of the new facility. Restored in its entirety to a familiar location, the frieze at the apex of the original Yankee Stadium from 1923-1973 was replicated perfectly, yet enhanced with steel and zinc to protect it from rust. (In the original stadium, the frieze was copper.) Returning my vision to the bleacher seats, I loved the space behind the white walls that showed #4 subway trains as they passed by, just like at the old place.

Another throwback from the old Stadium was the manually operated auxiliary scoreboard built into the left- and right-field fences. Seeing it situated in the same locations it existed in the pre-renovation model of the old ballpark, the image of Don Larsen's ninety-seventh and his last pitch of his '56 World Series perfect game immediately came to mind.

Modern machinery, construction and technology meets the Yankee way, I enthusiastically concluded. Oblivious to the dreary morning sky and numb to the drizzle coming down, the kid in me couldn't stop taking pictures of the ballpark on my cell phone. Once I finished soaking in the novelty of my surroundings, those childhood memories and high hopes I owned were replaced with the fortune of having a job.

About ten or so minutes later, another reality set in...by way of the responsibilities of the job. After Alliance Company President Michael Rodriguez detailed his ambitious journey from high school flunky to affluent business guru and how it could happen to anyone of us present, one by one the many Alliance staff supervisors addressed the daily upkeep of this big ballpark in the Bronx.

Speaking in English and Spanish, their tongues translated an authoritative unison. Painting a truthful picture about what the maintenance positions entailed—restroom cleaning assignment responsibilities; the daily wipe down of the Yankee Stadium seats section by section; the power-washing and scrub-brushing of everything concrete; massive wipe downs of the many blue stadium columns; major squeegee work on rainy days; the transport of large bins of food and trash to garbage and recycling dumpsters—the brush they used on the job description disrupted my rose-colored canvas.

From their view, being a maintenance attendant at the new Yankee Stadium was a monotonous mixture of madness in janitorial, custodial and sanitation form.

"We want this stadium looking brand-new every day," one of the main bosses sternly directed. Then he gave the ultimate marching order: we were instructed to focus on the job, not what happened between the white lines of the beautiful baseball diamond in their background. The intimidating manner in which he, and the ensuing controllers, spoke altered that initial feeling I had of being blessed.

Surveying the blue seats and studying the faces of my colleagues, I wondered if anyone else shared the feeling of discouragement now running through me.

In return, I saw listless looks of defiance, hopelessness and "I'm-just-here-for-the-paycheck" mentalities.

In different shades and ethnicities, the pain was the same.

I don't know about this, I texted to Cheryl.

Give it a shot, came her reply. *God wouldn't put you in a position to fail, William. He has you here so you can glorify Him, with your goodness and love. Remember our mission statement at Church. It applies to everything we do.*

The passion in her text leapt from the screen and into my heart, causing me to recite the declaration.

We are an ever-evolving community of visionaries and dreamers who have been CALLED BY GOD to live the lives we were created to live; COMMANDED BY GOD to love beyond the limits of our prejudices; and COMMISSIONED BY GOD to serve!

For the next five minutes, the last portion of our statement, *COMMISSIONED BY GOD to serve*, blocked out the voices of the supervisors. Forming a protective shield from the pain-filled neighboring eyes and destroying whatever cynical thoughts I may have developed about what lay ahead, a smile fortified by faith creased my face. The task, as unenviable as it may have been to many of the people sitting in those stadium seats—including me for a short span—was an opportunity given by God for me to shine.

And given the dreary unemployment climate, I was grateful.

From that point forward, I approached job responsibilities with a mentality to serve, with everything that God had given me to work with. The road ahead would have its bumps and potholes, but I was determined to make the experience fun to whoever crossed my path.

Feeling blessed to be a Yankees fan working the inaugural season at this new stadium, I thanked my Heavenly Father for this opportunity with a quick prayer.

Once that mindset was established, the very next day God again intervened. After being given a maintenance uniform (blue slacks, pinstriped blue shirt, matching bowtie and vest with the Yankees logo) I was assigned to a men's room area in left field.

Immediately, I went to the maintenance office for supplies.

"Where do I find the cleaning agents for my restroom?" I asked.

A distinguished-looking gentleman wearing a blue suit with thin white pinstripes, one I would later find out was an administrative official from the company's Manhattan office, looked me over imperceptibly, searching my eyes for sincerity.

Then he turned in the direction of one of his well-dressed peers.

"Do you think he's cool?" he asked his partner.

Fighting off a sudden rise in my heartbeat, *cool for what?* I thought.

Before his colleague could utter a word, he faced me once more and said, "Come with me."

With a blatant hesitance, "Are you sure he can handle it?" the other man asked coyly.

"I think so," his partner responded.

Growing weary of all the "around-me-but-not-to-me" chatter, I finally spoke.

"With all due respect, could you let me in on the decision process? Maybe I can share some input about who I am."

Where that query came from is anyone's guess, but in hindsight, the direct yet professional manner in which the words left me served as confirmation to the powers-that-were.

Smiling, the brown-haired Caucasian man, now proud that he endorsed his own intuitiveness, escorted me down a stairway, then through a long, concrete tunnel-like corridor. Though his name presently escapes me, he introduced himself and told me about the sudden reassignment to the 000 level of the stadium.

"I think you can handle the cleaning responsibilities of this area, William. Many of the players' families will come by, and on occasion you'll see a celebrity or two."

"I'm honored that you chose me," I humbly replied.

Taking me to a premium, all-inclusive lounge area along the first base line complete with private restrooms, high-definition television monitors and grab-and-go dining foods, The *Ketel One* Lounge became home number one. Working there during the season's introductory batting practice and two exhibition games against the Chicago Cubs—both Yankee victories, I might add—I established an immediate rapport with the bartenders, waiters, security guards and fellow cleaning colleagues.

Chris, aka Buddy Love, one of the recycling dumpster runners, and I connected immediately. A holdover from the old stadium, his smooth wit, innate sense of humor and easy rapport eased away whatever trepidation I may have owned about my promotion.

"You're the 'Chosen One,'" he kept calling me that Saturday after-noon. "There's something special about you."

Startled while lowering my head in humility, "You think so, man?" I mumbled.

"Pick your head up, brother. You have what it takes, man. I can just tell."

Hearing those words was like good gumbo for my soul, though on this particular game day, I couldn't visualize his assumption:

April 4 was a tough one.

About the seventh inning of the exhibition game versus the Cubs, a part of the sewage system malfunctioned, causing half of the lounge to be flooded with water, urine and...

Let's just say it wasn't a fun day.

Trying to clean as much of it as I could, sadly my efforts were futile.

But they weren't unnoticed. On April 15, a day before the home opener, I was moved once more, into the lower level of an exclusive area demanding premium cleaning and care.

In an irony that paralleled Yankees lore, I was the benefactor of some timely fortune: Like Lou Gehrig substituting for Wally Pipp, I was replacing someone who had called in sick.

"Do you want to man this area during the season?" Angel Chavez, my new supervisor, asked me. "It'll take a lot of work to clean this place."

Not wanting to usurp the job of another, I hedged.

"What about…"

"Don't worry about him," Angel assured me. "I like your work ethic."

Like the office representative, he, too, went on a hunch. However, upon closer examination, maybe, just maybe, he, too, was a sign from above.

After all, his name was *Angel*.

God sure works in many mysterious ways.

Surveying the spacious lower region of the restaurant, then the dimly lit restroom, its five ceramic urinals and three stalls, I paused for five seconds, said my fastest prayer ever, then smiled at my boss.

"Let's do it," I responded.

Finally adjusted to the rigorous details of my occupation, it wasn't one behind a desk like in my past, but it was a job nonetheless.

Unbeknownst to me, it was the beginning of a season where dreams came true.

HOME SWEET HOME? 1

Moving slowly along the infield grass of a brisk November evening, the ground ball hit by Philadelphia Phillies outfielder Shane Victorino took forever to reach second baseman Robinson Cano. In those precious milliseconds before the World Series-clinching putout was recorded and Queen's "We are The Champions" replaced Frank Sinatra's *New York* theme throughout the stadium, I tried to imagine what Joe DiMaggio must have felt in 1936, or Derek Jeter some sixty years later.

Like those pinstripe legends, I was a rookie with my favorite professional sports team, the New York Yankees, and about to celebrate a world championship.

To say that my one season working as a maintenance attendant in the exclusive Legends Suite Club at the new Yankee Stadium was merely a job is a tremendous understatement. Right at the season's inception, from those initial April exhibition games against the Chicago Cubs, a voice from *somewhere* told me that I would be part of a special experience that would alter the course of my life. Principal Owner George Steinbrenner had built the Yankees a spanking new, $1.5 billion construction complete with state-of-the-art amenities, and Alliance/First Quality Management, the cleaning company contracted to maintain the newness of the ballpark, stationed me in the lower men's restroom of their exclusive, bi-level restaurant.

Cognizant of the less-than-glamorous duties that came with the position, I felt fortunate to have been chosen to provide service in one of the most important venues of the sports ground; for the Legends Suite Club was a breathtaking provider of service that transcended any entertainment or dining venue. Embodying the spirit of *The House That Ruth Built* by blending Yankees tradition with the new millennium, seeing a century's worth of Yankees images posted throughout the extravagant event space made employees and patrons feel as if they were a small part of history.

Discussing that point with Kevin Michaels, a Yankees historian masquerading as a Legends bartender, I could see from the gleam in his eyes that he too had taken residence in pinstripe paradise.

"Man, this makes up for all those games I longed to go to," I told him Opening Day.

"I want to show you something," Kevin responded. Flipping open his cellular phone, he punched the keys that led to his pictures section and showed me two bleacher seats from the old stadium.

"These cost me a pretty penny," he crowed.

"Trust me, buddy, this season you'll get back your return handsomely."

Sharing a knowing smile, we embraced.

A black man from Jersey City, New Jersey and a bearded white man from Suffolk County, walking different lives yet on the precipice of sharing a season-long bond of Yankees love through trivia tests, T-shirts and championship pins. As if our union was ordained, I had found a kindred spirit, a blood brother in faith willing to join me on the magic carpet ride.

What was the color of the blood running through our veins?

Yankee Blue, of course.

For me, the opportunity to contribute to the hallmark of greatness that was the New York Yankees for one season was a dream come true. And with that honor came the responsibility of making all that I associated with feel right at home in that restroom.

After all, I thought, *we're family*.

And sometimes being part of a family means recognizing that its members need reassurance that no matter what happened in the upcoming baseball season, it would be one to remember. Sensing the trepidation of Yankees season ticket-holders paying exorbitant prices, supreme optimism and faith shielded the nervousness I possessed about the task ahead.

Besides, I knew the Bronx Bombers had history on their side: Herb Pennock, Joe Dugan, Wally Pipp, Bob Meusel and some guy named George Herman Ruth christened the Old Stadium with a world championship in 1923, some eighty-six years earlier when John McGraw evicted the future dynasty from the Polo Grounds.

Despite this nugget of information, I could understand the tension many felt: After an off-season in which the Yankees missed the playoffs for the first time in thirteen years; and the management threw caution to the wind and shelled out almost a half-billion dollars on free agents C.C. Sabathia, A.J. Burnett and Mark Teixeira, anything short of a 40th American League Pennant and 27th World Championship banner flying amongst the façade would have been unacceptable.

Championship perfection was also the expectation of the hundred or so servers, busboys, hosts, in-seat waiters, the Food Network performance cooking chefs, kitchen staff, bartenders and maintenance team of the Legends Hospitality LLC unit, as per the directive of its manager, Margaret Ann Quinlan. Firmly entrenched in her commitment to excellence by way of thirty-plus years of experience, the woman affectionately known as "Mugsy" preached chemistry, togetherness and teamwork all season long during her inspirational pre-shift meetings. Wanting the whole staff to be a shining example of the very best Yankee Stadium offered to ownership, CEOs, entertainers and hard-working season-ticket holders, the end result was a finely tuned two-tiered, dining extravaganza that made for an evening of comfort watching what Yankees faithfuls hoped would be the best team in baseball.

Or so we hoped.

Many positive feelings for the upcoming season were transformed to cynicism and fear with the March 5th report of Alex Rodriguez's torn hip labrum. That he would miss the first twenty-eight games only added insult to a rapidly diminished legacy in desperate need of an overhaul. Already mired in grinding times, his mid-winter encore to a 2008 season where he was a magnet of distractions and turmoil was the startling revelation, then tearful admission, of a failed steroids test five years earlier.

A Hall-of-Fame reputation has gone up in smoke, with a torn hip to boot. What a way to start a season, embattled Yankees Manager Joe Girardi must have thought. A man of strong Christian faith, he too, was under intense scrutiny. Replacing former skipper Joe Torre, a man whose resume had ten American East Titles, six American League Pennants, four World Series Championship Rings and a postseason berth for all twelve years he managed the Bronx Bombers, Girardi's inaugural campaign at the helm of sports' most successful franchise consisted of 89 wins, a third-place finish in the American League East, and a spot next to me on my sofa as we watched the playoffs without pinstripes for the first time since 1993.

With all the money spent on the new ballpark and player acquisitions, he understood the unspoken ultimatum:

This was the first year in a fancy, pricey new stadium.

A half-billion dollars of new talent was brought into the fold.

The Yankees had a third-place finish in the best division in baseball in 2008.

You had better win the damn thing this year.

Or else.

Other than Mayor Bloomberg, Joe Girardi was easily the most watched man in a city that never sleeps.

While many fans were blown away by the wide array of services in this new version of the old stadium, many of the guys relieving themselves in my home away from home wanted to take their eyes off the product on the field; especially after the Yankees' opening series to the Cleveland Indians. Bookending a 6-5 Friday afternoon victory were two humiliating losses. Our 10-2 homecoming loss on April 16th had fans emptying out before the seventh-inning stretch after the Tribe put up a nine-spot in the top of the frame.

"I paid all this money for this?" one patron asked sarcastically.

"It's a long season," I responded while cleaning out a flooded stall. *(How's that for stadium initiation?)* "Have some faith, man." Before that first home game, I boldly said to all that I hoped our season would end on November 4 or 5, with us winning that last game for our 27th World Championship and holding our seventh Commissioner's Trophy. (The trophy, initially awarded to the last team standing in baseball in 1967, was given to the Yankees in 1977, 1978, 1996, 1998, 1999 and 2000.)

After a 22-4 nationally televised embarrassment two days later left the Yankees with a .500 record (6-6), my autumn aspirations looked particularly gloomy. Playing a mock psychotherapist when the Indians lit up a struggling Chein Ming-Wang and others in a 55-minute, 13-hit, 14-run second inning, I heard many a disgruntled fan voice their displeasure in that men's room that afternoon.

"Two hundred million doesn't get you very much these days," one man said.

"We better make the playoffs this year, or I won't be back," another added.

Calmly hearing the frustrations of many, then, bravely speaking optimism to the early-season cynics, "It's a long season," I again encouraged to all that listened.

Others, finding solace in the exquisite services provided in the Legends Club, shared in my levity by accepting consolation hugs.

Oprah Winfrey would have been proud of the many I talked down from their ledges.

Somehow, I knew the Yankees would be okay. Despite early season heroics by outfielders Johnny Damon, Nick Swisher and Melky Cabrera, slumps (Mark Teixeira: 3 home runs, 10 RBIs and a Mendoza-line .200 Batting Average, C.C. Sabathia's 1-3 record in his first four starts); injuries (Jorge Posada, Ian Kennedy, Chein Ming-Wang, Brian Bruney, Damaso Marte, Xavier Nady and Jose Molina were all disabled); home rainouts; and losing skids (which included five straight defeats at the hands of the hated Boston Red Sox, something that hadn't occurred in twenty-four years) left many impatient fans wondering if the team would ever locate its groove.

A rare blown save by Mariano Rivera (via back-to-back ninth-inning homers by Tampa Bay Ray stars Carl Crawford and Evan Longoria) in an 8-6 loss left the team in fourth place in the AL East with a 13-15 record, some 5-1/2 games behind the first-place Toronto Blue Jays. Further amplifying the early-season woes was a sluggish 6-7 record in their new abode, the *House That George Built* them.

Skip Bayless, a well-respected sports columnist turned contro-versially opinionated debater on ESPN's *First Take* show, gleefully predicted on his *First and 10* segment of the program that the Yankees wouldn't make the playoffs, even audaciously suggesting that Joe Girardi might be fired by mid-season.

And to top it all off, the archenemy Boston Red Sox were surging.

The outlook on a season filled with promise looked bleak, and a bad taste was forming in the mouths of an entire organization.

The date was May 7.

On May 8, one swing of a bat by a tormented man determined to reclaim everything he had lost turned it all around.

FINDING THEIR STRIDE...

How did the Yankees jump-start their season?

The answer is simple.

With a single swing.

A single swing coming from a man searching for peace and happiness.

On his first swing of the season, at the very first pitch he saw.

Amazing.

That one word describes the skill set of a man, when focused and hungry, rivals St. Louis Cardinal slugger Albert Pujols as the most imposing hitter in the game.

That man was Alex Rodriguez.

What goes through the mind of superstar baseball player stepping up to home plate for the first time, twenty-eight games into a season after arthroscopic hip surgery? Could he be effective, or would he be a shell of the player he once was? Could he remove the stain of a damaged legacy and restore credibility under harsh media scrutiny? Could he overcome destructive chatter his name brought after a year of being a tabloid punch line?

With a team steeped in winning tradition, one would think that redemption stories wearing Yankees pinstripes are hard to find.

However, they do exist.

One account that comes to mind is pitcher Ralph Terry. Best remembered for serving up the Game 7 round-tripper to Bill Mazeroski that won the 1960 World Series for the Pittsburgh Pirates, the Yankees' gods smiled on him two years later. Given the ball in another Game 7 against the San Francisco Giants, he did some serious soul-searching and took the mound with a fierce determination in his eyes.

Silencing a raucous Candlestick Park crowd, he wasn't a San Francisco treat that afternoon. Completely stifling the home team's powerful lineup, he went into the bottom of the ninth inning protecting a slim 1-0 lead. Giants pinch hitter Matty Alou led off the frame with a bunt base hit. After striking out the next two batters, Willie Mays laced a hard double into the right-field corner, putting the tying and series-winning runs in scoring position.

Facing Willie McCovey with two outs, Terry's second-pitch fastball was hit on the button by the Giants' slugger, who later said it was the hardest ball he ever hit.

Initially, the line drive appeared headed to right field, over the head of second baseman Bobby Richardson.

Would Ralph Terry be a goat once more?

Intervening quickly, the Yankees' gods said *no*. Not allowing Terry to revisit Heartbreak Hotel, somehow the hard-hit missile sank fast, and Richardson made the catch without leaping to end the game and series.

Yankees redemption, on that October day in 1962, was named Ralph Terry.

And on May 8, 2009, nearly forty-seven years later, a special season-long meal of redemption was prepared by the Bronx Bombers for the rest of the American League. One person in particular, Alex Rodriguez, began serving the dish with one incredible appetizer in Camden Yards.

Lee Riley, the father of Hall of Fame basketball Coach Pat Riley, once said, "Somewhere, someplace, sometime, you're going to have to plant your feet, make a stand and kick some ass. And when that time comes, you do it." As a first-inning, 97-mile-per-hour fastball from Baltimore pitcher Jeremy Guthrie approached A-Rod, you couldn't help wonder if during his Colorado rehabilitative stint, his girlfriend, Kate Hudson, had given him Riley's *Fire From Within* novel as reading material.

Maybe he simply realized that it's an honor being able to play the game of baseball at the highest level.

Or, maybe, just maybe, those screaming Oriole fans seated behind home plate in Camden Yards waving rubber foam syringes pissed him the hell off; so much so that he felt the need to shut those sonofabitches up with action.

They pissed A-Rod off so much that a combination of past frustrations and a newfound focus resulted in a swing unencumbered by months of personal baggage; a swing that not only produced solid contact, but put Major League Baseball on notice with this message:

To cynics, pundits, and whomever this may concern:

I am Alex Rodriguez, and my chosen identity is that of a baseball player. Contrary to the reports of my demise, not only am I focused on being a great one, I'm also trying to be the best teammate that I can be. More importantly, I'll be the best human being I can be, and go from there. You can conjure up my past all you want, but you won't see where I, or the New York Yankees, are going.

Peace.

Leaping up from my living room sofa in my Jersey City apartment, I watched the ball land in the left-field seats some 375 feet away. Unable to stifle screams of amazement, that intuitive thought I owned about something magic in the Yankee air was confirmed.

My fiancée, Cheryl, positioned in the back of our railroad flat listening to gospel music, ran into the room.

"Are you okay?" she asked, her eyes wide-eyed in worry.

Smiling, my response was this: "God must be up to something very special, honey."

After telling her about A-Rod's storybook start to the season, with the coolness I have known and loved throughout our journey together through life, all she said was this:

"So when are you going to write a book about the season? You know as well as I do that the Yankees are going to win the whole thing."

Looking at her with a scary, maybe-you've-been-reading-your-Bible-too-much-look, I shook my head.

"I wouldn't go that far just yet," I responded.

She then quoted a scripture that stayed with me throughout the season.

"Faith is the substance of things hoped for, and the evidence in things not yet seen."

"Hebrews 11:1, Cheryl. And…"

With a sly yet glittering grin, as if she knew something I didn't, "Enjoy the game, baby," she said in an unfamiliar, tender tone.

Now at this point, I know you readers are thinking exactly what I was at that moment. The following letter, written in my mind, went as follows:

Cheryl Faye Smith,

I've known you for years, and we've had a relationship over the years that transcended logic. In fact, one might say that we rival the union of Spencer Tracy and Katharine Hepburn in that only those two knew the depth of their connection, and couldn't give a damn about what others thought. I love you with all my heart, so that gives me the right to say, in complete, transparent honesty, what I think.

I think that you're nuts.

Now your temporary insanity does not diminish my affection for you. But your May prognostication of Yankees victory in November based solely on faith is, dare I say, unrealistic.

Baby, baseball is a funny game. Big innings and rallies end with sudden swiftness, as one swing of the bat can produce two, and on those rarest of occasions, three outs. Perfect games and no-hitters aplenty, defeat can be snatched away from the jaws of sure victory with homers, hits, errors, balks, blunders and Lord knows what else; for each day on the diamond brings joy for one team and pain for the opposing squad. Crowds that have cheered in anticipation of baseball's ultimate victory have been rendered moot, mute and melancholy in milliseconds.

The beauty of baseball is in that wonderful three-hour-a-day roller-coaster experience that lasts from the onset of spring till the leaves fall in autumn. America is addicted to the agony and ecstasy between the lines of its diamond, and nothing illustrates this more than the euphoria players, coaches, an entire organization, its rowdy fans, and an entire city feels when the last team standing after 162 regular season games and eleven postseason cliffhangers is the team from your city.

But you can't predict who's going to win the whole thing in May, that's all.

So again I state, while the conviction of your prediction might be a little off, I still love you.

Love Always,

William

So there I was, about to lick my mental envelope and leave the missive on a pillow next to Cheryl with a rose; when a funny thing happened.

Following A-Rod's spectacular cue, C.C. Sabathia pitched a complete game, four-hit shutout.

And a five-game Yankees losing streak was gone, just like that.

Alex Rodriguez, a constant point of interest once obsessed with securing his place amongst baseball's greats, took self-inventory while in Colorado and decided to do things differently in 2009. Liberated from a lifetime's worth of drama crammed into twelve months, he felt a need to be "just one of the guys."

And in this one instance, being Clark Kent and fitting in with a team instead of trying too hard to carry one, was a whole lot better than wearing a kryptonite green Superman outfit tailored by a media looking for its next story.

Something else happened with that swing: the switch to a dark room that was the Yankees' season to that point was located. Flicked on, the missing piece to an incomplete jigsaw puzzle was immediately found, and things fell into place for the team as a whole.

The deep early-season fog now lifted, our Yankees started to jell.

This season's about to get interesting, I muttered aloud. Our next home stand couldn't come soon enough.

That would start on May 15. Returning to the stadium for a 10-game stretch with a .500 record (17-17), the Bombers increased a modest two-game win streak at the expense of the Minnesota Twins. Developing a penchant for in-the-nick-of-time heroics, the Yankees had three straight walk-off victories that weekend, courtesy of Melky Cabrera (two-run single), Alex Rodriguez and Johnny Damon (game-winning homers). Every win in their final at-bat was punctuated with a celebratory "pie-in-the-face" towel of whipped cream, compliments of pitcher A.J. Burnett.

Completing the series sweep on Monday with another triumph, three more wins against the Orioles followed, and the winning streak swelled to nine games.

Another incredible thing that happened around this time the Yankees were finding their stride was the connection being made with many of the season ticket holders whenever they visited my restroom.

In hindsight, the common link to us all was the New York Yankees.

But, oh, what a connection it was.

Before working at the new Yankee Stadium, a small part of me couldn't understand why fans paid stratospheric amounts of money for expensive season-tickets. But the more I interacted with people from all walks of life: Former Yankees ballplayers and executives, entertainers and celebrities, professional athletes from other sports, CEOs of some of America's major companies, Armed Services officials, major city politicians, and fellow colleagues in service, one thing became clear to me: The baseball team at River Avenue and 161st Street in the Bronx united us all.

And like a fairy tale under construction, the shared romanticism for the New York Yankees brought us together to share what could be a special moment in all of our lives.

Young and old, black and white, the haves and have-nots: they all love the New York Yankees. Rich, poor and everyone in between live or die with every pitch, fielding gem, blown-save opportunity or game-winning home run. While doctors, movie directors and dentists engaged in animated debates about team strategy, bartenders and construction workers argued with the affluent about the definition of a "True Yankee" and the unique toughness needed to, in Sinatra's words, "make it here."

Just the way I studied their history through the years like it was a required lifetime course, the man owning an important role in society may not have, yet loves the Bronx Bombers so much he's willing to pay the hefty ransom for as many games in the beautiful new ballpark as possible.

And there's absolutely nothing wrong with the indulgence of watching the best team in professional sports in the best seats money can buy.

Additionally, in those seats lay business opportunities as well. Simultaneously enjoying a perennial winning franchise and utilizing networking skills, an important transaction can be completed; or, alternatively, a key client acquisition can be garnered because of a mutual passion: the players in those pinstripes.

The rich history of the New York Yankees resides in many of us, so much so that we'll go to great lengths to maintain this passionate love fest. Words cannot fully describe the joy that filled my bones when father, son, and many times *an entire family* visited me in my deluxe "hole-in-the-wall" completely decked out in pinstriped paraphernalia. The beauty of seeing generations of Yankees fans coming together to enjoy: a dining experience from the best chefs our city offered; the thrill of our new ballpark; and of course, the daily excellence of Derek Jeter, Jorge Posada and the rest of my favorite team, sent chills down my spine. Hearing the amazing tales of lore from elder statesmen about Ruth, Gehrig, Dickey, DiMaggio, Rizzuto, Berra, Mantle, Ford, Munson and Jackson were illuminating and inspirational. Interacting with fans that were in attendance at some of baseball's most historic games, and living vicariously through their exciting memories, did more to my spirit than you can ever imagine.

It was easy for me to transform what one might view as a thankless job of restroom attendant into an exhilarating experience, because I am a passionate Yankees Fan that inhaled its hallowed tradition, exhaled the love I possess for the organization, and thoroughly enjoyed the presence of finding a long-lost extended family.

And when in the company of family, people you love, making them feel right at home is innate.

Finding joy in helping people wash their hands, cleaning a floor, commode or the restaurant's lower level (*family always needs a clean home*, I surmised); exchanging passionate hi-fives; remaining animated, optimistic and upbeat whether the Yankees won or lost; sharing life stories through jokes and insight; offering advice and wisdom to those in need; talking sports; and basically constructing a lounge out of a restroom was as effortless as a smooth dance step.

Playful jousting with the opposition only added to the fun we Yankees fans had in the restroom. Engaging in witty games of verbal one-upmanship with visiting baseball owners and fans from other American League cities, respect was earned when I recognized their allegiance and loyalty was on par with the passion we shared for the home team. The other team was given their props…but not until after a little teasing from the regular patrons and their resident lounge host.

That I experienced moments that I'll share for years to come with people from all walks of life merely confirmed that the most famous and expensive franchise in professional sports is public trust; a stock bond owned by a special place in all our hearts.

But for every Yankees fan, the satisfaction of quenching a nine-year thirst for a championship remained unfulfilled. In spite of the club's recent fortune, they were right where they finished the year before.

Third Place.

And the defending champions were coming to town.

PHILLIES, METS AND FIRST PLACE FOR A TICK. OH MY.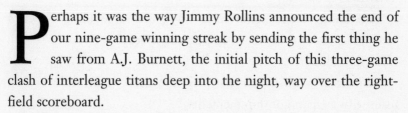

Perhaps it was the way Jimmy Rollins announced the end of our nine-game winning streak by sending the first thing he saw from A.J. Burnett, the initial pitch of this three-game clash of interleague titans deep into the night, way over the right-field scoreboard.

Perhaps it was the pitch Jason Werth blasted into orbit later in that game that found its resting place in the left-field second deck.

Perhaps it was the way they recovered from the Yankees' 5-4 come-from-behind walk-off Saturday afternoon special by delivering a Sunday punch of their own: a thrilling, 11th-inning, 4-3 victory that clinched the series.

Perhaps it was the way they strutted their championship swagger around our ballpark like they were the baddest baseball team on the planet; and for some portions of that series, played like it.

Perhaps it was the way a strong contingent of Phillies fans, many of whom made the two-hour Turnpike trip to the Bronx, had transformed Yankee Stadium into Citizens Bank Park with their invasion.

Perhaps it the way I said to our season-ticket holders that we would see this team again while respectfully saluting Philadelphia fans visiting the restroom by announcing the end of our friendship in late October.

Perhaps it was simply blind faith, but I was aware, way back in May, that the culmination of all championship aspirations would go through the Philadelphia Phillies.

Perhaps I knew, right then, with about 115 to 120 games left, that my one season of work at Yankee Stadium would include World Series baseball.

Kevin, my bartending brother, had the same premonition.

"We'll be playing them in the Series," he announced during our post home stand chat.

My eyes grew wide.

"You know, I was about to tell you the same thing. There's something about them that I respect too much."

Kevin nodded.

"They're a tough bunch that plays the game right, a throwback team with a championship mentality."

"Like us, right?"

"Which year? There's so many to pick from."

"1996. Over the Atlanta Braves, four games to two."

"I was thinking 1943 or 1978," Kevin said.

"The Cardinal series of '43? How's that possible? That was a rematch series, Kevin. After the Cardinals won the first game, we ran the table, much like they did to us the year before."

"The same with the 1978 World Series, Will."

"We lost the first two there," I argued.

"You don't get it, do you?" Before I could respond, Kevin continued. "When we get to the series, we're going to encounter a minor problem, figure them out quickly, and put them away. It'll take five or six games."

Understanding his *Yankeeosophy* completely, I nodded in agreement. "You're right. Then again, you could have chosen 1958 as a better example."

"The Milwaukee Braves, when we were down 3-1, and came back. That was Stengel's sweetest series victory; his finest hour."

"His last one, too," I added. Next challenging him with trivia, "Who was the pitcher that bailed them out?"

"C'mon, William, give me something harder. It was Bullet Bob

Turley. He lost in Game 2, pitched a shutout in Game 5, saved Game 6, and pitched 6-2/3 innings of two-hit ball in Game 7."

"Okay, so I tried."

Sharing a laugh, another embrace and knowing glow, if anyone walked by us and overheard the conversation, they would have thought we were joined at the hip.

We were. Kevin Michaels was my blue blood brother, sharing my hope for October Yankee glory.

Still, work on the playing field needed to be done to make it possible. Despite winning eight of ten games on the home stand, we remained in third place, a game behind the first place Red Sox and a half-game behind second-place Toronto.

Somehow I knew we wouldn't remain there.

Toronto usually fades away right about now, I assumed.

Further confirming my assumptions was a unique newness about the 2009 New York Yankees being constructed that captured the affection of millions in the Big Apple. Maybe it was the whipped-cream walk-off pies, or the awarding of a toy-replica WWE championship belt to the hero of each victory; but I noticed this group of Yankees was different from the last few teams in that it seemed looser, more supportive and comfortable with one another than in previous years. New personalities A.J. Burnett, Nick Swisher and C.C. Sabathia seamlessly meshing with old stalwarts Jeter, Rivera, Posada and Andy Pettitte *(a fact confirmed as early as spring training when C.C. generously purchased Orlando Magic tickets for his new teammates; A.J. Burnett's fishing trips; and Manager Joe Girardi's bond-building billiards parlor excursion)*, the chemistry on this club was easy to see in their willingness to sacrifice for one another.

Another thing under transformation was the way Yankee baseball was being played. For so long, the perception was that they bludgeoned opponents into submission with a balanced long-ball attack. Given the additions of Nick Swisher and an awakened-from-April hibernation

Mark Teixeira (thirteen homers in May); and the early-season, record-setting pace balls flown over the stadium fences, the Bombers could in fact, bomb away. Lethal from one-to-nine in the batting order, by season's end, eight Yankees would reach double figures in home runs.

However, the reality screamed that team, in spite of its production at home plate, needed late-game toughness, timely hits, and clutch fielding as much as the air needed to breathe.

Whether it was with offense or defense, the New York Yankees of 2009 were relentless. Early-season pitching, however, was another story.

Because of the struggles of end-of-the-rotation hurlers Joba Chamberlain, Chien Ming Wang and Phil Hughes, there was no depth in the starting alignment. Supplying the Yankees with his usual reliability, Andy Pettitte, the fifth starter coming out of spring training, played a more prominent role in the mix as he moved into third place on the franchise all-time wins list. Filling in with superb mid-season long relief, Alfredo Aceves and his cut fastball ate up innings as he kept the Yankees in games in which the starters bombed. Aceves joined a long line of pitchers who provided double-digit victory support from the bullpen: *Luis Arroyo (15 wins, 1961), Ron Davis (14, 1979), Sparky Lyle (13, 1977), Goose Gossage (13, 1983, 10 1978), Dave Righetti (12, 1985), Lindy McDaniel (12, 1973) and Lee Guetterman (11, 1990).*

A two-time Gold Glove first baseman, Mark Teixeira solidified an infield that went eighteen straight games without an error—a Major League record. Whether he was flipping balls to first base or turning double plays with ease, silky-smooth second baseman Robinson Cano fielded so effortlessly that many times it seemed unfair, and in the words of many pundits, nonchalant. Derek Jeter ignored all statistics saying he was one of the worst fielding shortstops in baseball and produced a Gold Glove caliber season. And upon his return, third sacker Alex Rodriguez produced only nine errors, his fewest since moving to third base in 2004.

The glue to the Yankees' improved infield defense however, was Teixeira. Whether stretching or leaping to receive an errant toss, or scooping up a short-hopped throw, his stabilizing presence was undeniable to the infield.

And, of course, there were the walk-off wins. A direct signal to the fans to maintain their enthusiasm and faith, the end-of-the game triumphs were momentum builders of confidence and chemistry between New York City and its ballclub. Victories at home in this fashion helped a legion of fans who couldn't come to the games because of more pressing commitments (rent, school tuition and outstanding bills) embrace this team; for they needed the joy of the Yankees to absorb the hurt of jobs lost and a failing economy.

For a respite, a thrilling Yankee victory was an enjoyable distraction.

Additionally, a fear was put into the mind of opponents that in spite of any lead, the Yankees were never out of any game. Restoring the "five o'clock lightning" days of yore, the notion that the losing team could play well and have the game won until a dramatic come-back proved damaging to their psyche. In some instances, the Yankees won two games: the walk-off victory that unfolded; and the day after, if the losing team remained forlorn.

If you made a mistake against the Bronx Bombers, sooner or later they made you pay.

May 24 would be the Yankees' last day in third place; taking two of three from the AL West-leading Texas Rangers on the road would see to that. With the Blue Jays permanently in our rearview mirror, by week's end we moved atop the division for the first time since the end of the 2006 season, passing those hated Red Sox on May 29.

Those antagonists from Yawkey Way passed us again, flexing their baseball muscle with yet another three-game sweep in Fenway in early June. As much as were playing good baseball, it seemed like the Yankees were clueless when handling their biggest problem: how to beat the Boston Red Sox. Inclusive in their eight-game win streak was one of every kind: We lost to them in extra-inning games, blowouts and all demoralizing fashions in between. The Pinstripes hadn't experienced such misfortune against their bitter rivals since 1912, when they were losing fourteen straight as the New York Highlanders.

For the next fifty-five days, the disturbing notion that we couldn't win the games that mattered most would be a continuous thorn in the Yankees' side as they fell two games behind in the American League East.

✪ ✪ ✪

Every now and then, the game of baseball gives you a moment that reveals a certain destiny. If your intuition is on high alert, as mine was after that conversation with my fiancée, you'll gladly accept the gift moment with a smile, keep the premonition others might find as absurd to yourself, and keep it moving.

Having said that, it's now time to share a moment of destiny you might find amusing.

Consider the date of June 12, 2009 as my initiation into the spirit of the Subway Series:

My workday at the stadium was proceeding as normal when I took my daily half-hour break. Leaving through the Legends Suite entrance, I walked east, along 161st Street with my supervisor and colleagues, greeting Yankees fans awaiting the opening of the gates with hi-fives and enthusiastic cheerleading. Noticing the blue-and-orange T-shirts as well as black or pinstriped replica jerseys of our cross-town rivals, the New York Metropolitans, all I could do was smile.

The New York Mets.

Saying their name softly as I continued my stroll, I couldn't help but think about how *Sports Illustrated* had picked them to win the 2009 World Series; this coming after they gift-wrapped the 2008 National League Eastern Division with a late-season collapse for the second year in a row, and presented it to Philadelphia Phillies Fanatics in a neat bow.

Also coming to mind was a team embroiled in controversy, bickering, inner turmoil and confusion.

The way they terminated Willie Randolph in June 2008 left a rancid aftertaste with me as well. Fired because the speculation of him losing his job created a tense atmosphere around the ballclub, the move was announced via e-mail press release at 12:14 a.m. Pacific Standard Time (3:14 EST) when the Mets were on the coast.

What made this move appalling was the fact that Randolph, as classy an act in baseball as there ever was, and realizing his inevitable end was near, had asked team General Manager Omar Minaya for his release prior to him flying west with the ballclub.

"I know there's a lot of pressure on you, but if I'm not the man to lead this team, then please don't let me get on that plane," Randolph said.

How honorable is that request? A man calmly asking for a blindfold and cigarette before bravely facing the firing squad, I seethed.

Imagining the class in which a spiritually and emotionally worn-down Randolph handled the situation, the memory of how this whole thing played out, an abomination to the Mets and the organization as a whole, left me feeling nauseated. Couple that with the fact that long before Willie Randolph was a manager, he was a Yankees second baseman, a co-captain, then bench and third-base coach after his retirement, and...

You never screw over a Yankees legend, a captain nonetheless, when the Yankee gods are watching, became my battle cry.

At that point, my silent musing was interrupted by the shrill of an annoying tone.

"The Yankees suck! They suck! Go back into the Stadium and watch the Mets kick ass tonight! The Yankees suck!"

Why this bad-breathed, caramel-skinned fool, wearing a faded Mets T-shirt and an even dingier Red Sox cap, made the decision to pick me out of the thousands entering the stadium of fans to go nose-to-nose with is beyond me.

But he picked the right Yankees Fan to pester that day. Moving past him briskly, the memory of a blue T-shirt with orange-and-white script lettering being sold by a River Avenue street vendor came to me.

Feeling a surge of "benevolence" run through me, *He needs a new shirt*, I thought.

Seeing the mischievous dance of my eyes, "Don't do it, William," my supervisor, Angel, ordered, laughing when seeing me pull a crisp twenty-dollar bill from my wallet. My other colleagues, futile in trying to conceal their humor, nearly doubled over in hysterics.

After purchasing the top, we went to McDonald's, where we devoured our meals in record time and hoped my tormentor was still by the Stadium gates with his shtick.

He was still there, torturing hundreds of Yankees fans with his blistering combination of halitosis and hatred.

Politely tapping on his shoulder, with all the goodwill I possessed in my heart, I said, "This is for you. Please have a nice day."

Then, I handed him his gift.

Opening the shirt in front of hundreds, I watched his chest heave in frustration and his face redden in humiliation as he threw the shirt down.

Ever the gentleman, I picked up the object of my affection, and gave it to him once more.

"No, sir, I insist you take this shirt as a token of my appreciation of your hospitality." By now a cluster of Yankees fans, curious to see why passersby were laughing, gathered around.

The Yankee agitator dropped the shirt once more, and this time, one of my colleagues joined in the fun.

"Sir, sir, you dropped this." Picking up the shirt, he made sure all that neared saw its inscription:

The New York Mess. 2007 and 2008 Back to Back NL EAST Collapses: Let's Go, Mess!

Smiling as I walked away and hearing the laughter left behind, I silently thanked the Yankee gods for giving me a cool wit. Returning to my work post, about an hour later, five Yankee fans entered the Lower Legends restroom, laughing about what they had witnessed.

"You should have seen the look on the guy's face when the worker handed him the shirt. That was classic," one of them said.

Then, he saw me.

"That's the dude that did it!" he screamed.

All of them, after washing their hands, hugged me.

"Thank you so much," one said. "Hearing him hate on the Yankees got under my skin."

After they left, I pointed to the sky and said, "Thanks."

Stuff like this only occurs during that one season when dreams are coming true.

More strange things happened that evening: In what had to be one of the most unlikely, utterly unbelievable ways to lose a baseball game, Mets second baseman Luis Castillo dropped a pop fly and apparent final out against the Yankees, giving us an improbable 9-8 victory.

Down by one in the bottom of the ninth with runners on the corners and sitting on a 3-1 fastball, a slumping Alex Rodriguez lofted a pop-up to shallow right field, slamming down his bat in disgust. But Castillo, staggering like a drunk to his left to make the play, had the ball pop out of his mitt, scoring Derek Jeter, the runner from third. When Castillo compounded his error by throwing the ball to second base, Mark Teixeira, who had been intentionally walked, motored around the bases with the winning run.

I laughed for at least five minutes immediately afterward, as well as on the southbound *D* train to Manhattan.

My night got even better once I arrived at the Port Authority Bus Terminal.

Boarding my bus home to Jersey City Heights, I saw a sea of blue and orange; Mets fans who had come across the Hudson to watch the game.

Giggling while finding a seat in the middle of the vehicle, for the duration of my twenty-minute ride, I was the subject of merciless taunting by the psychologically wounded legion of Mets fans.

And like a notorious villain wearing Yankee pinstripes, I loved every second of it.

As the bus made its way through Lincoln Tunnel, through the maze of streets and hills that was Weehawken, Union City, then Jersey City Heights, I pointed to the interlocking *NY* logo on my vest.

"They don't like where I work very much," I said with a smile to the attractive woman next to me.

Meeting my smirk with a wide grin of her own, the gorgeous blonde put on her Yankees cap, then extended her hand for a hi-five.

"Don't worry. They don't like me much either."

Laughing together for the remainder of the ride home, all we kept saying to those within earshot of our chatter is that *you never screw over a Yankees legend, a captain nonetheless, especially when the Yankee gods are watching.*

By the end of the fourth inning of that Sunday game (the Mets won the middle game of the series 6-2), it was apparent to everyone that the two New York baseball franchises were taking trains in opposite directions. The Yankees never let Mets ace Johan Santana out of the frame, blasting him for nine runs and nine hits in a 15-0 shellacking.

After a three-game sweep of the Mets in their new Citi Field ballpark later in the month, the Mets were never the same. Santana bravely pitched with low velocity on his fastball until mid-August, when it was discovered that he had bone chips in his elbow. He had season-ending surgery. Infielders Carlos Delgado and José Reyes had already suffered season-ending injuries, and All-Star center-fielder Carlos Beltran missed half with a deep bone bruise on his knee. The one person Mets fans could cheer about, third-baseman David Wright, went into a deep power drought. Though he finished amongst the National League leaders with a .307 average, he only hit ten home runs.

The Mets would finish the season with a 70-92 record, good for fourth place in the NL East, while the Yankees continued their hot pursuit of the Red Sox.

You never screw over a Yankees legend, a captain nonetheless, especially when the Yankee gods are watching.

Yankees fans found solace in the misery of the Mets; that is, until they figured out a way to beat Boston.

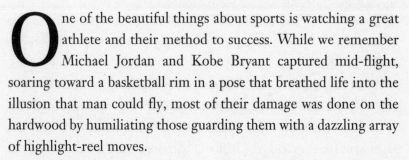
One of the beautiful things about sports is watching a great athlete and their method to success. While we remember Michael Jordan and Kobe Bryant captured mid-flight, soaring toward a basketball rim in a pose that breathed life into the illusion that man could fly, most of their damage was done on the hardwood by humiliating those guarding them with a dazzling array of highlight-reel moves.

You gave Gale Sayers, Marcus Allen, O.J. Simpson and Barry Sanders a football and eighteen inches of daylight, and instinct and intuition took over. Possessing electrifying elusiveness, startling stutter-steps and spectacular stop-and-start movements, their success was magnetically magical and mesmerizing all at once.

To watch Pernell "Sweet-Pea" Whitaker practice the sweet science of boxing was akin to watching a three-card monte player take the money of a hapless sucker. Pure poetry in motion as he taunted, teased and tamed opponents while paying tribute to the timeless hit-but-not-be-hit mantra, his controlled contortions left fans paying homage to his now-you-see-him-now-you-don't antics.

These great athletes are defined by their variety.

Other great ones, however, don't just have a style. Thriving in simplicity and solitary repetition on a stage when everyone's watching, they have a distinct, permanent stamp that signifies exactly who they are. Seeing the signature play over and over again, everyone knows what's coming, yet are unable to stop the end result.

Like the monster in the horror movies, you can lock all the doors, barricade all the windows, grab a sawed-off shotgun and hide in the basement. No matter what you do to avoid the inevitable, it still gets you.

For some, the stamp might be performed by many thinking as one. An example of such is Vince Lombardi and the Green Bay Packers' famed power sweep. Transforming that one play into something innate, part of their reflexive being, it symbolized the example of eleven minds and bodies working as one to achieve the ultimate goal of an NFL championship; something that happened five times in the 1960s.

While not the inventor, whenever you think of the skyhook, you can only see Kareem Abdul-Jabbar and the image where: his left leg is straight, his right knee comes up, the left arm extends out, the right arm rises up with the ball and with a casual flick of his wrist, a basketball rotating through the hoop.

Continued success with a go-to play or bread-and-butter move can not only build a team's confidence, but instill a sense of calm in an entire city as well.

Sometimes, in the example of Yankees closer extraordinaire Mariano Rivera, the signature to history is in one pitch.

Carl Hubbell's devastating screwball led him to 24 consecutive wins between 1936 and 1937, the longest such streak ever recorded in Major League Baseball. The big curveball of Sandy Koufax produced four no-hitters and one of the best six-year runs (1961-1966) a starting pitcher ever had. Nolan Ryan's blazing fastball produced 5,714 strikeouts, 324 wins and seven no-hitters. Bruce Sutter's split-fingered fastball produced a Hall of Fame career as a reliever.

All those great pitches by great pitchers were complemented by a secondary pitch in the chamber, one of a different spin and velocity. Ryan had the circle-changeup, Sutter a brilliant curveball, and Koufax and Hubbell brought heat.

For Mariano Rivera, it has, is, and always will be that dastardly darting, dipping, devastating cut fastball.

The same pitch, from the same easy delivery, for a decade and a half.

Here's the anatomy of that one pitch: From its release, the fastball comes in hard, almost always in on the hands of an opposing hitter. Then suddenly, the ball moves as if it has a mind of its own. Breaking late, as if it were scuffed or defaced, the late movement rivals the infamous spitball, a pitch banned more than eighty years ago. When he adjusts his fingertip pressure along the seams, Rivera can determine how dramatic the break is. Usually, the right-handed batter gives up, and the left-handed hitter stands frozen as a called third strike blows past him.

And if you swing and make contact, the end result is a feeble ground ball or pop-up; or alternatively, a broken bat. Yankees fans have lost count in the number of bats he's shattered; though, by estimation, it's probably enough wood to keep scores of fireplaces lit forever.

In the long history of relief pitching, Mariano Rivera is considered by many baseball experts and past and present bullpen specialists to be the greatest relief pitcher in baseball history. While the role of the modern closer has come under heavy criticism for becoming too specialized (in the past they often entered games at crucial points and pitched multiple innings, while modern closers are usually called upon to only pitch the ninth inning), his combination of focus; self-discipline (no matter what, he sticks to his routine of arriving to the bullpen in the sixth inning of close games, stretching in the seventh, the weighted ball arm circles to loosen his arm, then hard throwing after a few warm-up tosses in the eighth inning); durability (in a role best known for its high turnover rate, his decade-and-a-half tenure as the Yankees' stopper has exceeded the ordinary lifetime of a closer); consistency (he has an almost 90% success rate on his save opportunities); and professionalism (avoiding the New York City limelight, this God-fearing man is as quiet off the field as he is calm on it), it seems fitting that he will be the last Major Leaguer to wear the uniform number 42, which was retired throughout baseball in 1997 (in honor of Jackie Robinson), he has won over everyone with his near-automatic efficiency.

While he's been successful in the regular season, what makes Mariano Rivera transcend generations is his impact on October baseball. The proud owner of numerous postseason records, *(lowest ERA (0.74), most saves (39), most consecutive scoreless innings pitched (34$\frac{1}{3}$), most consecutive save opportunities converted (23), and most appearances (88))*, his dominance in postseason games has seen him utilized in many two-inning appearances, where he has recorded a record 14 saves of this variety. If ever there was a peace within the ninth-inning storm, it is the sight of a batter flailing away in futility at a cut fastball.

If there is one expression that defines Yankee cool, it would be Mariano Rivera in the ninth inning. As Metallica's "Enter Sandman" fills the stadium with anticipation, the Yankees' bullpen door swings open, and a slender frame wearing the home pinstripes trots slowly to a job that requires his trademark pitch, incredible focus and steely determination to slam the door of hope for many a team. Taking the mound while the crowd roars its approval and opposing players dread, instead of flashing menacing looks at the batters he must face, the countenance of the best closer in the history of baseball wears the same peaceful look.

That same peaceful look, throwing the same unhittable pitch over and over; from the same fluid delivery; producing the same result time and time again.

On May 17, 1996, Mariano Rivera induced a double play ball from the Angels' Garrett Anderson for his first save.

On June 27, 2009, against his cross-town rivals some thirteen years later, he delivered a message to Yankees fans that all's well for the 500th time, the second most all-time.

Five hundred saves.

And more fires to put out.

More peace for Mariano Rivera to deliver to the city that never sleeps.

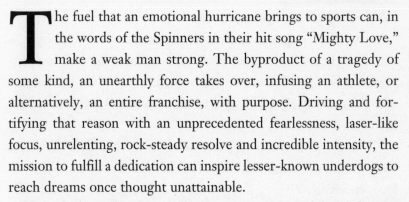

A TALE OF TWO
BASEBALL TEAMS
5

The fuel that an emotional hurricane brings to sports can, in the words of the Spinners in their hit song "Mighty Love," make a weak man strong. The byproduct of a tragedy of some kind, an unearthly force takes over, infusing an athlete, or alternatively, an entire franchise, with purpose. Driving and fortifying that reason with an unprecedented fearlessness, laser-like focus, unrelenting, rock-steady resolve and incredible intensity, the mission to fulfill a dedication can inspire lesser-known underdogs to reach dreams once thought unattainable.

The unlucky opponent, usually an unsuspecting prohibitive favorite in the moment, bravely tries to weather a storm of something more spiritual than physical. Dealing with someone determined to complete a mental mission, they never see, nor fully understand, what hit them.

James "Buster" Douglas provides proof of how an emotional hurricane moves. On February 11, 1990, four months after being abandoned by his wife of two years and grieving over the death of his mother twenty-three days earlier, entered Tokyo Japan's Korakuen Hall against undisputed, undefeated heavyweight champion "Iron" Mike Tyson.

A chiseled assassin full of arrogance, Tyson, an imposing menace, was a ferocious monster who stalked the ring with bad intentions. Beating up everyone with his hulking arms, brutal power and savage intensity, he piled up knockout after knockout with terrifying swiftness. Defeated by an aura of invincibility long before the first punch, many of his opponents were actually coaxed from the locker room to fight the bully.

"Buster" Douglas was supposed be nothing more than another quick knockout and easy payday for Mike Tyson. Countries were bidding as much as $6 million per appearance for his ring savagery *after* this tune-up. That only one betting parlor in Las Vegas held odds on the fight (listing Douglas as a 42-1 underdog) only confirmed what the world thought:

No one gave him a prayer.

Just before the first bell, someone shouted for the challenger to win the fight for his mother. Probably remembering their last conversation two days before her death when he shared his confidence, Douglas nodded, closed his eyes for an instant, and strode forth into the heart of his storm.

Meeting the "monster of his demise" in the middle of the ring, from the onset of the fight, his stiff left jab found its mark in Tyson's face repeatedly.

Referring to Tyson, "Nothing there," Douglas' trainers screamed with a minute left in that initial round. However, something was there for "Buster" Douglas on that early morning overseas: a fearless inspiration brought on by a tidal wave of emotion, thus producing a once-in-a-lifetime experience.

Capitalizing on this moment in time, Douglas followed up those stinging jabs with powerful right hooks and uppercuts; then skillfully danced out of harm's way after getting his punches off. By the end of the fifth round, the menace was gone from Mike Tyson as his left eye was swelling shut.

As the Japanese crowd of 30,000 sat in stunned silence, Douglas, continuing his brilliance, hammered away with crisp combinations, emphasizing the intent of his arsenal with solid right crosses.

By round eight, he was treating Mike Tyson like an old sparring partner. That all changed with six seconds remaining in the round when one fierce uppercut from Tyson knocked the confident challenger on his back. Douglas, pounding the mat in frustration at his own lapse, ignored the crisis and picked himself up at the count of nine, and went back to work.

Launching another fearless assault in the ninth round, Douglas rocked Tyson into the ropes with punches that caused the champion's head to move up and down loosely on his pillar of a neck. Backing him up to the ropes with a series of right crosses, by round's end, Tyson's left eye was completely shut, leaving the half-blind fighter more vulnerable than at any point in his career.

Even with his helpless, outclassed state, it was difficult for many observers to conceive what happened next to "Iron" Mike Tyson. Just over a minute into the tenth round, James "Buster" Douglas— thought so much of an afterthought that he could not garner the attention of *one* photographer at the weigh-in the day before—landed a huge uppercut into Tyson's chin, snapping his head back like a bobble-head doll wobbling from the impact of a sudden stop.

A rapid four-punch combination followed.

Punctuating the moment with a chopping left hook, there went a heavyweight champion once thought of as invincible toppling horizontally onto the canvas. Skidding on his backside, the image of Mike Tyson struggling on his knees, searching, then finding his mouthpiece and placing it crookedly into his lips while falling into the arms of Octavio Meyran, is enduring.

The fight was over.

Jubilant Douglas supporters poured into the ring, as well as a throng of reporters wanting to know how the greatest upset in boxing history was made possible.

"My mother," Douglas told the interviewers as he choked back tears, "My mother. God bless her heart."

Inspired by an emotional hurricane, James "Buster" Douglas reached for the stars, and grabbed them, if only for that night.

Sometimes, an emotional tide of inspiration is fuel for a team to reach for heights previously unknown. While the 1990 NCAA College Basketball Championship was won by UNLV and Jerry Tarkanian's Running Rebels, the tournament is also remembered for a spirited run by the Loyola Marymount Lions in the West Regional.

Coached by Paul Westhead, the team adopted a fast-paced style of offense that encouraged opponents to shoot layups so Loyola could get the ball back quickly and score, mostly from three-point range. This breakneck style had produced two of the nation's top scorers in Bo Kimble, and his childhood friend from Philadelphia, Hank Gathers.

Tragedy struck the Lions on March 4, 1990. In the semifinals of the regular season-ending West Coast Conference tournament, Gathers, the team's star forward, suddenly collapsed on the court and died due to an abnormal heart condition. The WCC competition was immediately suspended, with the regular-season champion Lions given the conference's automatic bid.

After taking a players' vote to continue their season, the Loyola Marymount Lions entered the NCAA tournament as an 11th seed in the West Regional, on a mission. Upsetting the sixth-seed New Mexico State 111-92 in the first round, the Lions went on to destroy defending national champion Michigan 149-115 in the second round to reach the Sweet 16.

Fully embodying everything about March Madness (the catch phrase used to describe the rash amount of upsets in college basketball's ultimate tournament), by now the world shared in their momentum. Shooting guard Jeff Fryer was spotting up and raining three-pointers from everywhere; and Kimble, the team's undisputed floor leader in the wake of his fallen comrade, paid tribute to his friend by attempting his first free throw in each game left-handed despite being right-handed.

Kimble made all of his left-handed attempts in the tournament.

Convinced that they would win the national championship for Hank Gathers, Kimble and his teammates squeaked by Alabama in the West Regional Semifinals 62-60.

Three more wins, and an emotionally charged destiny of a national championship would be fulfilled.

Alas, the dream died one win short of the Final Four, when the eventual champion UNLV Rebels beat Loyola at its own frenetic game 131-101 in the West Regional Final. In spite of the loss, the death of a teammate sparked one of the most improbable tournament runs in the history of college basketball.

✪ ✪ ✪

On Tuesday April 7, 2009, Los Angeles Angels rookie hurler Nick Adenhart, making his fourth career Major League start the next evening, called his father, Jim, in Baltimore, Maryland. Suggesting that he make the cross-country trip to mark the occasion, "something special is going to happen," he told him.

Jim Adenhart was there at Angels Stadium that Wednesday night, beaming proudly as he watched his son give the best performance of his brief career. In pitching six scoreless innings against the Oakland A's, young Nick escaped a pair of bases-loaded jams while striking out five. Though credited with a no-decision for his brilliance—the Athletics rallied for six runs against Angel closer Brian Fuentes in a 6-4 victory—the young pitcher shared a budding confidence with Mike Butcher, his pitching coach.

"I've got it," he joyfully exclaimed when asked about how the ball felt leaving his hands.

The potential of a breakthrough season looming, Nick Adenhart decided to celebrate the birth of his limitless possibilities. So he gathered three friends, Courtney Stewart, Henry Pearson and John Wilhite, and went riding in Stewart's silver Mitsubishi Eclipse. Heading to a country bar in nearby Fullerton, one could only imagine the happiness they felt as they neared.

Fast forward twenty-four hours later…

The Los Angeles Angels, numb and shell-shocked, postponed their scheduled game against the Athletics. Jim Adenhart was standing on the very pitcher's mound where his son unknowingly said "I Love You" and "Goodbye" to him, peering upward at God with one question…

Why?

Why did Andrew Thomas Gallo, an allegedly drunk twenty-year-old motorist with a suspended license, run a red light in his red minivan and blindside the Mitsubishi, driving it into a telephone pole, and then try to leave the scene of the crime? Why couldn't the Eclipse have been fifty yards ahead, already at the bar, or fifty yards behind, watching the speeding vehicle whiz right by? Why did his son, blossoming with limitless promise, have to go away in a blink of his eye, way before his time, in such a senseless manner?

Why God, why?

The impact of Nick Adenhart's death sent shockwaves throughout baseball. Agent Scott Boras, whose ruthless negotiation tactics came directly from a page of Sun Tzu's *Art of War*, was overcome by emotion. Sobbing uncontrollably, he couldn't make it through his press conference. Equally shell-shocked was Angels Owner Artie Moreno, who said he felt like he'd been hit in his stomach. His 2008 teammates with the Angels' Triple-A team in Salt Lake City were as grief-stricken as the Major League club.

Nick Adenhart, a decent young man and top pitching prospect, was gone.

With an unfamiliar pain in his stomach, Angels Manager Mike

Scoiscia offered this perspective: "We've lost a teammate and a friend. However the Adenharts have lost a son." In his eight years at the helm of this franchise, he produced six postseason berths, including a World Series title in 2002. However, nothing would compare to his delicate navigation of his grieving clubhouse; a testament of perseverance that would result in 97 victories, another American League Western Division title and a well-deserved Manager of the Year award.

Slumping early on from a combination of mourning, lack of starting pitching and crippling injuries, the Angels gathered on April 23 for a private memorial service. Encouraging them to move on in their own way, Scoiscia drew on Adenhart's performance in that final game as motivation. In those early innings of his epitaph, he fell behind several A's hitters and struggled with his command. But somewhere around the middle of the game, he developed a feel for his changeup and began moving through the Oakland batting order with ease.

Battling his way through, on the last day of his life Nick Adenhart gave the 2009 Angels organization the gift of mental toughness, a point emphasized by the manager's last words. Insisting on accountability between the white lines of a baseball diamond, "We *will* move on," he said.

The words were said in a soft tone, but strong enough to deliver a message: The best way to overcome this tragedy is to transform his memory into a driving force. Struggling early on, much like the New York Yankees, the Angels were in third place in the AL West with a 13-14 on May 7. A month later, they moved over .500 and into second place, 3-1/2 games behind the front-running Texas Rangers.

However, something was happening to that early-season sorrow. Teammates became closer, hanging out together, communicating words of encouragement when one saw another slipping.

Brothers bonded together in grief and inspiration, the Angels, already an aggressive base-running unit, were infused with even more urgency; no team in Major League Baseball went from first-to-third or second-to-home more than the 127 times the Angels did so in 2009. A sound defensive ballclub, they focused even harder on flawless execution, and played even better. The pitchers on their makeshift staff threw first-pitch strikes, refused to walk anyone, and the fundamentals instilled in them by Scoiscia seemed sharper, more defined.

And if anyone let up, they needn't look too far for motivation. Upon entry into the clubhouse, directly to the right was Nick Adenhart's clean No. 34 jersey on a hanger in his locker, and cleats and shoes side by side on a shelf. On the centerfield wall, there was a picture Nick Adenhart, hurling a strike. And outside of Angels Stadium was an ever-expanding montage of caps, photographs, stuffed teddy bears and rally monkeys.

Nick was gone physically, but his spirit lived vicariously through the Angels organization. Growing bigger with each win, by June 27, 2009, the emotional hurricane that was the Los Angeles Angels had moved into first place of the American League West.

✪ ✪ ✪

Fight on my men, Sir Andrew said,
I'm hurt a little but not yet slain.
I'll just lie down and bleed awhile,
And I'll rise and fight again.

By July 10, the New York Yankees were flying high. Feeling confident in spite of their 0-8 record against the Red Sox, their sluggish start, and "diabolical hater" Skip Bayless' off-target prognostication, they rode a .667 winning percentage over 57 games

(38-19 record) into a solid first half of the season. Going into Angels Stadium for their last series before the All-Star break, they were tied for first place in the American League East.

Angels Stadium, *a personal house of horrors*, I thought as I watched the first pitch of the series leave Joe Saunders' hand. Over the past decade, the ballclub on Gene Autry Way was pure torture to the New York Yankees. Merciless playoff assassins to Yankee aspirations for higher ground, the favored Bombers were ambushed by the Angels in the divisional round. From Garret Anderson and Tim Salmon to Howie Kendrick and Mike Napoli, while passengers on the West Coast Express changed over the years, the train kept steamrolling the Bronx Bombers—especially in the hostile confines of Angels Stadium, where they won sixteen of twenty-one games against the Yankees. Presenting problems to the Pinstripes with great defense, aggressive base-running and timely hitting, I prayed things would be different this time around. And after four innings of the first game, things looked different. Ahead 5-1 going to the bottom of the fifth, the Yankees appeared to have removed the Angels from their collective heads.

Then suddenly, without warning, those annoying little things that the Angels always seem to do against the Yankees surfaced. Patiently working the pitch count, hitting doubles within the outfield gaps, running the bases with reckless abandon and executing rally-ending double plays on defense, the Halos again played the role of tormentor. Scoring nine runs in three innings against Joba Chamberlain, Mark Melancon and Brian Bruney, they lit the Yankees up for a 10-6 victory.

Continuing their relentless assault on Yankees pitching, they sent balls all over the yard the next two games. Erasing another 4-run deficit by pounding Andy Pettitte and others in a 14-8 victory in the Saturday matinee contest, on Sunday Angel ace John Lackey outpitched C.C. Sabathia 5-4 to complete the mind-numbing sweep.

Once again, the mission to recapture championship glory had been stalled.

Also turning Yankee confidence to concern was Boston's three-game sweep of the Kansas City Royals, which left them three games back as the season reached its three-day break. Hurting but not yet slain; bleeding, baffled but not unbowed; they were at 51-37, with the third best record in baseball.

Good, yes, but not good enough to still the mouth of Skip Bayless and other cynics.

A half season remained. Hopefully, it would be enough time for the Yankees to rise off the canvas, dust themselves off, and make a serious move.

I had faith that they would.

Once upon a time, Iowa farmer Ray Kinsella was asked to build a field of dreams. Twenty yards left of Gate 4 at the new Yankee Stadium, you will see an entrance; an entrance to a club of dreams. If you own a blue, gold-lettered ticket, little do you know you are in possession of a key to something special, provided the blue velvet ropes aren't revealing. Receiving blue resort-like wristbands, you pass a few levels of security and two blue smoked-glass doors bearing the famous Yankees logo, and you've crossed the threshold and are in the top level of a warm, comforting house of dreams.

Inundated with an embarrassment of riches, to the naked eye, there's so much to savor that my suggestion is to schedule an arrival time of two hours before any home game. To the right of the blue-tinted staircase is a sleek bar area complete with more flat screens per square foot than any sports bar in the city. To the left of the steps is a cavernous, yet cozy dining room complete with interactive food stations. There, a keyboard musician plays Sinatra, Michael Jackson and everything in between while toque-wearing performance chefs and staff prepare exquisite meals buffet style.

Serving you the highest quality of everything, from the sensational sushi created in front of you to the delightfully delicious Wild Bison Rib Eye steak, the first-rate food literally snatches your taste buds and takes them on an endlessly pleasing journey.

More food, you say? Venture down the plush blue staircase, and, after entering the massive downstairs level of the suite club, try the filet mignon, and the roasted chicken or turkey, or the butter-smothered lamb chops. The chicken, butternut and squash ravioli station is equally appetizing, not to mention the Scottish salmon and lobster rolls. From a meaty paella, chicken and sausage sandwiches and slow-cooked pork ribs conveniently cut into bite-size pieces to pretzels, hot dogs and…get this…a dessert bar with made-to-order ice cream sundaes served in little blue Yankees helmets, they have it all in their dining mall.

And to top it all off, on your way to the 1800 or so Legend seats that go around the horn (first- to third-base lines), there is a "grab-and-go" snack area with free sodas and peanut bags, M&M's, cotton candy, Cracker Jacks, Twizzlers, Twix, Skittles and Starburst. To call it a scrumptious smorgasbord or a dining place of dreams doesn't fit the descriptive bill.

A five-star dining extravaganza, The Legends Suite Club at the new Yankee Stadium is, simply put, a feast.

So have a seat, and enjoy the electric ambiance. Brown custom-designed walls bearing the interlocking Yankees logo are accentuated by an archival art gallery of pinstripe lore handpicked by the Steinbrenner ownership. Also meshing with the steakhouse-like décor are carefully constructed white patterns that spell out *New York*, as well as the hundred or so flat-screen high-definition televisions covering bar and dining room walls. And again, that spectacular blue staircase that breaks up the two-tiered, seven hundred-seat Suite Club is absolutely incredible.

While the price to enter the private, members-only palace of dreams may be expensive, the Yankees organization goes above and beyond to ensure that you are pampered to the fullest. Passing through those glorious blue doors, you see nothing but happy, friendly faces busing tables; taking martini, drink or wine orders (from a vast collection that rivals any Napa Valley wine cellar); immediately refilling your water or drink; and escorting you to your seats in time for the first pitch. You needn't worry about touching a door; it is opened for you by a restaurant representative.

And if it was raining outside, we wiped your wide recliner seats for you.

Margaret Ann Quinlan, the manager of Legends Suite Club, wouldn't have it any other way. Known throughout the stadium as "Mugsy," she is the pulse of Legends. Compassionate, fair and professionally driven, her motivational pre-game shifts came directly from her heart, as well as everything she does to make the suite club a place of dreams. Seeing endless attention to every square foot of the establishment and commitment to excellence was something to behold. If you ever fantasized about watching Leonardo da Vinci quench his insatiable thirst for perfection in a portrait, if you ever envisioned yourself in a room watching Beethoven, Mozart, Brahms or Handel toil away on an artist creation, the cleverness of Margaret Ann Quinlan, to the naked eye, is comparable.

Feeding off of her tremendous work ethic, seeing her tireless work to make the establishment an unforgettable experience for every patron, makes her staff work even harder to ensure the patrons' pleasure.

It made me work just as hard on the maintenance of the five-star dining extravaganza, as I never, ever, wanted to let her, or her excellent supporting staff down.

From the time the doors opened for the fans, they received the best of everything: "Mugsy" and her warm, wondrous smile, the high-quality food, sincere hospitality and the pinstriped product on the playing field.

Then, whenever you needed a restroom break, for that one season, you went to either the restrooms upstairs, or you came to "My House" on the lower level of the restaurant. Brown-bricked, dimly lit and luxurious, there were sterling silver stalls complete with soft tissue and air fresheners; ceramic, non-scented urinals; two HDTV monitors embedded within the mirrors so you wouldn't miss a second of the game; and the respective network announcers covering the game blaring over an expansive speaker system.

Even relieving yourself was done in Yankee class. And I felt obligated to add to the Yankee way in the best way possible; by giving everything I had from my heart. Upon entry, you were greeted with a smile, a passionate pregame analysis and prediction, and a joke or two about the opposition.

As the season progressed, something special was not only happening in the Legends Suite Club, but in that lower-level men's restroom as well. Instead of it merely being a place to relieve, it transformed itself into a chic lounge, a hip hangout spot. Servers and busboys looked to me for wisdom and guidance, and were supplied with words from a place deep within my soul.

As if I knew a happy ending beforehand, "Cherish this moment, guys," I would tell many of them. "This season will be something you can tell your grandchildren about."

Season-ticket holders would, upon entry into the Suite Club, come directly to the lounge to chill after a long day at work. Young kids were sharing birthday cakes and stories of neighborhood home runs with me. Teenagers would share their scholastic, then summer experiences, and during the games, passionate Yankees fans from eight to eighty would look to me for optimism when things looked bleak for the home team.

"Hang in there," I often responded. But more often than not, we were exchanging hi-fives and laughter, because on that newly con-structed baseball diamond was a New York Yankees team playing great baseball. Soon, it came to a point where I predicted walk-off victories and sweeps, home runs and big innings. Calling shots the way the Bambinos did with regularity, membership club patrons and support staff would shake their heads in amazement.

The merger of action and awareness, basketball players often describe being in a "zone" as the hoop being as wide as an ocean, everything around them moving in slow motion, and having mastery over the moment in time.

For the inaugural season at the new Yankee Stadium, I was in a complete zone.

When you're in that one season when your dreams are coming true, life seems to be one constant zone.

Every day spent in that restroom was a new experience to me. Interacting with a heavy mix of New York's most powerful minds, from Yankees ownership and investment brokers to major political officials and entertainment entrepreneurs, you learn a great deal about ambition, determination and dreams realized.

Alas, you wouldn't think this was the case when reading blog reviews of the Legends seats, most of them written by individuals sharing a "once in a lifetime" experience. Dripped in sarcasm and jealousy, subjective in rooting for the everyday guy, I totally understand what "Joe Fan" might think of the lavish surroundings as overindulgence; to be perfectly candid, a project-reared-kid-from-Staten Island-turned-Yankee-Stadium-restroom-attendant originally thought this as over-the-top as well.

However, by the end of my initial home stand, like Malcolm X returning from his pilgrimage to Mecca, I saw things quite differently.

Entering the doors to my lounge were some of the most humble, benevolent men I have ever encountered. Each day and its success seemed irrelevant when sharing the common denominator of being a Yankees fan. Case in point: During the season, I had the honor of befriending former New York City Mayor Rudy Giuliani. While he may have been reviled in some parts in the Big Apple, my rebuttal to those who only follow politics is "Have you ever had a conversation with him?" Politics is his chosen profession, not him as a person. Engaging in animated discussions with him throughout the season and sharing our Yankee passion through laughter and game analysis, behind the steely veneer known throughout the Big Apple, lay a compassionate, kind spirit.

He's a very cool dude.

The same goes for many of the powerful movers and shakers of the city. While not privy to mention all their names, investment brokers, real estate developers and consultants, talent agents, general partners of major Broadway plays, executives, CEOs, and presidents of schools shared their triumphs and breakthroughs with me, and offered many words of encouragement. Soon, those handshakes turned into righteous hugs and hand pounds, hi-fives and playful back-slapping every time our paths connected.

So many of them touched my soul, but only one, Roy, knew of my origins. Throughout the season we would share stimulating con-versations, yet he never revealed his place within the Yankees organization.

(NOTE: *I assume he was part of the Yankee family because on two occasions when he encountered critical cynical fans everyone in the lounge felt his passion for the franchise.*)

"You're going places," he said to me one day in April.

"I'm lucky to have a job." After confiding in him about my adversities, faith and good fortune, "God works in mysterious ways," I concluded.

"You're right about that," he agreed.

Offering advice and positive words every time he visited the lounge, perhaps the best bit of wisdom he imparted came on a late evening in May.

"Don't miss the train of opportunity when it passes by. Hop on, and enjoy the ride. You'll be amazed at the possibilities life presents."

Watching him leave the restroom that evening, for the remainder of the season, I asked myself: *Who is that guy?*

That question would never be answered, but if one had a query about the liveliness in the men's restroom, the response would be this:

WE HAD A BLAST!

The funny hi-jinks, shared by the suit-wearing boys at heart and the resident ringleader, were an experience in itself. Whenever fans from other cities entered the club, he was given a ten- to thirty-second time limit to relieve himself. Special blue hand sanitizer was placed on the counters to combat the "Red Sox Flu." Yankees T-shirts with our championship history were given to owners from visiting cities as a reminder of our glory. And for the major trash-talkers—almost always a Mets or Red Sox fan—a vote was taken when the restroom lines were at their longest. A resounding *NO* would be yelled in unison by the Yankee fans, resulting in a cup being passed down the line, eventually reaching the loud-mouth.

(NOTE: Yankee fans did show their cross-town rivals compassion, for one day. Two days after the New York Mess…oops… Mets were mathematically eliminated from playoff contention, on September 15, we had Hug-A-Met-Fan Day in the Legends Lounge. What made this account funny were the reports from Kids and CEOs I received during that Tuesday night home game. Throughout the day they really showed compassion to Mets fans by hugging them at school and at their place of business. This was really amazing stuff that couldn't be made up.)

Athletes past and present and celebrities were granted inclusion as well. The day Tino Martinez stopped in, we gave him a rousing ovation for his Yankee exploits. Offering words of support to New York Giants Coach Tom Coughlin when dealing with the win-now demands of the New York media, I could tell he appreciated the sincerity of my tone. Justin Tuck, Giants defensive end, was one of the coolest guys around, as was NASCAR legend Jeff Gordon.

I hold a special place in my heart for former New York Giant wide receiver and Pro Bowl special teamer David Tyree. Author of the greatest catch in Super Bowl history, he entered the lounge reading

The Shack, the national bestseller by William P. Young which speaks of the author's encounter with God. Seeing the novel, I mentioned that it was the book of the month with the Youth Ministry of my church.

"My spiritual adviser asked me to read this," he responded with a smile.

Upon name recognition during our formal introductions, he told me the story leading up to his moment in time.

"I couldn't catch a cold that Friday in the practice before the Patriots game," he said, referring to Super Bowl 42.

"Bad dress rehearsals usually lead to tremendous performances," I responded.

"My spiritual adviser said the same thing!" Sharing a brotherly hug, I felt so happy for him.

"God has some plans for you, William. Just you watch," he stated before he left.

(NOTE: *At publication time, David Tyree had retired from football to focus on ministry. God is going to continue to use him in awesome ways.*)

When rags-to-riches entrepreneur Christopher Gardner came into the restroom, I wanted to share the story of how I could totally relate to his determination while in *Pursuit of Happyness*. On the tip of my tongue was a brutal Friday night in August 2007, when after thirteen hundred dollars was erroneously missing from my law firm paycheck, I came home to find myself evicted from my Bronx apartment. Experiencing a real-life page from his bestselling autobiography, the irony of it all was the very next day, at a breast cancer function I had donated books to—one day after one of the most humiliating experiences of my life, with no place to lay my head after my appearance at this function—I was supposed to meet *him!*

Though I wanted to share my story about the challenges I had faced while in pursuit of my literary dreams, all that escaped my lips was this: "I read your book, and I can relate to your story more than you'll ever know."

While my struggles remained silent in my soul, his presence alone served its purpose. The perfect motivational chip, even today I think: If Christopher Gardner could triumph over the adversities that life brings, then why should I expect any less of myself?

Keith Olbermann, NBC news anchor, sportscaster, writer, political commentator and season-ticket holder, and I spent many a moment analyzing the Yankees season as it unfolded. Both of us, worrying that the end-of-the-pitching-rotation wouldn't hold up, agreed that there would be October baseball in the Yankees future.

Going into the concrete gray hallway outside the lower level of the Suite Club left me near the clubhouses. There, I would rap with some of my favorite sportswriters and featured columnists, former players, play-by-play analysts and broadcasters. A roll call would be a Who's Who in American sports media: Dave Campbell, William C. Rhoden, Joe Buck, Dick Vitale, Bill Rafferty, Tim McCarver, Bob Ryan, Tim Smith, Joe Morgan, Orel Hershiser, Tim Kurjian, as well as the Yankees team of Michael Kay, John Sterling and Suzyn Waldman. That these down-to-earth voices and writers offered smiles, handshakes and were approachable in conversation, meant more to me than you could possibly imagine.

Yankees ownership and family, as busy as they were constructing a championship dream for millions, even came by the lounge to say hi. Many of them, while brief in their stay, always shared their love for the Yankees, as well as for the job I was doing. Their words of encouragement kept me positive on those rare days where my energy was low. Reminding them that they needed to order new championship rings to accompany the impressive diamond baubles they wore, the hopeful smiles I received from them warmed my soul.

Always offering General Manager Brian Cashman a kind word of encouragement whenever our paths crossed, to my surprise, he would stop, and engage in friendly conversation, if but for a respite.

"There's a championship mandate this year," I told him one early June evening as he entered the Lower Legends Suite entrance.

"I know. The pressure's on us to win," he responded with an unexpected candor.

"The ballclub you built, it won't let us down." Sensing his guard was down by the I-sure-hope-you're-right look on his face, I continued, "We got this, man. *Faith*, remember that word. As always, it's a pleasure. "

Exchanging handshakes, into the restaurant he went with the weight of the world on his shoulders.

And off I went, to clean up another mess.

Hall of Fame catcher Yogi Berra, our greatest living Yankee, has to be the most lovable man in the organization. Warm, inviting and approachable, whether assisted by golf cart or walking with special assistants, he would always take time out to say hello. The occasions where we spoke, our usual, ten-second conversations always ended in laughter, or us exchanging a hi-five.

It was a pleasure interfacing with Yankee family, as well as some of the major celebrities that came by that restroom. Never one to be star-struck or badger anyone for an autograph, an innate security mode usually took over. They were Yankees fans for a day or night, and needed the peace of enjoying the ballgame, and when they were in my presence, my silent admiration morphed into a protective cloak.

A fan of the *Die Hard* movies, when Bruce Willis came by the lounge, I smiled. While no words were exchanged (I spent a couple of minutes warding off autograph-hounding waiters trying to say hi), our paths crossed as he neared the exit to return to his seat.

"Yippee ki-yay," I said with a wink. Seeing the glow of his beam would have been enough for me, but he went one better.

"Thanks, man," he said as we shared a fist-bump.

"I can't wait to see what you do next," I said to movie and TV actor Taye Diggs, greeting him with an embrace.

"I can't wait to see what I do as well," he said.

"Whatever you do, continue to dip it in your greatness," I encouraged.

After a warm embrace, he went on his way.

Paul Simon, a kind, genuine man, frequented the place, and we would talk about his partner Art Garfunkel and other musical inspirations as if we were long-lost brothers. Patrons would look at us like "Wow, he's talking to him"; sometimes interrupting our discussions for an autograph or two. Film director Spike Lee, wearing a Yankees cap with the twenty-six championship years on it, often visited my lounge. And on one occasion, I had the opportunity to meet his father, and present an autographed novel and media kit to him. Emmy Award-winning actor Michael Imperioli, aka Christopher Moltisanti from *The Sopranos*, is another cool dude. Talking about his roles in cinema, I made him laugh when I mentioned that his portrayal of Jojo, from the movie *Bad Boys*, may have triggered his fame.

Hip-hop artist Fat Joe and I had a skull session about the rap game, and how much it's changed. After we both admitted missing Big Pun, his late partner in crime, "Keep makin' it happen," I said as we shared a hug.

"Yo, you're real peeps. I feel your love," he said after the embrace.

Encountering some of the world's most creative talents was an awesome experience, but there were two moments—one hilarious, one very revealing—that I'll cherish for the rest of my life:

During the Subway series, on Saturday, June 13, 2009, a distinguished eighty-something-year-old man entered the restroom to relieve himself. Recognizing him immediately, I thought of how he was a Calypso giant and handsome cinema star in the 1950s. He'd probably had my grandmother swooning, yet passionately had touched my mother's soul by risking everything he accomplished standing up for the Civil Rights Movement in the 1960s. This was a man who provided for activists during times of struggle, raised thousands of dollars to release many that were imprisoned simply for the color of their skin, financed the Freedom Riders and spoke loudly at any slight against people of color. In more recent times, he was very critical of former President George W. Bush and his faulty administration. A musician, actor, social activist, and a man who stood for everything right for many generations, to say that I felt a sense of pride to be in the restroom with this man alone was a gross understatement.

Speechless as he approached the sink area, I greeted him with a warm smile.

Turning on the motion sensitive faucets, I asked him, "Are you a Yankee fan, sir?"

"No. I'm a Mets fan," he responded. Clasping my hands, then, pausing while peering deeply into my eyes, what next came from him completely rattled me. "God has a message for you."

My mind whirling between confusion and shock, in those precious milliseconds, I went from friendly to completely naked and vulnerable as a myriad of thoughts ran through me. *How did he know I was a man of deep faith? Oh, God, I hope I didn't offend him by helping him wash his hands? Can I start over by admitting my recognizance and saying that I'm privileged to be in his presence? God, if you're listening, help me out.*

My fears, of course, were unnecessarily unfounded. Perhaps he saw it in my eyes, or alternatively, an intuition spoke to his soul, but the tone of what came next was as soothing as much as it was spiritual.

"You should never settle, for you have too much going for you," he said.

"You can tell, huh?"

With a smile, the man nodded.

"It comes across to anyone that comes in here."

I lowered my head as he sang part of my life with his words.

"To be honest, I feel like I'm on assignment from God. Something wonderful is happening here," I confessed.

"You're supposed to be here. But you're never to settle. You're anointed for greatness, so walk with the faith and confidence of a King," he added.

"I will, sir."

Like a son does to a father that loves him so, I dried his hands. After a pause, we shared a ten-second hug and I kissed his forehead in reverence. By this time, a couple of awestruck Yankees fans who witnessed the forming of a deep, intimate relationship invaded the moment as he left.

"Don't you know who that was?" one asked.

Smiling, "Just another guy that needed a little help," I said, deflecting my knowledge of the very famous man.

The man would come to three more games during the season, and every time we saw each other, the love of two spirits surfaced unashamedly by way of embraces and pleasant conversation. In fact, the "Never Settle" message that he delivered is one of the reasons why my ruminations of the past year now appear on paper.

And whatever blessings God may have in store for my obedience, I have Harry Belafonte to thank for carrying out what Our Father put into his spirit.

God bless you, Mr. Belafonte.

When Ken Griffey Jr. and the Seattle Mariners invaded town in early July, I had the honor of meeting a man whose Cheshire-cat grin, only-the-devil-may-care attitude, magnetic charisma and versatile talent as an actor, has made him an American icon. Known for his astounding portrayals of dark-themed characters, I often wondered how much of him did this three-time Academy Award winner put into the character portrayals to make them believable.

I would find out on July 2.

Around the fifth inning, as I was refreshing my lounge, he came with one security guard, walked up to me, and says, "Hey."

Smiling at his down-to-earth greeting, I went, "Hey, how are ya?"

"Fine," he responded, exchanging a hi-five with me.

"I know why you're doing well, sir."

"Why's that?"

Instinctively, I broke into an impersonation of my movie favorite characters, Col. Nathan Jessup, from *A Few Good Men*. Fixing my face to resemble the person in my presence, I then let loose. "'Cause I eat breakfast three-hundred yards away from four-thousand Cubans who are trained to kill me, so don't think for one second you can come into my restroom, flash your thing, and make me nervous."

Seeing his tribute by way of a big grin was more than I bargained for, but what happened next was the most hilarious moment of the season. As we chatted, suddenly we're bum-rushed by cameras and star-struck Yankee fans; about ten to twenty. Seeing this popular man go from calm to unnerved bothered me, so I said, "C'mon, man, you better go use the urinal."

Nodding nervously, he agreed. Soon, the restroom was packed with guys behaving like kids, trying to get a look at him. A couple of them were running their mouths non-stop next to him as he tried to release.

For a split second, I felt sorry for this renowned icon, and was about to scream "For crissakes, will you let him pee in peace!" Before my thoughts could leave my lips, I heard this loud announcement:

"Alright, camera people, you want to take a picture of something, take a picture of my dick!!!"

Laughing along with everyone present for this only-in-the-new-

Yankee-Stadium moment, I wanted to run out of the restroom and fall out, but I was only reduced to letting out that chuckle. Quickly regaining my composure, I escorted him past his throng of admirers, out of the lavatory, and toward Mugsy and the security officers that were waiting for him. Watching him walk away, all I could do was smile and think:

Jack Nicholson isn't acting. That's really him.

The irony of both moments is that the Yankees lost both of those games. But somehow, I was winning, for my dreams were becoming a reality.

Soon, my one season in pinstripes would get even better.

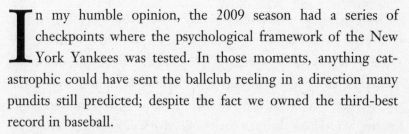

FIRST PLACE:
BACK WHERE WE BELONG

I n my humble opinion, the 2009 season had a series of checkpoints where the psychological framework of the New York Yankees was tested. In those moments, anything catastrophic could have sent the ballclub reeling in a direction many pundits still predicted; despite the fact we owned the third-best record in baseball.

(NOTE: *Skip Bayless, still believing that the Yankees would fall apart and not come out of the AL East, suddenly became enamored with the surging Tampa Bay Rays, announcing on his First and 10 show that they would pass us in the standings.*)

The initial checkpoint came early. For all the newfound chemistry developed during spring training, it appeared that the steroid revelation and subsequent hip-surgery of Alex Rodriguez would tear apart the unity.

It turned out quite the opposite.

Bringing the team closer, the entire squad formed a protective shield over its troubled slugger by coming together to the news conference where A-Rod came clean. Finally allowed to fit in as opposed to always standing out, on May 8th, the maligned superstar-turned-underdog thanked the team for its support by hitting a home run on the first pitch he saw that season. Like a jolt of electricity, he triggered a nine-game, early-season charge that was highlighted with the walk-off wins against Minnesota.

Another checkpoint came on June 24. In Atlanta for an interleague match-up, they had lost four out of six to the Washington Nationals and Florida Nationals, then got blanked by four Brave pitchers in the series opener.

Taking a page right out of George Steinbrenner's time-honored "Sense of Urgency Handbook," General Manager Brian Cashman cancelled a trip to Triple-A affiliate Scranton, then rerouted to Atlanta to see the team up close. Giving no indication to the growing whispers concerning Manager Joe Girardi's job security, before the second game of the series he used positive reinforcement. Letting the players know that "We're all in this together"—meaning managers, coaches, ownership and players—he simply told them they were an exceptional ballclub good enough to win a championship, but needed to look through their collective windows and believe in themselves to perform at an optimum level.

At first, the surprise visit and speech had the Yankees sleepwalking. For five innings of that second Atlanta game, they went hitless. Trailing 1-0 in the sixth, Brett Gardner led off the sixth with a walk. He didn't stay there very long, thanks to a missed call by first-base umpire Bill Welke on a pickoff play. With scoreboard replays clearly showing that Gardner was safe, out of the dugout came Joe Girardi, who argued the call until he was ejected. The Yankees fans in attendance cheered the embattled skipper as he left the field, but they would have roared even louder for what happened in the dugout.

Turning the card over to bench coach Tony Pena and making his way to the clubhouse, the banished manger was startled by a gentle hand on his back. Turning around, he saw Yankees captain Derek Jeter. It was a small gesture, yet the volume of it was deafening in its message: Let's get the party started again and turn this thing around.

It happened immediately: reserve catcher Francisco Cervelli drilled his first big-league homer on the next pitch, and by the inning's end, three more runs had crossed the plate, propelling the Yankees to an 8-4 victory and another winning streak.

A critical checkpoint of the season came by way of a two-and-a-half-week stretch following the All-Star break. How would the Yankees respond after being swept by the Los Angeles Angels? Would an extended losing streak follow, thus flushing the Yankees' title hopes down the drain? Or would they make their move?

If this were a horse race in...let's say the year 1973, the Yankees would have been comparable to the legendary Secretariat running the second leg of the Triple Crown, the Preakness Stakes. Breaking from the starting gate slowly, by the beginning of the first turn, jockey Ron Turcotte had the horse running last. Then Turcotte and Secretariat made their move. Sensing that no other horses seized control of the race (the other five horses dawdled along, seemingly trying to save something for a stretch run), the jockey boldly moved his hands in along the reins, and the horse responded with a spectacular back-stretch run. Moving from last-to-first, he passed by noted rival horse Sham and others. Rival riders went from loping along to running their horses faster than they wanted in an effort to keep up. Assuming the lead horse was going too fast, when Secretariat faltered down the home stretch, they figured, one of them would pick up the pieces.

He never did. Surprising the other riders with that daring midrace move and the stamina-filled, sprinter's kick finish, by the time they knew what had hit them, the race was over, and Secretariat was two-thirds of the way to his Triple Crown.

The 2009 Yankees, like Secretariat in the Preakness, broke from the gates slowly. By the season's first turn, they were still finding themselves, jockeying for position as the division rivals either lauded themselves for being in the divisional race; or in the instance of the rival Boston Red Sox (the horse Sham in the analogy), failed to run away and hide with a dominant stretch of good baseball. As the 2009 baseball season entered into its crucial back-stretch, so with it came another critical checkpoint.

How would the Yankees respond?

Playing the Detroit Tigers at home in their first game after the All-Star break, they trailed 3-2 in the bottom of the seventh. Battling Tiger hurler Joel Zumaya, rally igniter Derek Jeter fought off a fastball and punched it into right field for a single. Then Johnny Damon jumped on another fastball and drove it past right fielder Clete Thomas for a double. Sensing another late-game miracle, the Stadium rocked as Zumaya quickly fell behind Mark Teixeira. With a 3-0 count, he threw the slugger a fastball right down Broadway, then turned to watch his pitch soar deep into the right-field stands for a three-run homer and a 5-3 Yankees victory.

The Saturday afternoon contest brought pitching aces C.C. Sabathia and Justin Verlander together for a mid-season, pitcher's duel, and the two didn't disappoint the 46, 423 fans in attendance. Matching each other pitch-for-pitch and scoreboard zeroes for 6-1/2 innings, once again the Yankees struck in their half seventh. Leading off, Alex Rodriguez lofted what appeared to be a routine fly ball to the opposite field. Perhaps accustomed to the spacious dimensions of their Comerica Park, Verlander, centerfielder Curtis Granderson and other Detroit Tiger teammates in the dugout expected the innocent-looking fly to produce an out.

Only one problem, however: Things didn't usually work that way in the new Yankee Stadium. The seemingly lazy pop-up found the glove of a fan one row deep into the right-field stands for a home run, breaking the scoreless tie. An ensuing insurance run rendered Tiger outfielder Marcus Thames' eighth-inning blast moot as the Yankees won 2-1.

Sunday, Old-Timers Day, brought out Yankee Legends past and present. Experiencing the moment live for the first time, tears flowed as I viewed the ceremony alone in the restroom; for I received another blessing within this season where my dreams came true.

Composing myself, I had to see the event up close.

Sneaking outside and finding great joy in watching the player introductions of Don Larsen, Yogi Berra, Whitey Ford, Ron Guidry, Mike Mussina, David Cone, Willie Randolph, Bucky Dent and of course, Reggie Jackson, it surprised me to see an ageless Mickey Rivers speed around the bases after stroking a double.

I found greater joy over what transpired in the regular game. Striking out eight batters through seven innings, a refreshed Joba Chamberlain pitched his finest game of the season and was supported with solo homers by A-Rod and Teixeira in a series-sweeping 2-1 victory.

A third consecutive 2-1 triumph came against the Baltimore Orioles. Hideki Matsui, battling balky knees and a reluctant transition from outfielder-to-designated hitter, turned on a Jim Johnson fastball and launched a walk-off moon-shot into the right-field seats. Rounding third base and throwing his batting helmet into the night sky after the circuit-tripper, there was a bigger reason for Matsui and the Yankees to celebrate: The Red Sox were in the process of losing its third consecutive road game.

The American League East leading tie placed around the neck of the Pinstripes fit oh-so-good.

The next night, Tuesday, July 21, 2009, the Yankees were tailored and suited with a whole new outfit; one I hoped they would wear for the remainder of the regular season. Fifth starter Sergio Mitre allowed three earned runs over 5-2/3 innings, Alfredo Aceves, Phil Coke and Mariano Rivera slammed the door on the Orioles with 3-1/3 innings of scoreless relief, and second baseman Robinson Cano drove in four runs in a methodical 6-4 win.

Meanwhile, in Texas, the Red Sox bats continued to slump. Having been stifled in the two previous games by Roy Halladay and Kevin Milwood, respectively, rookie Tommy Hunter held Boston's lagging offensive in check as the Texas Rangers extended their losing streak to four games.

That 4-2 Red Sox defeat, and a .194 team batting average during their five-game skid was defense, and a current five-game winning streak. Stirred and shaped, the recipe was poured into a bowl, and the meal looked like this: For the first time since June 8, the New York Yankees were in first place.

The meal was delightfully appetizing for Yankees fans, and atrociously nauseating for anyone from the New England area.

The Yankee winning streak would continue to eight games before Oakland pitcher Gio Gonzalez silenced their bats, hurling 6-2-3 innings of one-run, two-hit baseball in a 6-4 Athletic win. Regrouping quickly to take four of their next five—including two of three from the third-place Tampa Bay Rays, the team Skip Bayless thought would surpass us in the standings—on July 29 they were sitting pretty, 3-1/2 games ahead of the reeling Red Sox.

What occurred next was the resolve-testing portion of this checkpoint. Just as quickly as they overtook their bitter rivals for first place, the Yankees almost returned the favor. While the Red Sox rediscovered their hitting stroke in Baltimore, New York was losing three straight in Chicago to the White Sox in an ugly, frustrating fashion. A Saturday afternoon 14-4 shellacking of A.J. Burnett and other hurlers reduced their lead to one-half game.

Reaching a crisis point once more, the call went to C.C. Sabathia to stop the bleeding.

The big left-handed ace gutted through seven-plus innings, allowing five runs and ten hits. Staked to an early 3-0 lead, then relinquishing it in a four-run third, Sabathia angrily stormed off the U.S. Cellular Field mound. Normally a jovial spirit, perhaps he and the Yankees knew they had reached an important moment of the season.

Now, there he sat, in the dugout seething. Glaring at catcher Jose Molina, "That's it. That's all they get," he announced.

Molina co-signed.

"No more for them," he echoed.

Locked in for the remainder of his outing, the Yankees lefthander was in shut-down mode, allowing just one more run through four innings.

Centerfielder Melky Cabrera bailed him out. Igniting the Yankees with a three-run homer in the second inning, he doubled and scored a run in the fourth, then singled home a run in the fifth off White Sox pitcher Mark Buehrle—a man who one month earlier had pitched a perfect game. Coming to the plate in the top of the ninth inning, Cabrera only needed a triple to accomplish what no Yankee had done since 1995—hit for the cycle.

Lacing a liner over the head of Jermaine Dye—who aided Cabrera's effort by misplaying the drive—he motored around first base, and sprinted toward second. His teammates rooting him on in the dugout, Melky found an extra gear, stormed by second, ran even faster, and slid into third just ahead of the relay to complete a rare cycle.

The already raucous Yankees bench went wild. Not only did they witness a remarkable feat of batting power, base-running speed, hitting prowess and great fortune, they avoided a four-game sweep with a huge 8-5 victory.

The leak in the dam now fixed, the Yankees had made it through the season's third checkpoint with a half-game lead. Three nights, two more road victories over the Toronto Blue Jays—including one over ace-on-the-trading-block Halladay—and two more Red Sox road losses—compliments of Bayless' new love, the Tampa Bay Rays—and the cushion was back up to 2-1/2 games.

The stage was now set for a showdown in the Bronx, a four-game series that I had circled on the calendar way back in March. The Yankees and Red Sox, with the balance of power in the American League East at stake, were going head-to-head.

Not wanting it any other way, a certain restroom attendant was ready.

A YANKEE-RED SOX REFLECTIVE, FROM MY EYES

ACT ONE: THE JOY

As a matter of fact, all my life I had been groomed to walk onto the stage of this rivalry.

Ever since I was seven years old, I've been a sports enthusiast; especially, a baseball fan. Collecting baseball cards, I remembered how I owned the whole 1973 Topps set. In order to complete the 660-card collection, the last original card I had to get was Willie Mays. Finally receiving that blessing in late September 1973, I ran down Fenimore Street in the Flatbush section of Brooklyn screaming, "I got Willie Mays," at the top of my lungs, rejecting a twenty-dollar offer for the card, going upstairs...and watching highlights of his retirement ceremony.

The next month on television, I sat glued in front of my mother's black-and-white television, expecting something spectacular from the "Say Hey Kid." Playing in the World Series for the New York Mets, he was still producing game-winning hits (two-run single in a 10-7 Game 2 victory); however, what I remember most is his battle with the sunny Oakland California skies.

Watching him struggle, stagger, then stumble when misplaying two extra-inning fly balls, "He doesn't look good," I said to my mother.

Seeing the tears well in her eyes, she sighed. "Yes, son, but he was the best."

The day before, in Game 1, I saw Henry Aaron throw out the first pitch of the series. After my mother shared with me his proximity to breaking the most hallowed record in sports, Babe Ruth's home run total of 714 (at the end of 1973, Aaron had 713) and his difficult journey against racial hatred, April couldn't come soon enough.

Sure enough, Monday, April 8, 1974 came, and once I witnessed Aaron launch a 2-1 Al Downing fastball over the left-field fence at Atlanta's Fulton County Stadium and into the glove of bullpen reliever Tom House, I became obsessed with baseball.

For the next few years, I read everything about America's Pastime. Whether it was the back of baseball cards for statistics to increase my recall of numbers, books that compiled biographies of the game's greatest stars, or preview periodicals that projected yearly outlooks, nothing went untouched.

Moving to Staten Island at age nine, another fond childhood memory is when a Bookmobile—a public library on wheels—came into my Park Hill neighborhood. Racing across the Fox Hill shopping area to the vehicle once a week, my favorite book was the *Baseball Encyclopedia*. Borrowing the dense book on numerous occasions and perusing the year-by-year narratives (usually a two-page synopsis of each league), it was at that age I became familiar with a deep, personal rivalry between two East Coast baseball teams and their respective cities. Unmatched in its intensity on the baseball diamond and its fervor and history off of it, the most famous rivalry in all of professional sports is between the New York Yankees and Boston Red Sox.

Reading about the 1904 season, I identified with the frustration New York Highlanders fans felt way back then when spitball pitcher Jack Chesbro's 40-win, 454-inning, 48-complete game, 239-strikeout, 1.82 ERA season went for naught. Locked in an American League pennant struggle with the world champion Boston Americans (*also known as the Pilgrims, they didn't adopt the Red Sox nickname until 1907*), it came down to a dramatic doubleheader at the Highlanders home field, Hilltop Park.

Needing two victories to win the pennant, Chesbro pitched and won the first game, but went into the top of the ninth inning of the second game deadlocked at 2. With runner Lou Criger on third base, one of his spitballs got away from him in the top of the ninth. Sailing over catcher Deacon McGuire's head, Criger scored the winning Boston run, and the Highlanders meekly went down in the bottom frame.

That one moment epitomized the rivalry for the first eighteen years of the twentieth century. While the Highlanders—renamed the Yankees in 1912—wallowed in the American League's second division, the Red Sox were winning six pennants and five world championships. Fielding stars like Cy Young, Jimmy Collins, Tris Speaker, Harry Hooper, Duffy Lewis and Smoky Joe Wood, the Red Sox, along with Connie Mack's Philadelphia Athletics (six pennants, three world titles), ruled the league.

After the Red Sox world championship in 1918, things began to change. Owner Harry Frazee, mired in tremendous debt after purchasing the franchise on credit and producing shows, stripped away the Red Sox aura bit by bit. After a sixth-place finish in 1919, he sold legendary pitcher-turned-slugging-outfielder Babe Ruth for $125,000 and a loan of $300,000, a security amount on Fenway Park, the Red Sox' home stadium.

(NOTE: *So when those Fenway Fools—remember their self-given nickname of the early twenty-first century, "Idiots"; no further elaboration necessary—start blabbing about recent history, merely present the facts as referenced. We owned them in more ways than you ever dreamed: between the white lines of a baseball diamond and, for a brief time, paid the mortgage on Fenway Park!*)

With some of the money, Red Sox Owner Harry Frazee financed a non-musical play, *My Lady Friends*, a production later put to music and renamed *No, No, Nanette*. Opening on Broadway in December 1919, the play had simultaneously launched the beginning of the Yankees' dynasty while leaving Boston raped of its nucleus.

The Red Sox total of five World Series championships, a record at the time, would remain unchanged for eighty-six years. Soon after the Ruth heist, Frazee, for reasons only known to him and the baseball gods, sent player after player to New York, either by trade, or in the alternative, more money. The list reads like a who's who of dynasty-building Yankee lore: Sad Sam Jones, Bullet Joe Bush, Everett Scott, Waite Hoyt, Herb Pennock, George Pipgras, Joe Dugan, Wally Schang, and Carl Mays. Even Edward Barrow, the manager of the last Red Sox champion in 1918, abandoned ship. Hired by the Yankees in 1920 as a general manager, he constructed Ruth and the additional fleeced parts into fourteen pennants and ten world championships over the next quarter-century.

The Red Sox soon became a baseball laughingstock. Finishing dead last nine times in eleven seasons, at one point, they averaged over 100 losses a year over an eight-year stretch (1925-1932). Re-establishing stability with his $1.2 million purchase of the ballclub in 1933, for nearly a half-century, Tom Yawkey devoted his finances, time and passion to building the Red Sox into a competitive, championship-caliber ballclub.

Yet as I continued reading baseball history into my adolescence, it became evident that as much as the Red Sox tried, in terms of history, they always came up short against the Yankees. Despite the fact that many greats—Ted Williams, Lefty Grove, Jimmy Foxx, Vern Stephens, Bobby Doerr, Mel Parnell, Johnny Pesky, Carl Yastrzemski, Carlton Fisk, Jim Rice, Bill Lee, Fred Lynn, Luis Tiant, Jim Lonborg, Dominic DiMaggio, Dwight Evans, Wade Boggs and many, many others wore the Red Sox uniform, it seemed there was something magical missing in comparison to a Yankee list of legends: Ruth, Lazzerri, Gehrig, Joe DiMaggio, Dickey, Berra, Mantle, Maris, Ford, Howard, Guidry, Munson, Chambliss, Nettles, Jackson, Guidry, Gossage, Randolph, Winfield and Mattingly.

It was that way on the playing field as well. A sportswriter once said that the Yankees' rivalry with the Red Sox was akin to the rivalry "between a hammer and a nail." With the Yankees constantly hammering away, by century's end, the facts overwhelmingly supported the statement. From 1920 through 2003, the Yankees won thirty-nine American League pennants and twenty-six World Series championships, compared to only four pennants for the Red Sox. Further analysis showed that in every year that the Red Sox won the pennant—1946, 1967, 1975 and 1986—they lost the World Series; all in deciding seventh games, and in the most painful ways imaginable.

In 1946, the St. Louis Cardinals won the World Series in the seventh game when Enos "Country" Slaughter scored the ninth-inning, go-ahead run all the way from first base on a single to left field. The throw from the left-fielder was cut off by Boston shortstop Johnny Pesky, who hesitated ever so slightly, then fired the ball to home plate a split-second late.

In 1967, after the Red Sox won the American League Pennant on the season's last day, they battled the Cardinals again in a classic. In another seventh game, ace Jim Lonborg, pitching on two days' rest, was shelled by Cardinal batters. Hall of Fame ace Bob Gibson completely shut down the Red Sox with a dominant three-hit performance in a 7-2 victory.

After a dramatic 12th-inning victory over the Cincinnati Reds in Game 6 of the 1975 World Series, *(recalling staying past midnight to watch this game, I distinctly remember the teams being fatigued when Carlton Fisk drove a shot toward the Green Monster. Fisk started to run toward first, but stalled as the ball appeared to be heading foul. Jumping up-and-down waving his arms fair, the Red Sox catcher willed the ball off of the foul pole for the 7-6 game-winner)* Game 7 appeared to have left off right where Game 6 had as Boston seized a 3-0 lead in the third inning.

The Reds were not about to go quietly into the night, however.

Determined as well, they fought back to tie the game. In the top of the ninth, Ken Griffey led off with a walk and managed to reach third on a sacrifice and a groundout. Reliever Jim Burton intentionally walked Pete Rose, but Joe Morgan knocked a clutch single up the middle for the 4-3 lead. Red closer Will McEnaney silenced the Fenway faithful with a three-up, three-down bottom frame, and the Reds emerged as World Champions.

The 1986 Series was the most painful of all. Facing a heavily favored New York Met team that won 108 games in the regular season, the Red Sox won the first two games but lost the next two at Fenway, knotting the series at two games apiece. When pitcher Bruce Hurst recorded his second victory of the series in Game 5, the Red Sox returned to Shea Stadium looking to win their first championship in sixty-eight years.

However, Game 6 would go down as one of the most devastating losses in club history. After pitching seven strong innings, Roger Clemens was lifted from the game with a 3–2 lead. After the Mets then scored a run off reliever and former Met Calvin Schraldi to tie the score 3–3, the game went to extra innings, where the Red Sox took a 5–3 lead in the top of the 10th on a solo home run by Dave Henderson, a double by Wade Boggs, and an RBI single by second baseman Marty Barrett.

Recalling how after recording two outs in the bottom of the 10th, a message appeared briefly on the Shea Stadium scoreboard congratulating the Red Sox as World Champions, I remember how quiet Shea Stadium was that Saturday night; it was funereal. After so many years of frustration, Red Sox fans all over could taste the flavor of sweet victory.

And I was fuming. Having finally confessed my Yankee allegiance to friends and family and regretting that the Don Mattingly and Dave Winfield-led Yankees came up short during the regular season, I would have been happy to see anyone win other than the Red Sox; even the Mets.

After all, our annoying little cross-town brothers need a victory every now and then, I lamented.

With the Mets down to their last strike, I was about to drown my now twenty-year-old sorrows in a beer (the drinking age in New York was nineteen then) when Mets catcher Gary Carter, down to his last strike, hit a single. Ensuing singles by Kevin Mitchell and third baseman Ray Knight plated Carter.

Receiving my Heineken from the local bartender as the Red Sox changed pitchers, I noticed the beer tasted better than ever as I sipped from it.

With centerfielder Mookie Wilson batting, a wild pitch by Bob Stanley sent Mitchell racing home with the tying run.

Drinking my beer even quicker, each swig grew more amazing than its predecessor.

Then, the improbable happened: Wilson then hit a slow ground ball to first, and to the joy of many a Yankees fan all over, the ball rolled through first baseman Bill Buckner's legs, allowing Knight to score the winning run from second.

Considering the fact that a bad-kneed Buckner was in the game at that point was incomprehensible, though one might say that Red Sox Manager John McNamara was trying to repay Buckner for his outstanding career by leaving him in the game.

Placing the empty bottle on the counter, as if on cue, the bartender, perhaps caught up in the euphoria that went from announcer Vin Scully's depiction to the out-of-their-mind ecstasy that was Shea Stadium to the screaming New Yorkers seated right next to me, asked me if I had enjoyed my drink.

With a big grin, I responded, "The best beer I ever tasted in my life, sir."

With that, I received a free one.

Two nights later, the Mets rallied from an early 3-0 deficit and won Game 7 with an 8-5 victory, concluding the devastating Red

Sox collapse. By now, I was a walking sports encyclopedia that could recite all of their collapses...

As well as their second-place finishes to the Yankees. During this time, the Red Sox finished second in the standings to the Yankees on twelve occasions—in 1938, 1939, 1941, 1942, 1949, 1978, and every year from 1998 to 2003. Over an eighty-four-year period (1921-2003), the Yankees finished with a better regular-season record than the Red Sox an amazing sixty-six times.

Two of those seasons immediately come to mind; one I read about in my youth and one I witnessed. The 1949 season featured a dramatic finish between the Yankees and Red Sox. The Red Sox, managed by former Yankees skipper Joe McCarthy, were the favorites while the Yankees, battling through a tremendous amount of injuries under first-year skipper Casey Stengel, were painted as the underdogs. After trailing the Yankees throughout the campaign, the Red Sox found themselves up by one game with two games left against the pinstripes at Yankee Stadium. Needing only one win, they came up empty: The Yankees swept them to capture the pennant, and then started a record run of five straight World Series titles.

In 1978, the Red Sox, led by MVP Jim Rice, Fred Lynn, Carl Yastrzemski, catcher Carlton Fisk and George Scott, seemed destined for a trip to the Fall Classic for the second time in the decade. Leading the Yankees in the standings by 14-1/2 games by mid-July, the Red Sox were a shoo-in while their chief antagonists were in a controversial state. The Yankees were in a season-long slump, and the public and media seemed more concerned about what happened next in the "Bronx Zoo" than they were about winning baseball games.

With less than three months to go in the regular season, Yankees skipper Billy Martin resigned on July 23, and was replaced with Bob Lemon. The Yankees responded to the managerial change by winning nineteen of twenty-seven games in August, while the Red Sox, now ravaged by injuries, hit a rough patch.

By Thursday, September 7, the Yankees had chopped down the once insurmountable 14-1/2-game deficit to four games, and went to Fenway Park for a four-game series. In a mind-boggling sweep, the Yankees won all four games in the series by the scores of 15–3, 13–2, 7–0 and 7–4 for a combined score of 42–9. Carrying their red-hot momentum past Boston and into first place, on September 16, the Yankees held a 3-1/2 game lead over the hated Red Sox.

But this Red Sox team, perhaps their greatest ever, won twelve of their next fourteen games, including the last eight in a row. Forcing the Yankees to play flawless baseball, the two teams went stride-for-stride during the last week. The Yankees won seven straight games, but had to win the season's last game—and *their* eighth in a row—to capture the American League East title. The win would be their 100th of the season.

Remembering that Sunday afternoon and how I rushed home from the Kingdom Hall (the church I attended in my youth), I couldn't wait to see the Yankees complete their great comeback. Turning on WPIX-11, the local Yankees network, to hear Frank Messer, Bill White and Phil Rizzuto, I was ready to watch the completion of a historic comeback.

Cleveland Indian pitcher and noted Yankee-killer Rick Waits wasn't having it. In pitching a five-hitter, Waits beat the Yankees 9-2. With the bitter division rivals now possessing identical 99–63 records, a one-game playoff was scheduled that Monday afternoon to determine who would get that elusive 100th victory.

Ron Guidry, the Yankees outstanding 25-game winner and the eventual 1978 American League Cy Young winner, started for New York on three days' rest. Mike Torrez, a former Yankee who acquired Red Sox DNA and was now a 16-game winner for Boston, took the hill for this showdown. Watching the game on ABC as opposed to the local broadcast, I was a twelve-year-old bundle of nerves. While not a Yankees fan just yet, the sheer magnitude of a one-game season had me tense.

The winner moves on.

The loser goes home.

Sports at its very best found a deeper place in my heart that afternoon.

Immediately, the Red Sox jumped out to an early 2-0 lead. In the second inning, Carl Yastrzemski jumped all over a Guidry fastball, and deposited it just inside the right-field pole for a solo home run. In the sixth inning, a run-scoring single by that year's MVP Jim Rice and an intentional walk to Carlton Fisk placed runners on first and second. Threatening to break the game wide open, Fred Lynn cracked a tiring Guidry fastball toward the right-field corner. Lou Pinella, the Yankees right-fielder, snared the drive just before it hit the wall.

"Phew," I said. But relief was drenched with reality: With nine outs remaining in the Yankees' season, I wondered if God that day was a Yankees Fan.

Then, in the top half of the seventh, with Chris Chambliss and Roy White on base, Yankees shortstop Bucky Dent, who hit five home runs that year, came to the plate. After fouling a pitch off his foot and receiving a new bat from Mickey Rivers—a bat with a home run in it, Rivers told him—Dent lofted a Torrez pitch just over the Green Monster in left field to put the Yankees ahead by a score of 3-2. The images of left-fielder Carl Yastrzemski's knees buckling, as the baseball found its resting place in the screen, and the ensuing silence of Fenway Park that screamed shock, are remembered as if it happened yesterday.

Without delay, the New York Yankees, like a shark smelling blood in the water, attacked. Thurman Munson doubled home another run, and Reggie Jackson homered in the eighth to put the Yanks up 5-2.

You might find this hard to believe, but as I watched Reggie's shot reach the center-field seats and then the camera shot of Yankees Principal Owner George Steinbrenner celebrating in his box seat, my youthful intuition told me the game wasn't over.

Sensing that the game was a mirror reflection of the entire season, "That run will decide the game," I said that Monday afternoon.

It wouldn't be the last time I predicted a Yankee-Red Sox outcome.

Bravely, the Red Sox closed the gap to 5-4 in the bottom of the eighth inning on run-scoring singles by Fred Lynn and Carl Yastrzemski, and had an opportunity to either tie or win the game in the ninth. With one out and Rick Burleson on first in the bottom of on in the ninth, Jerry Remy turned on a Goose Gossage heater and hit a laser to right. With the late afternoon October sun glaring, Lou Piniella couldn't locate the ball.

Miraculously, the baseball landed in front of him, sprang up to his left, and Piniella flashed out his glove and trapped it on that one bounce. Had it caromed by him, the Kansas City Royals' opponent in the 1978 American League Championship Series would have been the Boston Red Sox.

The play, a lucky one, was proof that God wore pinstripes that day. After Rice, the next batter, flied to deep right center, the Red Sox had runners at the corners. The season for two teams was all set up for one last showdown: a dramatic two-out, bottom-of-the-ninth encounter between two future Hall of Famers.

With an autumn sun serving as a spectacular backdrop, I held my breath as I watched the duel. On the mound was Richard "Goose" Gossage, the premier flame-throwing relief pitcher of his time; and waving an imposing bat sixty feet, six inches away, was eighteen-year veteran Carl Yastrzemski, arguably the best fastball hitter of his.

My young heart couldn't take it.

The first pitch, a high fastball, was taken for ball one. Years later,

I heard that Peter Gammons, future Baseball Hall of Fame sports-writer but then Red Sox journalist for the *Boston Globe*, mentioned that "Yaz always wins in these moments."

Was this one of those moments?

Gossage's second pitch, another 90-plus-miles-an-hour fastball, had nasty movement to it and ran inside on the Red Sox great. Swinging, one city groaned, and another celebrated. The seconds the pop-up stayed in the air seemed like hours. Landing in the glove of Yankees third baseman Graig Nettles somewhere near the third base coaching box, Yankees fans all over went berserk, then packed their bags for Kansas City, Los Angeles (the World Series) and a second straight world championship.

The Boston Red Sox, one win and one run short of being the best team in baseball, went home.

By the time these two teams faced off in the 1999 American League Championship Series, an arrogant sense of entitlement inhabited my frame of mind. Unable to fathom a Red Sox victory, though I hadn't completely bought into the "Curse of the Bambino," I knew the franchise was snake-bit. Encountering passionate Red Sox fans at the law firm where I worked, a mere shaking of my head spoke words my mouth didn't ever need to say.

Finally, when pushed to speak, "We own them. They'll never, ever beat us," I boldly announced.

My sentiment was shared by members of the Yankee family, for legend has Bernie Williams quoting Yogi Berra at the start of the series, when the famed catcher visited the Yankees' clubhouse.

"He said to us, 'They've been trying for eighty years, but they can't beat us,'" Williams said.

Years later, when Berra was asked if he recalled telling the story, he gave his answer with a simple smile. When asked if winning the 1949 pennant was that much sweeter because it came at the expense of those Red Sox, his smile evolved into a chuckle.

Like the Hatfields and McCoys, the feelings of the rivalry only intensified with age…

And for the Fenway faithful, total frustration. What happened in the series served as an exasperating exercise in *frustration*. After winning two one-run games at the Stadium *(Game 1 featured a tenth-inning walk-off blast by centerfielder Bernie Williams off closer Rod Beck)*, in Game 3, the Yankees sent former Red Sox ace Roger Clemens against a team he had won 192 games for from 1985 to 1996.

Clemens, making his first appearance at Fenway with the hated Yankees, got shelled. Pitching against Pedro Martinez, his top-of-the rotation replacement, to the delight of the Fenway faithful, he gave up five runs on six hits in two innings. Mercifully removed after facing one batter in the third, Red Sox fans chanted *Where is Roger?*, then a response chant of *In the Shower*.

Meanwhile, Yankee-killer Martinez was sensational. In an effort to keep the Yankees' bats off stride, the fire-balling hurler effectively changed speeds and turned in a brilliant performance, striking out twelve and surrendering just two hits in seven innings. By the time the Yankees scored their only run of the game in the eighth, Boston had a 13-0 lead.

Game 4 was a tight 3-2 contest headed into the top of the ninth when Yankees reserve outfielder Ricky Ledee highlighted a six-run stanza with a grand slam. After second-base umpire Tim Tschida blew a call on a phantom tag of Red Sox Jose Offerman by second baseman Chuck Knoblauch in the bottom of the frame, things got ugly. Livid, Red Sox skipper Jimy Williams got ejected for fiercely arguing the call, and the fans responded by littering the field with debris.

Chuckling to myself as I watched the game, *perhaps they're frustrated because they can't beat us*, I mused.

The only thing that remained was a coronation, and a Yankees 6-1 victory the next night was a mere formality. Derek Jeter, as usual, got the Yankees started with a two-run homer in the first inning; and two more runs in the seventh and ninth ended the baseball season at Fenway Park for 1999.

Beating the Red Sox in 1999, that was great. But nothing... absolutely nothing, compared to the 2003 American League Championship Series. Though separated by six games in the regular season standings (Joe Torre's Yankees won 101 games to the Grady Little-led Red Sox 95), the series was a titanic struggle between two evenly matched baseball powers, as evidenced by the slim, regular season 10-9 Yankee advantage when the teams squared off. The Pinstripes, having been embarrassed and eliminated in the 2002 playoffs by the Anaheim Angels, were determined to go their 39th World Series. And all season long, the Red Sox players, particularly pitcher Pedro Martinez, openly talked up "The Curse." To a man, they made a vow to the City of Boston to end Yankee supremacy and win the World Series for the first time since the peace agreement signing ended World War I.

Sure enough, from the onset of Game 1, passionate Yankees fans reminded the Red Sox of their most recent World Series championship. Serenading the Sox derisively, before the first pitch, a brutal "1918!" chant echoed throughout Yankee Stadium.

Oblivious to the hatred surrounding them, the Red Sox, backed by three homers and solid pitching by knuckleballer Tim Wakefield, stunned the 56, 281 in attendance with a 5-2 opening-game victory. Bouncing back quickly, Andy Pettitte scattered nine hits over 6-2/3 innings as the Yankees evened things at a game apiece 6-2.

The series now shifted to Fenway, the intense, combustible nature simmering between two historic franchises finally erupted. Handed a first-inning 2-0 lead, Pedro Martinez gave it back with solo runs in the second and third. Noting that Martinez's fastball had no life to it, the Bronx Bombers pounced. Leading off the fourth, Jorge

Posada walked and moved to third on first baseman Nick Johnson's hard single. Swinging aggressively, Hideki Matsui ripped an RBI ground-rule double, breaking the 2-2 tie.

Clearly frustrated in his inability to hold the lead, the next pitch Martinez threw violated baseball's unwritten brush-back code. Intentionally whistling a heater behind the right ear of outfielder Karim Garcia, the ball hit him in the back, clearing both teams' benches as the two engaged in a heated argument. Later in the inning, the rattled Red Sox ace pointed a finger at his temple when shouting at Posada in the Yankees' dugout; something the Yankees interpreted as a blatant threat to bean someone else.

In the bottom of the frame, Yankees hurler Roger Clemens retaliated with a high fastball at Boston outfielder Manny Ramirez, who took exception to the pitch by walking toward Clemens waving his bat in anger. Once again, the dugouts and bullpens emptied. Yankees bench Coach Don Zimmer, rushing the mound on seventy-two-year-old legs, raised his hand at Martinez as he reached for him.

Grabbing his head, the Red Sox ace threw him to the grass.

Hitting the ground and rolling over, Zimmer suffered a cut on the bridge of his nose.

Adding to this theater of the bizarre, later in the game Garcia, scaled the right-field wall and joined reliever Jeff Nelson in a fight with a member of the Red Sox grounds crew. All of this overshadowed the fact that Roger Clemens outpitched Martinez, giving the Yankees a hard-earned 4-3 victory and 2-1 series lead.

(NOTE: *Check this out: I read somewhere that at the moment of the bullpen skirmish, the time on the scoreboard clock above them read 7:18 p.m.—7:18 in the evening in military time is 19:18. Think about it.*)

Watching the game in my Bronx apartment that Saturday afternoon, I felt the emotions of both teams in my soul. Trying to keep my emotions in check, the strong dislike I felt for anything having to do with the Red Sox grew by leaps and bounds. The battle between the two best teams in the American League was now a war, with the survivor going to the World Series.

And the war went back and forth.

After a rainout, the Red Sox evened things with a 3-2 victory in Game Four behind Tim Wakefield's second series win. Shutting the Red Sox down in Game 5, Yankees pitchers David Wells and Mariano Rivera held the Bostonians to six hits in a 4-2 triumph. With their backs to the wall, the Red Sox lit up starter Andy Pettitte, losing pitcher Jose Contreras and three other Yankees hurlers with a 16-hit barrage. Their stirring 9-6 victory tied the American League Championship at three games apiece.

The grueling obstacle course completed, the stage was now set for what baseball begged for, something America's Pastime wanted since Jack Chesbro uncorked that wild pitch almost a century earlier: Baseball's grand cathedral, Yankee Stadium, would play host to the New York Yankees and the Boston Red Sox in a seventh-game showdown.

So many elements made this game a classic before the first pitch was ever thrown: On the line was a trip to the World Series; the starting pitchers, Roger Clemens and Pedro Martinez, two of the greatest pitchers of the era, brought a combined nine Cy Young Awards to the party; and the Boston Red Sox and the New York Yankees, bitter rivals for the past century.

Turning on the television that Thursday night in October, to that point, the greatest baseball game I had ever seen was played in October 1986, when those hated Red Sox valiantly staved off postseason elimination at the hands of the California Angels. In Game 5 of the series, the Red Sox were trailing 5-4 and down to their last strike when Dave Henderson launched a Donnie Moore forkball into the left-field seats. After playing spectacular defense for the next inning or so, Henderson's sacrifice fly in the 11th won the game for Boston. It was a shocking defeat for the California Angels—who dropped the next two games in Boston and lost the series—and specifically, Manager Gene Mauch *(who goes down in history as the manager in baseball with the most wins never to have piloted a team in the Fall Classic, the 1986 ALCS being his last opportunity at the brass ring)* and reliever Donnie Moore *(forever linked to the Angels' loss of the pennant, three years later he committed suicide.)*

That 1986 classic is now in second place, for what I viewed alone in my Marble Hill, Bronx apartment on October 16, 2003 had a little bit of everything: twists and turns, adversity and triumph, bit characters, accurate and questionable decisions, and of course, a dramatic ending for the victor and heartbreaking finish for the team that went home.

Again silencing the hostile Bronx crowd, the Red Sox came out swinging. Jump-started by a two-run Trot Nixon home run off Roger Clemens, they scored three runs in the second inning. Padding the run cushion, Boston first baseman Kevin Millar boomed another circuit-tripper to start the fourth, and after a walk to Nixon and single by third baseman Bill Mueller, with runners on first and second with no one out, the Red Sox, fueled by eighty-five years of agonizing futility, seemed poised to slay their personal demons.

Slamming a homemade Long Island Iced Tea down on my coffee table, "He has nothing," I screamed at my brother Jeff over the phone, referring to Clemens. "Torre's got to make a move before this gets out of hand."

(NOTE: *One of my two younger brothers, Jeff, five years my junior, used to steal my baseball cards when we were kids. Furious at him way back then, I am so grateful now, for like his older brother, he is a sports junkie. A boxing guru that rivals Bert Randolph Sugar and Teddy Atlas, we get together for every super-fight, or alternatively, engage in first round, mid-fight and post-fight analysis over the phone. However, in this unique instance, like so many others over the years—Michael Jordan's game-winning shot in game one of the 1997 NBA Finals comes to mind—we both have built-in radar that tell us when we're witnessing sports history.*

With that innate intuition is this loving tribute of brotherhood.)

His telepathy taking over, my younger brother spoke in a calm tone, like he knew something I didn't: "This one is far from over, bruh. The Yankees are going to stage a late rally, battle deep into the extra innings, and the least likely of heroes will emerge."

There was an awkward pause.

Finally, "How do you know?" I asked.

"Fred," Jeff said, using my middle name, "The Red Sox haven't won a damned thing in eighty-five years. What makes you think tonight will be any different? It may take all night, but the Yankees will find a way to win."

Yankees Manager Joe Torre must have owned a silent earpiece to our cross-city phone conversation. Left with no choice but to remove a great pitcher that had absolutely nothing, he walked slowly to the mound and waved his right hand.

The big, blue bullpen doors opened, and out came Mike Mussina. Making his first ever Major League relief appearance after more than 400 starts, he responded to Torre's all-hands-on-deck mantra by slamming the door on the Red Sox hurricane. After striking out Catcher Jason Varitek, he induced an inning-ending, double-play ball from then-Red Sox Johnny Damon. The storm now quelled, Mussina locked that door and tossed away any blowout possibilities by pitching two more scoreless innings.

Meanwhile, Pedro Martinez was making the most of his opportunity to pitch in baseball's ultimate showdown. Pitching magnificently, he baffled New York batters by moving his pitches all around the plate, changing speeds and locations on call. Though he appeared to struggle with his fastball earlier in the series, the velocity of his two-seamer increased inning by inning, eventually topping out on radar guns at 94 mph. Nullifying Mussina's valiant effort with his own brilliance, his one-run, three-hit, seven-strikeout performance through the first six innings was extraordinary...

Extraordinary, yes, but also very taxing.

Putting everything he had into his mastery of the Yankees' lineup, I noticed the enormity of the moment was slowly beginning to take its toll. In the bottom of the seventh, the Yankees began wearing him down. After a hard-hit outs by Hideki Matsui and Jorge Posada, a solo blast by Jason Giambi—his second of the game—narrowed the Bomber deficit to 4-2. Hard singles by Enrique Wilson and Karim Garcia put the tying runs on base, and though second baseman Alfonso Soriano struck out swinging to end the frame, as Pedro and shortstop Nomar Garciaparra hugged in the Red Sox dugout, I saw the beginning of his end.

Picking up the phone once more, "Do you see what I see?" I screamed to Jeff.

"Yeah, Fred. Pedro's tiring fast."

"They better take him out or we're gonna get him!"

No sooner than those words left my lips, back came the Sox in the top of the eighth. David Ortiz's solo shot took the air out of our conversation, and probably allowed all of New England to jump for joy.

With my confidence again wavering, my brother next uttered these exact words: "It looks good for Boston, but now's the time where they screw it up by going with Pedro one inning too long."

"They gotta see he's done," I countered. "He got roped last inning, and besides, that camera shot of him hugging Nomar says he's done. The bullpen has to win this for them."

"The curse lives, Fred. Just you watch."

The Curse lives. Thinking of Babe Ruth's sale being a voodoo hex as merely media fodder, up until then, I just thought 1946, 1949, 1967, 1978 and 1986 was merely bad timing. The National League's Chicago Cubs hadn't won a baseball championship since 1908, so I just figured it was all a coincidence.

Was it merely a coincidence that the Yankees, just five outs from elimination, staged a rally for the ages in their half of the eighth? Was it a mere coincidence that Derek Jeter, always in the middle of Yankee greatness, started things off with a ringing double? After Bernie Williams singled him home and Hideki followed with a ground-rule double, was it a mere coincidence that Red Sox skipper Grady Little came to the mound, ignored his bullpen, and left a dead tired pitcher in the game? Left-handed relief pitcher Allen Embry was ready to pitch to Hideki Matsui, and while Little may have attempted to take a page from history (*in Game 7 of the 1964 World Series, St. Louis Cardinals Manager Johnny Keane refused to relieve a fatigued Bob Gibson in the ninth inning, even after giving up two homers in the frame. After the game—a hard-fought 7-5 Cardinals win—when reporters asked why he stuck by his tiring ace, Keane, responded, "I made a commitment to his heart"*), his failure to remove Pedro Martinez was, without a doubt, the most questionable lapse of judgment in the history of the rivalry.

With Martinez clearly laboring, was it a mere coincidence that Matsui and Bernie Williams raced home with the tying runs courtesy of Jorge Posada's broken-bat, two-run, bloop double? Then and only then, did Grady Little remove Martinez. Was it a mere coincidence that the Boston Red Sox—only five outs away from breaking the shackles of their fated history, only five outs away from putting Johnny Pesky's late throw, Bucky Dent's homer and Buckner's gaffe in their rearview mirror of ancient memories—threw it all away?

Calling my brother once more, instead of hearing "I told you so," the sound of laughter moved through the cable lines and into my ear.

"You know, you could make us some money, Jeff," I said, breaking up his amusement.

"The Red Sox are done, bruh!"

"Done in by a curse?" I asked.

"Yup."

Wow, the curse still lives. Fixing myself another drink, I watched the rest of the game in calm, knowing the end result before the team from

Boston did. Waiting patiently as the bullpens got stingy, Yankees closer Mariano Rivera, determined to pitch the Bronx Bombers to the World Series, decided he was going to stay on the mound until the dawn of a new day or a Yankees victory, whichever came first. Imposing his shut-down will on the game, he pitched three scoreless innings of two-hit ball.

The Red Sox countered with Mike Timlin's blanket effort in the ninth. When knuckleballer Tim Wakefield took the mound in the bottom of the tenth inning, I noted the time. The clock on the wall struck midnight.

Thursday night was now Friday morning.

Calling my brother back, incredibly, it seemed I had awakened him.

"Man, how could you fall asleep during a game like this?" I asked.

"Because the Yankees are gonna win. Goodnight."

On my own the rest of the way, I fed off my younger brother's unwavering faith. Noting the speed of Tim Wakefield's bread and butter pitch and how the effectiveness is reliant on whether it floated or danced just enough, I wondered for the life of me how Knuckle-ballers Phil and Joe Niekro, Charlie Hough, Wilbur Wood, Tom Candiotti and Wakefield forged successful careers throwing a 45- to 50-miles-an-hour pitch, and shook my head in disgust. That Wakefield, with his sparkling 2-0, 2.08 ERA series portfolio built on that slow pitch could possibly walk away with playoff MVP honors (if the Red Sox won) irked me further.

Someone must keep their hands back on that freakin' knuckleball, time its boogie, and hit it a long way.

Mariano Rivera was thinking the same thing. After pitching through the top of the 11th to complete his longest relief outing in seven years, *we have to get this game*, Rivera mumbled while checking the scoreboard.

Aaron Boone, before leaving the dugout for his turn at the plate, was approached by Derek Jeter (even when he's not batting, he's always cast central in Yankee greatness.)

"There are ghosts in this stadium, and they're alive and well," he said to Boone.

Maybe my younger brother was right: Perhaps I really was the last one on earth to believe in *The Curse of the Bambino.*

If I still needed convincing, the first pitch of the bottom of the inning, and what followed, happily hit me over the head like a two-by-four. Playing it in slow motion as if it had happened minutes ago, I can see Wakefield's high knuckleball spinning in the October air toward Boone…coming inside, right into his wheelhouse…it's not dancing enough…just make contact, Aaron, and it's all over.

My mind calculated this in milliseconds, and what happened in real-time was this: Boone steadied himself as the darting ball neared him. Swinging aggressively, he took a vicious cut, and a small white object was sent on a new orbit, soaring and spinning through the brisk New York night. Heading toward the left-field stands, you could see the transformation of baseball's horseshoe cathedral into a raucous celebration. As the ball disappeared into a sea of wild-cheering Yankees shirts and caps, an entire baseball team that endured made a mad dash to home plate as their new hero rounded the bases.

Between second and third, Frank Sinatra joined the party. He had news to spread through song; about a melody, moment and town we all want to be a part of…

Everyone, that is, except the gallant Red Sox team that fell just short of exorcising its demons. As tears filled Yankees Manager Joe Torre's eyes and a bawling Mariano Rivera collapsed on the pitcher's mound thanking the Good Lord once more for being a Yankee, home run victim Tim Wakefield walked slowly to an emotionally deflated dugout, clubhouse and sleepless night, passing Pedro Martinez along the way. Martinez, having pitched the game of his life for six innings, sat there in a gray sweatshirt, inebriated by his demoralized stupor. The rest of the stunned team that was the Boston Red Sox filed by, one-by-one, staggered and speechless.

Sinatra still sang through the stadium loudspeakers, announcing to all his fantasy of waking up as king of the hill in a city living wide awake, sitting on top of a heap of Yankee joy. However, on this October morning, the chairman of the board's wish, as wonderful as it sounded to him, had already been granted to a pinstriped hero about to touch home plate and be swallowed alive by Yankee euphoria.

FOX- TV cut to the announcer's booth, where Joe Buck and Tim McCarver let the picture say words they needed not speak. Standing between them, in a colored shirt, was a guest announcer. He was a Seattle Mariner and former league MVP, and at that moment, the tears in his eyes were real. His name was Brett Boone. In keeping *The Curse of the Bambino* alive, his brother had joined a long list of Yankee Legends.

Sitting there with a smile, after the better-than-advertised contest I had just witnessed and ensuing post-game show, I turned off my TV and realized that I had become a believer.

There is a curse, I kept thinking.

It was a curse that was reversed in 2004, in the most humiliating way imaginable.

✪ ✪ ✪

ACT TWO: THE PAIN...

By 2004, I was a firm believer in *The Curse of the Bambino*. If you asked any Yankees fan if they actually thought the Boston Red Sox would ever defeat the Yankees when it mattered most, the answer most assuredly would have been in bold print, capitalized and capped off with an emphatic exclamation point...

HELL NO!

Audaciously arrogant, I put my belief system to the ultimate test. On Friday, October 8, 2004, a friend of mine, Dr. Linda M. Battle, asked me to come to Boston to participate in a lecture at a class she taught at Bunker Hill Community College. An outstanding woman on the precipice of her doctorate degree in nursing, Ms. Battle taught a class at the facility, and needed someone to break down clinical phrases concerning human nursing and sexuality in layman's terms.

Feeling honored to assist in the endeavors of future health care professionals, I was more than happy to oblige.

En route to Boston, not only was I focused on the job at hand, but the 2004 American League Playoffs. In one Divisional Series bracket were my Yankees, even with the Minnesota Twins at one game apiece in their best 3-of-5 series. And in the other matchup, the Red Sox were on the verge of sweeping the Anaheim Angels.

As fate would have it, Fenway Park would host the third game of the Red Sox-Angel series that night, a point I had emphasized to Linda right before the class.

"The Red Sox are going to win it all this year," she said.

"You believe that, and I have a bridge to sell you," I mocked.

"We're going to beat the Yankees."

"Don't put the cart before the horse. When they face the Yankees..."

"They still have to beat the Twins."

"C'mon, Linda," I growled. "You know it's going to come down to those two, the Yankees and the Red Sox. And we'll win, like we always do."

"I'm not really a baseball fan, William, but I'll say this much: This year will be different."

Dismissing her opinion, "Talk to me when they win a Game 7 at Yankee Stadium," I said.

Those were my exact words.

Upon my introduction to her class, I addressed the mostly adult students with my Yankee allegiance.

"Being that I'm from New York City, I can't wish your team success tonight," I razzed.

"Where do you live?" someone asked.

"The Bronx," I quickly answered.

A chorus of boos followed, which encouraged me to take another swipe.

"It's been a long time for you guys, huh?"

A blonde-haired woman, proudly attired in Boston red, finally spoke up.

"This is our year," she boldly announced.

"Y'all have been saying that for eighty-six years!"

Conjuring up the reason why Babe Ruth landed in New York, "No, No, Nanette," I chanted in two-three rhythm.

More boos.

Thoroughly receiving pleasure from their pain, the trash-talk eased my nervousness about the candor, caution and consciousness needed when openly discussing sex, and the doctor/client confidentiality group sessions I diligently prepared for.

Even as I talked about this crucial part of a person's identity, one that is a central characteristic to our emotional, physical and psychological being, I couldn't resist needling the students a little more. When mentioning some of the erotic pleasures surrounding sexuality, romantic expressions of warmth, comfort and affection like hugging, touching, and holding hands, "I would never hold the hand of a Red Sox fan, much less make love to one," I quipped.

My snipe produced another derisive chorus of different opinions.

"I hope you marry one!" someone screamed.

Receiving great reviews from the deans of the school's Chelsea campus and the staff participants, it was an amazing three-hour experience. However, many present in the class, once the passion of furthering their future waned, immediately turned their attention to the baseball game on television in a nearby cafeteria/lounge area.

The Fenway faithful, as well as the night students at the Community College on New Rutherford Avenue, were primed for a victory celebration when the Red Sox built a 6-1 advantage heading into the seventh. But three walks and a single by shortstop David Eckstein enabled the Angels to close the lead to 6-2 and bring their top hitter, Vladimir Guerrero, to the plate against reliever Mike Timlin with the bases loaded.

After a first-pitch strike, Timlin hung a 92-mile-per-hour slider.

Receiving a gift pitch to his liking, Vladimir made him pay. Connecting with an uppercut swing, the Angels All-Star crushed it, and the ball flew over the wall in right-center field for an opposite field grand slam.

Just like that, a five-run deficit was swiftly erased.

And Fenway Park went from the brink of euphoria to a stony silence. Feeling the same eerie somber in the cafeteria that was at the ballpark, I scanned the room and saw genuine fear in the eyes of the most passionate Red Sox fans.

The silence from a New England fan base battered by history had a voice of its own, saying, "Oh, no, not again."

Their sure victory was now in doubt.

That one swing might turn this whole series around, I thought. *They're haunted by the echoes of a tortured legacy. They'll choke, just like they've done in the past.*

With a series of devastating setbacks supporting my musing, I figured this game would be the beginning of another collapse, one of many that created the dark legacy that hung over the franchise.

It's only a matter of time, I assumed.

There's a saying that goes with assumptions; they're the mother of all screw-ups. My assumption, which came about 8:45 p.m. that

Friday evening, may have been the beginning of the biggest screw-up in baseball history.

As with many screw-ups, it all starts with a warning that usually goes unnoticed. Yankees fans were put on notice in the bottom of the tenth inning of Boston's playoff duel with the Angels. Future Yankee Johnny Damon started the frame with a leadoff single up the middle against Anaheim reliever Francisco Rodriguez. After Damon was forced at second on a bunt by Mark Bellhorn, Rodriguez struck out the dangerous Manny Ramirez looking.

With two outs, Angels Manager Mike Scioscia brought in left-hander Jarod Washburn to face David Ortiz and try to get the game to an 11th inning. The southpaw, who lost Game 1, was the manager's only option; for the Angels had no left-handed relievers.

Ortiz, just trying to reach base, swung at the first pitch he saw. That one swing clobbered the fear the Red Sox Nation owned over the Green Monster for a game-winning, two-run homer. Crossing the plate after his series-clinching clout, the man they affectionately called "Big Papi" was engulfed by his teammates on the Fenway lawn. As the stunned Angels filed off the field, the Standells' "Dirty Water" blared from the public address system and a wild celebration ensued. It reached its peak when first baseman Kevin Millar and winning pitcher Derek Lowe sprayed fans in the lower-box seats with champagne.

Smirking while watching the utter bedlam on television, then, in the cafeteria, it was at this point where I boldly made my assumptions known. As the students reveled in happiness, I totally overlooked the fact that this year's unit from Boston was very different from the 2003 edition. Wearing "New Sox," these were grinders who looked disaster in the face and reached deeper into their resolve tank. New Manager Terry Francona had instilled a loose persona in the clubhouse, and the team nicknamed itself "The Idiots." Playing fearlessly, their singular purpose of bringing the New England area its first World Championship since Woodrow Wilson's presidency was now an obsessive crusade.

And if presenting the heads of the New York Yankees on a platter to the Red Sox Nation was part of the plan, then so be it.

Unflinching in the face of pressure, this was a team who took your best shot in the gut, and kept coming.

They never quit.

Totally ignorant to their resiliency, all I saw was the Yankees beating them when it counted as they always did. The Minnesota Twins would be dealt with, then the Red Sox.

Or so I assumed.

"I must admit, this was impressive," I confessed to the students. "But get back to me when they win a Game 7 at Yankee Stadium."

Another chorus of derision met my announcement, but they collided with a smug arrogance forged from nearly nine decades of head-to-head success.

Again, with more conviction, I repeated my assumption. "Wyle E. Coyote never caught the Roadrunner and Charlie Brown never kicked the football or kissed that red-headed girl, for that matter. Hell will never freeze over, and the Boston Red Sox will never, ever beat the New York Yankees."

"This is our year," one student argued.

"Again, talk to me when you win a Game 7 at Yankee Stadium. It'll never ever happen."

I swear, those were my exact words.

✪ ✪ ✪

"They wanted us, so now they got us!" I screamed after outfielder Shannon Stewart grounded out to second to end the Minnesota Twins' season. Although it had taken extra innings in Game 4 to usher in the winning run, the New York Yankees secured their annual date with Armageddon.

And truth be told, the balance of power in the American League was exactly as it should have been. The Yankees, finding themselves down 4-1 and wanting to avoid a deciding fifth game in the Hubert H. Humphrey Metrodome, staged a desperate eighth-inning rally out of their glorious past to send the fourth game in extra frames. Then a new face in baseball's greatest rivalry, one for dramatic reasons worshipped in one city and lustfully booed in the other, delivered an 11th-inning performance that gave a whole nation— especially the 230-mile Northeast Corridor which separates New York and Boston—exactly what it wanted: Another Yankee-Red Sox showdown.

It seemed fitting that Alex Rodriguez made certain the Yankees would get ample rest to prepare for Boston. From the end of the 2003 season till the night before Christmas, it seemed that the reigning American League Most Valuable Player and the man recognized by all as the best player in baseball would be wearing a white Red Sox jersey and matching dark blue cap with a bright red "B" on the front. The Texas Rangers, determined to move Rodriguez and his $252 million contract—the most expensive pact in baseball history— initially agreed to a trade with the Red Sox. Including "Yankee Killer" Manny Rodriguez and pitching prospect John Lester in the deal, Boston also wanted A-Rod to take a voluntary reduction in salary.

The MLBPA (Major League Baseball Players Association) swiftly rejected the deal because of the latter. Both sides tried reworking the deal—as opposed to the salary reduction, Boston would send $13 million in cash to Rangers Owner Tom Hicks—but the talks broke down.

In an ironic twist of fate, on January 16, 2004, Yankees third baseman Aaron Boone, who just months earlier provided a swing for the ages, severely injured his knee playing in a pickup basketball game near his Newport Beach, California home, and would be lost for the upcoming season. With their two best replacement options being utility players Miguel Cairo and Enrique Wilson, the Yankees had to make a move.

I can imagine how it all went down:

(NOTE: *Conference Call: February 14, 2004*)

OPERATOR: *Hello, Mr. Cashman, this is the Digital Bell Conference Operator. I have all parties on the line.*

BRIAN CASHMAN *(New York Yankees GM): Great.*

OPERATOR: *Would you like for me to do roll call?*

MR. TOM HICKS *(Texas Rangers Owner): That's not necessary.*

ALEX RODRIGUEZ *(Texas Rangers Shortstop): Mr. Cashman, Mr. Hicks, it's an honor that you've allowed me to sit in on this conversation.*

CASHMAN: *It's about your future, Alex. (Chuckle)*

RODRIGUEZ: *Well, let's make it happen then.*

HICKS: *Okay. Let's rap, Brian.*

CASHMAN: *Alex, we have a rich tradition here in New York.*

RODRIGUEZ: *Well, according to baseball history, the Mets have only won two World Series championships. That's some tradition.*

(Tom Hicks laughs.)

CASHMAN: *Are we getting a third baseman, or a comedian?*

RODRIGUEZ: *Well...*

HICKS: *Only if we get Alfonso Soriano. Now he's a real talent.*

RODRIGUEZ: *Hellooooo... Didn't I hit .298 with 47 homers and 118 RBIs last year? I Won a Golden Glove and Silver Slugger Award to boot.*

HICKS: *Alex, you definitely put up numbers here. But I think a change of scenery is necessary at this point.*

RODRIGUEZ: *Mr. Hicks, you can be real with me. You want to get from under my contract, don't you?*

(It's Brian Cashman's turn to laugh.)

HICKS: *Touche.*

RODRIGUEZ: *By the way, Happy Valentine's Day, Mr. Hicks.*

(Hearty laughter from all)

CASHMAN: *Now before Mr. Hicks and I agree to this trade, Alex, there are a couple of stipulations you must agree on.*

RODRIGUEZ: *Shoot.*

CASHMAN: *Well, as you know, we're already set at shortstop.*

RODRIGUEZ: *I hear he's a pretty good one too.*

CASHMAN: *Seriously, are you willing to accept the challenge of learning a new position? The transition to the "hot corner" can be pretty tough.*

RODRIGUEZ: *I'm up for it.*

CASHMAN: *Cool. There's just one more thing.*

RODRIGUEZ: *I know, I know. Babe Ruth wore number three, so I'll switch numbers. Is number "13" available?*

HICKS: *Lucky "13," huh, A-Rod?*

RODRIGUEZ: *I'll make it lucky there.*

CASHMAN: *I'm holding you to that. Tom, do you agree on what we discussed earlier?*

HICKS: *Yes. I'll pay $67 million of the remaining $179 million on his contract.*

CASHMAN: *Cool. Then we're all set. You get Alfonso Soriano and a player to be named later (which turned out to be Joacquin Arias, who was sent to Texas on March 24th), and you pay us $67 million. Once we get the agreements of the trade on paper, we'll overnight them to you.*

HICKS: *(sighing) I think that sounds about right. Alex, it's nothing personal, but that contract your agent Scott Boras suggested you sign…He did us no favors.*

RODRIGUEZ: *It's all in the past. As soon as we go "click," I'm officially a New York Yankee.*

CASHMAN: *I can't wait till Theo (Theo Epstein-Boston GM) and the rest of the Red Sox Nation hears about this one. All of New England is going to want his head.*

HICKS: *You snooze, you lose.*

CASHMAN: *That's right. You move your feet, you lose your seat.*

RODRIGUEZ: *You got that right.*

CASHMAN: *Very well then. Alex Rodriguez, welcome to the Yankee family. I think you'll look very good in pinstripes.*

RODRIGUEZ: *Sounds good to me. Now let's go out and win number 27.*

To that point, the reloaded Red Sox had swung the balance of power in their favor with the off-season acquisitions of starting pitcher Curt Schilling and bullpen closer Keith Foulke. They had the first opportunity to wrestle Rodriguez away from the Rangers, but they could not close the deal.

In a matter of days, the "Evil Empire"—a nickname given to the Yankees by Boston President and CEO Larry Lucchino—executed a trade that the Red Sox had months to complete. Extending its powerful tentacles, they laughed at the luxury tax threshold (because of their $188 million team payroll, the Yankees would pay almost $26 million in taxes), opened their wallets, re-directed A-Rod's trade destination to the Big Apple, and dealt a crushing blow to the psyche of Red Sox Nation.

Just another reason for them to hate us, I mocked when hearing the good news.

And while the move paid dividends during the regular season—A-Rod produced 36 homers, 106 RBIs and 28 stolen bases in his first season in pinstripes—the biggest pay-off came in the fourth game of the American League Divisional series.

With the Yankees and Twins deadlocked in a 4-4 struggle, A-Rod led off the top of the eleventh inning by lacing a double down the left-field line off Minnesota right-hander Kyle Lohse. While he could have waited for cleanup man Gary Sheffield—another off-season Yankee acquisition–to drive him in, but after noticing Lohse's elaborate leg kick, he stole third base on a 2-1 pitch.

With Sheffield still at the plate, Rodriguez took a big lead off third base. Lohse, clearly rattled, fired a ball past Pat Borders to the screen, allowing Rodriguez to score with the winning run.

With pure hustle and instinct, Alex Rodriguez ensured that the last two teams standing in the American League, teams 1 and 1A in baseball, would engage in a another dance to the death.

There could be no other way, no other resolution to American League supremacy. All season long they were at each other's throats; literally.

From the off-season battles and the Yankees stealing A-Rod from under the Red Sox to a midseason clash at Fenway Park where he formally announced his arrival into Baseball's Great Divide by reaching for the jugular of Red Sox catcher Jason Varitek, the tension between the teams was combustible.

And once again, the fuse had been lit.

The Yankees had won 101 regular-season games.

The Red Sox won 98, and the head-to-head season series 11 games to 8.

These two teams were even in every way.

Every way that is, except one. It was a matter of historical record that we owned them. This, despite the fact that Boston became better defensively with the mid-season trade of one of their best players, Nomar Garciaparra, to the Chicago Cubs for shortstop Orlando Cabrera and first baseman Doug Mientkiewicz. It didn't matter whether they added outfielder Dave Roberts, who gave them more team speed. Who cared if they owned two of the best starting pitchers in baseball in Curt Schilling and Pedro Martinez. So what the Bosox nearly erased a 10-1/2 game deficit in the American League East after trading Garciaparra; that the Yankees held them off underscored my point. Despite that many observers saw our antagonists as a more complete team than the Bronx Bombers, we had an intangible that transcended logic.

For eighty-plus years, victory against the Boston Red Sox in October was our right. Thirty-nine American League Pennants and twenty-six World Championships told me so.

Bucky Dent and Aaron Boone also supported my argument.

We have the Curse on them, I thought, before Game One.

They'll never beat us.

Game One proved that; or so I thought. Blowing open the game early, the Yankees pounded an ineffective Curt Schilling for six runs in three innings, his shortest outing of the season. Adding two more in the sixth, courtesy of a Hideki Matsui two-run single off Boston knuckleballer Tim Wakefield, the Yankees held a commanding 8–0 lead. Matsui, knocking in an ALCS record-tying five RBIs in the game, led a Bomber attack that saw the top four hitters in the Yankees' lineup go 9-for-18 against Red Sox pitching.

Meanwhile, Yankees pitching ace Mike Mussina was magnificent. Unlike his Boston counterpart, he had total command of his pitching arsenal. Setting the Red Sox down with great location on his curveball, he breezed through the first three innings by getting first pitch strikes on seven of the first nine batters. Then, in the fourth, he got Johnny Damon, Mark Bellhorn and Manny Ramirez to all look at called third strikes. Continuing to throw hard through the middle innings, his better-than-normal fastball had the oldest Yankees fans in attendance recalling an October afternoon in 1956 when Don Larsen retired twenty-seven straight for the only perfect game in postseason history.

Through 6-1/3 innings, Mussina had set down 19 straight batters.

He looked unhittable.

Then a funny thing happened.

The Red Sox bats came alive.

With one out in the seventh, Boston second baseman Mark Bellhorn ended Mussina's bid for a perfect game by ripping a double to the base of the left center-field wall. After Ramirez grounded out, David Ortiz singled, Kevin Millar hit a two-run double, and Trot Nixon singled him home.

It was now 8-3, Yankees.

Removing Mike Mussina, Yankees Manager Joe Torre elected to bring in reliever Tanyon Sturtze.

The first batter he faced, catcher Jason Varitek, blasted a two-run homer to right.

In the blink of an eye, it was an 8-5 game.

And the Yankee Stadium crowd, loud and boisterous at the first pitch, was growing quieter and quieter by the second.

In the next inning, Yankees reliever Tom Gordon gave up singles to Bill Mueller and Manny Ramirez to put runners at first and third for David Ortiz. Waving a menacing bat, "Big Papi" drilled a drive off the wall in left-center. Mueller and Ramirez scampered home and Ortiz stopped at third with a triple.

In less than twenty minutes, the Yankees went from flirting with history in an 8-0 laughter to a tension-filled, 8-7 eighth-inning white knuckler.

With the tying run ninety feet away and needing four outs for victory, Yankees Manager Joe Torre, wanting the Game One door slammed shut, called for his closer to do what he always did.

As "Enter Sandman" blared from the PA system and a cheerful explosion of faith filled the stadium, I tried to read the makeup of the game's best relief pitcher. Over the years, Mariano Rivera had been through many save situations.

None, however, would ever compare to the extraordinary circumstances surrounding this opportunity.

Earlier in the day, Rivera had flown to his native Panama to attend the funeral of his wife's cousins who were tragically electrocuted on his property three days earlier. Sobbing uncontrollably under a sweltering Puerto Caimito sun, after an emotionally exhausting day, any and everyone in the stadium would have understood if he had stayed home to be with his family.

But he had a job to do.

Arriving to the ballpark in the second inning and the Yankees bullpen in the fifth, three innings later he realized that twenty-five players in pinstripes, as well as the 56,000 fans in attendance needed him to do his job in the worst way.

Get the Bronx Bombers into the clubhouse with a 1-0 series lead.

Courageously, he obliged. Facing first baseman Kevin Millar, he threw two balls, then produced an inning-ending pop-up to Derek Jeter. After Bernie Williams doubled home two runs against Mike Timlin in the bottom of the frame, Rivera gave up two singles in the ninth, but was able to induce Bill Mueller into a game-ending, 1-6-3 double play.

I watched the Yankees' hard-fought 10-7 victory in my Marble Hill apartment alone, and when the Red Sox chipped away at the Yankees' lead, I remained calm, as if the game was never in doubt.

Sure, Boston always made things interesting, I reasoned.

Instantly, I thought of Affirmed and Alydar, thoroughbred race horses who staged an epic rivalry in the 1970s. Racing ten times, Affirmed emerged triumphant on seven occasions, including three classic Triple Crown confrontations. In the 1978 Kentucky Derby, Affirmed made his move on Churchill Downs' far turn, as Jockey Steve Cauthen steered his horse into the lead. Down the stretch, Affirmed held off Alydar's late, but furious close to win the race by 1-1/2 lengths.

Two weeks later in the Preakness Stakes, Affirmed set the pace early by immediately taking the lead, and felt the presence of his archrival when Alydar rushed near from the outside on the far turn. Down the stretch, they battled. Driving relentlessly, Alydar pushed Affirmed to the bitter end, yet lost the race by a neck.

The Belmont Stakes was even closer. Because the last jewel of the Triple Crown was the longest race—the 1-1/2-mile distance of the Belmont was a quarter of a mile longer than the Derby and 5/16 of a mile longer than the Preakness—most figured Alydar would finally vindicate his legacy with a win that would deny Affirmed the Triple Crown.

At the onset, Affirmed was able to get to the lead and pace the race slowly. Staying close, at the halfway point of the race, Alydar moved alongside Affirmed, and engaged in a speed duel for the ages.

For three-quarters of a mile, the two colts raced neck and neck, pulling away from the rest of the field. At the turn to the stretch, Affirmed had a slight lead. With a burst, Alydar got his nose in front by mid-stretch.

Affirmed was tiring, but had one last push left. Reaching deep, Jockey Steve Cauthen went to a left-handed whip, something he had never done before. That bold, risky move got just enough from his horse and at the finish, it was Affirmed by a nose to become horse racing's eleventh and last Triple Crown winner.

Alydar always made things interesting against Affirmed, but always fell short. Just like the Red Sox. They push us to the brink, but always go away when the lights burn the brightest. They'll never win when it counts.

Once again, ignorance fueled my assumption. On the verge of a humiliating defeat, the resilient Red Sox displayed a championship mettle never before possessed. Fighting back, they made a game of it and were ninety feet away from changing the complexion of this series with a dramatic comeback.

This was a team that wouldn't go away.

But I figured they would.

History showed they always did.

The mosaic law of the baseball universe, created when Harry Frazee put Broadway before baseball and *The Babe*, was crystal clear to all.

The Curse always prevailed.

They'll never beat us.

And Game Two of the series did nothing to disrupt my belief system. For the second day in a row, a New York starter stepped up and outpitched his Boston counterpart. John Leiber, making just his second career playoff start, out-dueled Pedro Martinez with seven-plus innings of one-run, three-hit ball.

Martinez, tuning out the derisive "Who's Your Daddy" serenade, pitched six solid innings of his own. Throughout the night, he kept the Yankees off-balance with a fastball that registered 95 miles an hour on the radar guns on several occasions; not to mention a devastating breaking ball.

He was terrific, but beatable. Allowing a walk and stolen base to Derek Jeter to open the game, Pedro hit Alex Rodriguez to put two runners on base. The next batter, cleanup hitter Gary Sheffield, lined the first pitch he saw to left-center, scoring Jeter to give the Yankees a quick 1-0 lead. Then, after Jorge Posada worked a one-out walk in the Yankee sixth, Martinez left a 1-2 fastball over the plate for John Olerud that the first baseman lined into the right-field seats for a two-run homer and a three-run cushion.

Leiber pitched into the eighth, allowing a leadoff single to Red Sox Outfielder Trot Nixon. After pitcher Tom Gordon got two out—but not after a run scored, courtesy of a Jason Varitek double and Orlando Cabrera groundout—Yankees Manager Joe Torre again summoned Mariano Rivera to get the last four outs.

And once again, the backbone of Yankees relief pitching came through. Freezing Johnny Damon on a called third strike to end the eighth, the ninth saw him give up a one-out double to Manny Ramirez, then blow third strikes by David Ortiz and Kevin Millar to earn his major-league record thirty-second postseason save.

With the Yankees making this series look like another stroll through the park, *Two down, and two to go*, I thought. With a commanding 2-0 lead in the best-of-seven series, even recent history showed the ditch the Red Sox were digging: Since 1985, the last thirteen teams to win the first two games of Championship Series play had advanced to the World Series.

Further accentuating their dire circumstance was the revelation that the ineffectiveness of Game One starter Curt Schilling was due to a torn tendon sheath in his right ankle, an injury that happened during his start against the Angels in the American League Divisional Series. Walking in a boot cast, Schilling's season was in jeopardy, along with the rest of the Red Sox organization.

The only thing going for Boston was that the series traveled north to Fenway Park, where the Red Sox were 56-26 in 2004. The swagger that fueled them to New York to begin the series: All that talk about how much they'd love to change the course of history; all that was now ancient history. Battered and bruised by *The Curse of the Bambino*, at least they were going home to friendly confines to turn it all around.

Or were they?

Pounding baseballs all over Fenway in Game Three, the Yankees pushed Boston to the brink of elimination with a blistering offensive barrage. Led by Alex Rodriguez (3-for-5, a home run, two doubles, and five runs scored); Gary Sheffield (4-for-5 with a homer and four RBIs) and Hideki Matsui, (5-for-6, two doubles, two homers and five runs), the Bombers plated 13 runs in the game's first five innings in a 19-8 annihilation.

It wasn't pretty. Assaulting Red Sox pitching to the tune of 19 extra-base hits, the Yankees quickly turned the game into an extended batting practice session. They hit everything the Red Sox hurlers threw, everywhere. Doubles down the foul lines, hard hit drives off of the Green Monster, and moon-shot blasts onto Lansdowne Street, you would have thought no place in Kenmore Square was safe.

I was at a Harlem nightspot with a couple of friends from out of town, Sonya Allen and Trish Hill, both Yankees fans from Columbus, Ohio. Watching the game from the bar area, we kept commenting on the eerie silence heard throughout the ball park, and that the quiet only amplified the hideous sound an entire New England area must have heard each time a baseball crashed against their green, thirty-seven-foot-high landmark.

"This is getting real ugly," I announced, gleefully sipping from my Long Island Iced Tea.

"Let's not celebrate until the Yankees get the last out of that fourth game," Sonya cautioned.

Trish nodded her head in agreement, then, quoted Yogi Berra. "It's not over till it's over, William."

Watching another ball crash against the Green Monster, I found it difficult to believe in miracles.

"Ladies, the series is over."

To me, each thud symbolized another nail in the coffin. For the eighty-sixth consecutive autumn, the Boston Red Sox were not going to win the World Series. No baseball team in history had ever recovered from a 3-0 playoff deficit, and this embarrassing defeat, a rout without a single trace of competition, dignity or honor, was gospel to the souls of the Evil Empire.

City officials could appeal for judicial intervention, religious leaders could pray for a new divine order and Red Sox Nation could stick pins in Yankee Dolls forever. But they will never, ever beat us, I thought.

Once again, their entire franchise and its legion of followers throughout the New England organization were receiving last rites from the baseball gods. If it wasn't Bucky Dent off Mike Torrez, it would be Aaron Boone off Tim Wakefield. If it wasn't Buckner's inability to handle a slow roller or Johnny Pesky hesitating, it would be something else. So what the Yankees had holes in their starting pitching; so what their defense was merely adequate in this series. The Red Sox would never, ever beat us. Because they sold the greatest player the baseball diamond had ever known, the Boston Red Sox were cursed. And when they faced the New York Yankees, the pain of their futility would be *in their face;* and, like slow torture, all the more excruciating.

They will never, ever beat us.

✪ ✪ ✪

Three outs away.

We were three measly outs away.

Up by one run, 4-3, in the bottom of the ninth, with the best closer in history on the mound, the bottom of the Red Sox batting order was due up. With thirty-two saves in thirty-six postseason opportunities—including six-for-six against Boston—Mariano Rivera was all set to nourish the body of the *Curse of the Bambino* once more.

I was at the 40/40 Club sports nightspot with Sonya and Trish, ready to celebrate another Yankees pennant, their fortieth.

Bring on the Cardinals or Astros, I thought, munching on one of those mini hot dogs from Jay-Z's menu.

They'll never beat us.

And then, a walk, a pinch runner, a stolen base and a base hit changed everything.

In his second inning of work, the game's ultimate closer, trying to paint the outside corner with his cut fastball, began the bottom of the ninth by walking Boston first baseman Kevin Millar on five pitches. Once pinch-runner Dave Roberts entered the game, the apprehension and downright dread the 34,826 fans in Fenway Park must have felt gave way to the slightest ray of hope.

It was a hope that increased ever so slightly when Roberts promptly stole second; a hope that morphed into a good feeling when the next batter, Bill Mueller, lined a single up the middle, scoring Roberts and squaring things at 4.

And a hope that grew into joy and relief some three innings later, when David Ortiz blasted a twelfth-inning pitch off reliever Paul Quantrill over the Green Monster for a game-winning, walk-off home run. Defeating the Yankees 6-4, all of New England was spared the ignominy of an embarrassing sweep at the hands of their smug, superior archrival.

"Damn," all three of us said in unison.

Feeling more dejected that I couldn't celebrate with my friends from Ohio than demoralized over a single loss, I assumed the dancing in the streets of Boston would be for a moment. Any Red Sox fan who thought a miracle was under construction was sadly mistaken. Publicly they may have hoped so, but privately they knew the truth: Ever since 1903, when postseason play began with the World Series, no team had ever scaled the mountain completely from a three-game deficit to win a postseason series. That the Sox hung in for over five hours to get their parting gift, a single series win, was irrelevant. A comeback against the New York Yankees, baseball's aristocrats, remained in historical terms, improbable and impossible.

This was a new torture Red Sox fans have to endure, I smirked. *Aaron Boone's home run in Game 7 last October was too good for them. This one has to be a slow death, so they can feel every bit of the pain.*

Remembering a response Winston Churchill made to a woman who insulted his drunken state—"You are ugly, but tomorrow I'll be sober"—the analogy seemed fitting to Yankees fans in reference to their New England counterparts. We were royalty, and the Boston Red Sox were our minions, our personal, perennial stepstools. And after Monday night's Game 5 victory, I assumed Yankees fans would be sober in triumph, while the Red Sox Nation would remain Cinderella before the ball, enduring another ugly winter of anguish, pity-parties and an inferiority complex the size of an elephant. Wearing the same blue dress made from bile and frustration from fed-up fans and know-it-all sports talk hosts, the sad, bizarre opera they always attended would sing loudly for the deconstruction of the team.

Tomorrow, I thought, *order will be restored*. Like death and taxes, I assumed the inevitable pain still awaited the Sox.

Quoting Little Orphan Annie to Sonya, "The sun'll come out tomorrow. Bet your bottom dollar that tomorrow there'll be sun," I sang in a horrible voice.

Again, like they were prophets with a vision, my buddies stifled a premature celebration.

"William, let's hope the day away isn't *days or months* away, like in 2005," Trish cracked. "They should have ended it."

Sonya reinforced this point. "The way the Red Sox won was like a desperate team that will fight you till their last breath. They just might make things very interesting, babe."

Still, my body language remained confident, saying, *we got this*.

"That win was their last breath," I countered. "This win took everything they had inside. Watch what happens tomorrow. It's all over, tomorrow."

Only the tomorrow I spoke of saw the impossible dream of the Boston Red Sox gain a little more life. For the second straight night, a Fenway Park crowd witnessed its second straight dramatic game, and was rewarded with another heart-stopping, come-from-behind, extra-inning victory; this one 5-4 in a 14-inning extravaganza that took nearly six hours to complete.

Yankees starter Mike Mussina, who pitched six perfect innings to start Game 1, wasn't as effective this time out. In a thirty-four-pitch first inning, he allowed two runs to score, compliments of three straight singles and a bases-loaded walk. After his shaky beginning, Mussina regained the focus he owned just five days earlier and shut Boston down over the next five innings, allowing only two meaningless singles.

His counterpart, Pedro Martinez, allowed one run through five frames, but in the sixth, Derek Jeter drove a stake into the heart of the Red Sox Nation with a bases-loaded double into the right-field corner on Pedro's 100th pitch of the night. Clearing the base paths with his three-run dagger, the Yankees now owned a 4-2 lead. Relievers Tanyon Sturtze and Tom Gordon took over for Mussina and got three outs in the seventh, leaving the Yankees only six outs from the pennant.

Once again, I could taste sweet victory in my glass of triumph.

And once again, the dead team walking, this time down two runs and six outs away from fishing and golf tee times, kicked over the glass.

"Big Papi," the lifeline of the Fenway Faithful in the series, led off the bottom of the eighth by drilling a solo homer off a billboard sign atop the Green Monster to cut the deficit in half, to 4-3. Tom Gordon, who surrendered the David Ortiz blast, then walked Kevin Millar. And like the previous night, speedy Dave Roberts bounced out of the dugout to pinch-run for Millar. Clearly rattled, Gordon quickly fell behind in the count to Trot Nixon; and on a 3-1 pitch, Nixon laced a single to right, giving the Sox runners on first and third with nobody out.

Taking no chances, Yankees Manager Joe Torre again went to his stopper to close the deal.

And for the second straight night, Mariano Rivera couldn't close the door on the Sox season. Given the precarious predicament he inherited, it seemed unfair that a blown save was in order as Catcher Jason Varitek lifted a sacrifice fly to center to tie matters at 4.

But things were different now. For the first time in nearly ninety years, everything was going the way of the Red Sox. Sitting in my apartment dumbfounded, watching these Boston ghostbusters reach deep, then deeper, it was at that precise moment I recalled my smug superciliousness, my supposed superiority by way of Yankee tradition in that Bunker Hill lounge. With unrestrained, unwavering arrogance, I just knew the running punch line that New Englanders endured since the sale of Ruth would continue.

To me, the 2004 American League Championship series was simply another in a long-running episode of futility for the Boston Red Sox. Surely, something freakish would happen—a slow roller through the wickets, some fluke fly ball barely clearing the Green Monster, a sure groundout bouncing crazily around the infield— something confirming the Sox impending doom usually happened right about now.

What happened was this: After Derek Jeter's double, the Red Sox bullpen shut the Bronx Bombers down for eight innings. Knuckle-baller Tim Wakefield, already forfeiting his Game 4 start when he was hit like a gong for three innings and change in that 19-8 debacle, volunteered to pitch in Game 5. It was a selfless act, one that per-sonified the character, guts and determination of a city desperate to reverse a curse that lived as long as Methuselah. Pitching three one-hit, four-strikeout scoreless innings, he was locked in an extra-inning duel with Yankees hurler-turned-hopeful hero Esteban Loaiza.

Loaiza, having pitched brilliantly for three innings himself, finally bent ever so slightly in the bottom of the fourteenth. With one out, Sox centerfielder Johnny Damon walked. After whiffing shortstop Orlando Cabrera, Loaiza issued another free pass to Manny Ramirez.

"Shit!" I screamed at my television.

Waving his daunting bat once more, David Ortiz stepped in the batter box. After drilling a 1-2 pitch foul, "Big Papi" fouled off five straight sinkerballs from Loaiza. Then on the tenth pitch of the at-bat, he sent all of Fenway into a state of euphoria by looping a broken-bat single into center, scoring Damon with the winning run.

Watching the ensuing bedlam in Boston, my mind screamed the first three letters of the word "assume."

Sometimes you become an *ass* when you *assume.*

Finding myself halfway to the former, it was at that moment I realized the magnitude of what could possibly happen. No team in baseball history had come back from three games down to even force a seventh game; much less win one. And there the Boston Red Sox were, on the threshold of something that seemed utterly preposterous merely days ago. Rejecting fear and replacing doubt with collective will, strength and faith, they were one win away from forcing another ultimate showdown.

And heaven forbid they won a Game 6 *and* 7 in the hallowed cathedral known as Yankee Stadium. It would be like walking into your home, punching your mother, wife and other loved ones who were in your face while smiling, then taunting you while doing it again.

The mere possibility of that would make the most conservative Yankees fan vomit.

But there the Red Sox Nation were, passengers on an Amtrak train of momentum to the Bronx, threatening to knock the world off its axis, and prove after centuries of facts that it was indeed flat.

They were one win away from another showdown, two wins away from the unimaginable; a precedent-busting miracle.

And for the first time in my life, I hoped *against* something special.

✪ ✪ ✪

Depending on your vantage point, the beauty and beast of sports is that every once in a while when you watch an event, you can tell by what is unfolding before your eyes that time has run out on the destiny of a particular team and its loyal fan base. The fortuitous bounces and breaks received over a lifetime are now steered toward the opposition, and every call once received like it was your birthright now goes against you.

Sometimes the hands on the clock of fate run slowly, with each tick giving you small doses of the bad fortune others may have experienced throughout years, and sometimes decades, of agony. And alternatively at times, the reversal of fortune drops on your head without warning and with sudden and unexpected quickness, much like an *ACME* anvil from the sky in a Bugs Bunny cartoon. Like a building avalanche of snow going down a hill destroying everything in sight, the change is devastating, embarrassingly painful and unconscionable, for it all happened so fast.

You and the team you root for passionately are left in a stupor, puzzled and perplexed, asking yourself this: What in the hell just happened? Thinking you've merely experienced a bad dream, you awaken from sleep the next morning to find that the nightmare was terrifyingly real; and reverberations of cataclysmic failure might be felt for years, decades, and centuries to come.

For the long-suffering benefactor, the teams and its ardent supporters, the joy of their long-awaited success is eternal compensation; an abundance of blessings being made for all those years and tears of futility. The joy of the landmark breakthrough defies description, and leaves a team, its fans and an entire city partying for generations on end. But even more gratifying might be the experience of finally facing your defeat-inflicting tormentors and screaming in their faces: Now we're even!

As I turned on my television that October evening to watch Game 6 of the 2004 American League Championship Series, I was looking over my shoulders at a possible tidal wave. Deeply troubled by the sudden turn of events, the prospect of witnessing the improbable left me mortified. Feeling my trepidation, the intense jitters that enveloped me left my Bronx apartment, traveled down the Major Deegan Expressway to the ballpark on River Avenue, entered the clubhouse and into the collective psyche of the team wearing pinstripes.

Everyone in the stadium that evening must have identified with my worst fears as well; by game time, many of the fans in attendance were incredibly tight as they bit the fingernails of their crossed digits.

An eerie hush kidnapped their enthusiasm, and the taunts and derisive chants that usually sounded a death knell to the opposition were muted by a sense of panic.

Under a cold October drizzle, Yankee Stadium, once a graveyard for the championship designs of the Boston Red Sox, became the "away-field advantage" of the team from Beantown.

Playing the first few innings of the game in a tense, scoreless fashion, the Sox began realizing their tremendous fortune in the top of the fourth. After working over Yankees starter Jon Lieber for fifty pitches through the first three innings, Kevin Millar ignited a two-out rally with a double down the line in left. After fighting through ten pitches, Catcher Jason Varitek next laced a single up the middle, plating Millar with the game's first run. After Orlando Cabrera kept things going with a single to left, up stepped second baseman Mark Bellhorn, who to this point was having a dreadful series (3 for 20, with 10 strikeouts in 20 ALCS at-bats).

Hitting a fly ball to deep left, much like Bucky Dent some twenty-six years earlier, the ball landed about three feet over the wall, hitting a fan in a navy blue sweatshirt square in the chest, then bouncing back onto the field of play.

At first, the ball was signaled in play by left-field umpire Jim Joyce, thus producing a two-run double. Irate with the initial ruling, Boston Manager Terry Francona ran out of the dugout and protested vehemently.

With television replays clearly supporting Red Sox skipper's argument, it was then we witnessed a new twist in this century-old rivalry. The officiating crew huddled, then overturned the initial call.

Mark Bellhorn was now the proud recipient of a three-run homer.

And the Boston Red Sox had a 4-0 lead for Curt Schilling to protect.

In an inspirational pitching—his performance that will go down in Red Sox history as a testament of will, competitive fire and just how badly he wanted to help exorcise the Yankee ghosts—Schilling, ignoring the prognosis that his season was over, shunned the specially designed shoe Boston team doctors thought would protect his torn tendon sheath. Opting instead for a suturing process in which the skin around the dislocated tendon was cut and connected to ligaments, tissue and bone, he took the Yankee Stadium pitching mound in his regular cleats and fired away. By the end of his gritty, seven-inning masterpiece—which he allowed one run on four hits, striking out four without a base on balls—Schilling's white sock was partially red; drenched in his own blood.

He and the rest of his Boston teammates were rewarded for their resiliency in the bottom of the eighth. After a Derek Jeter single drove in Miguel Cairo (who had doubled with one out), the whole stadium came alive. Cheering crazily, you sensed the inevitable change of tide.

Here it is: that weird moment that always strangles the Sox, I thought. *It always happens right about now, at the most critical point in the game.*

Something strange did occur, all right.

And like yours truly, millions of Yankees fans born with a sense of entitlement were in for the shock of their lives.

Alex Rodriguez, all season long the source of Red Sox frustration, hit an innocent looking tapper between the mound and first base line. Converging on the ball simultaneously, pitcher Bronson Arroyo and first baseman Doug Mientkiewicz both realized no one was covering first. With no other options, Arroyo, charging aggressively, picked up the spinning roller and went to tag A-Rod.

Suddenly, the ball came flying loose, making its way down the right-field line while Jeter tore around the bases with the Yankees third run.

The stadium went berserk.

I went berserk.

We're gonna win, I assumed once more. *It may have taken longer than I thought, but…*

My musings were interrupted with a different type of madness; the madness that occurs when a professional sports team and an entire city, a little over eight million strong, is on the verge of a mind-bending meltdown of historic proportions.

Convening once more, the umpires and baseball gods huddled, then cited rule 7.08 of the baseball handbook, which goes a little something like this:

"Any runner is out when he intentionally interferes with a thrown ball; or hinders a fielder attempting to make a play on a batted ball… Offensive interference is an act by the team at bat which interferes with, obstructs, impedes, hinders or confuses any fielder attempting to make a play. If the umpire declares the batter, batter runner, or a runner out for interference, all other runners shall return to the last base that was in the judgment of the umpire, legally touched at the time of the interference, unless otherwise provided by these rules… In the event the batter has not reached first base, all runners shall return to the base last occupied at the time of the pitch."

With a left-handed chop straight from Mr. Miyagi's *Karate Kid* manual, Alex Rodriguez had altered the course of *the Curse*. Completing their long conference, the umpires ruled A-Rod out and Jeter was ordered back to first.

The Yankee Stadium crowd, perhaps unaccustomed to the new wrinkles of the rivalry, went berserk once more; this time in a really bad way. Already incensed about the controversial fourth-inning homer, they were livid when the umps overturned the play. Throwing batteries, balls and other debris, the litter that decorated the baseball diamond was not only a reflection of the evening's chaos, but it was also a strong indicator that the New York Yankees and their fanatical loyalists, not the team from Boston creating wine from water, were in fact spooked.

Four outs later, after Tony Clark struck out swinging with the tying runs on base to end the game, the Boston Red Sox were twenty-seven outs away from the greatest baseball story ever told;

and the possibility of the Pinstripes authoring the most colossal collapse in the history of professional sports loomed large.

And a stunned, stone-faced man who watched the game from his Marble Hill living room—one who a mere week and-a-half earlier crowed to a Bunker Hill Community College lounge that the Boston Red Sox would never, ever beat the New York Yankees— was 27 outs from feeling like a complete ass.

✪ ✪ ✪

At 12:01 a.m. on October 21, 2004, New York batsman Rubén Sierra hit a routine groundball to second baseman Pokey Reese, who threw to first baseman Doug Mientkiewicz for the final putout of a dominant 10-3 victory. As catcher Jason Varitek leaped into the arms of pitcher Allen Embry, everyone from Hartford to Maine, including those who invaded their House of Horrors in the South Bronx to witness history, danced on the grave of Babe Ruth as they rejoiced.

A cosmic curse had been lifted, and the strange sight of the Boston Red Sox celebrating in Yankee Stadium left fans across the New York region—from the Bronx and Bensonhurst, Brooklyn to Bayonne and the furthest suburbs of New Jersey—stupefied, shell-shocked and slack-jawed at witnessing the most inglorious loss in their team's104-year history. Manny Ramirez held his right index finger high, signifying the Red Sox were No. 1 in the American League, and Trot Nixon sprinted out to right center-field and laughed loudly at the Bleacher Creatures.

For the first time in nearly ninety years, the Boston Red Sox had gotten the last word.

And my phone kept ringing.

Throughout the game, ingenious messages from Boston flooded my answering machine.

"The Yankees suck, dude," a Boston fan announced.

"This makes Cinderella look like a horror movie!" another proclaimed.

"A funny thing happened to the World Series this year that was supposed to be in the Bronx. It ended up at Fenway Park!" one more person cracked.

"A very dark cloud over Yankee baseball," another crackpot screamed.

"How do you feel being the owner of the single greatest collapse in the history of American sports?" another message said.

"Attention, Yankee Universe! Please be advised that your world is being taken over by aliens from the Red Sox Nation!"

That one was good.

One person counted down the outs one-by-one, and another played back the game highlights as they happened, including the history-changing last out.

Like Sinatra encouraged us to do one year earlier, the Red Sox Nation gleefully spread the news of their ground-breaking achievement. And as disgusted as I was about the most humiliating experience of my sports life, even I had to smile at the creativity of the crank calls.

That smile quickly disappeared as I replayed the magnitude of the moment: Up three games-to-none with three outs to go, and the game's greatest closer on the mound to wrap things up. And now this: the biggest piece of the apple caught in the throat of a city too depressed to sleep on a night like this.

Perhaps the message that things would be different came in that Yankees Game 3 demolition job, a 19-8 victory that proved to be their last in 2004. The Boston Red Sox last won a world championship in 1918, and that number mirrored the final score of Game 3; with one notable exception.

The "One" was missing.

Days later, the Yankees found that one victory.

It was neatly tucked in the back pocket of the Boston Red Sox.

The Bronx Bombers thought they would receive it in that seventh game. In fact they were so sure that *the Curse of the Bambino* still lived that they trotted out Bucky Dent, who homered to slay the Red Sox in 1978, to throw the ceremonial first pitch to Yogi Berra. Further support came from Yankees Owner George Steinbrenner, who showed up in the clubhouse some six hours before the first pitch.

All of the championship karma from the gift of Ruth was in place to taunt, torment and torture all of New England, and baseball's eternal justice would reign supreme once more.

Only this time, a funny thing happened: Someone forgot to tell *the Idiots* about the order of nature in these parts.

The shaggy-haired leader of the Red Sox pack, Johnny Damon, started things off immediately. Ignoring his .103 batting average through the first six games of the series, he singled to left off a 94-miles-an-hour, Kevin Brown heater to open the game. Stealing second with one out, he tried to score on a Manny Ramirez single to center, but was gunned down at the plate on a perfect relay throw by Derek Jeter.

Jeter coming up big under the bright lights is a great sign, I thought as I watched the game at home. *We have nothing to worry about.*

That would be my last assumption.

The very next pitch Kevin Brown threw completed my transformation from arrogant Yankees fan to a complete ass.

And as he did throughout the Series, it was "Big Papi" who made me pay for my bravado.

Completely dialed into the moment, David Ortiz cemented his curse-busting, playoff MVP legacy by rifling his third homer of the series deep into the right-field stands for a two-run homer.

For Yankees fans, it was the faith-crumbling beginning of an eight-decade mystique.

For the Red Sox Nation, the completion of a baseball miracle was in sight; a miracle made sweeter because it came at the expense of their hated rivals in a place where they were always subservient to baseball history.

Growing tougher and tougher as the game progressed, the Boston knockout punch came early. Loading the bases in the second inning (a single and two walks) against Kevin Brown, they forced Yankees Manager Joe Torre's hand. Emerging from the dugout, he took the ball from Brown and placed the remnants of the curse into the hands of Javier Vazquez, a pitcher who gave up two home runs in a game in June to Boston's next batter, Johnny Damon.

His first pitch, a fastball straight down Broadway, left Yankees fans mumbling to themselves and cursing the baseball gods. Damon, looking fastball all the way, lifted a fly ball that carried into the first row of right-field seats for a back-breaking grand slam.

Boston now led 6-0.

Tumbling headfirst into a disillusioned doom, the countdown to the most devastating loss in Yankees history had officially begun. Traveling along this treadmill to pitchers and catchers in Tampa, the journey to "Spring Training, 2005" picked up momentum in the fourth. With a runner on, Vazquez threw another first-pitch fastball to Damon, who promptly sent it soaring into the upper deck in right field, where a fan with a Red Sox cap gleefully caught the souvenir.

It was now 8-1, Red Sox.

The home run was the culmination of a complete unraveling, and the Evil Empire, one that ruled since Armistice Day, was no more.

Derek Lowe, pitching against the Yankees on two days' rest, ran the victory lap. Allowing the Bombers one run through six innings, he gave way to Pedro Martinez in the seventh. Though the Yankees touched him for two runs—and brought hopeful "Who's Your Daddy" chants for one last miracle—the game was over long before then.

It seemed fitting that there would be a fourth homer to right—this one by Mark Bellhorn—in the eighth. Right field in Yankee Stadium was first occupied by a slugger who patrolled the stadium lawn and launched many a moonshot into its bleachers.

What was his name?

It was George Herman "Babe" Ruth.

For the first time in eight-and-a-half decades, a Yankees season would end listening to a Boston Red Sox celebration at their expense.

And when it was over and the 10-3 victory was officially recorded in the American League history books, it would be done with an asterisk. An egregious gag job like no other, amplified by the fact it came against their most ancient, bitter rivals, no longer could Yankees fans conjure up Bucky Dent or Aaron Boone; nor could they humiliate Red Sox Nation with an awful chain of events. Banished forever from the New England lexicon, never again would the word "curse" be uttered in one-upmanship, or used as against the Red Sox like garlic to ward off vampires.

The mental hold that New Yorkers held over a city five hours away was gone forever.

This was a choke job of the grandest proportions, one that would flap in the wind alongside twenty-six championship flags.

That alone was enough to make millions of Yankees fans feel like I did.

Like a complete ass.

✪ ✪ ✪

THE AFTERMATH...

Things were never the same since that dreary Wednesday night in October six years ago. The Red Sox, flying high, banished the Curse forever by sweeping the St. Louis Cardinals in the 2004 World Series.

The night they won their first championship in eighty-six years was another night I failed to answer my phone.

"Guess what they're doing in Boston, William?" Linda Battle asked in her message. "They're partying like it's 1918!"

(NOTE: The good doctor, now residing in Texas, actually holds a special place in the hearts of Red Sox Nation if they purchased a copy of this book, for she helped reverse the curse by having a Yankees fan give a lecture in her class. Her contribution to New England lore is one of baseball's unknown stories...until now. I can see it now: much like Ralph Branca and Bobby Thomson after "The Shot Heard 'Round the World," we'll go on tour together reliving the moment. NOT!!!!)

Surprisingly, that was the only message left on my machine that fateful night.

While the Yankees continued winning the American League East (their 2006 triumph included a five-game sweep of the Sox in Fenway that effectively ended their season), even their regular season dominance ended in 2007; when the Red Sox collected an AL EAST CHAMPS banner en route to its second world championship of the new millennium. And in 2008, the Red Sox and Tampa Bay Rays ensured that there would be no postseason baseball in New York City for the first time since the baseball strike of 1994.

And for the first time since 1919, Yankees fans endured slanderous taunts while losing all baseball debates against anyone from the New England area.

The New York Yankees of 2009 had to fix things. That the baseball world was spinning the wrong way on its axis for five years was too long.

Now it was time to restore order.

HOME SWEEP HOME: THE STORY OF HOW THE EAST WAS WON

T he scores were as follows: 5-4, in eleven innings; 16-11; 4-1 (this one included an embarrassing steal of home by Jacob Ellsbury); 6-4 (in a rain-delayed game at the new stadium which finished a little after one in the morning); 7-3 (in the ninth-inning a drunk Red Sox fan poured salt in an open wound by clogging one of my toilets.); 7-0; 6-5 and 4-3.

Despite the fact that they were two-and-one-half games out of first, the Boston Red Sox came into this showdown feeling all the psychological arrows pointed in their direction.

Eight straight wins over the hated Yankees told them so.

It even convinced Skip Bayless to announce on *First and 10* that the Yankees would split the four-game series, and the Red Sox would eventually catch and surpass the Pinstripes during the stretch run.

I hoped for more than a split, and boldly stressed such from the minute I entered the Legends Suite Club the afternoon of Thursday, August 6.

"We need a sweep," I said to Kevin Michaels, my favorite bartender.

Smiling, my blood brother knew as well. Feeling the October-like electricity as well, "We're gonna get it too," he countered. He lifted up his uniform to display an anti-Sox T-shirt. "I'll be wearing these every day."

I had T-shirts of my own: Yankees T-shirts to give to the members of the Red Sox Nation who talked the most trash. Fussing and fighting with the visiting Fenway Faithful during that initial two-game set in May, many of them actually silenced me with memories of 2004, as well as the fact that the Yankees championship pedigree of the twentieth century was, in their opinion, archaic.

"We're just giving you a head start, just like last century," I defended.

Fanning the flames of revenge that burned within me, "It's *the Curse of A-Rod*," A Sox fan quickly responded. "The Yankees will never win again. A-Rod shouldn't have used PEDs. He put a black mark on the Yankee tradition."

It didn't matter that A-Rod's missteps occurred in a Texas Ranger uniform; nor did it matter to him that the Yankees sat atop the division going into this showdown. The Boston Red Sox and its nation of loyalists had adopted that same disposition—a smug, arrogant attitude screaming its self-importance loudly—that we owned until the ninth inning in Game 4 of the 2004 American League Championship Series.

This was a perfect trap, the ultimate set-up; a golden opportunity for the Yankees to restore some of their swagger. In this age of communication by action, merely splitting or winning the four-game series was not an option. A statement had to be made to the Boston Red Sox and the rest of the American League, and it had to be done emphatically.

And the time to strike was now. Back in June, after sweeping a three-game set from the Yankees at Fenway Park to extend their winning streak to eight against the Pinstripes, the Sox were two games in front in the AL East and looking superior to the Bombers in every way: hitting, starting pitching, bullpen, speed, depth and, most notably, youth.

Seven-and-a-half weeks later, the psychological needle had tipped in favor of the New York Yankees.

With the Red Sox hurting (All-Star outfielder Jason Bay would miss the first three games of the crucial showdown with a strained right hamstring and starting pitchers Daisuke Matsuzaka and Tim

Wakefield were on the disabled list), hittable (end-of-the-rotation pitchers Brad Penny and Clay Buchholz were joined in their in-effectiveness by future Hall of Famer John Smoltz, who was coming off shoulder surgery himself) and hemorrhaging badly, the possibilities of what lay ahead fascinated me.

A sweep will finish them, I mused.

Sure, over seven weeks remained, and as reporters and announcers loved to say, "That's a lifetime in a 162-game season." But something deep within told me that the Red Sox Nation was wounded and wavering, and if the Yankees found a way to put them down, they would not get back up.

The American League East would be decided right here, in August, at the new Yankee Stadium.

However two questions remained unanswered: Were the Yankees ready to deliver? Were they ready to end the longest losing streak against their bitter rival since a time when they played their home games at Hilltop Park and answered to the name "Highlanders"?

Before a sellout crowd which included Muhammad Ali, the first game supplied some of those answers; but not immediately. Joba Chamberlain, effective since the All-Star break, struggled with his command early. And his teammates missed a scoring opportunity in the second inning when Jorge Posada, trying to score on a Nick Swisher single, missed Melky Cabrera's slide signal and was thrown out at the plate.

Capitalizing on their early momentum, the Red Sox struck first in the top of the third. Second baseman and reigning MVP Dustin Pedroia, making the stadium look small, led off the inning by hitting an opposite-field solo homer into right-center-field seats.

For a half inning, the stadium was hushed, but the Yankees restored life to their Homer Depot when Johnny Damon evened the score with his twentieth blast of the season; his thirteenth at home. Striking back quickly, the Red Sox went back ahead in the fourth, when new acquisition Casey Kotchman hit another Chamberlain offering over the wall in right; giving Boston a 3-1 lead.

By now, it was clear to everyone in the stadium that Joba Chamberlain was laboring. Fighting through his sloppy, 108-pitch performance, he gave up four runs and six hits while walking a career-high seven batters. Pitching in-and-out of jams and constantly dodging danger, it was his gutsiest effort of the season.

And, as it turned out, those five innings were just what the Yankees needed from him. In the bottom of the fourth, the Bombers went to work against Red Sox starter John Smoltz. First Robinson Cano rapped a single up the middle to plate Jorge Posada from second. Then after a walk to Nick Swisher, Melky Cabrera stepped into the batter's box.

Smoltz, looking like Christy Mathewson pitching for the Cincinnati Reds or Warren Spahn for the New York Mets—painfully out of place at the end of an illustrious career—served up a batting practice fastball to Cabrera on a 1-2 count.

Unloading on his gift, Melky launched a three-run homer into the second deck in right, giving the Yankees a 5-3 lead and an irreversible shift of the tide.

As the batting order turned to the top of the lineup, the onslaught continued. After finally retiring a batter, Smoltz gave up a single to Johnny Damon, then a ringing double to first baseman Mark Teixeira. After intentionally walking Alex Rodriguez, Red Sox Manager Terry Francona came to remove this once great pitcher.

Watching him amble off the mound from the HDTVs in the men's room, I felt sadness for a moment. The John Smoltz I remembered was the big-game Atlanta Braves starter that matched zeroes deep into an October night with Jack Morris with a World Series title on the line, way back in 1991. As was the case many times in his career, he always came up big when the lights shined bright.

Not on this night, however. Going against an unforgiving lineup, the forty-two-year-old right-hander got knocked from pillar to post. Far removed from the days where he, Greg Maddox and Tom Glavine formed what arguably was the best trio of arms for one team in baseball history, John Smoltz looked more like a player hanging on than one of the best of his generation.

A 2-5 record with an 8.33 ERA in eight starts for Boston also supported my case.

If this were the last of John Smoltz, I thought as my compassion quickly returned to a beating-Boston-at-all-costs mindset, *then I won't hold this against him.*

(NOTE: *After the game, Smoltz was designated for reassignment and picked up by the St. Louis Cardinals. After a flaw in his mechanics was uncovered by pitching coach Dave Duncan, he pitched a little better; going 1-3 with a 4.26 ERA. But these stats won't be remembered once he's enshrined in Cooperstown. The diversity of an arm that produced over 200 wins and 150 saves will.*)

A former Yankees reliever, left-hander Billy Traber, followed Smoltz, and induced a bouncer to first from designated hitter Hideki Matsui. Hustling down the line, a weak-kneed Matsui turned a routine double-play into a fielder's choice; allowing the Yankees to increase the lead to 6-3.

Up to the plate stepped Jorge Posada, who to that point had been thinking about another catcher in the long line of Yankee greats, Thurman Munson. Paying tribute to the Yankees captain who died in a plane crash on Aug. 2, 1979, the current Yankees backstop decided to paint "No. 15" on his catcher's mask before the game.

His third hit of the night, a long, three-run home run that landed between the stadium's ambulance entrance and Monument Park, would have pleased the former captain. Punctuating a brilliant game with his blast, the shot concluded a 34-minute inning which saw the Yankees send thirteen men to the plate. By the time it was all over, the Yankees scored eight runs and had a commanding 9-3 lead.

Padding the advantage, Mark Teixeira smacked a solo blast of his own, his 28th (and 18th at home) in what was turning into an MVP-caliber season. Hideki Matsui later added a two-run double as part of his own three-RBI night, and the Yankees coasted home to a 13-6 victory.

The eight-game Red Sox winning streak against us was now in the Yankees' rearview mirror, and all questions about losing to them time and time again were answered in a resounding performance.

While all of us in the Legends Suite Club were happy that the Yankees had ended the streak, our celebrations were muted by the fact that it was only one game. Pure euphoria would come if we somehow found a way to get those remaining three games.

It was a long way till Sunday, and that 6-1/2-game lead Yankees fans hoped for.

Friday night's game would make that vision seem years away.

✪ ✪ ✪

In this generation of small ballparks, high-scoring slugfests, middle infielders with power numbers (where have you gone, Mark Belanger and Ozzie Smith?) and the game's never-ending romance with the four-bagger, the thing I love the most about baseball is a good old-fashioned pitcher's duel.

When two pitchers are in top form and their teams are supporting their efforts with fielding gems and game-saving putouts, every play and every swing takes on the magnitude of the moment. As the innings progress, the tension rises, matching the heightened drama of each pitch, and by game's end most fans leave the ballpark knowing that they witnessed something truly special.

To me, a pitcher's duel represents everything that's right with baseball. The mere thought of being at a game where two hurlers matched zeroes for innings on end gave me goose bumps. Longing to join 50,000 fans on the edge of their stadium seats for three, sometimes four hours, a pitcher's duel was like that woman of my deepest fantasies: the one I dreamed of making love to over and over again, only to have the pestering shrill of an alarm clock bring me back to reality.

Feeling like a forty-year-old virgin, I had never witnessed a pitcher's duel in person.

And I always wanted to.

I blame my seventh-grade English teacher at Staten Island's Prall Intermediate School, Mr. Hofferman, for that obsession. Seeing my passion for sports knowledge, every now and then he junked an English lesson and had me read an article of sports history to the class. Soaking up these moments in time like a sponge, I learned that the New York Jets' 27-23 win over the Oakland Raiders in the 1968 AFL Championship may have actually been a tougher battle than their 16-7 history-making victory against the Baltimore Colts in Super Bowl III some two weeks later. And to my surprise, I learned that Andrew (Rube) Foster, the founder of the Negro Leagues, was a great pitcher at the turn of the century that taught Christy Mathewson his famous fade-a-way pitch.

One day, after my first-period class had ended, my English teacher gave me something to peruse that still brings a fond smile to my face. The article was about two pitchers who hooked up on a mid-season Tuesday night in San Francisco and treated the nearly 16,000 fans in attendance at Candlestick Park to an unforgettable baseball experience.

That game, played on July 2, 1963 between the San Francisco Giants and the Milwaukee Braves, featured seven future Hall of Famers, including the two starting pitchers, Juan Marichal and Warren Spahn. The left-handed Spahn, forty-two years of age, began his career in 1942, five years before Jackie Robinson integrated the game. Twenty-one years later, he was in the middle of a season which saw him win twenty-three times; the thirteenth and last twenty-win season of a remarkable career with him winning more games (363) than any southpaw in baseball history.

Marichal, twenty-five years of age at the time, pitched his first no-hitter a couple of weeks before this game, becoming the first Latin player to accomplish that feat. A strong, right-handed fire-baller from the Dominican Republic, he was at the halfway point of an incredible season which saw him post a 25-8 record with a sparkling 2.41 ERA and 248 strikeouts.

(NOTE: Neither Marichal or Spahn, who would finish his season 23-7 with a 1.88 ERA, won the 1963 Cy Young Award. That honor went to Los Angeles Dodgers left-hander Sandy Koufax, who went 25-5 with a 1.88 ERA and struck out 306 batters.)

As much as they were polar opposites off the mound, Spahn and Marichal, utilizing high leg kicks in their windups and both possessing a vast array of pitches, were mirror images of each other on the hill.

What were their records going into that July 2 game?

Spahn was 11-3; and Marichal was 12-3.

As much power was in the ballpark that Tuesday evening (the Braves had Henry Aaron and Eddie Mathews and these were the Giants of Willie Mays, Willie McCovey and Orlando Cepeda), this would not be an evening for a barrage of tape-measure blasts. The sluggers would be silenced by an amazing pitching exhibition that should be gift-wrapped with a bow and delivered to Major League Baseball as a presentation to a generation of coddled pitchers and pitch-count wary managers paying more attention to statistical data than to a pitcher's strength at certain points within the game.

In complete mastery of the lineups they were facing, the young workhorse and old lion put up eight sets of matching zeroes on the Candlestick Park scoreboard. Then, in the bottom of the ninth, Warren Spahn hung a curveball that Giants first baseman and fellow future Hall of Famer Willie McCovey absolutely crushed. Traveling far over the right-field foul pole, the ball appeared to be a game-winner, but was ruled foul by the first-base umpire Chris Pelekoudas.

Smiling as he shrugged off the near miss, Spahn escaped the inning unscathed, and continued pitching deep into the night. For 200 pitches, the longtime mainstay of the Braves staff was extraordinary. Allowing a mere nine hits and one intentional free pass, the crafty legend held the potent San Francisco attack scoreless for 15-1/3 innings. It was an amazing performance which moved Hall of Fame pitcher Carl Hubbell, who was in attendance that night, to say that Warren Spahn should have his body donated to medical science.

As astonishing as the forty-two-year-old Spahn was, he was matched zero-for-zero by Juan Marichal, who was firing fastballs past the Atlanta hitters with an alarming ease. Yet in spite of his outstanding pitching, the tension was building: both in the field behind him, where the defense was fearful that one mistake might doom his spectacular gem; and in the San Francisco dugout, where Giants Manager Alvin Dark worried about the possible permanent harm he might be doing to his ace by leaving him in.

In the 9th, 10th, 11th and 13th innings, Dark visited the pitcher's mound to remove Marichal from the game, only to be talked out of it time and time again. Perhaps sensing that the pitcher's duel would be talked about for years to come, Giants catcher Ed Bailey became the voice in his pitcher's ear.

"Don't let him take you out. Win or lose, this is great," he kept telling him.

Finally in the top of the 14th, the San Francisco manager came to the mound with his mind made up.

"No more for you," Dark said to Marichal.

The Giants pitcher made his last valid argument. Pointing at Warren Spahn, who was sitting in the Braves' dugout, he said, "Do you see that man pitching on the other side? Do you know that man is forty-two years old? I'm only twenty-five. If that man is still on the mound, then nobody is going to take me out of here."

Why shouldn't he have kept pitching? The San Francisco Giants right-hander had held the Milwaukee Braves scoreless. Matching the ancient left-hander inning-for-inning and pitch-for-pitch, by the time he left the mound after the top of the 16th inning, he had hurled 227 pitches at Braves batsmen; allowing eight hits, and four walks. Striking out ten, he came within two innings of a complete game shutout that was the equivalent of a doubleheader.

After Warren Spahn retired Harvey Kuenn to start the bottom of the frame, Willie Mays stepped to the plate. It was a little past midnight by the bay, and the air was cool. Spahn's first pitch to the "Say Hey Kid" was a screwball that didn't break. Mays connected, and as the ball ascended into the night sky toward left-field, Spahn slowly walked from the mound, his shoulders slumped in defeat. His 201st and last pitch was his only mistake, and it proved fatal as the ball sailed over the left-field fence.

After four hours and ten minutes, the historic pitcher's duel had finally ended, with Juan Marichal besting Warren Spahn in a 1-0 classic.

Infatuated about that wonderful matchup and other classic confrontations throughout the years, how I wished I could be in a ballpark, any ballpark, for a gut-wrenching nail-biter that could be talked about with my grandchildren years from now.

On August 7, 2009, I would get my chance.

As soon as I saw the pitching match-up—A.J. Burnett and Josh Beckett, former teammates for a Florida Marlins team that shut down the Pinstripes in the 2003 World Series, were now facing off for the Yankees and Red Sox, respectively—that little voice of fate I heard all season told me that this Friday matchup had the word "classic" written all over it.

The night was pleasantly warm, and the electricity in the air produced a playoff-type atmosphere.

After the debacle the night before, Boston needed this game desperately.

The Yankees wanted to build on their momentum by landing another haymaker to the Red Sox title hopes.

And a certain restroom attendant in the Legends Suite Club had donned the outfit of a psychic.

"Runs will be at a premium tonight," I announced to everyone who entered the men's room.

"Yeah, right," a Yankees fan said while urinating. "We're going to cream Beckett tonight."

"A.J.'s gonna pitch like Carol Burnett," a balding fat dude from the Red Sox Nation countered.

As they both approached the motion faucets, I became even more clairvoyant.

"This is the most important game of the year, so we might be here for a while. Get comfortable; both of these pitchers will have their best stuff tonight."

Begrudgingly, both men agreed.

"I'll take your word for it."

At that instant, a familiar patron named William Ramonas vouched for me.

A tall, distinguished man, in a booming voice, he said, "You better listen to him; he's been right all year."

On this night, however, my call would be nearly perfect.

At 7:09 p.m. on Friday, Boston leadoff hitter Jacoby Ellsbury stepped into the batter's box at Yankee Stadium and stroked a hard single to left field off A.J. Burnett. It would be the very last hit Boston would get off him. Utilizing a fastball with outstanding movement and a nasty slider, Burnett stepped up and turned in the signature performance the Yankees expected when they signed him over the winter. Stingy, steely-eyed and spectacular, while he walked six, he fanned an equal number; and no other baserunner besides the leadoff batter

Ellsbury—who was left stranded in that first inning—reached third. After his 118th and final pitch produced 7-2/3 innings of scoreless, one-hit baseball, the Yankees hurler walked off the mound to a lusty standing ovation.

On any other night this season, he would have recorded a win for his efforts.

This night would be different, however; his counterpart on the mound, Boston ace Josh Beckett, was throwing darts as well. Possessing his sharpest stuff of the season, the big right-hander limited the Pinstripes to four hits in a brilliant 115-pitch, two-walk/seven-strikeout performance over seven innings.

By the bottom of the fourth inning, one of the gentlemen who initially doubted my prophecy came to me and nodded his head in amazement.

"You were right, William. These guys are not yielding anything."

Smiling, I proceeded to tell the long line of Yankees fans, busboys and waiters waiting to relieve themselves how I thought the game would end. (Oops, I forgot; there were a few Red Sox fans I allowed to use our facility. *Wink*.)

"One run is all we'll need tonight, gentlemen. One run will win this game tonight."

It would be a phrase I used with so much redundancy that I grew tired of saying it. But I had to keep saying it, because the Bombers discouraged their supporters with squandered opportunities and near-misses.

In the bottom of the fifth inning, Hideki Matsui and Jorge Posada singled, and after Beckett retired the next two batters, he walked ninth-place hitter Melky Cabrera to load the bases. With the sellout crowd of 48,262 on its feet and imploring Derek Jeter to come through in the clutch, the captain was unable to deliver, grounding out softly to third.

Opportunity knocked again for the Yankees in the ninth, but again they contributed to both teams combined 0-for-19 batting with runners in scoring position. With Yankees on second and third, Boston reliever Daniel Bard struck out Jorge Posada on a late-breaking slider in the dirt.

As I stepped out of the lower level men's room and saw the Yankee faces coming toward me, instantly I lifted a page from my Vince Lombardi motivational manual.

After all both he and I shared the same Gemini zodiac sign.

"All right, guys," I shouted in my best rah-rah voice. "It looks like this one may take a while. But mark my words: One run is all we'll need, and I'm willing to stay here all night to get it. How about you guys?"

Exchanging hi-fives with some of the familiar season-ticket holders, I heard a roar from all the Yankees fans in the restroom line.

"Are you sure we got this, William?" one asked.

"We get this one, and we break the back of the Red Sox Nation."

Another roar came from the little boy's room.

As the marathon progressed, those initial extra-inning roars gave way to mounting tension and growing frustration. Patrons and Legends support staff, coming back for second, third and fourth visits, were growing more exasperated by the inning. After Red Sox closer Jonathan Papelbon fanned Jeter with a runner on third to end the 10th, and Alex Rodriguez to finish the 11th, once again I repelled feelings of worry with supreme confidence.

"How long is this going to take?" an older gentleman with glasses asked me.

Stilling his uneasiness, "As long as it has to, sir," I responded. "One run is going to do it tonight. And the Yankees will get that one run."

My friend William, who always came right on time that evening, again backed me up.

"Listen to this man," he echoed. "He knows what he's talking about."

Also supporting my unwavering belief system was the Yankees' bullpen. Finding their shine after Burnett's departure, over the next 7-1/3 innings they further exemplified the two buzzwords needed to take one of these teams to October glory: *Great pitching.* Slamming the door completely on the Sox was Phil Hughes, who got the last out in the eighth inning; Mariano Rivera, who worked the ninth against the heart of the Red Sox batting order; Alfredo Aceves, who was summoned to throw three truly underrated innings; Brian Bruney, who in recording six outs gave the crowd a scare in the 14th when newly acquired Red Sox catcher Victor Martinez sent one of his pitches to the wall in right field, where it was flagged down by reserve outfielder Eric Hinske; and Phil Coke, who got three quick outs in the top of the 15th. Together, the quintet held Boston to three harmless singles.

As the epic struggle breezed past midnight, the Yankees threw away another chance to end matters in the 14th. When I saw Red Sox manager trot out Junichi Tazawa to pitch the 14th, I smiled and looked at Elton Ottley, one of my favorite Legends employees. Tawaza, a twenty-three-year-old rookie from Japan who was promoted from the minors earlier in the day, was making his major-league debut.

He was all the Red Sox had left in their bullpen.

"It's only a matter of time," I said boldly. "One run is all we need."

"You've been saying that for the past ten innings. But you know what? You've been calling it all year. I believe you, man. "

Sharing a high-five we invented just for the staff, we returned our attention to the restroom HDTVs showing the classic everyone in the stadium was now a part of.

We almost got Tawaza in that inning. With two on and one out, Hinske hit a ball directly on the screws. Producing a sizzling line drive, Boston right-fielder J.D. Drew raced back, stuck his glove up and made a game-saving, highlight-reel catch.

You could hear the capacity crowd groan all the way in the restroom.

Then Melky Cabrera came up next and scorched a laser down the right-field line. Bidding for his fourth walk-off hit of the year—and the Yankees' 10th overall—everyone thought his drive ended the game.

Everyone, that is, except first base umpire Jim Joyce; who saw the sinking liner hit just outside the white chalk and emphatically waved the "foul ball" signal. When Cabrera was sent back to strike out swinging on the next pitch, almost everyone in the stadium sighed in frustration.

Smirking as I watched the drive curve just foul, I remained composed.

Knowing that the top of the Yankees' order was due up, I remember being in the men's lounge with about ten guys. Looking at the weariness in their eyes, and knowing that the game was approaching the American League suspension time (in the Junior Circuit, an inning cannot start after 1 a.m.), I reached deep into a bag that my fiancée, Cheryl, had packed for me.

It was my magic bag of faith.

"This is the last inning, guys, and someone's going to end it here with a walk-off homer."

When pushed for a name, I wouldn't answer immediately.

However, as I saw Tawaza warming up in the bottom of the 15th, I smiled.

This would be a perfect time for A-Rod to start getting some of the love that he longs for so much from Yankees fans, I thought. But the thought was immediately dismissed when I remembered that someone would have to get on base for A-Rod to deliver; he was due up fourth in the inning.

As soon as I finished pondering, Derek Jeter, who to that point had been 0 for 6 and had failed three times with a runner on third in the contest, hit a bloop single to left-center.

I just shook my head in amazement.

A-Rod will end this.

The glow would not leave my face, even as the rookie Red Sox hurler retired the next two batters.

A-Rod will end this.

As Alex Rodriguez approached the plate, I couldn't help but think of Hebrews 11:1, the scripture that Cheryl had me quote when the beleaguered Yankees launched his 2009 season in dramatic fashion. *Faith is the substance of things hoped for, and the evidence in things not yet seen.* Then, I immediately thought of Michael Jordan, and what he said to Chicago Bulls Coach Phil Jackson after hitting that dynasty-ending shot in Utah way back in 1998.

During a heartfelt embrace, he said, "I had faith. I had faith."

As two pitches breezed by A-Rod, I thought of times in my life where God made a way out of none; with my literary career, and up to this point, turning this simple maintenance job into a transforming experience where many of my childhood sports dreams were coming true.

In life, a mustard seed of faith is all you need, as anything is possible.

And I had faith that A-Rod would end this classic contest.

It had been 72 at-bats since his last home run, the longest single-season power outage of his career. But on a 2-1 fastball that Junichi Tazawa grooved into his wheelhouse, A-Rod broke the deadlock by launching a walk-off rocket that landed in the left center-field bullpen.

It was his 573rd round-tripper, tying with Harmon Killebrew for ninth place on the all-time list.

After five hours and thirty-three minutes of intense struggle, a game where time seemed to have no jurisdiction had finally ended, and the Yankees, with their epic 2-0 triumph over Boston, had a season-high, 4-1/2 game lead over their bitter rivals.

Instead of one run, I had gotten two.

Raising a fist in triumph, the minute I heard the crack of the bat, I knew it was over. Instead of joining in a walk-off celebration in the Suite Club as I had done numerous times throughout the season, I just started my cleanup, as if nothing had happened.

It was 12:42 a.m. Saturday morning, and an afternoon contest awaited me.

Many of the patrons who stayed the entire game stopped by before their long journey home and thanked me for my unwavering faith in the Yankees. William F. Ramonas, the man who supported my boldest prediction yet, gave me a big hug.

"We've come a long way since that 22-4 game, huh?" he said.

Though weary from the longest night of the season, I gave him my biggest grin.

"We most definitely have, my friend. We most definitely have."

Although I didn't know it at the time, but while doing research for this book, I came across something that served as confirmation as to how beautiful life is. According to ESPN and the MLB Network, Alex Rodriguez's parting shot that summer night in August was just the fifth game-ending home run in a scoreless game in the 15th inning or later. He joined Adrian Garrett (Angels, Sept. 22, 1975), Earl Averill (Indians, Aug. 24, 1935) and Old Hoss Radbourn (Grays, Aug. 17, 1882), all of whom contributed to baseball history with their walk-offs.

The fifth person was Willie Mays, who ended the classic Spahn-Marichal duel with his "Drive Home Safely" blast.

Thank you, Mr. Hofferman, wherever you are.

✪ ✪ ✪

And on Saturday, the Yankees bullpen rested.

Because in Game 3 of this pivotal line-in-the-sand staredown between ancient rivals, C.C. Sabathia was in the house.

And when you really think about it, it seemed fitting that the ace of the Bronx Bomber staff, another fruit of the Yankees' winter spending spree, would be next in line to leave his mark in this showdown series. His scoreless, 7-2/3 inning pitching performance—to that point his best outing of the season—could not have come at a better time; as the classic marathon one night before left the Yankees' pitching staff fatigued.

Dominant and overpowering, for the first six innings the durable southpaw wearing baggy pants flirted with a no-hitter, eventually settling for a two-hit, nine-strikeout masterpiece and a standing ovation from the 49,000 Yankees fans.

No Red Sox runner advanced past second base. Other than leadoff hitter Jacoby Ellsbury, who was 4-for-9 at the plate, Boston bats went strangely silent over two games. Collectively hitting 4-for-67 (.060 average) Yankees pitching put a stranglehold on the series with a 24-four-inning scoreless span.

From the power pitching of A. J. and C.C. to the lights-out bullpen and timely hitting of Derek Jeter—his opposite-field two-run homer in the bottom of the eighth supplied a five-run cushion—the swagger and identity that the New York Yankees lost was being reestablished in a hurry.

And with that 5-0 whitewash of Boston that increased their winning streak to six games, came more role reversal. Now 5-1/2 games ahead, it was the Bronx Bombers who were threatening to turn the American League East into a two-month victory lap. It was the Yankees who were winning not only the battles on the diamond, but for in the front office battles as well, where General Manager Brian Cashman flat out-schooled Boston counterpart Theo Epstein.

It was the team in pinstripes feeling good about themselves and their ever-growing momentum.

And it was the free-falling Red Sox, losers of five-in-a-row and struggling, who now had a player under major scrutiny for steroid use. Before Saturday's tilt, David Ortiz held a news conference concerning his appearance on a list of players who tested positive for performance-enhancing drugs in 2003. Denying that he had ever used or purchased steroids, he admitted that he had been lackadaisical in his use of supplements and vitamins.

Sneaking into the press conference room to watch the circus, *Yeah right, can someone say Winstrol?* I sarcastically thought.

At least A-Rod came clean.

At publication time of this book, we Yankees fans are still waiting to hear more about those vitamins and supplements he used.

I guess we'll have to settle for the sounds of silence from Boston.

Let's revisit the Brian Cashman-Theo Epstein debate for a tick. That the tide changed so dramatically from June, when the Yankees were still finding their way, to the verge of putting the Sox to sleep with one more victory, was a testament to the winter moves of their GM. Paying tremendous dividends, the back-to-back performances of Burnett and Sabathia epitomized the 1-2 pitching punch that characterized the championship teams of 1996-2000. Their frontline dominance transformed a glaring weakness that kept the Yankees from postseason play in 2008 into a strength that could match zeroes with anyone.

In the most important series of the season, two of the Pinstripes' new additions stepped up and applied their chokehold on a team that once owned an eight-game winning streak against them. Like trained assassins, the top-of-the-rotation tandem had done their part in leaving their most bitter adversary bloodied, bruised and battered, lying in a pool of mounting frustration.

To finish the hit and kill off any remaining aspirations owned by the Red Sox Nation for AL East supremacy, we needed one more contribution from our off-season acquisition puzzle.

✪ ✪ ✪

Call me weird, but sometimes I believe in sports euthanasia. When a team is down to its last breath, as the Boston Red Sox were going into their most important game of the season, my sympathetic nature tells me that you must do what's best for them.

You put them out of their misery.

The New York Yankees had an opportunity to show its bitter archrival and the rest of the baseball world its unique sense of compassion, and I shared this thought with everyone at the new Yankee Stadium on Sunday, August 9, 2009.

Kevin, my kindred Yankee spirit, smelled Boston blood in the water as well. Visiting me before the ESPN-televised Sunday night battle, his face wore a look of anticipation.

"We win tonight, and they're done," he said, his eyes brimming with excitement as the words left him. "This one will be better than the Boston Massacre, or that five-game Fenway sweep in 2006."

"The game is going to have a playoff feel to it, because the Red Sox are fighting for their lives. It's gonna feel a lot like the old place tonight," I predicted.

And it did.

All season long, the brand-new baseball diamond on River Avenue had awaited a formal christening of sorts; a galvanizing, legacy-cementing moment that would have the place rocking, just like the old place across the street. A sellout crowd in attendance and millions of Yankees fans watching at home had waited all season for that initial moment when an eruption of delirious New Yorkers echoed off the stadium concrete to create an intimidating experience for opponents, just like the old place across the street. All season long, our triple-decked palace of a place had been searching for a reverberating thunder that would shake its foundation with a passionate frenzy, just like the old place across the street.

And on a Sunday night in August, before a nationally televised crowd of millions and a sold-out crowd longing to see sports euthanasia, the roar would be restored to the Bronx.

You could feel the energy in the Legends Suite Club, as many of the patrons who came by the men's room knew the night would be something.

"Alright, gentlemen," I announced in a fake Southern accent to a pregame crowd in the restroom, "Okay, guys, the Red Sox dog can't walk."

One of the season-ticket holders must have read my script, for he added, "That damned dog can't see either."

By now, everybody got involved.

"What are we going to do to this dog, gentlemen?"

About five men yelled in unison, "We're gonna put that dog down."

"Yessir, gentlemen, we gotta put that old Red Sox dog to sleep."

An energetic laughter came from the men's room, rippled out into the Suite Club and through the ballpark, where a congregation of fans came to cheer their hearts out. The electricity felt when rapper Eminem spit the lyrics of "Lose Yourself" over the Yankee Stadium speaker system before the first pitch was contagious. This was a tantalizing moment that the New York Yankees owned: the first of many opportunities to seize a chunk of things they wanted to accomplish in their inaugural season in a new ballpark.

Would this mixture of youth, battle-tested veterans, superstars seeking redemption and expensive new additions capture the moment, or let it slip away?

The answer came quickly, as Yankees starter Andy Pettitte walked onto the stadium mound, reached into a past that produced over 220 career victories, and pulled out a vintage five-hit,/two-walk/four-strikeout performance that Manager Joe Girardi called his strongest start of the year. Magnificent and mesmerizing, for seven shutout innings, the thirty-seven-year-old left-hander magically mixed movement and velocity while matching what hurlers C.C. Sabathia and A.J. Burnett had done in the previous two games. In his masterful outing, his only hiccup was leaving the bases loaded in the fourth inning.

Like a fine wine, Good Ol' Andy seemed to be better with age.

But on this night, we needed him to be outstanding, for his Boston counterpart, Jon Lester (the hot-shot prospect the Texas Rangers wanted from the Sox in the proposed-then-aborted A-Rod trade), was throwing 95-miles-per-hour bee-bees at the Yankees' batsmen. Cognizant of the fact that the Red Sox season was hanging in the balance, Lester was lights-out. For six innings, every zero his ageless rival put on the scoreboard, he matched with his own brilliance.

Doubling my pleasure, I came into this weekend clash-of-titans without ever having witnessed a pitcher's duel.

Now I had two birds in hand.

Again, worried patrons coming to release tension looked to me for support.

Donning my prognosticating suit once more, all I said was this: "The team that scores first will win this one. And the New York Yankees will be that team."

"C'mon, man, how can you be so sure?" a man asked me in the bottom of the fifth.

Glancing over my shoulder, I saw a young man from the streets of Brooklyn, one I deeply admired for turning a simple dream of spitting rhymes into a financial empire. From rapping to Rocawear clothing, later in the season he and a fellow New York icon would introduce a new Big Apple anthem, a reality-based, chart-topping single that would become one of the biggest songs of the year as well as a tune that best captured October baseball magic in our city of dreams.

That would be later; at this particular moment, he and the bodyguard that accompanied him into the men's room were simply out taking in a ballgame. He had been a spectator many times throughout the season, and each and every time I wanted him to feel the respect and love I owned. Feeling honored just to tell him to "Keep making us proud," this Sunday night my affectionate tribute would be a little different.

Beaming proudly as he approached the motion-sensitive faucets, I said, "Mr. Carter, the Yankees might have ninety-nine problems, but the Sox ain't one." Making sure he had foamy soap/sanitizer on his hands, I continued. "And your New Jersey Nets had better get LeBron James."

As I continued aiding others that needed my attention, I felt a gentle, playful tap in my ribs, as if someone was giving me respect.

Turning around, I saw a quick smile from Jay-Z.

And then he was gone.

It was another moment in this ever-growing list of memorable ones to cherish.

Another person that stopped by the men's room was a person I knew on a more intimate level. Having attended the same high school on Staten Island, we used to talk sports trivia all the time, stumping each other with knowledge beyond our years. Going in different directions after our brief connection in time, while my life pursuits turned literary and legal, this gentleman went from being the sports editor of our Susan Wagner High School newspaper to a lead anchor on ESPN's *SportsCenter*, then eventually, the face of the NFL Network.

I was so happy to see him, and I surprised him.

"Sir, you went to the University of Michigan, am I correct?" I asked as we began talking.

The look of amazement on his face made my day.

And it got bigger as I continued.

"Susan Wagner High School as well."

"Do you know me?"

I had to end the charade.

"Yes, I do, Rich Eisen. I am so proud of you."

When he saw my face, he was astonished.

"William Cooper, what are you doing here?"

"I'm supplementing my literary dreams by working."

"You write books?"

Nodding, I felt a twinge of sadness as I looked at him. There were so many words threatening to gush forth, but so few to say in a men's restroom. Life is about choices, and while I had made some ill-advised decisions in pursuit of my accomplishments, I am thankful that God is one who redeems constantly, and turns rags to riches in ways that many who don't know Him find incomprehensible.

And at that moment, I found wealth and great pleasure in self-lessness.

"Fulfilling your dreams takes a lot of work, man," I responded.

"Don't I know it," my former classmate agreed.

"Man, I am so proud of you."

Exchanging a hearty handshake, he said, "I want to read your books, William."

Well, Rich, not only will not you get to read one, but...

You get the picture.

That night, however, we had more in common than merely being old classmates; we were witnessing another classic contest in the most intense rivalry in all of American sports. Heading into the home half of the seventh, the Yankees and Red Sox were still locked in a scoreless duel. Placing the game's outcome in the hands of the rest of his teammates, Pettitte had departed the fray, having thrown the last of his 112-pitches, Unflappable as always, when the bright lights of the new ballpark shined brighter than at any point of the season, he refused to flinch.

His opponent, John Lester, blinked ever so slightly.

Up to that point, the game had seen a combined 13 zeroes placed on those old-fashioned scoreboards.

Alex Rodriguez made sure the game wouldn't see any more.

Watching him step into the batter's box, a familiar feeling gripped my senses.

Here's where Lester makes his mistake, I thought.

And right on cue, the Red Sox hurler tried to come inside with a 94-mph heater and left it out over the plate.

Putting a good swing on Lester's fatal offering, A-Rod crushed it.

The ball went flying over the centerfield fence, over 400 feet away.

And the whole stadium, to this point sitting on their hands, came alive once more.

With his 574th career tater, A-Rod moved into sole possession of ninth place on the home run list, and more importantly, broke the deadlock.

The team wearing pinstripes was ahead 1-0, and the hated Red Sox and their struggling lineup had been held scoreless by Yankees pitching for thirty-one consecutive innings.

Between innings, I greeted many of my favorite ticket-holders with hi-fives as they came into the restroom. Guarding my confidence closely, I told them this: "We still have six outs to get, and the Red Sox are playing for their season. It won't come easy, but we'll win."

"It's over, William," one of the Legends' attendants screamed. "We have this victory all wrapped up."

"Let's get these six outs first before we celebrate," I replied.

Just as I had predicted, the Red Sox would not go quietly into the South Bronx night. After nearly seventy-one hours without scoring a run, they finally broke through. With Yankees reliever Phil Coke pitching in the eighth, Dustin Pedroia laced a one-out single to center. The left-handed Coke quickly got ahead of the next batter, Victor Martinez, then grooved a fastball on a 1-2 count.

The newly acquired Sox catcher hammered a long drive into the left-field seats, and the sellout stadium crowd, incredibly fired up only minutes earlier, was suddenly stiff and silent in grief.

And the Boston dugout went bonkers.

Jolted with an impactful momentum, it was filled with a great feeling; the kind of joy they hoped would propel them to a much-needed victory.

Martinez's dramatic shot turned a 1-0 Bombers lead into a 2-1 deficit.

Martinez's dramatic shot also made my job as resident Yankee cheerleader harder to do. Having to deal with a sudden shift in emotions between innings, in the blink of an eye I went from cautiously optimistic to soothing patrons with another dose of my certainty. I knew we were going to win the game, but how could I convince the passionate regulars riding an emotional roller coaster?

Here's how: confronting their frustration with *faith*—there's that word again—I told the Yankee clientele that we had them where we wanted them.

Wearing looks of somber cynicism and panic only New Yorkers could recognize, a couple of busboys spoke up for everyone in the restroom.

"Come on, William. How's that possible?" one of them asked.

Another voice chimed in.

"Yeah, man. What are you talking about?"

Remaining stone-faced with conviction, I wanted to share my thoughts. Over the weekend, we pounded the Red Sox 13-6 on Thursday, beat them in a 2-0 extra-inning instant classic on Friday, and blanked them in a 5-0 Saturday matinee where the only thing that showed up was great Yankee pitching.

Why not come from behind to beat Boston on Sunday? I mused. *We beat them this way tonight, and they're finished psychologically.*

Instead of sharing my confidence, in a brisk, clipped tone, I announced to all that would listen, "You guys had better get outside, so you won't miss the comeback."

Met with skepticism once more, in a matter of seconds I saw the looks of disbelief multiply by five.

"I sure hope you're right, William," Mitchell, another season-ticket holder, said.

Feeling another smile of faith light on my lips, I couldn't resist what came next.

"I know I am. And after tonight, the Boston Red Sox will be an afterthought for the remainder of the season."

On the mound for Boston in the bottom of the eighth was reliever Daniel Bard, a fireballing set-up man who had been dominating batters for a month. Owning a 99-mile-per-hour fastball, he and closer Jonathan Papelbon—provided they made it to the ninth inning with a lead—were the hooks the Red Sox hung their season on.

Looking like a safe bet, Bard retired the first two batters, but then fell behind one ball to Johnny Damon. Feeling the need to even the count with his best pitch, his next offering was a fastball registering 98 mph on the speed guns.

It was a fastball left out over the plate; right in the hitter's zone.

And with that blur of white came the end of all competition for the American League East championship.

The Boston Red Sox would never challenge the Yankees during the 2009 season again.

With a quick healthy cut, Damon sent a line drive rocket through the night sky that landed just over the wall in right-center field, squaring matters at two.

At the crack of the bat, I was struck with a bolt of excitement. Darting out of the men's room and through one of the doors leading to the Legends seating area right behind home plate, I searched for someone—a server, police officer, team official, anyone—to exchange hi-fives with, and bumped into a Yankees fan that was in the restroom when I made my bold forecast.

"You were right," he screamed. "You were so right! How did you know? How did you know?"

Smiling, all I said was "I have faith in my Yankees."

While a thunder roared in celebration of a tie score, what happened next brought an even louder sound from the capacity crowd, one that rivaled cheers inspired by legends that made history across the street. No sooner than Damon finished receiving congratulations in the Yankees' dugout, Mark Teixeira sat on curveball Bard left high in the strike zone, and sent a shot soaring toward the right-field foul pole.

Holding his bat aloft while jogging slowly down the first base line, one might say that Teixeira was sending a text message to many New Englanders while the ball was in flight.

The passage read as follows:

To the Red Sox Nation:

Please be advised that your reign of dominance in the American League East has officially ended. Clearly forgetting that we once paid the mortgage of Fenway Park, over the past few years you held what was once ours, a stranglehold over divisional and rivalry supremacy, with more arrogance than we owned since the Sale of Ruth. All of New England can conjure up 2004 and 2007 until your hearts runneth over with joy, but you will be doing so in vain. The New York Yankees have reclaimed what is rightfully theirs, and we hope that you enjoy the view of our power and determination from your familiar second-place position.

We'll see you in playoffs; that is, if you get there.

Mark Teixeira.

P.S. By the way, you should have signed me last winter.

By the time the slugging first baseman had typed and sent his memo to millions, the crushed curveball had found a place in the upper deck in right field; landing fair into a new delirium.

Finally flipping his bat, Teixeira happily rounded the bases as an unfamiliar energy gripped the new ballpark. Filling the stadium with chants of "Sweep, sweep, sweep," concrete-cracking cheers rocked the new palace. Attendants were hugging baseball fans and police officers exchanged hi-fives with maintenance team members. And as proud as the security guards stood doing their jobs, you could see many smiles that matched the brightness of their light-blue shirts.

A dark cloud that hovered overhead since last season, one that filled anyone associated with the best professional organization in American sports with somber skepticism, had been lifted.

Shaking with an electric passion, much like the place across the street, the new Yankee Stadium finally felt like home.

Completing my search of the stands, one more sighting made this moment memorable. Five rows above the concrete moat (the section separating the Legends section from the *more affordable expensive seats*—kind of an oxymoron, isn't it?) was an ardent Red Sox supporter. All decked out in the gray road "Boston" jersey complete with blue cap, he sat glumly amongst a happy mob of pinstripe maniacs.

Making eye contact with this man, I traced my right hand across my neck, as if slitting my throat while sympathetically shaking my head.

"It's all over. You're finished," I passionately mouthed toward him.

Instead of a trash-talking rebuttal, he nodded his head in agreement.

"I know," he mouthed back.

That the Yankees busted the game open was a mere formality. The next four men reached base against Bard and reliever Hideki Okajima, with two of them scoring on a two-run single by Nick Swisher.

The score was now 5-2, New York.

With all the air now out of their balloon of hope, the Red Sox went quietly in the ninth, as Mariano Rivera set them down quickly to complete the Yankee sweep.

In my heart and mind, this was where the American League East was won.

But you couldn't tell that to the beat writers making their way to the Red Sox clubhouse. Assuming many were from Boston or other parts of New England—I saw Bob Ryan and Howard Bryant, familiar faces from the many ESPN shows featuring sportswriters—all I saw was red-faced dejection as they walked by briskly. While they might have said the politically correct "there's plenty of baseball left" answer had they been asked about the fate of twenty-five men from Beantown, the truth was embedded in their psyche.

History also supported this truth. According to the Elias Sports Bureau, the Yankees had never lost a division lead of more than six games this late in the season. That the distance between the two teams was a season-high 6-1/2 games screamed a reality to New England sportswriters that many did not want to hear.

The race for the American League East was all over.

Peering down the hallway, I saw the man who rebuilt the Yankees' pride, Brian Cashman.

Walking up to him, he had his back to me talking.

Placing my arm around his shoulder, "We beat them in every way this weekend," I said.

Smiling through his professionalism, "Yeah, it's been a good weekend," he responded. Seeing the twinkle in his eyes, perhaps he knew what I knew then; that we were both passengers on a train leading us to an incredible destination.

"I'm so happy for you, man. Congratulations."

"Thank you."

Off he went, to receive more well-deserved kudos.

And off I went back into the Legends Suite Club, to tend to my restroom.

If anyone doubted that the race for the American League East crown was done, then the three-game series in Fenway Park two weeks later proved in convincing fashion that the Yankees' early-season futility against the Red Sox was a distant memory. Led by a red-hot Derek Jeter, who was finishing a road trip which saw him go 19 for 36 (.527 batting average), the Yankees took two of three from the Red Sox. Pounding out 23 hits in the first game, they blasted the ball all over the yard in a 20-11 Friday night pounding of Boston.

When the Red Sox responded to the Yankees' rout that Saturday afternoon with a 14-1 drubbing of A.J. Burnett, it was the Yankees captain who took matters into his own hands the very next evening. Punishing the game's first pitch from Josh Beckett, Jeter set the tone for the Bombers' 8-4 victory by sending the opening fastball over the wall in right field. His 2,700th career hit was the first of five homers and eight earned runs the Red Sox ace allowed through eight innings.

The eight-run outburst gave the Yankees the luxury offset a less-than-dominant mound performance by C.C. Sabathia, who lasted just long enough—118 pitches over 6-2/3 third innings, striking out eight while giving up four runs—to secure his Major League-leading fifteenth victory.

Wrapping up a 7-3 road trip with their sixth win in seven games against Boston, the two victories were the Yankees' first at Fenway Park since opening the season winless in six tries. With clinical precision, the Yankees extended their lead over the Red Sox to 7-1/2 games in the American League East, and reduced Boston to fighting for a Wild Card berth.

They had a one-game lead over the Texas Rangers for that playoff berth.

Though more than a month remained in the season, the race for the American League East was all over.

A team from the Bronx had already won.

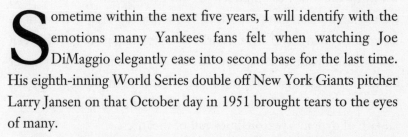

REACHING THE HIGHEST GROUND: A DEREK JETER TRIBUTE

10

ometime within the next five years, I will identify with the emotions many Yankees fans felt when watching Joe DiMaggio elegantly ease into second base for the last time. His eighth-inning World Series double off New York Giants pitcher Larry Jansen on that October day in 1951 brought tears to the eyes of many.

One last time, baseball purists saw that flat-footed batting stance and the incredible follow-through of his sweet, picture-perfect swing. Patrolling the great green lawn that was his center-field domain for a decade-and-a-half, never again would the deepest part of Yankee Stadium outfield be roamed with the long strides and exquisite grace of a man who made covering its expanse of ground look so easy. Never again would a generation of fans see a complete artist at work; a man who played the game so beautifully that often his intangibles far outweighed his statistical value. *(Something many find ironic considering that he is the owner of what many consider baseball's most untouchable record—a fifty-six game hitting streak that captivated a country in the summer of 1941).* While many were left awestruck by his vast array of skills—timely hitting, his great throwing arm, brilliant fielding and smart base-running—the man they called Joltin' Joe and the Yankee Clipper was always more than the sum of his parts.

Prolific, proficient and productive, yet effortless in his excellence, Joe DiMaggio was the ultimate symbol of cool, both on and off the baseball diamond. The consummate gentleman, he clearly epitomized Yankee pride and tradition as he became an American icon. Handsome enough to make Marilyn Monroe swoon and classy enough to maintain a regal presence in the American conscience long after his playing days ended, an inner nobility meshed seamlessly with his impeccable taste and quiet dignity, producing a celebrity that transcended the fame most presidents owned.

Along the way to becoming an enduring figure for generations to come, by the time he completed his wondrous journey in pinstripes, the most dominant team in professional sports captured ten American League Pennants and nine World Championships in his thirteen full seasons with the ballclub. Leading the Yankees with quiet efficiency, DiMaggio fashioned action and example into Yankee hallmarks, as opposed to operating with the flamboyance, fuss and fanfare of dynamic personalities full of theatrics.

A man that millions young and old admired and emulated, no one put it all together in his own special package like Joe DiMaggio.

But there is someone playing in those pinstripes today whose very aura matches the DiMaggio mystique.

About six decades after Joe DiMaggio first wore the pinstripes, a skinny shortstop from Kalamazoo, Michigan took the field in the Seattle Kingdome in the gray Yankee road jersey for the first time. Filling in for an injured Tony Fernandez on May 29, 1995, he was given the number 2 by Yankees clubhouse Manager Nick Priore.

The single-digit numbered uniforms of the New York Yankees are deeply entrenched in the team's sacred lore. All of them, save the numbers 6 and 2, have been retired, never to be worn again by anyone ever wearing the famous pinstripes. Billy Martin and his managerial prowess led to the retirement of Number 1 in 1986. Numbers 3, 4, 5, 7, and 8 (retired twice) belonged to players that landed in Baseball's Hall of Fame: Babe Ruth, Lou Gehrig, Joe DiMaggio, Mickey Mantle, Bill Dickey and Yogi Berra—Berra and Dickey, both catchers, wore number 8—respectively.

(NOTE: *Joe Torre, winner of six pennants and four world championships, wore number 6 during his managerial reign; so until that number is officially hanging amongst the single-digit famous, it's another untouchable.)*

Number 2 is the only active single-numbered uniform that was not retired. However, with great intuition, Priore said to anyone that would listen, "Someday, that kid's number will also be retired."

The kid who inherited number 2, Derek Jeter, had a pretty lackluster performance in his big league debut. Hitless in five plate appearances, which included an extra-inning strikeout with the go-ahead run on third base, the most memorable part of Jeter's night might have been when the youthful Yankee call-up and his father ambled past the darkened windows of closed restaurants in the Emerald City; eventually settling for a postgame meal at the only place that was open, a McDonald's.

While the Yankees lost that evening, 8-7, in 12 innings, then-Manager Buck Showalter was instantly impressed with the youngster. Already smitten with his natural fluidity on the field, his multi-sport build—at six feet three inches, 185-190 pounds, he owned the lanky, lean body of an NBA point-guard—he loved his athleticism and ability to play any position on the baseball field. Also, Showalter concluded that Jeter studied every nuance of the game on the diamond, in the dugout; and possessed poise beyond his years, as if this young man was born to wear the Yankee pinstripes.

What Showalter and others failed to realize on that Seattle night is that from birth, Derek Sanderson Jeter was *always* a Yankee. From the womb, he was taught to win, and that the word *can't* would not be used a single day of his life. By the fourth grade, he was telling his teachers and all that would listen, that his occupation would be the shortstop position of the New York Yankees.

Never hearing a discouraging word about his ambitions, all you need to do is trace his aspirations back to his parents, the white daughter of a New Jersey church sexton and the black son of a single mother in Alabama, and you'll see everything. Instilling humility, a quiet self-confidence and a healthy dose of respect for others, Charles and Dorothy Jeter had young Derek sign a commitment letter every August regarding his behavior. Somehow, they knew he would be special, so with loving discipline they groomed him for greatness.

Hal Newhouser, a former two-time American League MVP in the 1940s for the Detroit Tigers, knew Jeter would be a great one, too. A Michigan area scout for the Houston Astros in his later years, he implored to the Astros to take the player the National Baseball Coaches Association voted as the 1992 High School Player of the Year with the first pick of the June baseball draft. Seeing his leadership qualities as well as a hungry intensity that matched his performance on the playing field, he kept telling them, "This kid Jeter is going to be something special. We can build a franchise around him." Ultimately, the Astros settled on Phil Nevin with that pick; a selection that infuriated Newhouser so much that he quit baseball.

The Houston Astros made a hell of a mistake.

So did the four other teams that followed.

But the New York Yankees wouldn't pass him up. Selecting him sixth overall, he spent three years in the minor leagues. Initially struggling with his storybook vision, he struggled a bit in the Rookie league, as well as with the Class A Greensboro team in 1993.

However, something clicked in 1994. Accelerating through three levels of the minor league systems, he got the attention of the big ballclub up north by improving his game as he rose. Reaching the Triple A Columbus Clippers by the season's last month, he hit a robust .350; completing a rapid ascension that propelled him to Minor League Player of the Year status.

Another man who noticed Jeter was the man he eventually replaced as captain of the Yankees. Taking a liking to the young shortstop in Spring Training camp of 1995, every now and then Don Mattingly would impart his wisdom by teaching him "The Yankee Way." Adding professionalism to Jeter's strong value system and work ethic, one might say that the classy first baseman, one who battled with a chronic back condition in his final year in pinstripes, was already passing the torch.

Starting the 1995 season at Columbus, on that day in late May when the Yankees needed a fill-in—and after their initial call-up Robert Eenhorn went 0-for-7—they promoted Jeter for a cup of coffee in the big leagues. The night after his hitless collar saw him get his first Major League hit, when he stroked a single off the Mariners' Tim Belcher just beyond the reach of a diving third baseman.

And although Jeter's stint with the Yankees ended after thirteen games—the team briefly considered switching Fernandez to second base so Jeter could stay at shortstop, but decided he wasn't ready—everyone knew that the Kalamazoo Kid was the future of the franchise.

Don Mattingly knew.

"You'll be back," he told him.

It was only a matter of time before that classic inside-out swing along with an innate understanding for America's Pastime would endear himself to millions by making Yankee Stadium its permanent home.

✪ ✪ ✪

The date was April 2, 1996.

The place was Jacobs Field, home of the 1995 American League Champion Cleveland Indians.

On that sunny afternoon in Cleveland, Derek Jeter was given an opportunity to win a job.

He said so himself.

How would he respond to the pressure of high expectations?

By taking a high, inside fastball by pitcher Dennis Martinez over the left-field fence for his first career home run; by making a spectacular over-the-shoulder grab in left-center, and by robbing catcher Sandy

Alomar, Jr. of a base hit with a diving stop between second and third base, then throwing strong to first to get the hitter by a step.

To say he has succeeded since that opening day performance is an understatement.

With respects to "the Scooter" Phil Rizzuto, you can't imagine anyone else ever playing shortstop for the New York Yankees. A throwback to its storied tradition yet possessing an alluring essence of modern times, Jeter embodies the Yankee persona: a quiet confidence that never appears overwhelmed with any circumstance on the exterior, yet on the inside has a white-hot hunger to win.

It's easy for a Yankee fan to recount the many sensational jump-throws after fielding a ball deep in the hole to nip a runner scurrying down the first-base line; not to mention a simple, successful free-swinging approach when taking his position in the batter's box, his great instincts on the basepaths, an extraordinary quality of always being in-the-right-place-at-the-right-time, and the ice-water that runs in his veins when the baseball calendar hits October and November that was put on display by way of diving catches and game-changing/winning at-bats.

Never one to miss a shining moment in pinstripes, his aura is akin to Denzel Washington doing Broadway and delivering a show-stopping performance 180 nights a year; provided you include the postseason, which under Jeter's leadership is an expected, annual pinstriped rite of passage in the Bronx.

But if someone twisted my arm for two Derek Jeter moments over the hundreds baseball fans have witnessed and told me to store them in a time capsule, one would be simple; the other spectacular.

Let's start with the former. In an age where players stand at home plate admiring their handiwork—whether it be a long drive over the fence or a hard ground ball at someone—here's what I saw many a time in the 2009 season: Jeter running all-out to many a ground ball in the late innings of a routine game in which the outcome had already been decided. Years earlier, the simplicity of this feat so impressed Oakland A's General Manager Billy Beane that he ordered his *entire staff* to show a video of Jeter's sprint to all of the organization's players in spring training.

So many players today sulk after a pitcher induces a weakly hit tapper; others sadly, just flat out dog it.

They could learn a lot from the Yankees captain.

The other Jeter highlight constantly replayed in my mind ranks as the greatest sense of instinct, intuition, athleticism and awareness I have ever seen on a baseball diamond; a play that ranks with many as his signature stamp on the game he loves.

Having lost the first two games of the 2001 American League Divisional Playoffs at home, the Yankees' season was on the line in Game 3. Starting pitcher Mike Mussina was clinging to a 1-0 lead with two outs in the seventh when he allowed a hard-hit double into the right-field corner by Oakland batter Terrance Long.

Running at the crack of the bat was Jeremy Giambi, who'd been on first base.

Everyone in the ballpark knew he was going to be waved home.

Rushing into the corner, Yankees rightfielder Shane Spencer fielded the ball and threw the ball toward the infield. High and off-line, the strike sailed over the head of the cutoff man, second baseman Alfonso Soriano, as well as the backup cutoff man, first baseman Tino Martinez.

"Oh crap," I remember muttering in my apartment. "If the run scores, the Yankees are finished."

With the crowd in the Oakland Alameda Coliseum going crazy over the prospect of a tie game, playoff elimination and the end of a three-year championship reign seemed imminent for the New York Yankees.

Only someone had forgotten to share this bit of information with Derek Jeter.

Roving the infield like a free safety in an NFL secondary, what Jeter did in milliseconds is the stuff of legends. Correctly reading the flight of Spencer's errant toss, he positioned himself in an area between Martinez and Jorge Posada, the catcher, and caught the ball on a hop with two hands in the foul territory. With all his momentum carrying him away from the plate, he miraculously shoveled a backhand pitch to Posada.

The flip reached Posada just in time for him to apply a tag to Giambi, who like Lou Brock did in a Game 4 World Series-changing play in 1968, ignored pleas from the on-deck hitter and tried to score standing up.

Screaming as loud as the announcers were, for the next hour or so, all I could say is "WOW!"

Jeter's play saved the game (which the Yankees won 1-0), and was the emotional impetus for a series-winning comeback. And while the Yankees failed to extend their run of championship titles in 2001, it was a breathtaking play that symbolized his ability to seize the moment when the lights burned the brightest.

Like all the great ones, Michael Jordan, Tiger Woods and others, there's a look in their eyes only true competitors and those destined for greatness realize.

Thriving, then excelling in pressure-cooker situations, they will do anything to win.

And like Joe DiMaggio, the descendant Yankee who left the footprints that Jeter stepped in bravely, proudly and gracefully, he looks good doing it. Shunning the bulk and mass build created by… ahem…*creatine and other supplements* (can you imagine the look on my face when I typed this?), Jeter seems like an anachronism because he owns the streamlined carriage and athletic build of his pinstriped forefather. Sprinkle in a little Jordan-like cool (after all, he wears the only baseball cleats designed by His Airness' footwear line), his disdain for wrinkles when stepping out postgame as if he were doing a male model portfolio; add a dash of manners and an uncalculated humility from a man free of tattoos, piercings all over and a sewer-mouthed vocabulary, and you have a wonderful ambassador for the game Abner Doubleday was mythically accredited for creating.

(NOTE: *How's this for a coincidence: Derek Jeter was born on June 26, 1974. June 26th happens to be the same birthdate as…Abner Doubleday.*)

The bridge between Ruth, Gehrig, Jackson and Cano, he is the future of what the Yankees look for in their players, a modern man with respect for its proud tradition. That he has steered clear of any major controversies while under the watchful eye of the New York media is remarkable. In an age of cameras on cellular phones, online communication and bloggers and an sports era tainted by the use of performance-enhancing drugs, he is an old-fashioned role model that not only teaches kids how to play the game with respect, but also how to avoid the pitfalls while perched atop a pedestal of notoriety.

In times where the youth of our country so desperately need to see an adult hang on to the innocence and boyish enthusiasm of his youth while living a dream with maturity, God gave us Derek Jeter, the eleventh captain in the history of the New York Yankees and a man carving out a first-ballot Hall of Fame baseball career in the hardest environment in sports to do this in. Goodness oozing from his pores, Jeter combines a distinguished, regal presence with an unassuming self-assuredness as he moves through life effortlessly.

To me, he is like watching Fred Astaire dance: Light on his feet, and his presence in our lives will be timeless.

When looking at him, you also see the end result of strong moral fiber forged by family unity. So many times in the black community—any community, actually—we look for men who we can show to our children and say, "All things are possible, but dreams do not come true without hard work. There's a price to pay when fulfilling what God promises us all, but trust and believe and you will live life abundantly when you have faith in yourself and The Most High."

God also gave us a man cognizant of the fact that to whom much is given, a whole lot more is required in giving back. Establishing the Turn 2 Foundation in 1996, an organization whose mission is to help young people live responsible drug- and alcohol-free lives, at last report it has awarded over $10 million in grants. More recently, Jeter launched an outpatient center in Tampa bearing his name that helps teens in need of individual or substance-abuse treatment. Like a real-life hero garbed in a red cape and boots, one would think the man fulfilling his life-long dream of playing shortstop for the New York Yankees was able to leap tall buildings in a single bound.

Well...

✪ ✪ ✪

Watching Derek Jeter up close in 2009 was an inspiration.

Seeing how he handled his business daily with respect and dignity meant more than you can possibly imagine. At about 5:00 is when I took my half-hour break from the rigors of cleaning. Leaving my Legends Suite Club restroom post, one minute later I was usually outside watching Yankee batting practice while talking to the fans in the section above the concrete moat. If recollection serves me correctly, about 5:20 or so is usually when Jeter entered the batting cage.

Aggressively spraying the ball to left- and right-center field gaps with a tailor swing made to find all the outfield gaps, I often wondered if this man was impervious to slumps. His career statistics and truckload of accomplishments (a perennial Most Valuable Player candidate, he owns a lifetime .317 batting average, seven 200-hit seasons, over 200 home runs and steals—the only lifelong shortstop ever to do so, four Silver Slugger awards naming him the best hitting shortstop in the league, four Gold Gloves, the only player ever to win the All-Star game and World Series Most Valuable Player Awards in the same season; and of course, going into the 2009 season, four world championship rings) are deserving of a ticket to Cooperstown with the highest voting percentage ever for a ballplayer.

Always marveling at his hitting prowess, it wasn't what I usually looked for. I always looked closely to see a smile of joy, one of such wattage you would think it could clear clouds away.

And more often than not, I wasn't disappointed.

The joy that I saw in his face was contagious, even for a restroom attendant doing what many perceived as a thankless job. Feeling his sense of pride and awe for the pinstripes he wore, how could I not feel the same for my job? Like our captain, for one season in pinstripes, I poked my chest out, held my head high and worked hard, making sure everyone felt the joy and love for what I was doing.

The only time I didn't see this look of sunshine in the eyes of Major League Baseball's foremost champion and ambassador, the only time I saw the slightest hint of him pressing, was when he was reaching for the Yankees' highest ground.

Lou Gehrig's franchise record with 2,721 career hits, arguably the most important record on the greatest sports franchise of America, was a mark that stood for seventy-one years. And as the New York Yankees were putting the finishing touches on their American League East Championship, the only suspense left in the 2009 regular-season was when the modern Yankee that best embodied the stories told by an older generation about Gehrig and DiMaggio would surpass the historic number.

Fully expecting him to do it immediately—entering a Labor Day doubleheader against the Tampa Bay Rays, he had moved within three hits of the record—I was hoping to see him accomplish the feat live, for my heart was heavy. While at church the day before, my fiancée, Cheryl, had received the news that her father had passed away.

Spoiled by Derek Jeter's acute sense of timing, somehow I knew that he would lift my spirits and come through for me, as he did countless other times.

Many of the regular Legends Club members that I shared my pain with rooted for Jeter to break the record, but as Monday went into Tuesday, then Wednesday night, the prevailing topic of conversation around the stadium—and all of baseball, for that matter—was that Jeter was working under a pressure that was even foreign to him. Normally the last one to leave the clubhouse, after a third straight 0-for-4 collar extended his hitless streak to a season-long twelve at-bats, the media-savvy icon rushed from the clubhouse without fielding a question.

While some may have been startled by this extremely rare, un-characteristic move, I wasn't. As with all transcendent athletes, there comes a time where they need to reach even deeper into their reservoir of greatness to accomplish something that means more to them than what they show on the exterior. And in order for them to get to that space where this untapped resolve lies, they use un-orthodox tactics to venture to that new, even stronger mental place.

To get to this place, sometimes they must *break their routine* to get their routine back on track.

That's what Derek Jeter did that Wednesday night.

Foregoing his usual, first at-bat-in-a-game gesture where he shows the opposing manager respect by way of a distant fist-bump, there were no salutations when he led off the bottom of the first inning. Keeping his head down as he stepped in the batter's box, he lifted it ever so slightly to peek at Evan Longoria, Tampa Bay's All-Star third baseman. Noticing that he was playing behind the bag in order to protect a hard-hit drive, in the next millisecond he must have turned the page in his mental scouting report and realized that the Rays' starting pitcher Jeff Niemann, an imposing-looking hurler who stood six feet nine inches and weighed 260 pounds, would look like a lumbering NFL lineman trying to field a slow roller: painfully out-of-place.

Once Jeter recognized Niemann's first pitch was the fastball that he hoped for, he surprised everyone in the stadium with his personal brand of small ball.

It was a perfectly executed bunt. Rolling slowly, the baseball found its resting place between the mound and the third-base line, where to the delight of the ghosts of Yankees past and the present crowd, it died a happy death. Charging in, Longoria immediately realized he had no chance at retrieving and hoped his pitcher would make the play.

Moving slowly, Niemann took a few steps toward the ball and never even bothered to scoop it up.

Just like that, Jeter's 0-for-12 funk was gone. Once again he was one of the best active hitters in baseball, seriously chasing the hallowed mark by the Iron Horse.

And in that same instant, the stadium crowd went from screaming encouragement to its favorite son to the reenergized roar that signaled the resurrection of a chase.

As if we needed reminding, the Yankees captain had showed us all once more that New York was his town.

Clearly relieved from the pressure built up from the hitless skid, Jeter felt reinvigorated as well. Though he grounded out in the third, he hit a booming, ground-rule double off the centerfield warning track in the fifth; and with two out and the bases empty in the home half of the seventh, he again made Niemann pay for throwing a first-pitch fastball. Stinging it hard, the grounder skidded past a diving Chris Richard and into right field for the equalizer.

As he reached first base, the humble Yankee captain felt uncomfortable. Because the Yankees were trailing 2-0, he didn't want to disrespect the opposition by basking in the moment too long. Ignoring the flashing cameras and thunderous waterfall of adoration from 45, 848 fans, he looked toward the Tampa Bay dugout.

Instead of seeing his awkwardness turn to shame, what he next witnessed surprised him.

In a tribute of respect and sportsmanship, the Tampa Bay bench players and coaches were on the top step, applauding with just as much approval as everyone in attendance.

It was then and only then that Jeter began cherishing the accomplishment. Holding his batting helmet aloft and waving it in several directions, he looked in the direction of the centerfield video board and saw Lou Gehrig and a skinny kid from Kalamazoo bookending a giant number 2721.

Serving as a strong rebuttal to Charles Barkley's famous "I am not a role model" Nike ad, the two-minute ovation Derek Jeter received that night spoke for every taxicab and busy sidewalk in the city; as well as every hard-working person in this town that goes about doing their job the right way. They applauded loudly for his leadership of the greatest team in sports history; an era that had produced six pennants and four championship rings. They applauded him for his "Jeffrey Maier Moment," a fluke home run in 1996 that a Jersey kid stole from a right-fielder's glove. They applauded him for the two home runs in Shea Stadium in the 2000 series, thus securing the franchise's last world championship. They applauded him for his dive into the third-base stands in 2004 against those hated Red Sox that left him bloodied, not to mention the incredible flip play in 2001 that galvanized the Yankees' postseason; and the walk-off series homer that disappeared into the Bronx night once the calendar showed us November baseball for the first time. They applauded him for his day-in, day-out consistency and effort.

But most importantly, they applauded him for being the antithesis of every self-promoting athlete in this look-at-me-era. In an era of loud noise coming from overrated media stars, the stadium applauded Derek Sanderson Jeter, a man whose results of an illustrious career spoke louder than any Twitter or Facebook blog.

Taking this moment in from the Legends' restroom, I could see that it was hard for Jeter to enjoy his accomplishment entirely. A game needed to be resumed; a game that the Yankees were losing.

But not for long.

Jorge Posada, Jeter's best friend on the team and significant lineup partner for fourteen years, gave him a personal gift that glorified Jeter's accomplishment. Pinch-hitting with two runners on in the last half of the eighth, he came to the plate against reliever Grant Balfour with the Yankees needing a run to tie.

Running the count full, he saw a pitch to his liking and deposited it into the right-field seats. Not only did the three-run blast propel the Pinstripes to a 4-2 come-from-behind victory which completed a four-game sweep of the Rays; it reduced the Yankees magic number for clinching the American League East title to 14; and gave Derek Jeter a chance to break the record.

When Jeter approached the plate, I immediately rushed outside, found a standing place in one of the Legends' aisles just to the right of home plate, clasped my fingers together, and hoped for history.

Then something that I never would have expected in a million years happened; an honor that I can share with my grandchildren.

After lining a hard foul ball down the right-field line, he stepped out the batter's box and looked right at me.

Smiling proudly, I gave him a discreet thumbs-up sign—after all, restroom attendants were not allowed to leave their posts—and received a slight head nod from the Yankees captain in return.

Now, I don't profess to say that he's a mind reader, but maybe, just maybe he saw that hopeful look in my eyes.

The season-ticket holders who saw the exchange were stunned.

"Do you know him?" one asked me.

Sheepishly, I shook my head no.

Oh, how I would love to share with you the stuff of dreams. In a perfect world, my storybook ending to this scene would read as follows:

Derek Jeter, realizing that I would miss the next game to bury my fiancée's father, sends an opposite-field drive deep into the right-center field alley. Cruising into second with a standup double, he is mobbed by his teammates as a parade of flashbulbs pop in celebration of his newly constructed penthouse; a place where only he resides as the man with the most career hits in the history of the New York Yankees. After sharing numerous hugs with his team, he points to the luxury box where his parents, Charles and Dorothy, and girlfriend, Minka Kelly, are seated.

Then to the surprise of many, his next salute completely shocks the capacity crowd. Looking in the direction of William Fredrick Cooper, male restroom attendant in the Legends Suite Club, he extends a fist, as if he's thanking him with a distant fist-bump gesture. The stadium crowd, in amazement of his salute, roars ever loader. In classic two-three rhythm, they chant not only Jeter's name, but that of an ordinary guy whose dream comes true.

That's actually how it went…in my dreams. The reality was a tad bit disappointing: Jeter saw seven pitches from Balfour, fouling off three before drawing a walk that brought a chorus of boos from the fans.

I wasn't disappointed at the end result, because family (or in my instance, my soon-to-be-family) meant more to me than any baseball statistic, or any dream job for that matter. Somehow, I think in spite of all that he has accomplished in a Yankees uniform, Derek Jeter would agree.

✪ ✪ ✪

It seemed fitting that new record would have to wait until September 11th. Eight years earlier to the date, a band of terrorists played a horrific melody in our powerful financial district. Invading generous blue New York City skies, two wayward planes (four, if you include the strikes to our military hearts—Pentagon— Washington, D.C.—and rural souls—Pennsylvania) conducted a work of terror; killing thousands and leaving millions more grief-stricken and speechless as a symphony of sirens and screams sang in awful unison.

On the anniversary of our city's worst day, New Yorkers desperately needed something positive to ease the pain that the murder, mayhem and madness that surrounded that fateful day in history. If but for a respite, someone needed to make us forget that torturous heartache that had taken a bite from the collective fiber of our Big Apple.

On a drizzly Friday night, a city still grieving from its most tragic moment looked to the new Yankee Stadium for comfort; and the lonely eyes of a sellout crowd looking to rid themselves from sorrow turned to Derek Jeter.

And as usual, the Yankees captain came through.

After waiting through an hour-and-a-half rain, the buzz and hoopla that surrounded the moment really began to swell in the bottom of the first, when the man whose graceful grind had him on the doorstep of history stepped into the batter's box against Baltimore Orioles pitcher Chris Tillman.

If the rookie right-hander seemed awed by the 46,771 fans chanting "Der-ek Jet-er" in roll-call style or the all-time Yankee great standing before him, he didn't show it. Hurling heaters that hissed with bad intentions, Tillman started Jeter off with two 94-mile-per-hour-fastballs; one of which our captain took for a strike and the other he missed completely. Down 0-2 in the count, Jeter took a pitch out of the strike zone for a ball, then fouled off another blazing fastball.

At one balls and two strikes, Hillman decided to change speeds and throw a curve. Completely fooled by the pitch, Jeter whiffed badly.

The stadium crowd groaned.

Hillman had won the first duel.

By the time the Yankees captain came to the plate in the home half of the third, the nighttime skies were letting us know that our city still needed help in the healing department. The tears of those that perished came from the heavens came by way of a persistent rainfall. Swirling steadily around the stadium while saturating it with an unrelenting mist, there were mud puddles throughout the outfield and along the warning track.

The soggy stadium crowd, and perhaps in tune with the irony, pleaded with those above who needed a moment to smile once more. Chanting Jeter's name with passion, the new place across the street had never sounded like this before.

Not only was it a sound from the soaked ponchos and raincoats of a sellout crowd, it was a sound from those innocent people who were at work eight years ago, drinking coffee or situated at water coolers, laughing, telling loved ones over the phone to "have a nice day" for the last time in their lives; those firefighters and police officers who rushed into those towers trying to perform miracles; and those families whose days ended with unconscionable, un-justified, inexplicable abandonment.

It was a sound from both past and present, not only from Yankees fans, but one that emanated from a city that desperately needed to smile once more.

The ovation did not cease once Jeter entered the batter's box, but something else did: the heavy downpour. Tapering off, then stopping for a bit, there was a wonderful stillness within the cheers; like heaven and earth were standing still, ready for a new milestone as their eyes were glued to their prize at the plate.

The clock on the Jumbotron scoreboard read 9:23 p.m. when Derek

Jeter took two fastballs from Tillman. With the count now in his favor 2-0, he waited on the next pitch, a fastball out over the plate.

With a vintage inside-out swing that was his personal signature to baseball, the Yankees captain stayed inside the baseball and sprayed a bullet the other way. Racing past a diving Luke Scott, the hard-hit ball eluded the Orioles first baseman and made it into right field on a single hop.

As Jeter rounded, then returned to first, he spread his arms wide and clapped. The Yankee Stadium crowd, already on its feet snapping photos of their captain, erupted like never before. Always supportive of their humble leader, the moment that Jeter became the most prolific hit-producer ever to wear the interlocking NY logo was theirs as much as it was his.

In a three-minute outpouring of love, Derek Jeter was told in the loudest, clearest way possible that we appreciated his unassuming dignity. Chanting his first and last name in that Bleacher Creature two-three rhythm, it cascaded from the heavens as well, and found its place into the heart of that skinny kid from Kalamazoo.

Smiling proudly, after his Yankee teammates spilled out of their dugout and engulfed him in hugs and hand-pounds, Jeter held his helmet aloft and waved it to all the corners of the new stadium. The love continued to come from the crowd as he pointed to the luxury box on the suite level above the Yankees' on-deck circle. There, his parents, sister and friends returned his affection with wide smiles.

The Yankees returned to the dugout, but the stadium refused to let go of its favorite son. They would not stop cheering, or chanting their captain's name. Once again, Jeter took off his helmet and tipped it to the crowd.

It only made the love louder.

Nick Swisher, the next batter, further accentuated the moment when he stepped out of the batter's box. The chief cornerstone of the Yankees' present, by now embarrassed by all this appreciation, waved his helmet once more and once again showed leadership by clapping a few times in Swisher's direction.

It was time to get back to the matter at hand.

There was a game to win, and more importantly, a championship goal to accomplish.

As if to emphasize his objective, the very next inning, Jeter followed his historic hit with yet another single the very next inning; a carbon copy replica to right that not only drove in the Yankees' final run of the evening—they lost the game 10-4—but put more distance between himself and the Yankee pantheon.

There were more hits to get; more games to win.

One more thing happened before order was restored. New York Yankee Principal Owner George M. Steinbrenner was not in attendance, but his publicist quickly issued a statement on his behalf.

"For those who say today's game can't produce legendary players, I have two words: Derek Jeter," Steinbrenner's statement said. *"As historic and significant as becoming the Yankees' all-time hit leader is, the accomplishment is all the more impressive because Derek is one of the finest young men playing the game today."*

I would humbly amend this statement by merely saying that "Derek Jeter *is* the finest young man playing the game today."

That historic night was an appointment made by baseball for a city needing a break from a painful anniversary; a horrific experience that brought so many tears of pain.

For one September 11th, Derek Jeter brought New York City tears of joy.

✪ ✪ ✪

That appointment in time was one that I could not keep. Cheryl's father was buried at Calverton National Cemetery in Long Island that day, and while my heart was filled with sadness, the very next day God made me smile.

The very next afternoon, one of my favorite season-ticket holders came into the men's restroom and handed me a framed picture of Jeter's historic achievement. Visibly moved to tears, I couldn't believe his kindness.

In retrospect, then again, I could.

After all, we were all Yankee family.

Because I was not in attendance for the historic feat, I wanted to experience the post-achievement pageantry, so once again, I went outside, and received another present.

After receiving another standing ovation that Saturday afternoon, the Yankees captain quickly added to his record total by rifling a single to left field. As he rounded first, out of the stadium loud-speakers came Michael Jackson's "Don't Stop 'Til You Get Enough."

My eyes grew wide in shock. If anyone knows me, they know that my idol was, is and always will be the late, great King of Pop. A perfectionist in song and dance and my kindred spirit in terms of emotional sensitivity, my only hope in life is to touch lives once with something I do the way he did with a truckload of otherworldly achievements.

Taken aback by this surreal moment, I rushed back into the Legends Club, and into the lower-level men's restroom, where I was alone. Feeling like I had received a gift from above, I said a quick prayer of thanks.

And yes, in that prayer I thanked the Good Lord for creating Derek Jeter.

THE SEPTEMBER STATEMENT GAMES: A PRELUDE TO OCTOBER

11

The beauty that professional sports psychology holds over these nonsensical, contrived reality shows is in the mental analogies that simply cannot be made up. Earlier in the book I quoted Lee Riley, the father of Hall of Fame basketball Coach Pat Riley, when he said, "Somewhere, someplace, sometime, you're going to have to plant your feet, make a stand and kick some ass. And when that time comes, you do it."

The time to kick some serious ass is in statement games.

What are statement games, you ask?

Statement games are those contests you circle on the calendar days, weeks, and months ahead of the actual date you do battle. The closer you get to the day, the more you salivate, because more often than not, the opposition has you zeroed in on their radar as well. And once the foes, or teams—usually two high-caliber units—lock horns, the contest or series is usually played at the highest level, for you've been waiting a long time for the barometer check.

There are two types of statement games. For starters, there's the *payback statement game*. Whether you've been embarrassed in humiliating fashion, or in the alternative, experience defeat in a nail-biting heartbreaking classic, you can't wait until you see that team again. Hurt and revenge invades our veins, giving our bloodstream a different type of oxygen. You can't wait to see this team again, because the motivation to make them feel the pain you felt the first time around borders on obsession.

In real life, I know this feeling all too well. Playing wide receiver for a team called the Falcons in a Bronx touch-tackle football league, on Christmas Eve 1994, we played a semifinal playoff game against a team called the Heat under a steady, heavy downpour.

The field, Rice Stadium in Pelham Bay, was a muddy quagmire, and everyone had trouble with the footing. This came into play on the game's first play, when our center, perhaps trying too hard to overcompensate for the treacherous conditions as well as the Heat's pass rush, snapped the ball over the head of our quarterback and through the end zone for a two-point safety.

Fighting back, our team moved the ball up and down the field all of the game, only to be stopped repeatedly when in the opponents' red zone. Slipping in the slop, throwing interceptions, fumbling away numerous chances to put points on the board; we just couldn't capitalize on our scoring opportunities.

Ultimately the game came down to our last possession. With five minutes remaining and eighty-five yards to go for the winning score, our offense huddled up at our fifteen yard-line. Because I was the team's third receiver, I trotted onto the field with all the starters.

Inordinately calm, there was a tremendous presence in our huddle. Everyone knew the deal, so not much was said. Determined but not desperate, as we approached the line as one, you could see the fear in the eyes of the defense.

Throwing the ball on every down, we marched up the field. A couple of times, we faced fourth-and-the-season plays. Both those times, our quarterback, Ron Rodriguez—a computer technician that I worked with at a midtown law firm by day—called my number, and I came up with two clutch grabs. (One was on a diving slant catch, and after hauling in a bullet pass on the second grab, I was slammed to the muddy turf by a cornerback and safety.)

Fiercely cheering us on, my soaked teammates on the sidelines were going hoarse.

Finally, with the rain coming down harder than ever before, we faced another four down; this time at their ten-yard line with fifty seconds left. Using our last timeout, we knew we had to go to the end zone. Ron was about to call my number once more, when another receiver demanded the ball.

Because this was a veteran club filled with police officers—I was a rookie—deferred.

Well, the fade pattern went to the other receiver, and he dropped the ball.

A lump the size of a walnut formed in my throat as I saw the end of our season unfold in slow motion; a tremendous wave of pain captured my body when I saw Ron's pass hit the receiver right between the numbers, then fall harmlessly to the ground.

My head felt like it was going to explode as I sat on Rice Stadium's muddy lawn and watched the Heat celebrate.

The deafening cheers of my Falcon teammates, screams of hope only seconds before that rivaled a roaring Yankee stadium crowd, became fast friends with silence as they were dragged headfirst into a horrific nightmare.

We lost the game 2-0.

Going home on the subway together, the agonizing defeat left Ron and me so demoralized that not a word was said during the hour-long ride. Replaying the fateful play over and over in my mind, I had easily beaten my defender on a post-corner move—he fell down—and saw everything unfold all alone in the right corner of the Heat's end zone.

Finally, as the train doors opened at my Bowling Green station stop—I lived on Staten Island at the time—Ron told me, "I should have thrown the ball to you. You were wide open."

The twenty-five-minute ride across the Staten Island Ferry felt like hours as the numbness of the moment I experienced finally thawed, resulting in an uncontrollable watershed of emotions the rest of the way home.

The tears I bravely held back came down in buckets.

That loss haunted our team for nine months, until we faced them in the second game of the following season. Delivering a payback message, all the pain we felt was released with vengeance. Routing the Heat 28-0, it was the first of three statement games we against the team that made our holiday season a major bummer.

After winning the second rematch game—a 14-7 midseason triumph—some 364 days to the date of our spiritually shattering experience, we faced the Heat once more with a championship berth at stake. As we warmed up, someone from our team actually played "The Big Payback"; James Brown's 1974 classic.

That game was another nail-biting contest, a 14-7 classic that went down to the wire. But unlike the year before, this game, played at Harris Field in Bedford Park, came down to our Steel Curtain-like defense. In an ironic twist, it was the Heat's turn to march down the field in the dying minutes, and the Falcons' turn to stop them.

On fourth down, the opposition's quarterback threw up a prayer in the center of the field that was batted down. Racing onto the field with joy, and at game's end, I shouted *Da-di-da-da* three times, just as Our Godfather of Soul had closed the powerful record, and carried on victoriously with my triumphant teammates.

Finding recompense and pleasure after failure, the journey of the Falcons' redemption statement was as sweet as sugar.

The second type of statement games I'll analyze are the ones that deliver psychological messages to a team that you might face in the future. During the encounters, you want to leave no doubt to the opposition, or prove a point to anyone watching that your team is better, tougher, and stronger.

And in the case of the Negro League players of the 1930s, equal. Easing the pain of the Northern inner-cities and small Southern towns during the Great Depression, black baseball teams bolstered the economies and brought communities together while becoming points of pride throughout the land.

Uniting a colored America with the talent and spirit, churches even amended their Sunday schedules so that thousands throughout the land could catch a different, exciting brand of baseball; one that was more faster and daring than their white counterparts.

However, nothing made the competitive juices flow through the veins of the Negro League players more than those head-to-head showdowns with the league that shunned them.

In 438 off-season exhibition contests against the yet-to-be-integrated Major Leagues, Oscar Charleston, Buck O'Neill, Josh Gibson, Judy Johnson, "Cool Papa" Bell, Satchel Paige and other players who may have been some of the greatest players the game has ever known—players whose deeds were relegated to the minds and hearts of many who saw them play—made a strong statement to then commissioner Judge Kenesaw Mountain Landis and the ignorant racists still breathing false superiority. By compiling a 309-129 record against the league that refused them only because of the color of their skin, they proved that while their league was separate, it was their athletic peer.

"Those games meant something to us," said Paige, a man who would finally get his opportunity to pitch in the majors at forty-eight years old. "We wanted to let them and the public know we were just as talented as they were, if not more so."

✪ ✪ ✪

Over the final three weeks of the 2009 baseball season, the New York Yankees had a series of these statement contests; the first of which was a Monday night September 14th showdown at the stadium against the team I feared the most; the Los Angeles Angels. A make-up game that was played in from a crowd of 44,701—this was rescheduled due to a May 3rd rainout—the nip-and-tuck struggle had postseason playoff preview written all over it.

Remembering that humiliating July sweep at the hands of our perennial tormentors—they had won thirty-four of the last fifty-five games against the Yankees—all I saw was the Yankees once again depending on the big innings, a philosophy which had never worked for them when playing against the frenetic, fast-paced brand of baseball of the American League West leaders.

Never was I glad to be so wrong,

With the score deadlocked at three runs each, Mark Teixeira led off the bottom of the eighth with his third hit of the game, a booming ground rule double that bounced over the right-field wall. After an A-Rod base on balls forced Angels Manager Mike Scioscia to remove starter Jared Weaver, Yankees skipper Joe Girardi countered the move by sending Brett Gardner to pinch-run for Teixeira.

With left-handed reliever Joe Oliver now pitching, Gardner gave no indication to anyone in the ballpark what lay ahead, but he noticed after two pitches that Angels third baseman Chone Figgins was playing off the bag. Already given the green to steal when possible, on the very next pitch, the fleet feet of the Yankees reserve outfielder made a daring dash.

He was the lead runner of an attempted double-steal.

Sliding headfirst into third, Gardner not only beat the throw easily, but received an extra award for his efforts. The throw from Angels catcher Mike Napoli went wide of Figgins' glove and skipped into left field. Springing back to his feet, Gardner raced home with the go-ahead run as A-Rod cruised into third.

Robinson Cano promptly singled off of a rattled Oliver, giving Mariano Rivera, who secured his fortieth save of the season by retiring the Angels in the ninth, a two-run cushion.

All too often, the New York Yankees stood still as the Los Angeles Angels, so notorious for applying pressure on the basepaths, ran circles around them.

Their "marbles on the wooden floor" type of baseball had driven the Bronx Bombers nuts.

Finally, the favor was returned in kind, by way of the Yankees' small ball.

Ecstatic as I was about the victory—which gave the Bronx Bombers an AL-best 93-52 record; six games better than the Angels 86-57 mark—my excitement was reserved, for I knew that three important games remained against the Angels. One week later, we would return west to the scene of the three-game mugging that happened some two months earlier.

And sure enough, my fears were realized when Angels hurler Joe Saunders opened up their three-game West Coast showdown by holding the Bombers to two runs and seven hits over eight-and-a-third innings. Andy Pettitte, pitching for the first time in ten days because of an ailing left shoulder, was shaky. Allowing two first-inning runs (three overall, through six) he had the Yankees playing catch-up from the start in a 5-2 loss.

While the loss reduced the Yankee lead in the race for home-field advantage in the American League to four-and-a-half games, another growing concern for the team to address cropped up on their things-to-do-before-season's-end checklist. After losing the first eight games to their hated rivals from Boston, the season's first issue was whether they could beat the Red Sox. Once that concern was crossed off the list by way of that climactic four-game sweep at the stadium, the next matter to deal with was whether they could beat the Red Sox in Fenway Park. Victories in two out of three late-August games took care of that.

However one mental hurdle remained. Losers for the fourth time in four 2009 meetings—and for the eighteenth time in their last twenty-three games since 2005—at Angels Stadium, the challenge of winning in a place that proved unkind to them for years was critical to postseason success. In the coming weeks, the Yankees knew that the road to the World Series could fly west and land in the Big A. Knowing the Los Angeles Angels could be their opponents, if the psychological hurdle was not conquered, their personal house of horrors could derail championship aspirations.

But before they could even think about October and possibly November, there was the mere formality of punching their ticket to the playoffs. With their magic number at one for clinching a spot in the postseason, the Yankees took the field in California looking to accomplish the first goal of many they had set during spring training.

And they took the field using force.

Exerting brutal long-ball hitting power, Alex Rodriguez and Jorge Posada drilled consecutive two-run homers off of Angels starter Ervin Santana in the third inning, staking Yankees pitcher Chad Gaudin to an early 4-0 lead.

Easing through the first four innings, Gaudin appeared to be in lights-out mode as he held the AL West leaders to three hits and a walk.

The game looked to be over when Hideki Matsui extended the lead to 5-0 with a solo shot in the top of the fifth and Gaudin quickly retired the first two batters in the Angels' half of the frame. To that point, Gaudin, needing only one more out to qualify for the win, allowed only one baserunner to advance beyond first base.

He never got the victory.

Battling with Angels leadoff hitter Chone Figgins, the count went full. Gaudin's next pitch was an inside fastball that Figgins pulled deep down the right-field line. Landing just inside the foul pole, his solo homer broke up the shutout and immediately ignited his teammates. The next batter, Maicer Izturis doubled. Then Bobby Abreu walked and cleanup hitter Vladimir Guerrero singled, scoring Izturis and cutting the Yankees lead to 5-2.

Refusing to take any chances, Joe Girardi yanked Gaudin.

Reliever Alfredo Aceves got the Yankees out of the fifth, but gave up two runs of his own in the sixth, pulling the home team to within one run.

Watching this game at home, I relived the July 10 and 11 games in this haunted house; games in which the Yankees blew four-run leads in disastrous losses, and wondered if history was repeating itself as the Angels loaded the bases with two outs.

With Vladimir Guerrero at the plate, the host team was threatening to bust the game open. Grounding sharply to third, he was robbed of a hit by a diving Alex Rodriguez, who immediately hopped to his feet to easily throw out Guerrero.

Sighing heavily, I knew the Yankees escaped trouble.

But in the eighth inning, they wouldn't be so lucky.

Thriving in their high-intensity environment, the Angels tied the score against Phil Hughes. Yankees second baseman Robinson Cano booted Howie Kendrick's grounder to open the inning; then Kendrick stole second and moved to third on Posada's throwing error.

With the tying run ninety feet from home with nobody out, Hughes got Figgins to pop out, but Izturis lined a single to right field, scoring Kendrick to tie the game and sending Angel Stadium into a sudden frenzy. Clearly rattled by the high intensity, Hughes walked Abreu to move the go-ahead runner to second, but survived the frame by striking out Guerrero and centerfielder Torii Hunter.

As the tie game moved to the ninth inning, the scoreboard showed an Oakland victory over the Texas Rangers, a win that clinched the Yankees fourteenth postseason berth in the last fifteen years. While the moment was sweet for Yankees fans, many of us knew that winning this game mattered more. For starters, we had not won a game this season in a place that we might visit in the playoffs. And then there was this bit about an early game five-run lead we flushed down the toilet.

This was a statement game where a Yankees victory would deliver a message to the Los Angeles Angels, Skip Bayless, and anyone else in baseball who questioned the resolve of the ballclub.

And like a team realizing the importance of the moment, the Yankees responded.

Leading off the ninth, Brett Gardner, quickly becoming a pain in the ass to Angel fans all over, singled off reliever Matt Palmer. Then after five pickoff throws in his direction, he ran on a 1-0 pitch to Derek Jeter and stole second. After Jeter walked, Johnny Damon perfectly executed a bunt with a two-strike count to advance the runners.

Angels Manager Mike Scoiscia brought in left-hander Darren Oliver, who walked Teixeira intentionally. Oliver then faced Alex Rodriguez with the hopes of forcing a double play. On Oliver's first pitch, Rodriguez hammered the ball to deep center for a sacrifice fly, scoring Gardner with the go-ahead run.

Once again the Yankees ripped a page out the Los Angeles Angel playbook.

What happened next made you think they stole the page the Angels were about to use.

In the bottom of the ninth, after Angels leadoff hitter Howie Kendrick worked out a walk against Mariano Rivera, Jorge Posada gunned down pinch-runner Reggie Willits to complete a strike-'em-out, throw-'em-out double play. One out later, Rivera secured his forty-first save in forty-three chances and the Yankees had a heart-stopping, message-delivering 6-5 victory.

With a playoff berth now secured, there was a subdued celebration for the Yankees that Tuesday night; no champagne showers or matching T-shirts and caps for becoming the first team in the majors to clinch a spot in the playoffs. While jazzed up about returning the postseason, they had a division championship to lock up, a pennant to win, and a twenty-seventh championship banner to hoist in their new ballpark.

Even before any of that, there was one more statement to deliver to the Angels, one that said this: "We can win a series in your ball-park."

And they would do so in compelling fashion. After spotting the Angels two early runs, the Yankees came back three of their own in the fourth; courtesy of Robinson Cano's two-run single and a Melky Cabrera double.

Once again displaying the versatility they would need in the coming weeks, after the 3-2 lead was secured, the game was put in the hands of the New York pitching staff. A.J. Burnett, sticking to a pregame plan concocted with catcher Jose Molina regarding the use of his fastball, pitched spectacularly.

Overpowering the Angel batters through 5-2/3 innings, Burnett struck out eleven Angel batters, and could have had more; he was still pitching strong when Manager Joe Girardi took the ball from him.

Using four additional pitchers to get to the ninth—most notably, Long Beach California resident Ian Kennedy, who took a major-league mound for the first time in thirteen months due to surgery to remove an aneurysm from his right arm—it was an unusual bridge to his closer extraordinaire, Mariano Rivera.

But the Yankees bullpen rewarded the skipper for his faith with 3-1/3 scoreless innings. The only nerve-wracking moment occurred in the Angels' half of the eighth, when they loaded the bases against Kennedy, who was pitching in front of twenty friends and family members. With the possibility of his inspirational story turning into a long night of second-guessing the manager looming large, the young reliever quelled the budding storm by inducing a harmless ball to left off the bat of Erik Aybar to end the inning. Mariano pitched the ninth, recorded his 42nd save, and the New York Yankees had answered all questions about their resiliency and determination.

In winning their first series in Anaheim in five years, a big state-ment was delivered to their Left Coast nemesis, a team that sent the

Yankees packing from the postseason in 2002 and 2005. The way they triumphed—in two back-to-back, one-run wins less than twenty-four hours apart—had their confidence sky high as they headed home. They faced a team that had been an annual thorn in their side, adopted the same brand of peskiness that the Angels had tormented them with for so long, and beat them with their own medicine.

That will definitely leave a mark, I happily thought as the series ended.

As giddy as that felt, I knew a more emphatic statement about their dominance in the AL East as well as to all potential postseason opponents needed to be made.

With the formerly big, formerly bad Red Sox coming back to Yankee Stadium, I could tell the ballclub from the Bronx was reading my mind.

✪ ✪ ✪

There was a feeling at the Legends Suite Club that the outcome of the forthcoming series against the Boston Red Sox had already been decided. With the magic number to clinch the American League East at five, you knew that by Sunday afternoon, the New York Yankees would be celebrating their sixteenth American League East Championship since the leagues went to a divisional format in 1969.

After winning their first eight head-to-head encounters with the Yankees this season for the first time since 1912, it seemed hard to imagine that the Red Sox wouldn't continue to steamroll over their hated rival en route to their third world championship of the decade. At this time, they were supposed to be setting up their pitching rotation for the playoffs and enjoying the fact they would own home-field advantage throughout the playoffs.

The August sweep at the hands of the Bronx Bombers altered everything. Being reduced to divisional also-rans and AL wild card leader (going into the series, they had a seven-game lead over the Texas Rangers, their closest pursuer) they would achieve a ninety-five win season. But on the evening of Friday, September 25, I saw something else while watching their pregame batting practice.

They lost their mojo, I mumbled. *They look finished.*

While playoff bound, the Boston Red Sox were a shell of the team that ran roughshod over the American League earlier in the season. Looking stale, injuries and poor pitching at crucial moments aided a wild momentum shift that now favored the hated Yankees.

The psychological grip they held over their fellow American League East heavyweight was now a distant memory.

However, what I saw was more than a potential red flag for the Red Sox Nation. Seeing no intensity or urgency in their eyes, they were a team with a foot off the accelerator, merely playing out the string of a long regular season.

At this point, my intuition began ringing like an alarm. I knew right then that not only would the Yankees sweep them again, but because the Boston Red Sox turned off their competitive engines too early, it would be very difficult for them to go to the whip once the playoffs started.

There will be no Grand Theater, or October feuds this fall, I mused. *The Red Sox won't be around long enough to face us in a real game next month.*

The three-game series in the Bronx was a regular-season victory lap. That Friday night, the Yankees blended their newfound base-running aggression with old standbys, good pitching and power hitting, to defeat the struggling Red Sox 9-5.

Setting a tempo of high-energy unpredictability that would last the rest of the game, Derek Jeter led off the game by hitting Red Sox starter Jon Lester's first pitch for a single. One pitch later, he

204 WILLIAM FREDRICK COOPER

stole second, then scored when Alex Rodriguez singled to left two outs later. Keeping the pressure on throughout the contest, Jeter's swipe of second was the first of a season-high, seven stolen bases the Yankees accumulated.

Alex Rodriguez, leading the Yankee attack with three steals (Jeter added two, and Robinson Cano and Johnny Damon one apiece), also added his 28th homer of the season to support a solid, six-inning performance by Joba Chamberlain. Responding to a meeting with Manager Joe Girardi and his pitching coaches, the twenty-four-year-old right-hander mowed down the first eleven Red Sox hitters he faced until Victor Martinez broke up the string with a solo homer in the fourth inning. David Ortiz would later clip Chamberlain for a two-run shot in the sixth, but it did little to damper Chamberlain's one-walk, five-strikeout quality start; a strong showing that produced his first win since the August 6th, my official *beginning of the end* for Boston.

One particular Red Sox fan who didn't see that his team's chances of winning the American League East—with that victory, the Yankee magic number to clinch had been reduced to three—were done.

Delusional, this fan, one who had harassed me all year with trash-talk, one who would be at all the games over the weekend, must have mistaken the powerful pinstripes the New York Yankees wore to those on the backs of the 2007 New York Mets. To even compare us to those choke artists—up seven games on the Philadelphia Phillies with seventeen games to play, they dropped twelve of those games and ended up losing the National League East on the last day of the season—was arrogant enough.

To admit that he clogged my toilets during that two-game showdown in May...well, let's just say that I seethed through my professionalism.

But I had something for him; something real good.

On Saturday, that team from Boston fired their last competitive blow of the season-long battle. Starting Red Sox hurler Daisuke Matsuzaka pitched a season-high seven innings, scattering six hits, five walks and allowing just one run while throwing 115 pitches. Mixing his pitches beautifully, whenever he found himself courting trouble, he exploited the hidden aggressiveness of Yankees hitters by getting them to chase pitches on the corners of the strike zone.

Like Houdini, for five innings he walked the tightrope of disaster, only to escape damage. In both the fourth and fifth innings, the first two Yankees reached base, but each time the Boston pitcher wiggled out of harm's way. In the fourth, he retired Robinson Cano, Cabrera and Jose Molina on a combined six pitches. In the fifth, he loaded the bases with no outs, Matsuzaka kept the Yankees off the scoreboard. Only one ball—a squibber by Alex Rodriguez—was hit in fair territory.

As good as the man the New Englanders know as Dice-K pitched, our guy, a fellow by the name of C.C. Sabathia, was even better. Striking out eight and walking only two in seven magnificent innings, the big left-hander was unhittable.

Well, almost unhittable. Coming in with his fastball, going away with his changeup, he yielded only one hit; a Mike Lowell single in the fifth broke up his no-hit bid. Shrugging that off, to say he was tough on the Red Sox batters was an understatement; after giving up the hit, Sabathia proceeded to strike out the next three batters.

So there we were, all of us in the new Yankee Stadium, intrigued by another pitcher's duel between these two bitter rivals, when Dice-K made his first and only mistake of the Saturday afternoon matinee. Leading off the bottom of the six, Robinson Cano got a juicy fastball over the plate and ripped a liner off the top of the left-field fence that caromed into the stands for a home run; thus snapping a scoreless tie.

Two innings later, the Yankees added insurance. Former Met-turned-Red Sox Billy Wagner, entering the rivalry for the first time, walked Nick Swisher to open the inning. Brett Gardner, in to pinch-run for Swisher, advanced to second on a wild pitch, then stole third. Cano struck out, but Gardner stole third and Melky Cabrera was hit by a pitch. Derek Jeter, attempting a suicide squeeze bunt, missed the pitch and Gardner, steaming down the line, got caught in a rundown between third and home. However, Boston catcher Chris Woodward dropped the ball, costing the Red Sox what would have been a big out as Gardner returned to third and Cabrera moved to second. Jeter eventually struck out, but Johnny Damon blooped a broken-bat single to right, driving in two runs.

The 3-0 victory—Mariano Rivera got another save—allowed the Yankees to reduce the magic number to one.

"Put the bubbly on ice," I announced after the game.

The first clinching celebration at the new Yankee Stadium was less than twenty-four hours away, and I couldn't wait to deliver a statement to my trash-talking, toilet-clogging Red Sox fan.

✪ ✪ ✪

Once upon a time, I had the experience of attending a title-clinching game. Back in October 2000, I went to Game 5 of the National League Championship Series. Wearing my Yankees cap, I went into Shea Stadium that Monday night to watch the Mets put away the St. Louis Cardinals.

Seated right above home plate, I was adjacent to a section of seventy or so people from St. Louis, hoping that their beloved Redbirds would somehow find a way out of a 3-games-to-1 series hole.

Unfortunately for them, Mets pitcher Mike Hampton had their number that evening. Hurling a complete game five-hit shutout, he never let the Cardinals in the game as he made it look too easy.

Around the fifth or sixth inning, with the Mets comfortably ahead and the Cardinals simultaneously changing pitchers and preparing their off-season golf plans, a victorious fan wearing blue and orange strolled by the Cardinal section, carrying a birdcage. In it was a fake redbird on a perch. Faced downward, the bird looked as dead as the team on the baseball diamond that night.

Needless to say, the visitors from St. Louis were furious. Throwing objects and hurling profanities, while privately worrying about his safety—because of heavy security, he escaped harm; however, I honestly think the police wanted to pour salt in the open wounds of Cardinal fans all over by allowing his stroll—I simply sat there laughing and marveling at the creative genius of the fan.

Nine years later, I would use my own creativity to silence a big-mouth Red Sox fan.

Silence.

Remember that word.

Silence wouldn't be the word of the day on September 27, 2009, at the new Yankee Stadium. There was an electric feeling around the Legends Suite Club. In anticipation of a celebration, many of the regular season-ticket holders were ready to whoop and holler along with an assemblage of talented baseball stars that put unity and cohesiveness over individualism in order to reach the precipice of championship glory.

My Yankee blood brother, one who along with me had a sense that we would be sharing this moment, was beaming.

"I told you that you would get a return on those seats you purchased," I mentioned to Kevin during an eighty-three-minute rain delay.

He smiled.

"Yeah, man. This is step one. Who would have thought in our first year at the season that we would win the AL East? And the clincher will come today against those damned Red Sox."

"Isn't that something?" Exchanging a hi-five, "One championship down, two more to go," I continued.

"Do you think we'll see Boston in the American League Championship Series?"

"I know it would be good for business here. But I don't think we'll be seeing the Red Sox anymore after today. They look dead, and like a hungry band of vultures, today we'll be picking over their remains. Then the Angels will stomp on their bones."

"They still need a win to get in the playoffs, right?"

Nodding my head yes, I then chuckled. "They won't get it today, that's for sure."

My Yankee buddy also chuckled.

"They won't be celebrating a damn wild-card berth in our house today."

Shaking our heads together with disgust, we both said *wild-card berth*, and laughed.

For three innings, however, it looked as if Boston might actually have a champagne shower in the visitor's clubhouse. With two outs in the first inning, outfielder Jason Bay doubled off starter Andy Pettitte, and Kevin Youkillis and David Ortiz followed with walks. Then third baseman Mike Lowell singled, plating Bay and giving the Sox an early 1-0 advantage.

My trash-talking buddy from Boston came to see me in the bathroom.

"Here it comes, the beginning of the end for the Yankees!" he shouted upon entry.

"You really believe that, don't you?" I answered.

"Hell, yeah!"

"You do know that the Yankees have forty-eight come-from-behind victories this season, right?"

My fact was met with silence, so I continued.

"Do you know that thirty-four of them have come at home?"

More silence.

"We're going to win, man. Face it, buddy, this is another day at the office."

I didn't think he even believed in his Red Sox anymore than I did; this in spite of the fact that they scratched across another run in the third. The feeling in the Legends Suite Club as well as the rest of the *House that George Built* was that it was only a matter of time before the Yankee wrecking ball—one that produced eight wins in the last nine games against their bitter rival— would swing through to destroy any remaining hope of a Red Sox miracle. This wasn't 2004, when the Curse of the Bambino was reversed by way of a mind-numbing, all-out collapse. Nor was it 2008, when baseball stopped in the Bronx in September.

This Yankee ballclub, one that had been in first place for seventy straight days, was one that stayed upbeat and refused to wilt when giving the American League—and the Red Sox, in particular—a head start in the early months. Honoring their talent by playing together, everyone on the roster bought into the positive atmosphere set by its leader, Manager Joe Girardi. The end result was an incredible season that would culminate with 103 victories, the most in baseball.

Victory number 100, the American League East clincher, would mirror their season. They gave the Red Sox an early 2-0 advantage; they shut the door on their hopes with solid pitching, clutch hitting, and of course, the long ball. After giving up those two runs, Good Ol' Andy settled down and gave the Yankees six strong innings.

His teammates responded to his efforts. In the bottom of the third, Melky Cabrera took a first-pitch fastball from Boston hurler Paul Byrd and deposited into the right-field seats to cut the deficit in half.

Byrd, pitching 5-2/3 brilliant innings himself, finally wilted in the sixth. After getting two outs, he gave up singles to Mark Teixeira and

A-Rod. The hits forced the hand of Boston Manager Terry Francona, who replaced Byrd with reliever Takashi Saito.

Smiling as I went out to watch the pitching change, I found my Red Sox tormentor seated in one of the back rows behind home plate, near the entrance to the Suite Club.

Tapping him on his shoulder, "This is where we clinch," I said confidently.

"You think so?" he responded.

"I *know* so."

Returning to my post after my little break, Saito made me look like a prophet. First uncorking a wild pitch—which moved the runners into scoring position—his next offering to fellow country-man Hideki Matsui put the rain-soaked Yankee crowd on notice that a long-awaited celebration was imminent. Swinging from his heels, the Yankees' designated hitter lined a clutch single to right-center, giving the Yankees a 3-2 lead.

From that point forward, it was countdown time.

We were nine outs away from our first celebration in our new ballpark.

And I was nine outs away from pulling my prank.

Yankees reliever Brian Bruney, once the primary eighth-inning option and now battling for a postseason roster spot, recorded five outs and left to an ovation so loud that it moved him to tears.

Next, Phil Coke came in, and struck out David Ortiz to end the eighth.

In the bottom of the frame, Teixeira turned back to a page from that August sweep, unloaded on another Daniel Bard pitch, and sent it soaring into the right-field seats for his thirty-eighth homer and 120th RBI of the season; and more importantly, a critical insurance run. Now the proud owners of a 4-2 lead, the sellout crowd at the new Yankee Stadium felt like Times Square on New Year's Eve;

festive and waiting for that ball to drop, thus signaling the dawning of a new era in Yankee annals.

While still on the clock, I was in party mode as well. Cleaning up the men's room quickly, like an excited kid, I rushed upstairs to purchase my gray AMERICAN LEAGUE EAST CHAMPIONS T-shirt from the Yankee Store, only to find a huge crowd awaiting that final out.

Mariano Rivera made things interesting—a single and an error put runners on second and third—but as usual, he delivered a message to Yankees fans that all's well in the Bronx. This save, however, indicated that for the first time since 2006, order was restored in the American League East.

The final out, while occurring in seconds, played out slowly.

And my mind freezed each frame of it.

Catcher Jose Molina leaped in victory from behind the plate, even *before* Rivera cleanly fielded the slow roller hit by Boston's Jacoby Ellsbury. After tossing the ball to Teixeira at first, a huge smile crossed his face as he pumped his fist. Teixeira, pumping his fist as well, joined Molina and Rivera in a group hug. Within seconds, they were swarmed by players and coaches alike. Exchanging hugs, hand-pounds, and hi-fives while matching their pinstripes with the gray divisional title T-shirts, they saluted the stadium crowd—which returned their appreciation with a rousing ovation of its own—then went scurrying into the clubhouse for eyeglasses.

They say that champagne burns the eyes.

Completing step one of their mountain climb, the 2009 New York Yankees hoped for three more eye-burning experiences in the coming weeks.

However, this first real bash at their new home, one that clinched a division title and home-field advantage throughout the playoffs, christened their palace with a familiar winning tradition; one that merely waited for a red light—'07 and '08 failures—to turn green so that it could cross the street.

We Yankees fans expected that light to stay green throughout October and November.

After purchasing, then putting on my T-shirt, I rushed back to the lower Legends men's room and found about a line of thirty or so people awaiting my arrival.

At the end of the line was my wisecracking Red Sox friend.

Thinking quickly, upon entry into the restroom, I politely told the front of the line to give our friend from Boston the silent treatment. Soon, my message filtered down the line, even to Yankees fans in front and back of this patron. Watching my prank unfold, even people engaging in trash-talking banter with the man suddenly stopped and acted as if he was never there.

For five whole minutes, the line moved in silence as the Red Sox fan kept running his mouth. Trying to agitate Yankees fans, he brought up the 2004 collapse, their two championships during the decade, A-Rod's tabloids, even Joe Torre's book, *The Yankee Years*, about his time in New York that criticized George Steinbrenner, Brian Cashman, and A-Rod.

Not one word was said to this man, who kept talking and talking.

Silence, I learned, screams volumes. In this instance it screamed sixteen American League East Championships since 1969, nine victories over the Boston Red Sox in our last ten games to deadlock the season series at 9-9, and two spirit-demoralizing back-to-back-sweeps at our new home that sucked the competitive life out of their organization.

And at that moment, it screamed Yankee victory to a member from the Red Sox Nation that wouldn't keep his mouth shut all season; one who purposely clogged up my toilet during the season.

He was making a fool out of himself and it was hilarious.

Finally, he reached the restroom.

More silence.

Finally, as he approached the motion sensitive faucets, he asked, "Why isn't anyone talking to me?"

Looking him in the face, I merely shrugged, then pointed to my new T-shirt.

As soon as he left the men's room, I led a victorious "Let's Go Yankees" chant in Bleacher Creature two-three rhythm.

Then, we all laughed.

Sometimes, statements in September are made without a word.

✪ ✪ ✪

There was one more statement made in the 2009 regular season; one that occurred on the season's last day.

Alex Rodriguez had hit a three-run homer on his first swing of the season, then defused any tension he created within the Yankee organization for his tumultuous 2008 season by rehabilitating his mind and body and embracing the team concept. The 2009 season would be not about compiling dazzling statistics, or in the alternative, being "the man." Playing with the joy that he came into the majors with, his focus sharpened like a laser and his teammates formed a protective cocoon around him, one that best exemplified the team's newfound unity.

A-Rod also learned a lesson that many of us have in this crazy thing called life: Whenever you stop looking for blessings from above, that's when they usually come. Because he had missed the first month of the season, Rodriguez's remarkable streak of reaching thirty homers and 100 runs batted in for eleven consecutive seasons was in jeopardy. Going into the last game of the season—versus the third-place Tampa Bay Rays—A-Rod began that Sunday afternoon with 28 homers and 93 RBIs.

And with Rays starter Wade Davis cruising into the sixth inning with a 2-0 lead, the possibility of extending his 30-100 streak didn't cross his mind when he came to the plate with two runners on. Finding a pitch he liked, he gave the Yankees a 3-2 lead when he hammered a drive into the left-field seats. Returning to the dugout after the three-run blast, he joked with reserve outfielder Erik Hinske.

"I may have one shot," Rodriguez told him. "We load the bases, I might pop one, you never know."

In order for that to happen, he would have to get by with a little help from his friends.

And like the famous group from England that made that song, the New York Yankees made some beautiful music.

Batting around, they plated three more runs and had two runners on with two out when Mark Teixeira stepped into the batter's box. Reliever Andy Sonnanstine, perhaps under orders from Tampa Bay Manager Joe Maddon, intentionally walked him. The only logical reason why I think this happened is this: the Yankees first baseman was tied with Tampa Bay's Carlos Pena, at thirty-nine home runs; this despite Pena's season ending on Sept. 7 due to an injury at Yankee Stadium.

As he set himself in the batter's box, perhaps A-Rod knew that God was shining on him. Perhaps he knew that because of the tabloid disgrace that was his 2008 season, a steroid revelation that soiled his legacy, and hip surgery that threatened his career, he was playing with house money in 2009. He had never expected to be on the field in 2009, and never expected to be this close to a milestone.

Or maybe, just maybe, Alex Rodriguez was making a statement by giving the baseball world a preview of things to come.

Steadying himself at the plate and swinging with nothing to lose, Rodriguez crushed a fastball over the right-center field fence for the eighteenth grand slam of his career. Raising his fist triumphantly as he rounded first base, the home run established many records for A-Rod, as well his Yankee teammates. Compiling thirty homers and

100 RBIs for the thirteenth time, Rodriguez broke a tie with Babe Ruth, Jimmy Foxx and Manny Ramirez for the most seasons, and tied Foxx's Major League record by accomplishing the feat in twelve consecutive seasons. A-Rod also became the first player in American League history with seven RBIs in an inning.

The Yankees' 10-2 season-finishing victory gave them a 103-59 record, their best season since 2002, when they posted the same record. It seemed fitting that Alex Rodriguez would deliver the final blow of an explosive season. The difference maker in a potent lineup that hammered a team-record and Major League high 244 homers— including five players: Mark Teixeira (an AL-best 39), Rodriguez (30), Hideki Matsui (28), Nick Swisher (28) and Robinson Cano (25) with at least twenty-five home runs each—the team was 13-15 with him on the disabled list, and 90-44 when he came back.

By no means were the New York Yankees one-dimensional. With timely base hits (Derek Jeter and Robinson Cano became the first infield tandem to collect 200 hits apiece in a season); stolen bases and contact hitters throughout batting order (they had the third fewest strikeouts in the American League), they wore out the opposition's starting pitching by working deep into the count; thus making every at-bat a grinding experience.

With C.C. Sabathia, Andy Pettitte and A.J. Burnett fresh for the playoffs, Manager Joe Girardi elected to go with a three-man pitching rotation in the playoffs; most often using his starters on three days' rest. With Joba Chamberlain now bringing his heat from the bullpen, the Yankees could turn an October baseball game into a six- or seven-inning chess match. And with Mariano Rivera now ready to get six outs if necessary, the 2009 New York Yankees were ready to count to eleven.

It would take eleven postseason wins to get the Canyon of Heroes parade.

And no Yankee was more ready to bring a championship to the

city than Alex Rodriguez. Knowing that there had been too many empty Octobers since his trumpeted arrival in 2004, he knew that the regular season would be a mere footnote in his Yankee legacy. In four American League Divisional Series in pinstripes, he batted .238 (15-for-63); .159 (7-for-44) if you discounted his .421 average against the Twins in 2004. What Yankees fans remembered him most for was Joe Torre batting him *eighth* in Game 4 of the 2006 ALDS.

While making a statement on the last day of the regular season, Janet Jackson's "What Have You Done For Me Lately?" thumped inside the head of A-Rod and the minds of his twenty-four team-mates. The organization had given the baseball players $201 million reasons why they should listen to that classic '80s groove.

And now that the September statements were made, it was time for the New York Yankees to dance for real.

A WHOLE NEW BALL GAME: THE AMERICAN LEAGUE DIVISIONAL SERIES

The summer breeze that we longed for in July and August gives way to the cool air autumn brings. The shorts, sleeveless shirts and tanning lotions are tucked away in favor of jeans, light jackets and fashionable sweaters; and the summer leaves, green and lively as they took residence on branches when the weather was warm, have turned brown and now call the lawns and the city sidewalks home. Somewhere between the wild and crazy beach parties of summer and the regal, festive holiday parties of winter, somewhere between our favorite time of the year and the most wonderful time of year is the most intense action of a baseball season.

On that playing field is a whole new ballgame once the postseason rolls around. The fans' cold beers of summertime are replaced by hot cocoa, coffee, and more importantly, championship hope. Gone is the pomp and pageantry of the regular-season, gone are the meaningless spring training Grapefruit games, or the mid-season lulls in the schedule.

Also gone are the days where players conjure up mysterious ailments just to get a day off; not to mention those September days where a manager is more interested in keeping his players healthy and rested for a championship run (you can thank the advent of the wild-card berth for this thought process.) Every single thought from March till the onset of October, all those things about statistical goals, taking a day off to recharge batteries and moral victories by way of close one-run losses, even all that talk about late-season pennant race fervor; all that junk is rendered moot by the quest to obtain that Commissioner's trophy.

It's a whole new ballgame all around when the stakes are raised. The playoffs are when every pitch, every swing, every fielding chance, every coaching move and every mistake gets placed in a frying pan, cooked properly with the blazing fire of a pressure-filled scrutiny— or improperly, depending on the outcome of your team—then placed under a microscope for years of further examination. The difference between good and greatness is a small one that can be defined by a bad bounce, a heroic swing, or a pitcher's mistake.

Under those harsh lights of postseason play, everything is magnified.

But the intense analysis and hope of success only begins with the media and loyal baseball fans.

I never fully understood how much pressure there is on baseball players to perform until I took a couple of tours around the new Yankee Stadium before Game 1 of the American League Divisional Series. Listening to fellow maintenance colleagues and security officers, many of whom were seasonal employees like me, you got the sense they wanted the playoffs to last as long as possible, so they could continue collecting work paychecks. During these grinding economic times, all of us needed the Yankees to travel deep in the playoffs, so that we could temporarily avoid the hassle of trying to secure unemployment benefits from a cash-strapped government.

Also dependent on the postseason Yankee success was the neighborhood surrounding the stadium, where many stores flourished when the Pinstripes played great baseball. Record crowds wanting to see an exciting team with new faces playing in a spanking new ballpark converged on the South Bronx looking to spend money; this in spite of our current recession. Opening their wallets and purses freely to purchase all types of Bomber Merchandise, local store sales went up as much as 30 percent from the year before.

Once the playoffs began, you add an additional 20 percent to those totals.

If 50,000 fans are coming to see a game at the stadium, about 20,000 fans are walking the streets looking for merchandise; not to mention they're doing a lot of eating and drinking.

And that means great business for the local taverns and restaurants.

Just down the street, on the corner of Gerard and E. 161st, is a local watering hole (my favorite watering hole, I must add as I still taste their Long Island Iced Teas in my mind—wink) that almost anyone associated with the Yankees—vendors, merchants, maintenance staff and crazed Yankee fans—hung out at pre and post-game. The Yankee Tavern, a part of the neighborhood since 1928 and the former stomping ground of Yankee legends Babe Ruth, Lou Gehrig and Mickey Mantle, was strangely silent in October of last year. While the regular patrons supported the establishment, a baseball postseason without Yankee baseball made for a grim atmosphere.

Not only was that the case in many of the pubs in the shadow of Yankee Stadium last year, but all over the city empty bar stools multiplied by the hundreds when the Yankees' 2008 season ended prematurely…for them, that is. Without a steady stream of patrons supporting them, so many places suffered. Cruelly crippling business, it made you realize the importance of what a triumphant postseason by the New York Yankees means to the Big Apple.

In Octobers past, the New York Yankees were real good for business.

Playing in a city whose only gauge of a successful year is one that ends with a World Series trophy, the question in 2009 was which part of the championship-or-nothing mantra would they fulfill?

✪ ✪ ✪

The answer to that question would begin on October 7, 2009, when the Yankees squared off against the Minnesota Twins. Winners of seventeen of their last twenty-one games, the American League Central Champions were the first team in Major League history to win the division after trailing by three games with four to play. Forcing a one-game showdown with the Detroit Tigers before their Homer-hankie waving Metrodome fans, it took four-and-a-half hours and twelve nerve-wracking innings for the Twins to emerge victorious.

The dramatic, tension-filled contest came to an end when Alexi Casilla singled to right field, scoring centerfielder Carlos Gomez from second base and giving Minnesota a heart-stopping 6-5 victory and its fifth division title in the past eight seasons.

Even as they celebrated their courageous victory, Frank Sinatra's warning crashed their party.

Did the Minnesota Twins truly want to be a part of the "New York, New York" that blared from their sound systems? In less than twenty-four hours they would do battle with a well-rested ball club that went 7-0 in the regular season against them; and they would do so without slugging first baseman Justin Morneau—out since mid-September due to a stress fracture of the lower back—and little lineup protection for soon-to-be-League MVP Joe Mauer. Were they sure they wanted to face a Yankee team that had eight hitters—Mark Teixeira, Derek Jeter, Johnny Damon, Alex Rodriguez, Hideki Matsui, Robinson Cano, Melky Cabrera and Jose Molina—with career averages of .300 or better against Minnesota pitching? Are they sure they wanted All-Star closer Joe Nathan to close out games against the Bronx Bombers? After all, he was 0-3 with a 4.20 earned run average in his career against the Yankees.

With all the strikes against this weary band of travelers (catching a late-night flight, they arrived in New York City around 3 a.m., and checked into their hotels two hours later), would Manager Ron

Gardenhire's scrappy, sleep-deprived unit be up to the challenge of facing the best team in baseball?

For the first 2-1/2 innings of Game 1, they certainly looked up to the task. With starting pitcher Brian Duensing looking solid over the first two innings—after allowing a leadoff single to Derek Jeter to start the game, the rookie left-hander set down seven straight Yankees—the Twins put a small dose of fear in the hearts of a sellout crowd and an entire city.

There were two outs in the visitors' third when second baseman Orlando Cabrera hit a hard single to right off of C.C Sabathia. Joe Mauer followed Cabrera's single with a ringing double to the gap in left-center, putting runners in scoring position for Michael Cuddyer, the Twins' hottest hitter during their September stretch run.

Continuing his torrid streak, Cuddyer delivered with a single to right, putting the Twins on the board and runners on the corners.

Two pitches later, the Twins added another run when Sabathia threw a fastball that crossed-up catcher Jorge Posada. Expecting the pitch to break toward the inner half of home plate, it tailed outside, glancing off Posada's glove and toward the Yankees' dugout.

Thinking that Mauer, the third base runner, had already scored, Posada took his time retrieving the ball. Mauer, believing that Posada would snatch it up quickly, hesitated slightly before racing home.

The end result was a close play at the plate, where a sliding Mauer eluded Sabathia's tag.

By the time Sabathia struck out Jason Kubel to end the inning, an eerie silence gripped the entire stadium. The faces of the men who entered into the Legends Suite Club men's room wore looks of panic.

Screaming in frustration, "It better not happen again!" one season ticket-holder said.

Another one concurred.

"It better not, or I'll burn my freakin' jersey!"

The "It" in reference was three straight Divisional Series losses, and in milliseconds I relived three painful memories:

2005 – Watching Game Five vs. the Los Angeles Angels in Cleveland with friends, I screamed at the television when Yankees outfielders Gary Sheffield and Bubba Crosby crashed into each other on Adam Kennedy's two-run triple in the second inning, and cheered with hope when Derek Jeter clubbed a seventh-inning homer off Erwin Santana to cut the Angels' lead to 5-3.

But what stood out prominently about that Monday night showdown was A-Rod going hitless to finish the series 2-for-15. The superstar who posted 48 homers and 130 RBIs in an MVP regular season didn't launch a single homer or drive in a single run in those five games. His parting shot in the series, a fatal double-play groundout in the ninth, sent me to the Amtrak station near the Rock-and-Roll Hall of Fame totally bummed.

2006—The Detroit Tigers?

That's what I said in the Dallas-Fort Worth airport on the morning of October 8th, with astonishment on my face. The day before, the Yankees, in the words of their General Manager Brian Cashman, "got what they deserved," when they were eliminated in four games by an upstart team from Motown playing with nothing to lose. Reviewing the New York Times at a newsstand in shock, all I kept saying aloud was…The Detroit Tigers?

As fate would have it, a couple from Michigan going home from who-knows-where observed that I had the wind taken out of me, danced with glee.

"Torre hit A-Rod eighth", they sang, reciting the batting order demotion of Alex Rodriguez, who ended the series with an .071 batting average; not to mention a clumsy third-inning error in the 8-3 final game loss. "Heads are gonna roll in the Big Apple," they continued.

In response, all I could say was…The Detroit Tigers?

2007—Facing a younger, more determined team in the Cleveland Indians, it was painful to watch what many thought of as the end of a

Yankee dynasty. Perhaps what I remember most about the Game Four, season-ending 6-4 loss was a season-killing, seventh-inning double play ball hit by a slumping Derek Jeter that turned Yankee Stadium into the world's largest outdoor funeral service; one that spelled the end of Joe Torre's twelve-year tenure as Yankee manager.

Jeter, hitting .176 during the series, came up with runners on the corners and the Yankees down 6-2. The 56, 135 in attendance chanted his name strongly, with the hope that the legend of so many falls could write a new chapter in pinstripe lore. Instead, Yankees fans all over were sent spiraling into a vortex of oblivion over a third consecutive, first-round playoff defeat.

And once again, that "it" feeling resurfaced.

Going into the Yankees' half of the third, I wondered if Derek Jeter remembered his fatal, final postseason at-bat at his old home across the street; or alternately, heard the hushed worry that had 49,000-plus fans sitting on their hands in the new house. With the Yankees trailing 2-0, the October paranoia of seasons past was slowly making its way down the aisles and corridors of the new palace, bringing with it an odor of terror that disrupted scents of potential success.

Taking a whiff of the possibility that this postseason might find the New York Yankees adding another chapter to an early-exit playoff legacy, an entire city was paralyzed by a familiar feeling of dread.

Someone had to remove that stench of recent playoff failure. Someone had to remind the New York Yankees organization and its million of fans that this postseason was going to be about redemption, rebuilding and the eventual restoration of baseball's most storied legacy.

Someone had to step up, set a tone and say, "enough of this losing foolishness, let's bring the noise back to the Bronx."

Someone had to get rid of that "it" feeling.

With one out, and Melky Cabrera on second, Jeter dug into the batter's box. In the first pitch of his first at-bat, the Yankees captain reminded everyone in the ballpark how much he despised that 2008 hiccup of postseason activity when he lined a hard single to left.

This at-bat, however, would wake up the new stadium.

With the count at one ball and two strikes, the slider that left Brian Duensing's hand came over the plate high.

Jeter must have smiled when he saw the pitch coming.

Taking a healthy cut, he sent it soaring through the brisk Bronx air. As the ball climbed high into the night, every seat in the stadium, every barstool in every pub, every den and every living room, every sidewalk and car radio; everyplace where Yankees fans chose to spend their first night's return to postseason play, came alive once more.

Once the ball found its destination in the left-field seats, everyone in the Big Apple felt a swagger return to their step.

Giving hi-fives to everyone in the Suite Club, "Here we go," I announced to all that would listen.

Once again, Derek Jeter did what he does better than any post-season player of his generation. Knotting the game at two with his eighteenth career postseason home run—his tenth in divisional series play—once again he ushered calm into the hearts of millions...

Not to mention, his Yankee teammates. Re-energized by the different sound and feel around the stadium—something called momentum gripped it—they changed things in a hurry. With Robinson Cano on first and two outs in the fourth inning, Nick Swisher lined a double into the left-field corner. Steaming around second, Cano picked up third-base coach Rob Thomson, who without hesitation, waved him around third.

It was a bold, aggressive play, but the third-base coach knew that only a perfect relay throw would nail Cano at the plate. It didn't happen. The throw was up the first-base line, and Cano slid in safely. Swisher, watching the developments while standing on second base, pumped his fist and pointed his two index fingers skyward.

His double gave the Yankees a 3-2 lead.

It was a lead Sabathia failed to relinquish. Struggling with his command while throwing seventy-seven pitches through the first four innings, the big left-hander finally found his groove and made life miserable for the Twins. Moving an unhittable cut-fastball around the plate effectively while complementing such with a devastating slider and wicked changeups, he began reconstruction work on his playoff legacy—in five previous playoff outings he posted a 2-3 record, a 7.92 earned run average, and never got past the sixth inning—by growing as big as the moment before him.

Striking out eight while allowing just one earned run in 6-2/3 innings, he threw strikes early in the count, and confused Twins batters so much that they couldn't differentiate pitches when they left his hand. By the time his 113-pitch outing was complete, Sabathia received a heartfelt standing ovation from Yankees fans that had longed to see postseason pitching dominance.

Lifting his cap to the appreciative applause, the Yankees ace handed the ball to Joe Girardi, who immediately passed it off to the Yankees' bullpen. Inheriting two runners in the seventh, Phil Hughes quickly got Twins leadoff hitter Denard Span to fly out to right to end the threat. From there, Hughes, Phil Coke, Joba Chamberlain and Mariano Rivera slammed the door on Minnesota, hurling two more scoreless innings.

With three runs in the bank by the end of the fourth, that would be all the Yankees would need; but they didn't know it at the time. More runs were produced, and one player in particular, finally began removing an albatross that weighed him down like an anchor on a battleship.

In the fifth, Alex Rodriguez came to the plate with two out and

Jeter on second. Hitless in his nineteen previous postseason at-bats, he was even worse with a man on base (0-for-29). In fact, if you went all the way back to his last three at-bats in Game 4 of the 2004 ALCS against the Red Sox, he had left forty runners on base for the Yankees in the playoffs, with no runs batted in.

Not a single one.

During that stretch of futility, his lone October RBI for the Yankees came in the last game of that Yankees-Indians series in 2007, when he hit a cosmetic home run in a blowout loss.

(NOTE: *Remember how frustrating it was watching him come through after the fact, I likened that solo shot to an NFL quarterback who pads his passing stats in a game already decided; inconsequential and irrelevant.*)

If ever there was a time for you to start turning things around, now's it, I thought as Minnesota pitching coach Rick Anderson visited the mound. Anderson, perhaps sensing my intuition, warned his rookie pitcher about throwing A-Rod a first-pitch fastball.

"Throw something away, in the dirt, so that he can chase it," he encouraged.

"I want to go at him," the rookie left-hander replied.

Stubborn like that kid having to touch a hot stove after his parents told him he would get burned if he touched it, Brian Duensing threw him a first-pitch fastball out over the plate.

It was his last pitch of the evening.

Stinging the fastball on the screws, A-Rod smoked a single to left, scoring Jeter and giving the Yankees a 4-2 lead.

Looking at A-Rod on the HDTV monitors, I could see him more relaxed than ever, like an enormous weight was lifted from his broad shoulders.

At that point, Twins Manager Ron Gardenhire removed Duensing.

Watching him signal for left-handed reliever Franscisco Liriano to face Hideki Matsui, my psychic bell started ringing like a fire alarm.

"The game is over right here," I said to Elton Ottey, my Legends friend who had stopped by the men's room.

After watching Lirano fall behind Matsui in the batter's count, "You think so?" he replied.

"Just watch."

No sooner than those words escaped my lips, a 2-1 fastball came right into the wheelhouse of the man Japanese sportswriters call "Godzilla."

The next thing I heard was Elton screaming, "Oh my God!"

He looked at me, and I looked at him.

Then I winked.

Teeing off, Godzilla crushed the Twin Cities with a blast to straightaway center, where it landed deep into Monument Park for a game-breaking, two-run homer. The tape-measure shot—Matsui's fourteenth against a southpaw in 2009, the most in the majors by a lefthanded hitter—gave the Yankees a commanding 6-2 lead.

"Game over," I announced, then went back to cleaning my bathroom.

It wouldn't be the last time I was right on target about a divisional series long ball.

A-Rod, continuing to give Yankees fans hope for greater things, supplied one more run in the seventh, when he again knocked in Jeter from second with a single off pitcher Jon Rauch.

The Yankees' 7-2 series-opening victory had everyone in the Legends Suite Club excited, but a guarded optimism still lingered. There was still more work for the team in pinstripes to do, more October legacies to rebuild, more stories about great Yankee moments to create.

One of those moments would come two nights later.

For me, that unbelievable moment confirmed everything.

✪ ✪ ✪

The team and the fans came in April, bringing along hopeful enthusiasm, pride and tradition in their suitcases.

The concrete-shaking roar of the crowd followed suit in August when the Yankees sealed the Red Sox fate; and its energetic brother electricity finally arrived, just in time for Game 1 of the ALDS.

One thing that hadn't made the trip across the street was the Yankee Mystique. Sure, during the regular season there were the 15 walk-off hits, a dropped fly ball, a dramatic blast here and there, and a magical milestone moment that made the inaugural season in the new Yankee Stadium memorable.

However, the ghosts that gave the New York Yankees an un-beatable aura of invincibility in the fall; the ones that coerced the umpires into strange calls that went against the opposition; the ones that caused teams to produce mental blunders; the dramatic home run in the bottom of the ninth that made getting those last three outs against the Bombers in October the hardest feat in baseball; and most importantly, an extra inning ...

Well, those spirits, four of them to be exact, were still living rent-free in the old place.

Alas, in Game 2 of the American League Divisional Series, the Ghosts of Yankees past arrived at their half-demolished stomping ground, only to find the place locked.

Praying that their denial of entrance was some huge misunder-standing, they flew around *The House That Ruth Built*, hoping they would gain access to familiar surroundings.

Alas, their efforts were not meant to be; in fact, a police officer rebuffed all their attempted bribes.

"I'll give you seats from the old Stadium," Ghost #1 pleaded.

The big, burly officer shook his head no.

The second ghost, more of a charmer than the first and normally adept at getting people to believe almost anything he said, began his shtick.

"I understand that you can't grant us entry. You have to do your job. But…"

Before he could continue, the cop cut him off.

"You guys are lucky I don't run you in. Here," he said, handing him a card, "You should call this guy,"

Seeing the tears well in their eyes, the officer offered one last bit of advice.

"You'll love the new place. Trust me."

Going to the Hard Rock Café in the new stadium's concourse to drown their sorrow over Coronas, Ghost #3 was so shook up by the sudden eviction that he knocked over his bottle, causing the gold beer to flow off the edge of the bar.

Ghost # 4 set the bottle upright while posing a question to his three friends.

"Should we call him?"

Reluctantly, his other constituents nodded yes.

Ghost # 2 started dialing.

✪ ✪ ✪

So there I was, in the Legends Suite Club, cleaning area rugs with a hand vacuum, when I suddenly heard my cell phone go off.

"Is this William?" the voice on the other end of the phone asked.

Standing straighter than I ever did before, "Who wants to know?" I asked.

"I am one of the Ghosts of Yankees past. I'm known as Ghost number two, but you could call me 'Babe.'"

Smiling like never before, my plan was working.

"Okay, Babe. Listen, you and your friends…"

"We don't like the place," he interrupted.

"Why not?"

"It's because you haven't won a damn thing yet!"

Leave it to the *Bambino* to rattle my cage.

Taking a deep breath, I responded.

"You're just jealous because it's not named after you. It's not the house that you built anymore. Besides, we won the AL EAST, Babe. And Wednesday, we won our first playoff game here at the house that George…"

"These damn tiered playoffs! That's kiddie stuff! Let's see you sons-of-bitches win an eight team division seven times, like we did," Babe argued. "Let's see you sons-of-bitches…"

I had to put my foot down. Game 2 was scoreless, but the Minnesota Twins were threatening in the fourth. With two outs, Yankees starter A.J. Burnett hit outfielders Delmon Young and Carlos Gomez with pitches. With runners on first and second, third baseman Matt Tolbert grounded a single to the right of Robinson Cano and into right-center field.

Rounding third, Young was sure to score the game's first run.

"Look, Babe," I interrupted firmly, "I need your help. Your Yankees are about to fall behind and I need you to do something right now."

After telling him my request and the urgency thereof, Ghost #2 and perhaps the Yankees' greatest phantom acted swiftly. Seeing Gomez race around second, he put a banana peel out on the base paths. Gomez, running swiftly with the expectation of reaching third, stumbled and tried to scramble back to second.

Seeing the play develop in front of him, Nick Swisher quickly scooped up Tolbert's single to right and hurried the ball back into the infield, where Derek Jeter applied the tag on Gomez *before* Young—who was a few feet away from home plate—scored.

It was a heads-up play by both Swisher and Jeter; one that was aided by the Ghost of the Bambino.

In reality, the rule cited for this play appears in Major League

Baseball's Official Rule book is under section 4.09, "How a Team Scores." Rule 4.09(a) reads as follows:

"One run shall be scored each time a runner legally advances to and touches first, second, third and home base before three men are put out to end the inning. EXCEPTION: A run is not scored if the runner advances to home base during a play in which the third out is made (1) by the batter-runner before he touches first base; (2) by any runner being forced out; or (3) by a preceding runner who is declared out because he failed to touch one of the bases."

Sighing with relief, I really appreciated this assistance in the matter.

"Yo, Babe," I said in a very thankful tone, "Good looking out."

Surprisingly, the Babe understood my slang.

"No doubt," he answered back, then paused. "You know something, William? I'm beginning to like this place."

"I knew you would, man. Now go catch a drink at the Mohegan Sun lounge. "

The Babe did just that.

While this conversation was wrapping up, the scoreless duel continued. Both pitchers—Burnett and Twins starter Nick Blackburn—were answering the bell by keeping their teams in the game. Allowing eight baserunners through his first five innings, Burnett struggled at times, but only surrendered one run—by way of a sixth-inning RBI triple to left by pinch hitter Brendan Harris—during his six-inning journey through the Twins lineup.

He pitched an awesome game.

But Nick Blackburn was even better. Holding the potent Yankee batting order hitless through the first four innings—the only pinstripe baserunner came via a second-inning walk to Hideki Matsui—he worked 5-2/3 innings, allowing one run on three hits while striking out three and walking only two. Owning great movement sinkerball and inducing many groundouts.

As brilliant as he was, his lone trouble spot, a sixth-inning jam, spelled the end of his evening.

Trailing 1-0, Jeter started the Yankees' brief rally with a one-out double to right-center and Johnny Damon walked. Mark Teixeira made the frame's second out on a routine fly ball to left field, only after barely missing a three-run home run down the right-field line on a shot that was only a few feet foul.

As Alex Rodriguez stepped into the batter's box, I went outside to watch the at-bat. Standing right behind home plate in the concrete section that divided the 000 section with the 100 seats, I engaged in a conversation with a couple of Yankees fans above me.

"So what do you think?" an older gentleman wearing a road Yankees jersey said to me.

My response came quick, and because of the groundswell of hope building inside the stadium, it was loud as well.

"Well, this is one of the biggest at-bats of A-Rod's Yankee career!" I screamed above the roar of the crowd. Seeing that they were met with head-nodding of agreement by four others who overheard my statement, I continued. "The New York fans want to show him love so bad, and this is the moment he starts receiving it."

Later on that statement would be amended; however, no sooner than those words left me, A-Rod delivered.

Rapping a hard single between third baseman Brendan Harris and shortstop Orlando Cabrera, he scored Jeter with the tying run. The base hit, Blackburn's only mistake in an outstanding, big-game performance, was A-Rod's third straight with a runner in scoring position.

Those people in the stands looked at me like I was crazy.

Giving them a wink, I returned to my post.

While tidying up the place, the shrill of my cell phone disrupted my groove and returned me to a fantasy.

It was the Babe, calling me from the Mohegan Sun. He sounded like a proud parent, and I could hear his chest puff up with pride.

"You like what I'm doing with A-Rod, don't you?" he asked.

"I most certainly do."

"My three friends, Joe D, Mickey, and Lou have decided to join the party. After I told them about how awesome the place is, their curiosity got the best of them. Say hi, fellas!"

In the background I heard three ghosts from Yankee past shouting in unison, "Hiya, fellas."

My eyes grew wide in amazement. Knowing that Gehrig and DiMaggio were loners while alive, I wondered how the preeminent ghosts of past Yankee glory pulled this one off.

"We'll talk later, Babe. I have patrons to tend to."

Hanging up, I had to finish doing my job as well as watch the game.

What I saw had me worried. Battling back, those resilient Twins regained the lead in the eighth inning. With two out and runners at the corners, Nick Punto hit an RBI single off Phil Hughes and Denard Span followed with another run-scoring single off Mariano Rivera.

The stadium crowd, shimmying and shaking with a swagger just two innings earlier, grew quiet as terror and trepidation resurfaced; especially after the Twins retired seven straight Yankees after Blackburn's departure. Once again, that familiar feeling of dread kidnapped the billion-dollar playground and threatened to crumble the fresh new joy Game 1's victory produced.

It sounded like a tomb in the Legends Suite Club. The happy heartbeat that frolicked through the dining venue all season had been replaced by the fear of a sudden offseason. I could see the frustration in the eyes of many of the support staff employees. Some had families to take care of, and the long hours during the season sure did help ease the pressure of growing bills. Anchored in the enormity of the situation, a loss here at the new stadium, and possibly two more in the Twin Cities, would not only mean a stunning finish to the season, but a dramatic readjustment to the lives of hundreds.

The patrons felt the growing frustration as well. Many of the season ticket-holders were simply tired of seeing the franchise spend all this money on the most expensive payroll in baseball only to see the product on the field die a quick death in games that really mattered. The place had changed, but the approach was old, some thought.

Once again, time appeared to be moving on without them.

With three outs to play, a sense of urgency enveloped the season of the New York Yankees; sooner than anyone expected.

And I bet any amount of money that somewhere Skip Bayless was smiling.

The men's room was silent after the top of the ninth. Workers and fans alike didn't know what to say.

Former Mayor Giuliani was as perplexed as everyone else.

"Let's hope they do something here," he told me as he approached the motion sensitive faucets.

Placing my arm around his shoulders, "They will," I said confidently. "I have faith."

"I do too, my friend," he said.

After he left, I distinctly remember repeating the word "faith" to all that entered the facility, as well as to my colleagues in the Suite Club.

"We will win this game," I added. "Just have faith."

Perhaps accustomed to our recent stretch of first-round exits, a tall gentleman with distinguished gray hair spoke what everyone was thinking.

"Yeah, right, man. It's another season down the toilet."

It was then where my heart, mind, body and soul met with Babe, the ghost of Yankees past.

Through me, he may have been calling another shot.

In a bold, confident tone, I said this: "Teixiera will lead off the inning with a hit, then A-Rod will deliver his biggest hit ever in a Yankees uniform. He's due. It's his time. Just watch. I guarantee it."

Those were my exact words.

At the time I said it three Legends employees, (one named Mike, another named Josh, and I can't recall the third person's name) happened to overhear me say it.

"You think so?" Mike asked me.

"Go see so for yourself," I said.

After everyone left, I went into one of the stalls, closed the door, and said a quick prayer.

Now some might think of this as crazy. But sometimes the reward of faith shows up in ways others deem incomprehensible. I remember after the night ended, the next morning I shared this story with Cheryl.

With a look that told me she thought I had lost it, "You prayed for A-Rod to hit a home run?" she asked.

I DID NOT PRAY FOR A HOME RUN. What I prayed for was a confirmation about what I was feeling at the time I felt it. It was a strange rush of certainty that couldn't be described in mere words. Never in my entire life had I spoken this way, with such faith and confidence in what was about to happen. It was a proclamation made with nary an ounce of fear in my body, something I had never done before.

I knew what was about to happen, because I had complete faith.

Smiling, I remember watching Joe Nathan warm up. Cognizant of the fact that he had 47 regular-season saves to share the Rolaids Relief Man of the Year Award with Rivera, I knew that while the Twins' right-handed closer was from Upstate New York, he was about to take a walk through a Bronx minefield and not make it to the other side.

As predicted, Mark Teixeira came up and rifled a hard single to the right-field corner.

When A-Rod came to the plate, my smile became a huge grin, and that rush that came over me caused me to feel so full. Much had been made of his remarkable streak of failure, and for the most part he had been successful in restoring the faith of fans all over.

But still, as he locked in to the most important at-bat of his Yankee career, he hadn't felt the love from all of New York; and the longing in his eyes reflected something the millions of dollars he was making couldn't assuage. Something, whether it was dating Madonna or some other tabloid fodder, a steroid allegation-then-confirmation, a failure to produce in the clutch, or an injury to stunt his season; something had always been in the way of the affection he had been searching for from the most ardent Yankee supporters.

Watching Nathan throw three straight curveballs out of the strike zone, *he's about to experience a love he's never received before*, I mused. Then, as he took a 94-miles-an-hour fastball for a strike, those intuitive alarms rang once more.

"It's time," I mumbled.

Nathan's next pitch was supposed to be a fastball down-and-away, but it went straight down Broadway.

Then there was that crack, a contact sound of bat-meeting-ball that lets everyone in the place know that it's okay to go crazy.

The minute I saw the swing, that rush threatened to set my chest ablaze. Barely able to breathe, I needed to get air, so I went outside for some air and watched the new place shake like never before.

There, I ran into someone that was in the restroom when I made my bold statement.

"You called it! You called it! How did you know?" he screamed.

"I just knew," was all I said, smiling.

From the moment the ball made contact with his bat, A-Rod knew it as well. Flipping his bat away, he looked into the Yankees' dugout and pumped his fist. This was the moment he had been waiting for ever since he first donned the pinstripes five years earlier.

Nathan knew also. Watching the mistake soar toward right-center field, the pain he felt must have been intense, because he almost doubled over. Recovering in a millisecond, he tried with all his might to will the ball back into the playing field as he started to back up home plate.

But nothing would bring this one back. Carlos Gomez, the Twins centerfielder, chased the blast all the way to the steak sign in front of the Yankees' bullpen and climbed the fence. His efforts too were in vain.

Ultimately, the ball landed in the glove of Yankees bullpen coach Mike Harkey, who caught the blast right in front of the big red Toyota sign behind the bullpen.

Breaking new sound barriers with sheer elation, the stadium was rocking like never before, and got even louder when Alex Rodriguez came out for his curtain call. All the love Yankees fans had held back from him for so long was given to him with interest. Watching him wave his helmet to the crowd made my eyes water. Sure these players made millions; and yes, some of their egos reflect such. But long before they put on the uniforms, they were human beings.

And the most compelling human story of October, one of sweet redemption, was being written before my eyes.

A-Rod's dramatic two-run homer not only tied the game, but in the eyes of many New Yorkers, he permanently washed away the sins of his baseball past.

That was the moment when Alex Rodriguez became a true Yankee.

Returning to my post with a huge grin and a tie score, not only had my faith been confirmed, but in my mind, my destiny as well.

This moment told me that the New York Yankees would be World Champions.

Greeting the Legends crowd at inning's end with enthusiastic hi-fives, some of them may have known this as well. Even if were to go into extra innings, like this contest, it was only a matter of time before the Yankees would find a way to win this one.

Before that would happen, I would have to make one more call to the Yankee Ghosts, as I needed help in the eleventh inning.

"Y'all must be having a party up in that lounge," I said.

This time, I spoke with the Iron Horse.

"Yeah, William. We like it here."

"Thanks for bringing that aura of invincibility over, Mr. Gehrig."

"No problem."

"Hey listen, Lou. I need your help…"

After telling him my request, he obliged once more. Leading off the Twins' half of the frame, left-handed Joe Mauer hit a opposite field line drive off Yankees reliever Damaso Marte. Chasing the ball down the left-field line was umpire Phil Cuzzi. Looking fair, the ball glanced off outfielder Melky Cabrera's glove and bounced away, giving Mauer what appeared to be a sure double.

The ball looked a foot fair, but then the Ghosts of Yankees past intervened once more. Obstructing the umpire's vision, Cuzzi ruled the ball foul, sending Mauer back to the plate. Though he would later single in the at-bat, you got the sense that the rhythm of the inning was disrupted; especially when television replays clearly showed that Cuzzi clearly missed the call.

After the game, crew leader chief Tim Tschida addressed the media and admitted what everyone knew; that "an incorrect decision was rendered." But the confession wouldn't change anything…

Or the fact that the Twins would blow yet another scoring opportunity. While they finished the game by leaving seventeen runners on base—the fifth-highest game total in postseason play—none would be as heartbreaking as the squandered chance they had in the eleventh. After the Mauer controversy, Jason Kubel singled to right, moving Mauer to second.

Changing pitchers, Joe Girardi brought in Dave Robertson, and the red-hot Michael Cuddyer greeted him with a single.

Suddenly, the Minnesota Twins had the bases loaded with no one out.

Reaching deep into his resolve tank, the twenty-four-year-old right-hander came up big. After getting Delmon Young to line to Teixeira to line out to first, he induced a grounder to the first baseman, who quickly fired home for a force play on Mauer. Then with two outs, he challenged Brendan Harris with three fastballs; eventually getting him to fly to center for the third out.

The 3-3 tie had been protected.

And now it was time for the Yankees to win it. They had already squandered an opportunity in the tenth, when with runners at the corners, Johnny Damon lined into a double play. Seeing the frustration in the eyes of some of the Suite Club members, I was reassuring once more while preparing them for the bottom of the eleventh.

"Go out there and watch the end of the game," was all I said.

In the ninth inning, the initiation of the new Yankee Stadium officially ended with A-Rod's titanic blast into the right centerfield bullpen.

Now we needed the stadium to shake once more; this time in victory. Leading off the frame, Mark Teixeira saw a 2-1 pitch from Jose Mijares that he liked and hit a rocket into the left-field corner. As the 50,000-plus in attendance craned their necks to see where the drive was going, the Yankees slugger ran hard to first.

The line drive stayed fair by two feet, landing just above the 318-foot mark in left field.

Suddenly Sinatra spread the news to the place, and the crowd let out a thunderous roar of approval. Young, the Twins leftfielder, paused for a second, then hung his head in defeat as Teixeira stuck his index finger to the sky.

The ball was gone, and never coming back.

The Yankees had won their first postseason classic 4-3, owned a 2-0 series lead, and now set their sights on closing the Hubert H. Humphrey Metrodome for baseball business.

Before I left the stadium, I placed one last call to my new friends, the Ghosts of Yankees past.

This time I got Joe D's and Bob Costas' favorite son on three-way.

Wishing that I could talk to them both about playing centerfield in the old place, I looked at my watch and saw it was now Saturday morning.

"So did you like your first game at the new place?" I asked them both.

"We sure did, William," Mickey Mantle answered enthusiastically. "Maybe I'll bring Billy and the Scooter over too."

"On the day Mr. Steinbrenner comes through those pearly gates, please try to keep him and Billy from ripping each other's heads off. When they were together here on earth, they didn't always play nice," I requested.

"Being up here changes things," Mickey stated.

"I bet it does."

Always the classy gentleman, Joe D put it best.

"There's no place like our new home," he said. "It'll be even better when the current club hoists that twenty-seventh banner."

"We'll bring it home, guys. We'll bring it home."

Returning to reality, as I hung up from my fantasy phone call all I could do is smile, for I was now convinced that the 2009 New York Yankees would do the one thing that would bring past and present together as one.

I knew from that moment on that they would bring it home.

✪ ✪ ✪

Desperate times call for desperate measures.

Down two games to the Los Angeles Angels, the Red Sox Nation pinned their divisional series playoff hopes on the memory of one of their most famous postseason moments. Reaching back twenty-three years to a point where their season was down to their last strike, the Boston Red Sox trotted out Dave Henderson to throw out the ceremonial first pitch.

On an October Sunday in 1986, Henderson drove a Donnie Moore pitch into the sunny California skies and over the left-field fence, starting an American League Championship Series comeback versus the Angels that proved that no game or series is over until the final strike is recorded.

Now twenty-three years later, here were the Red Sox facing elimination by the Angels again. And here was Henderson again, surfacing in Fenway Park on a bright autumn Sunday, hoping along with 38,000 screaming fans that his appearance would awaken ghosts.

Briefly, Henderson's presence revived the championship hopes of all New England. For eight innings, two outs and two strikes of Game 3, the 2009 edition of the Red Sox recaptured a swagger; one that helped them knock the Angels out of the playoffs three times in the previous five years.

They held a 6-4 lead with two outs and no one on base in the ninth, and needed one more strike to finish off the batter at plate, Angels infielder Erick Aybar.

For clarification sake, let me say that again.

The Angels' ninth-place batter had two strikes, with Jonathan Papelbon, one of the game's most dominant closers, on the precipice of pitching the Red Sox to Monday.

One more strike would keep Boston alive.

One more strike.

One more strike.

Three times in the inning Jonathan Papelbon delivered what he and all of New England thought would be the game's last pitch.

He never got that last strike.

Refusing to go quietly, Aybar slapped a single to left. Then leadoff batter Chone Figgins walked on another two-strike pitch.

The Angels' next hitter, former Yankee Bobby Abreu, also faced a two-strike count. Remaining cool, calm and composed, Abreu ripped a double off the Green Monster, scoring Aybar, moving Figgins to third, and placing the Red Sox in a quandary. Should they pitch to the third-place hitter Torii Hunter, who was 3-for-7 in the series with a monster three-run homer; or free swinging cleanup batter Vladimir Guerrero, who was 2-for-12 lifetime against Papelbon?

Gambling, Boston Manager Terry Francona rolled the dice. Intentionally walking Hunter, he wanted Papelbon to pitch to Guerrero.

The dice he rolled bounced off the Green Monster, came up snake eyes, and ended the Red Sox season.

Swinging at the first pitch he saw—a straight fastball right down the middle of the plate, a pitch many scouting reports said he couldn't hit, Guerrero ripped a single to center, scoring Figgins and Abreu with the tying and series-winning runs.

Just like I had predicted when I saw them in late September, the Yankees' bitter rival couldn't flick that switch back on. For the first time since 2005, the Los Angeles Angels were on their way to the American League Championship Series.

And the Boston Red Sox and their Nation were going home.

I watched the game at the ESPN Zone in Times Square, and was cheering along with many of the Yankees fans when the Angels came back. Once the last out was recorded and the Red Sox were eliminated, you heard a thunderous roar in the upstairs restaurant area that rivaled one you would hear if the Yankees were playing.

The very things many in the bar areas were cheering about then would be the very things they would fear; provided the Yankees handled their business in Minnesota later on. An incredible collection of contact hitters, they posted a Major-League best .285 team batting average—the Yankees were second at .283—and hit 173 home runs in 2009, their most in nine seasons.

Offensively speaking, the American League West champs covered the whole spectrum. Wearing pitchers out with patience from a balanced lineup and rattling them with their trademark aggression on the base paths, four Angels hit 20 or more homers, eleven drove in at least 50 runs, and as a team they were third in the American League with 148 stolen bases.

ThunderStix and Rally Monkeys (Angels Stadium hallmarks) aside, this was a very dangerous team that was intoxicated with Manager Mike Scioscia's team-first mindset and played smart baseball all season long. With timely hitting, good pitching—Boston only scored seven runs in the series; six in the last game—and great defense, there was nothing fluky about the way the Angels swept the Red Sox Nation into the offseason. They were clearly the better team.

And recent history showed that they gave the New York Yankees fits. Not only did they lose two divisional series to the Angels during the decade (in 2002 and 2005), but the Angels were the only team that owned a winning record against the Yankees from 1996 to 2009. Accentuating this point, they won 7 of 10 against Joe Girardi's team in 2008, and split ten games in 2009.

Those three September wins were important, I thought as I sipped from a Corona. *They were huge for us psychologically.*

Beyond all the statistics, the Los Angeles Angels were on a mission to bring a championship to Anaheim. Bonded with passion and purpose, they were driven to win as a tribute to the memory of their fallen comrade Nick Adenhart, the rookie pitcher killed in a car collision in April.

They overcame a lot as a team, yet still had a great deal to play for.

All of this told me that my Yankees would have to raise their level of their game if they were going to bring a World Series to their new home.

Before all of that, however, they needed to close the Metrodome by beating the Twins.

And for the first six innings of Game 3 that Sunday night, the Yankees had all of us at the ESPN Zone mad as hell. It wasn't so much that they were locked in a great pitcher's duel that had everyone pissed.

It was *who* Andy Pettitte was dueling with that irked us.

It was Minnesota starter Carl Pavano that had us all messed up. After the 2004 season, the Yankees signed the right-hander to a $39.9 million contract. Rewarding the organization with four controversial seasons filled with injuries and what many New Yorkers thought of as apathy, he made a mere 26 starts in a Yankees uniform, producing only nine wins.

We thought he took our money and ran…to Cleveland, of all places. After getting nine wins for the Indians, he was traded to the Twins in August and compiled a 5-4 record in 12 starts during the stretch run.

Now here he was, silencing the New York bats through six innings. Effectively tailoring his performance around a split-fingered fastball and changeup, Pavano looked every bit the starting pitcher we wished he was for us. Mixing the movement of his pitches, he went right after Yankee batters by throwing strikes early, then finishing them off by having them chase balls out of the zone.

As stingy as Pavano was, he was matched zero for zero by Good Ol' Andy. Utilizing a cut fastball of his own, Pettitte retired the first twelve batters he faced, ending his Don Larsen-esque stretch with five strikeouts in his last eight batters. The only blemish on his performance came in the sixth inning, when with two outs Minnesota outfielder Denard Span hit a two-out single to center, then stole second base. After walking Orlando Cabrera, the veteran Yankees left-hander then faced the American League Batting Champion, Joe Mauer, who lined the first pitch he saw through the hole at short for an RBI single.

With the Twins up 1-0 and threatening for more, Pettitte quickly shut the door by striking out Michael Cuddyer.

"Damn," I yelled as I placed my Long Island Iced Tea on the counter.

That was pretty much the sentiment of the whole sports bar, many of whom came in Yankee paraphernalia ready to celebrate them moving on.

The festivities would be put on hold; at least temporarily.

To that point, Pavano was spotless. Haunting and taunting Yankees General Manager Brian Cashman, through six innings he allowed only three hits while striking out eight; and punctuated his outing by striking out Johnny Damon to end the sixth.

The stadium that did not want to close its doors sounded louder than ever before when Pavano retired Mark Teixeira to open the Yankees' seventh. Rising to their feet, 54,735 fans screamed for the Minnesota hurler to continue his brilliance, so the place that provided so many baseball moments through the late Kirby Puckett, Kent Hrbek, Frank Viola and Jack Morris could stay open one more night.

A locked-in Alex Rodriguez, however, needed to hear silence.

Stepping in to face Pavano, A-Rod quickly fell behind in the count, 0-2. Battling back, he took the next three pitches for balls. Next, he yanked a hard foul ball on the next pitch of the at-bat.

Rodriguez had seen six pitches—fastballs, sliders and a changeup—and had worked the count full.

Pavano's seventh pitch to him was a fastball right where he wanted it.

And suddenly, what was once a noisy, hankie-waving crowd became an incredibly silent place.

One crushing crack off the bat of a revitalized slugger had done the trick.

The ball went soaring, high and far to the opposite field, where it landed over the right-centerfield baggie fence and into the idle football seats.

The score was tied, and somewhere Brett Favre began his warmup tosses.

Those football tosses would get more intense two batters later. After Pavano struck out Hideki Matsui, Jorge Posada came to the plate, looking to hit the ball hard. Connecting on a 1-0 pitch, the left-handed hitting catcher drove a rope to left. As I watched the ball carry, I couldn't help but think of Kirby Puckett's spectacular catch against the Plexiglas extension in the 1991 World Series.

As the ball continued its flight, *Did they remove the glass?* I thought.

My answer came in a millisecond, as the ball barely cleared the glass-less wall for a first-row home run.

"Yes!" I screamed.

There was absolute bedlam in the ESPN Zone.

Meanwhile, in the Metrodome, what was once a rocking place was now an indescribable scene of horror for the Minnesota Twins fans. In all of my years of watching games that were played there, I never heard the place so quiet.

Someone at the bar yelled, "It's closing time!!!"

I couldn't agree with him more; Yankees fans were primed to close the pinball palace in Minnesota.

Nine more outs and it would be a reality.

When Andy Pettitte struck out Jason Kubel to start the bottom of the seventh, he had thrown 81 pitches. Allowing just one run on three hits, he had been absolutely dominant to this point.

That's why it shocked us all to see Joe Girardi come to the mound and take the ball from him.

"What is he doing?" one patron screamed.

Another Yankees fan was less diplomatic.

"He's gonna fuck it up by overmanaging!" he shouted.

Reluctantly, the place applauded Pettitte as he walked off the mound.

"Good Ol' Andy!" I yelled while clapping.

My mind, however, hoped that Girardi knew what he was doing.

At first, his decision immediately looked bad when Delmon Young greeted Joba Chamberlain with a double into right-center. To his credit, however, Chamberlain recovered to retire the next batter, Brendan Harris, on a groundout to third and struck out Jose Morales to end the inning.

In the eighth inning, his move looked even worse when Twins second baseman Nick Punto led off the inning with a double off a struggling Phil Hughes.

You could hear the ESPN Zone groan when the next batter, Denard Span, hit a soft chopper behind second base.

It's a tie game, was my thought.

Derek Jeter didn't think so. After corralling the bouncer just before it got into the outfield, these defensive instincts that leave us all shaking our heads instantly kicked in. Alertly, the Yankees captain threw home to Posada.

Punto, who inexplicably rounded third with his head down, was halfway home when he saw third-base coach Scott Ullger's stop sign too late. Desperately trying to halt his brakes, he made a sliding stop on the Metrodome turf to stop his momentum and scrambled to get back to third.

Posada, scooping up Jeter's one-hop throw, fired a strike to A-Rod, who calmly slapped the tag on a retreating Punto, then pumped his fist a la Tiger Woods.

I pumped my fist, too, and let out a yell.

"The Metrodome is officially closed!" I screamed amongst the pandemonium surrounding me.

With the air now deflated from the Metrodome's Teflon roof, Hughes settled down and got Orlando Cabrera to fly out to center. With two outs and Joe Mauer coming to the plate, the whole sports world knew what Girardi was going to do next.

Enter Sandman.

And once again, Mariano Rivera brought peace amidst a storm. Inducing Mauer to hit a broken-bat grounder to first, the greatest closer in baseball history watched the Yankees tack on two insurance runs in the ninth ; the courtesy of three walks and bases-loaded RBI singles by Posada and Robinson Cano off a still shell-shocked Joe Nathan.

And when Brendan Harris grounded to Jeter to end the game, a baseball team celebrated on the Metrodome carpet for the last time. It had taken five years, some wild spending sprees and many a first-round heartbreak. But the New York Yankees were back in the American League Championship Series, and four wins away from the World Series.

And the new Yankee Stadium still needed its seasonal staff.

While the feeling was good for the guys wearing the gray "New York" road jerseys, you could tell that their revelry was somewhat muted. That restraint traveled thousands of miles, to a sports bar named after the worldwide leader in all of sports. While there were some Yankees fans at the ESPN Zone that held on to a sense of entitlement—believing that it's our birth right to win the World Series every year—I hoped the past five years made them understand the difficulty of winning and advancing.

Sure I was happy that we won. But I also knew that a dangerous opponent in the Los Angeles Angels lay ahead.

There was more work for the 2009 New York Yankees to do.

And, more importantly, more work for me to do.

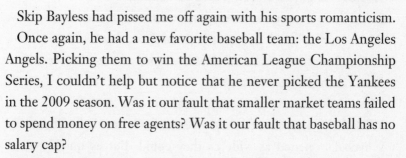

A HALO WAR: THE AMERICAN LEAGUE CHAMPIONSHIP SERIES

Skip Bayless had pissed me off again with his sports romanticism.

Once again, he had a new favorite baseball team: the Los Angeles Angels. Picking them to win the American League Championship Series, I couldn't help but notice that he never picked the Yankees in the 2009 season. Was it our fault that smaller market teams failed to spend money on free agents? Was it our fault that baseball has no salary cap?

While wondering why on earth this man had it in for the New York Yankees, my thoughts were interrupted by a phone call on my cell.

"William?"

"Yeah, Rick."

"Are you excited?"

"You better believe it. Again, I can't begin to tell you how much I appreciate what you did for me."

Sighing, the voice on the other end of the phone paused.

"Man, good people deserve good things. Now come meet me and my friend at the entrance of the Legends Suite Club at four-thirty."

"Sounds good. I'll see you then."

I couldn't believe it—I was going to Game 1 of the American League Championship Series.

Yeah, I had been to every game—save two—during the 2009 season.

But tonight, there was one small difference.

Instead of wearing my pinstriped shirt, polyester pants and matching vest with the Alliance Maintenance Company logo, on the night of October 16, 2009, I would be a Yankees fan in a suit.

And I had my friend Rick to thank. At the end of the Yankees' final regular-season night game—a 4-3 victory over the Kansas City Royals—a muscular man with dark hair and a confident smile approached me in the lower-level Legends men's room with an account executive of the Yankees.

"Here's the guy I've been telling you about," he says.

Befuddled, a myriad of thoughts ran through me. *Have I done something wrong? All I do is come to the stadium, do my job, root for the Yankees, then go home. God, it's William again. Are you listening?*

It was then the executive spoke.

"This gentleman here wants to treat you to a game."

With the excitement of a child given his favorite gift on Christmas, my eyeballs opened as wide as they could. But as quickly as an overwhelming joy filled me, it immediately turned to worry.

"I'd be honored, but I want to make sure it's okay with my company."

Rick gave me his number, and told me to call him in a couple of days.

On the way home that night, I thought of how sad I felt watching the various companies reward workers with Employee of the Month presentations behind home plate, and how the maintenance company never gave us any incentive for the hard work we did during the course of the season. Not that I felt unappreciated—hell, I was blessed to be working—but every now and then I wondered if they realized that some of us really put our heart and soul into what some people thought of as a thankless job.

Some of us were there for more than a paycheck.

Some of us also deserved more.

"Let's do it," I said to Rick the next morning. Ordering me a Legends ticket during the Minnesota playoff series, he also left me without an out.

The day before, I called in, only stating that "I had something to do."

Waffling back and forth as to whether I should go, Cheryl set the record straight over our midday lunch date.

"That man paid a lot of money for the ticket, so you better go," she said in front of her Park Avenue workplace.

"But what will the other workers think? The last thing in the world I want is anyone thinking that I'm better than them."

When they say behind every successful man is an even stronger woman cracking the whip, they were talking about my fiancée. Cheryl Faye Smith is a sweet woman with a bite that at times drives me crazy; but I know my entire being would be crazier without it. Whenever she detected my slightest fears, she would go into her phone booth, come out in her commando gear and feed me a healthy dose of tough love.

This was one of those moments where I needed to be bit.

Starting in a tender, yet stern tone, "William, you work hard as hell, and everyone deserves a break," she said. "You'd be a damn fool if you worried about what others think."

"But..."

"William, go have a nice time. Besides, you need to show those people at the stadium you're more than just a restroom attendant. You're a humble child of God, a fine man that's run across a little rough patch in life, a hell of an author, and you look good in that gray suit you're wearing. And above all else, I love you."

Well, damn, since she put it like that, how could I not go?

I felt like I was faster than a speeding bullet, more powerful than a locomotive, able to leap...

You get the picture.

Feeling like Cinderfella, I was going to the best ball in town: Game 1 of the American League Championship series at the new

Yankee Stadium. My iron horse and carriage, the Bronx-bound D train, would get me there, and the only difference at this party was that 50,000 people hoped the Los Angeles Angels would turn into pumpkins at midnight.

From the minute I met Rick and his buddy at the Legends Suite Club entrance, I experienced something that removed all of my concern. Eliminating my uneasiness was the fact that many of the Legends' employees showered me with kindness as they catered to my every need.

"It couldn't have happened to a nicer guy," was what many of them said.

Hearing that meant the world to me; Lord knows, I tried to make everyone from the Legends busboys and servers to Yankee ownership feel like the most important person in the world.

During my one season in pinstripes, I wanted the experience to be memorable to whoever crossed my path.

And for one night, the favor was returned a thousand times over.

Many of the season-ticket holders that I catered to in the men's restroom were buying me drinks throughout the evening, so much so that it got to a point where I was turning them away.

Mitch Modell, the CEO of the Modell's Sporting Goods chain, paid me a wonderful compliment that evening.

"You don't belong in a restroom," he said. "This is where you belong, right out here making people feel good."

It was an unforgettable experience dining in the Legends Suite Club, a moment made even greater when I watched the game from my fourth-row seat down the right-field line, just past the first base dugout. Sitting with so many familiar faces from the Suite Club, many of us were oblivious to the chilly forty-five-degree temperature.

That's because C.C. Sabathia, the Yankees' Game 1 starter, was blazing hot.

Firing fastballs fearlessly at the Angels lineup, the Yankees ace handcuffed a team that beat him twice during the regular season by working both sides of the plate effectively.

From where I was seated, you could see that the big left-hander had total command on his fastball and even better control of his sensational slider. Amazed by the velocity and crispness of his pitches—late in the game, he audaciously used changeups with two strikes—so powerful was his eight-inning/one-run/four-hit/seven-strikeout effort, that the crowd repeatedly chanted the initials of the big lefty when he got two strikes on an Angels batter.

It was a dominant pitching performance that made the 50,000 in attendance feel like the game was never in doubt. I spent more time enjoying the company surrounding me and looking at the left-field flags whip around in the wind than I did worrying about the Los Angeles Angels.

"Rick, this is amazing," I said. "Thank you, man."

"You deserve it, man," he kept saying.

About the fifth inning or so, I sat back in my blue cushioned chair, relaxed, and soaked in my temporary reality. Yes, I deserved this. For one night, I was seated with many of New York City's power brokers and brightest minds, and it felt good receiving the love from so many of my friends in the Legends Suite Club; the love I so desperately tried to give to them was being returned tenfold.

And to top it all off, the Yankees won.

Oh, for a second there, I forgot about the playoff game recap.

Because of C.C.'s dominance, the Bronx Bombers only needed two runs, and got them in the first inning. Derek Jeter started the game with an eight-pitch at-bat against Angels pitcher John Lackey, one that culminated with a sharp single to right. Johnny Damon flicked another single to left, sending the Yankees captain to third. He would take second when leftfielder Juan Rivera made a terrible throw to the middle of the infield.

Rivera's throw was a portent of things to come for the Angels, who uncharacteristically had a bad fielding day. After A-Rod drove in Jeter with a one-out sacrifice fly to center, Hideki Matsui lifted a pop-up that twisted in the wind above Angels shortstop Erick Aybar and third baseman Chone Figgins.

Aybar, wearing a bright red ski mask that covered his ears—a balaclava—couldn't hear Figgins yelling for him to make the catch, and thought the third baseman would corral it. Looking at each other with helpless, befuddled looks on their faces, the ball fell to the earth, finding its place on the edge of the outfield grass as Damon scored the Yankees' second run.

After the Angels closed the gap to 2-1—a Kendry Morales fourth-inning single drove in Vladimir Guerrero, who had earlier doubled—the Pinstripes made sure my dream night would end on a high note. Damon got his second hit of the night when he opened the fifth with a double to left-center; and after a one-out walk to Rodriguez, he came home on Matsui's double to left. Rodriguez, running with his head down, also tried to score, but was tagged out in a collision at the plate.

From there, C.C. just closed the show. The Yankees would add a run in the sixth—thanks to an RBI single by Jeter—however, the night belonged to Sabathia, who punctuated an inning-ending, seventh-inning strikeout of Angels catcher Mike Napoli by pumping his fist and shouting. One inning later, he placed his masterpiece on the shelf, and allowed Mariano Rivera to close the game with a hitless ninth.

With a 4-1 victory, the Yankees drew first blood in their "Halo War."

And because of a special friend—thanks, so much, Rick, wherever you are—I went home with an experience that best exemplifies how the New York Yankees bring people from all walks of life together.

The night belonged not only to C.C. Sabathia, but to a certain restroom attendant whose dream season in pinstripes was getting better by the second.

✪ ✪ ✪

The next afternoon, I was worried that I might be reprimanded for taking in a game.

Luckily, that was not the case.

"I would have done the same thing," one of my supervisors said when I arrived at work.

Between workers, news travels around the new Yankee Stadium like a brushfire.

"Why didn't you tell me you were going to the game?" Paula Collins, the general manager of the Stadium Cleaning Operations of First Quality Management, an Alliance Affiliate, asked me.

Lowering my head, I blurted out an excuse.

"I didn't want to upset the apple cart. I just figured I call in and come to a ballgame. Besides, I didn't want my colleagues to think I was better than them just because I was blessed with a ticket to a game."

"Let me know something next time, because people saw you having a drink and didn't realize you weren't working."

"I'm sorry, Paula."

Leaving her maintenance office before I knew whether she wrote me up or not, *some things in life are just worth getting in trouble for*, I mused.

✪ ✪ ✪

The Los Angeles Angels would be in a little trouble if they lost Game Two of the American League Championship series. Finding their vaunted running game neutralized by C.C. Sabathia, the one edge the Halos possessed over the pinstripes was non-existent in Game 1. It was strange seeing an Angels game sans the first-to-third dashes, stolen bases or the aggressive base-running high jinks that usually drove the Yankees crazy.

You could sense their desperation as they took the field for the start of ALCS Game 2. While going home to games at the Big A, a 2-0 hole against the Yankees would not be endearing to their California faithful. Such urgency would be reflected in their surprise starter, Joe Saunders.

In a move that left many people scratching their heads, Angels Manager Mike Scioscia bypassed Jered Weaver, a pitcher who gave him a superb outing in ALCS Game 2 against the Red Sox, for a left-handed sinkerball artist; one that would be pitching in a ballpark suited for the powerful Yankee lineup.

This point was immediately brought home in the Yankees' half of third, when Derek Jeter slammed a shot to right. Challenging strong winds, the drive cleared the fence, giving the captain his nineteenth career postseason home run—third most all time—and more importantly, the Yankees a 2-0 lead. (Robinson Cano drove in the game's first run with a two-out triple in the second.)

The stadium crowd, believing they had Saunders on the ropes, rocked once more.

Five innings later, however, you could hear a pin drop. Validating his manager's faith in him, Saunders pitched seven sparkling innings, allowing six hits while striking out seven. Working deep into the game to preserve the Angels' bullpen—as it turned out, they would need it later—he was not without his trouble spots; but the fact that he escaped trouble can be attributed to his sinkerball. Inducing ground balls at the most opportune times, in his final three innings he produced three double plays.

The first one came in the fifth. When Melky Cabrera and Jose

Molina opened the inning with successive singles, Saunders bore down and got Jeter to ground weakly back to the mound, starting a 1-6-3 twin-killing that took the air out of their rally. Another double play, started by Kendry Morales at first, got Saunders out of the sixth after a throwing error by third baseman Chone Figgins. And Saunders escaped trouble again when Hideki Matsui erased pinch-runner Brett Gardner with a third double play in the seventh.

By this point, the Angels had finally entered the series. Leading off the fifth, second baseman Macier Izturis hit a ground-rule double off Yankees starter A.J. Burnett; then scored one out later when Erik Aybar grounded a single to center to make the score 2-1, Yankees.

After Aybar stole second, Burnett hit Figgins with a pitch, putting two runners on. Bobby Abreu fouled out to left for the second out, then centerfielder Torii Hunter walked to load the bases. Burnett wild-pitched Hunter's ball four into the stands and the umpires had to send Aybar, who was trying to score from second, back to third.

Determined to make sure the Angels tied the score, Burnett threw another wild pitch to the next hitter, Vladimir Guerrero, one that he swung at and missed. The ball got away from Yankees catcher Jose Molina and Aybar raced home with the tying run.

When Guerrero grounded out to Jeter to end the inning, a chorus of boos rained down.

It wasn't pretty, but after one game and four innings, the Los Angeles Angels had joined the war.

I made mention of that point in the lower Legends men's room.

"It looks like we have a series, gentlemen," I announced.

"You had better believe it," a muscular man wearing an Angels polo shirt replied. Having met this man earlier in the season, he was a member of their organization—I assumed that was the case, because he traveled with a group that looked like Angel ownership—one that I had told in May that they would be returning for the playoffs.

"Welcome back, sir. But you know I can't wish you good luck," I said with a smile.

"Feels good to be back," the gentleman said.

"You know, I just wanted you to know that I respect the Angels ballclub more than you'll ever know. Over the years, you guys have had our number."

"Thanks," the man said.

Introducing ourselves, his last name was Jolly, and he confirmed my assumption—years later, I am fully recovered from the 2004 ALCS fiasco—by indicating he was a member of the Angels family.

When he mentioned family, I immediately thought of the Adenhart family.

"Mr. Jolly, I'm really sorry about the Adenhart family. It's another reason why I respect your organization so much."

Pausing, he seemed surprised that I would even know.

"Are all the people here like you?" he asked.

I smiled, but didn't answer the question.

I wasn't supposed to.

"I read about it in the papers," I said.

"The Angels dedicated the season to his family. It would be pretty cool to win it all," Mr. Jolly said.

My emotions agreed with him—he saw my eyes water—but I couldn't jump on the bandwagon.

He read my face, and continued.

"I know you're a Yankee fan, so you can't agree with that," he said.

"Thanks, man. You enjoy the game, sir."

That was the only time during my dream season where I wavered. But before he left the restroom, I admitted this.

"Hey," I said, gently placing my hand on his shoulder, "If the Yankees don't win this series, then the Angels are the team I would like to see win the whole thing."

That was our little secret...until now.

And so the game went on. Other than his fifth-inning lapse in control, A.J. Burnett was magnificent. Using a darting fastball that moved in, out and around the strike zone and a curveball that froze Angel batters, Burnett struck out four, allowed just three hits and held the Angels to those two runs in his 6-1/3 innings.

He left the Yankees in a pickle in the seventh: Burnett departed with one out, after Robinson Cano's error on Erick Aybar's grounder. Reliever Phil Coke walked Figgins and struck out Bobby Abreu. Joe Girardi then brought on Joba Chamberlain to face Torii Hunter, whose infield hit loaded the bases for cleanup hitter Vladimir Guerrero.

With the crowd screaming at a fever pitch, Chamberlain blew two fastball strikes by the Angels slugger, then got Guerrero swinging on a breaking ball to leave the bases loaded. It would be a long night for Guerrero, who left eight runners stranded on throughout the contest.

After the seventh, it was a battle of bullpens. Matching the Angels' brilliance was Mariano Rivera. Entering the game with two on in the eighth, Rivera struck out Aybar to end the Angels' threat, then pitched two more scoreless innings.

But here is where it gets tricky: As opposed to allowing Phil Hughes to pitch out his own trouble, Girardi used Rivera to end the eighth inning, a move that rendered him useless in the eleventh.

That was the inning the Angels finally made the Bronx Bombers blink. Alfredo Aceves, the Yankees' regular-season long-relief specialist, allowed a leadoff walk to Gary Matthews Jr., who then took second on a bunt. Chone Figgins, hitless in 19 postseason at-bats, finally broke through. Drilling a double to left to drive in Matthews, he pulled into second and punched his fist in the air.

His hit silenced the stadium.

The Angels now had a 3-2 lead, and were just three outs from taking a bite from the Big Apple, and sending the city into panic.

Matching the Yankees' bullpen effectiveness with their own stout relief, Kevin Jepsen (two scoreless innings) and Darren Oliver (a scoreless tenth) shut the Pinstripes down, and had the sellout crowd worried.

One of the things I learned early in this playoff season was that whenever the Yankees were in trouble, a true Yankee bailed them out or led them from dangerous waters. Before the 2009 postseason, I would only think that the Yankee gods smiled only on Jeter or Posada in pressure-packed moments.

However, this season in pinstripes was about redemption, in every way imaginable. The Yankees needed deliverance from the post-season doldrums; not to mention the 2008 absence from it altogether. Before my season in pinstripes, I needed a personal redemption; for before taking the job at the church, then the stadium, the potential of my life seemed unrealized.

And leading off the bottom of the eleventh, a certain Yankee, Alex Rodriguez, stepped into the batters box against Angels closer Brian Fuentes needed more redemption from his past. Fuentes led the majors with 48 saves, but also led the league with seven blow opportunities. Confident with the former, Fuentes went after A-Rod aggressively. Getting ahead of him with two strikes on fastballs, he wanted to get him to chase a high, hard one for strike three, but his next offering tailed outside.

A-Rod took the pitch up, up and away, to right-field and through a biting wind and intense rainfall. Having flashbacks to when he played right field for the Yankees, Bobby Abreu gave it a good chase, and leaped at the wall. But his effort went for naught: the ball barely cleared the fence and hit a fan in the first row for a game-tying home run.

A-Rod had done it again. Continuing his postseason power-hitting binge with his third homer—his second, game-tying blast—all eight of his playoff RBIs had come on hits that either tied or put the Yankees ahead.

With one swing, he took care of the Angels lead, and brought the love down from the Yankees fans all over.

The Legends Suite Club went crazy.

Jumping up and down, I was exchanging hi-fives with everyone in the place. I knew the Yankees were going to win.

And in the bottom of the 13th, after five hours of baseball, they made Dave Robertson a Game 2 winner for the second time in the playoffs.

In actuality, it was the normally fundamentally sound Angels who fashioned this finish. Leading off the inning, Jerry Hairston, in his first postseason at-bat, singled off Angels pitcher Ervin Santana. After Brett Gardner bunted him to second and Robinson Cano was intentionally walked, Melky Cabrera hit a bouncer between first and second base.

Fielding the ball, Maicer Izturis, looking for the force at second made an ill-advised attempt at throwing the ball across his body. Hurling it wide past shortstop Erick Aybar, the ball rolled behind third, where Chone Figgins, in a hurry to make a play at the plate, dropped it.

Hairston, running all the way from second, went flying around third once he saw Izturis' errant toss skip by Aybar and slid home safely with the winning run.

In another ironic twist, the Yankees' small ball produced a 4-3 victory and a 2-0 series lead.

While happy that the Yankees were traveling west with a commanding advantage, I felt bad for Mr. Jolly, who I saw leaving the stadium. Between our chat in the restroom and the Angels' implosion, he and his wife had been harassed so severely that I felt the need to apologize for the obnoxiousness of some of my Yankee family.

"I can take the taunting," he said. "But when it becomes personal, and they direct the insults at my wife..."

"I understand," I responded, cutting him off. "I'm so sorry."

Before I could say another word to him, he and his wife were gone.

I wanted to tell him this: the greatest feeling in the world is when after you've endured a bunch of crap in someone else's backyard, you render them silent with your sweet sound of victory. The triumph becomes extra special, because you keep your mouth shut while others ran theirs, and maintained that silent humility after you kicked their ass.

I wanted to share that information with Mr. Jolly.

And for some strange reason, I knew I would see him again.

✪ ✪ ✪

On the third pitch of Game 3, Derek Jeter took his first swing of the game and sent Angels starter Jered Weaver's offering into the left-field bullpen. The Yankees' captain's third career postseason lead-off homer was followed three innings later by another solo blast into the left-field bleachers, courtesy of Alex Rodriguez. And in the fifth inning, Johnny Damon connected with a drive of his own. Taking advantage of a short porch in right field, Damon's shot barely cleared the three-foot wall.

Angel Stadium was lifeless.

Deflating the crowd's Thunderstix—those inflatable plastic red tubes Angels fans banged together, creating a deafening sound that energized the home team—the Yankees had gotten off to another impressive start. With Andy Pettitte throwing strikes, their three-run advantage appeared larger to many of the Yankee faithful watching the game at ESPN Zone.

Already, some of the bar patrons were thinking ahead to bigger game.

"Wouldn't it be cool if we faced the Dodgers in the series?" someone asked me.

Before I could answer, an intrusive Yankees fan screamed, "Joe Torre's coming back to the Bronx!"

Chuckling to myself, I knew that the Philadelphia Phillies, the defending world champions and Los Angeles Dodgers' opponent in the National League Championship Series, wouldn't play the foil to what most baseball romantics wanted.

"The Dodgers aren't winning that series. The Phillies will be waiting for us," I responded.

Trying to become the fourth National League team ever to win back-to-back championships (joining the 1907-08 Chicago Cubs, 1921-22 New York Giants and Cincinnati's "Big Red Machine" of 1975-76), the Phillies were hungry to create a dynasty; and showed this to all of baseball with two midseason acquisitions: Cleveland's Cliff Lee, the 2008 AL Cy Young winner; and an old Yankee nemesis, three-time Cy Young Award recipient Pedro Martinez.

This was a team that kicked ass and took names.

They were ahead in their series, and would be waiting.

"Let's worry about finishing off the Angels," I continued.

Up 3-0 in the fifth and Pettitte seemingly on his way to his sixteenth career postseason victory, the Yankees were threatening to make short work of the ALCS. To that point, the Angels lineup hadn't done much against Yankee pitching. Hitting just .154 as a team, their power numbers were even worse: No one from the AL West Champs went deep in the entire playoffs.

Someone had to step up, end their power outage, and show the Yankees they weren't going to just roll over.

Enter Howie Kendrick, a part-time infielder and certified Yankee-killer. The proud owner of a career .400 batting average against New York pitching, the Angels' second baseman sized up a cut fastball from Pettite and blasted a home run to left to cut the lead to 3-1.

While Angels Stadium and their dugout were feeding off this in-fusion of hope, I immediately thought of how the Yankees squandered a pair of scoring opportunities in the second and fourth innings that could have blown the game wide open. With runners on first and third with one out in both frames, Nick Swisher and Melky Cabrera let Weaver off the hook by not coming through.

Those lost chances, coupled with Pettitte's constant attention to Angel base runners—attempting to stifle their aggression, he attempted nineteen pickoff throws through six innings—came back to haunt the Yankees in the sixth.

With two outs, Bobby Abreu singled, and cleanup hitter Vladimir Guerrero came up. Coming into the game, the slugging cleanup hitter had gone just 2-for-11 in the ALCS; leaving ten runners stranded on base in the process. In an effort to stir motivation within, hitting coach Mickey Hatcher approached him during a team workout the day before, and showed him what the media was writing about him.

Many sportswriters thought he was finished.

Riled up by the premature reports of his demise, Guerrero battled Pettitte in a situation where his team needed him to come through. Fouling off three great pitches, he took two more for balls, then received an inside fastball that was just off the plate.

The pitch, Pettitte said later, was a mistake.

With one swing, Guerrero made him pay.

Pulling the ball down the left-field line, there was never a doubt about the blast, one that not only tied the game, but sent Angel Stadium into pandemonium.

Damn! We just let them back in the series.

I shook my head with disgust.

Rejuvenated and revitalized, the big bash reminded me of that scene in *Rocky IV*, when the underdog Balboa, backed in a corner and being pummeled in the second round, landed a four-punch combination that bloodied villain Ivan Drago. Seeing the Angels' dugout, I could imagine what Manager Mike Scoiscia was saying to his troops.

It probably went something like this:

"They're hurting! They're cut! You see men, the New York Yankees are not a big, bad baseball machine…They're men just like us! Now let's go get 'em!"

And like sharks smelling blue blood in their waters, the Los Angeles Angels attacked their wounded prey. Pettitte, after getting the first out of the seventh, was removed by Joe Girardi. Summoning Joba Chamberlain, this was the first of two moves by the Yankees manager that called into question his use of his bullpen.

Chamberlain was greeted rudely by Kendrick, who boomed a triple off the right-field scoreboard. Pinch-hitter Maicer Izturis, whose error at second ended Game 2, followed with a go-ahead sacrifice fly to put the Angels ahead, 4-3.

The capacity crowd went crazy.

Fueled by their frenzy, in the eighth inning the American League West Champions correctly called pitchout when, with Jorge Posada batting, Brett Gardner attempted to steal second. They guessed right, and Gardner was thrown out at second. Nearly 45,000 Angels fans erupted, as they sensed that the Yankees were dead.

Jorge Posada thought otherwise. Two pitches later, the Yankees catcher blasted a Kevin Jepsen fastball to dead center. Raising his arm briefly as he sprinted past first, within seconds the stadium went silent once more.

The ball cleared the fence, and just like that, the score was tied at 4.

And it stayed that way through regulation and the tenth inning, in large part because the Angels were shooting themselves in the foot. Leading off the bottom of the eighth, Bobby Abreu laced a long double to center off reliever Phil Coke, but overran the bag and tried to scramble back. Derek Jeter, backing up the play, took the throw from center and immediately whirled and fired a strike to Mark Teixeira, who covered second.

By the time Abreu reached second, the Yankees first baseman was waiting for him with a tag.

In the tenth inning, another opportunity at victory slipped from their grasp. Leading off the frame, catcher Jeff Mathis hammered a double off Phil Hughes. After Girardi replaced Hughes with Mariano Rivera, shortstop Erick Aybar bunted Mathis over to third, and reached base when the Yankees closer tried to nail Mathis at third. The errant throw bounced past Alex Rodriguez, but Mathis couldn't advance, because Johnny Damon backed up the play.

With the Yankee infield in to cut off the runner at third, Chone Figgins grounded out to first. The next batter, Abreu, was walked intentionally to load the bases with the heart of their lineup coming up.

With the crowd pumped up, Rivera showed why he is the best relief pitcher the game has ever known. Effectively slamming the door on the Angels' rally, he induced ground ball outs from Torii Hunter and Vladimir Guerrero, ending the inning...as well as his stint on the mound. Because he was used to get seven outs on Saturday, manager Girardi did not want him to go any further, so he brought in Dave Robertson to start the eleventh inning.

The Yankees fans in ESPN Zone clearly understood Girardi's reasoning when removing Rivera from the fray.

But what we all didn't understand is his trip to the mound after Robertson retired the first two batters without incident.

What is he doing? I thought when I saw Alfredo Aceves take the ball. *Why tinker with something that's not broke?*

Quietly I thought this, but the collective groans in the sports bar understood my muse.

"What in the hell is he doing?" someone yelled.

"He's over-managing again!" another screamed. "He's gonna lose the game trying to play genius."

Facing a red-hot Howie Kendrick, Aceves threw him four cut fastballs, the last of which grounded up the middle for a single.

You should have heard the expletives fly then.

And you think they were bad then?

What happened next brought the place down. On a 0-1 fastball, catcher Jeff Mathis, a .211 hitter who was only in the lineup because of his outstanding defensive work and handling the pitching staff, blasted a double off the left-field wall. Motoring at top speed, Kendrick flew around the bases, scoring the game-winning run on a pop-up slide at home. Mathis, standing on second, threw his helmet to the infield dirt and pointed to his mother and grandmother in the stands.

As the Yankees trudged slowly off the field, victims of their first postseason loss, Angels Stadium exploded.

I can't say that I saw this one coming.

But with C.C. Sabathia taking the mound for Game 4, you better believe I knew how the Bronx Bombers would respond.

✪ ✪ ✪

They would respond with a vengeance.

For more than one reason, Game 4, a dominant 10-1 Yankee victory over a team with the second best record in baseball, wasn't pretty to watch.

If you were an Angels fan, that is.

One would have thought C.C. Sabathia, pitching on three days' rest, would find his effectiveness compromised.

Quite the contrary.

Gliding through eight innings and 101 pitches, Sabathia gave up just one run—a fifth-inning solo homer by Angels first baseman Kendry Morales—on five hits and a run while striking out five. With his fastball registering 95-miles-per-hour on the speed guns, his wicked sliders freezing left-handed hitters and a devastating changeup fooling right-handers, for the third time in the postseason he made Manager Joe Girardi look like a genius.

He only faced two jams; in the fifth and sixth innings. After giving up the Morales homer, he gave up successive singles to catcher Mike Napoli and Erick Aybar. With the Angel stadium crowd roaring for a comeback, Sabathia escaped further harm by getting Figgins to bounce into a force and Bobby Abreu on a fly ball.

In the sixth, the big lefty walked centerfielder Torii Hunter and allowed a bloop single to Vladimir Guerrero, but stopped the rally cold by getting Juan Rivera to ground into a double play and a red-hot Howie Kendrick on a lineout to first.

In contrast to Sabathia, his counterpart, Scott Kazmir, struggled throughout. The Angels left-hander, acquired from the Tampa Bay Rays in August, avoided trouble in the second and third innings, but the Yankees broke through in the fourth. Continuing his unconscious postseason, Alex Rodriguez started things with a single and took third on a double by Jorge Posada. Next up, Robinson Cano hit a slow roller to second. With the infield playing in, second baseman Kendrick charged the ball and threw home, but his throw was high as A-Rod slid under Mike Napoli's tag.

After Nick Swisher walked to load the bases, Melky Cabrera's gave the Yankees a 3-0 lead when he chopped a two-run single to left. The inning could have been worse, but Swisher negated Johnny Damon's sacrifice fly when he was called out for leaving third base early.

Kazmir would only last four more pitches; a line drive single by Mark Teixeira ended his night. His final line—four innings, six hits, four runs and four walks—was not what the Angels expected from him when they made that August trade.

On a hunch, Mike Scoiscia brought in Jason Bulger, a reliever who had struck out the next Yankee batter, Alex Rodriguez, in Game

One. Bringing heat, he got a quick strike on A-Rod, then uncorked another 92-miles-per-hour fastball.

That was a bad move, one that moved the Los Angeles Angels to the brink of playoff elimination.

Guessing correctly, A-Rod unloaded on it, and the Yankees had a five-run lead.

Trotting around the bases briskly, the one-man wrecking crusade that was Alex Rodriguez had his fifth homer in seven postseason games and had driven in a run in his eighth straight postseason game, tying the Major League record. Long considered a player who was smothered by the postseason pressure, in 2009 Alex Rodriguez was obliterating that label. By night's end, his 3-for-4 performance brought his playoff totals to the following: a .407 batting average (11 for 27) with five homers, 11 runs batted in and nine runs.

The Yankees would add five more runs—two of them coming on an eighth-inning long ball by Johnny Damonb—ut the game would be remembered more for C.C. Sabathia and his lights-out performance…And another whiff by the umpires. With runners on second and third and one out in the fifth, Nick Swisher bounced a comebacker to Angels pitcher Darren Oliver, who threw home to get Jorge Posada in a rundown. Posada got back to third but overran it, and Robinson Cano, the runner on second, stopped a few feet shy of the base. Catcher Mike Napoli tagged both runners off the bag, but umpire Tim McClelland ruled Cano safe at third.

Both runners were supposed to be called out.

Fortunately for Yankees fans, the blown call had nothing to do with the game's outcome, a rout that put the Pinstripes in a position they were last in way back in 2004.

And because all of New York knew what happened then, seizing the end of the series when the end was *this close* was critical. Wanting the New York Yankees to move far away from that moment as possible, while I would have loved to see the Bombers clinch a home—

another workday for all the seasonal workers, I thought—I also knew that the Los Angeles Angels may have been down three games to one but were definitely not out. They were still on an emotional crusade, and when battling more than a team on the baseball diamond, anything was still possible.

The sooner the Yankees finished them, the better.

The sooner the Yankees finished them, the sooner I would be going to my first World Series game ever.

✪ ✪ ✪

"Not in our house," the Angels said.

By the bottom of the seventh, there were twenty cases of champagne in the tunnel outside the visitors' clubhouse, ready to be popped.

I think someone made the Los Angeles Angels aware of them, and to a man who decided that the corks would remain sealed.

"Not in our house," they said as one.

Playing their biggest game of the season, the American League West champions had just received a knockout punch by way of a six-run Yankee seventh. Staggered, stunned and stupefied, they were struggling to rise from the canvas.

In the first inning, they thought the survival statement was made while showing the Yankees the difference between a team having the time of their lives, and one fighting for it. Coming out smoking, they immediately went on the attack against starter A.J. Burnett. After leadoff batter Chone Figgins walked on five straight fastballs, Burnett, continuing to follow his game plan of throwing strikes early in the count, served another fastball to Bobby Abreu, who promptly drilled a bullet to deep right-center. Figgins, flying around the bases, put on the brakes and stopped at third as Abreu cruised into second with a double.

Finally throwing a curveball, Burnett saw Torii Hunter rip a two-run single up the middle.

Nothing worked. Turning on another first-pitch fastball, Vladimir Guerrero smoked a double to left center, scoring Hunter. Now facing Kendry Morales, Burnett tried two curveballs, missed with them, then attempted to sneak a heater past him.

Morales smacked it over Derek Jeter's head, giving the Angels a commanding 4-0 lead.

With each Angel run, the sellout crowd at the Big A screamed, "Not in our house!"

Instead of a quick California celebration, A.J. Burnett and his Yankee teammates had walked into an ambush.

And the crowd at ESPN Zone was just as shocked as they were. In that first inning, you could hearing a symphony of groans, followed by a tense quiet as the Yankee bats, after threatening in the first inning—they started the game with two singles and came up empty—remained silent through the next five.

The Angels' starter on the hill had a lot to do with that. Pitching beautifully, John Lackey came up huge as his breaking ball kept New York off-balance and his heater produced seven strikeouts in six shutout innings. He was throwing so well that going into seventh, many of the Yankees fans in the lower level of the sports bar thought it was time for the Bronx Bombers to devise a recovery plan for Game 6.

Seated to my right were a couple of Angels fans—what they were doing in New York City is beyond me—and one of them yelled at the flat-screen monitors, "Put away that champagne and get out the Poland Spring water!"

Glaring at the red-haired gentleman, who was sipping a Long Island Iced Tea, a confidence invaded my bloodstream as I motioned to the bartender and turned to face my trash-talking friend.

"Excuse me," I said, politely interrupting his conversation while pointing to his drink, "Would you like another?"

Nodding yes, he responded, "That's very nice of you."

As the drink came to him, I responded to his arrogance, "You're going to need that."

Those close by laughed.

Three-thousand miles away, the Yankees heard that comment as well, and rewarded me for my faith. With one out, Melky Cabrera doubled to left-center, bringing Jorge Posada off the bench to pinch-hit for Jose Molina. With the count full at 3-2, Lackey threw a terrific fastball that appeared to catch the bottom edge of the strike zone.

All the replays would later indicate that the pitch looked like a strike at Posada's knees. But the pitch wasn't good enough for home-plate umpire Fieldin Culbreth, who called the pitch a ball. Protesting vehemently, Lackey spread his arms and screamed at the umpire, but his protest was in vain.

Clearly rattled, the Halos' ace walked Derek Jeter on four pitches to load the bases; but recovered to get Johnny Damon out on a short fly to left. He was about to settle in and face Mark Teixeira when Mike Scoiscia came to the hill. Protesting once more, Lackey pleaded with his manager to let him pitch out of the jam, but Scoiscia's mind overruled his own gut—he too thought about leaving in Lackey— and he brought in left-hander Darren Oliver.

There's a saying about following your gut that the Angels' skipper completely forgot about; one that says that your gut instinct is usually the correct instinct.

Reminding him of this, Teixeira blasted Oliver's first pitch to the wall in left-center, clearing the bases with a three-run triple. Taking no chances with A-Rod, the Angels intentionally walked the red-hot slugger, and Hideki Matsui made them pay with a game-tying RBI single to center.

That lower bar at ESPN Zone exploded. And when you thought the place couldn't get any louder, Robinson Cano's two-run triple into the right center-field gap had his teammates spilling onto the field.

The New York Yankees, nine outs away from their 40th American League championship, had knocked the Angels down with a mind-numbing comeback. Up two runs, they could taste the bubbly.

However, the team in the other dugout refused to quit.

After the rough start, A.J. Burnett had went into shutdown mode, pitching five shutout innings. His brilliance—only 80 pitches through sixth innings—placed his manager in a dilemma. Nine outs away from the pennant, should Joe Girardi use his bullpen to close the show, or should he stick with Burnett?

Opting to choose the latter, he let Burnett start the seventh.

The Angels quickly went back to work. Jeff Mathis, Game 3's hero, started the rally with a single; his sixth hit in a row in the playoffs. After Erick Aybar walked, Girardi brought in left-handed reliever Damaso Marte. Chone Figgins bunted the runners over to second and third and Bobby Abreu delivered a run-scoring grounder, cutting the Yankee lead to 6-5.

With two outs and runner on third, Joe Girardi summoned Phil Hughes to get the final out of the inning. But Hughes walked Torii Hunter, then left a two-strike fastball in the zone for cleanup hitter Vladimir Guerrero. Hacking away, the Angels' designated hitter sent bedlam through the stadium by sending a ball past a diving Jeter, scoring Aybar with his single and tying the game at 6.

Completing his meltdown, Hughes quickly fell behind Kendry Morales, who singled sharply through the right side, bringing home Hunter with the lead run.

Putting my head into my hands, I closed my eyes and muttered, "damn." The frenzied crowd cheered so loudly that it deflated the hopes of a pro-Yankees sports bar on the other side of the country.

"Girardi did it again!" one patron screamed.

"We better win this series," another warned. "Or he's gone."

Picking my head up to join in the frustration, I saw a drink in front of me.

I looked right, and saw a wicked smile.

"Touché," the Angels fan said.

After Jered Weaver further electrified the crowd striking out two in a 1-2-3 eighth, the Yankees had one last chance to close the ALCS show on the road. With the bases empty and two outs in the ninth, Angels closer Brian Fuentes walked Alex Rodriguez intentionally. Then he walked Hideki Matsui and hit Robinson Cano with a pitch.

Putting fear in the California air, he got two quick strikes on Nick Swisher, but ran the count full. Staying alive with a foul tip, the next pitch the Yankees right-fielder saw, an 89-miles-per-hour fastball right down the middle of the plate, was the pitch he was looking for. Swinging, all of Orange County, California screamed with the joy that came with a few more days of baseball added to their season. With the popup finding its place in the glove of shortstop Erik Aybar, the Angels held off the sunset of their emotional hurricane with a thrilling 7-6 come-from-behind victory.

The Halo war was not over.

Back to the Bronx we go, I sighed. While I was sad that we lost a closely fought battle, I found solace in the fact that Good Ol' Andy would be on the hill when we returned home.

✪ ✪ ✪

One of the best camera shots in recent baseball memory is when Andy Pettitte toes the pitching rubber. Total concentration oozing from his pores, his body is a portrait of intensity. And the vision of Pettitte's focused pupils sends a chilling message to those who dare suggest that he was merely a bystander of some fortunate timing in Yankee history.

Those eyes speak words he need not say; that he has the heart of a lion this time of year.

When the skies opened up and pushed Saturday's Game 6 to Sunday night, many in the media thought Yankee Manager Joe Girardi might again go with C.C. Sabathia on three days' rest. After all, Sabathia had given the Yankees two lights-out performances—three counting his dominant start against the Twins in the ALCS—and owned a sparkling 1.13 playoff earned-run average versus the Angels.

But could Big Lefty talk about a 1-0 1996 pitcher's duel with John Smoltz, a victory that put the Yankees on the brink of their first championship in nearly two decades? Before this season, did he have a resume that included fifteen postseason victories in thirty-seven career starts? Was he arguably the best postseason pitcher since Christy Mathewson?

With respect to the dominant October the nineteen-game winner was having, Sabathia just didn't have the pedigree of closing out teams in the playoffs.

Another Yankees left-hander on his way to Cooperstown did.

And when Sunday came, the Yankees stuck with Pettitte. He was the Yankees' guy.

And how would Andy respond?

For 6-1/3 innings, he was solid, steady…Good Ol' Andy. Allowing just one run on seven hits, he walked a single batter and had six strikeouts while endorsing his fellow southpaw as ALCS MVP. The way this master of October pitched, you knew he wanted Sabathia's next start to come on an even bigger stage: The World Series.

But his start did not come without some tense moments; moments that made everyone in the Legends Suite Club hold their breath. Leading off the Angels' third, Jeff Mathis, their blazing-hot catcher, led off the inning with his fifth double of the postseason. Two outs later, Bobby Abreu gave the Angels an early advantage.

To that point, the potent Yankee offense was like the 1968 Baltimore Colts in the first half of Super Bowl III: squandering one scoring opportunity after another. Leaving two runners on in the first, they loaded the bases against Angels starter Joe Saunders in the second; only to come away empty again.

Sensing the trepidation of many of my friends, once again I preached calm.

"Nothing good in life comes without a little adversity," I told Elton. "We are going to the series. I promise."

The Yankees made good on my promise in the fourth. After falling behind in the count one ball and two strikes, Robinson Cano worked out a walk to lead off the inning; then moved to second on a single to left by Nick Swisher. The runners moved up on a Melky Cabrera sacrifice bunt, and Jeter's battling Saunders through an eight-pitch at-bat, worked out his second walk of the game to load the bases.

The largest crowd in the new Yankee Stadium's history came to its feet as Johnny Damon stepped into the batter's box. Damon confirmed the cheering when he stroked a 2-1 fastball to left-center for a two-run single.

Raising a fist in the air, "Yeah, baby!" I screamed as the new Bronx palace went crazy.

It would get even louder after an infield hit by Mark Teixeira loaded the bases again.

And up to the plate stepped A-Rod and his five homers this postseason.

Building the drama was Angels Manager Mike Scoiscia, who chose to stay with Saunders. Sensing that his struggling sinkerballer was on the ropes, the sellout crowd screamed for more playoff magic. In so many times in his October past, Rodriguez would have gone for a knockout blow and swung for the fences. However, this was the 2009 version of A-Rod, one that exhibited patience at the plate.

Forcing a wild Saunders to make pitches, he took two balls, a strike, then another ball. With the count 3-1, A-Rod became a 90-foot hero when he laid off an inside fastball; drawing an RBI walk on the left-hander's last pitch of the night.

It wasn't a tape-measure blast, but it was enough to give the Yankees, and Good Ol' Andy, some breathing room.

Pettitte, living up to his big-game reputation, got through the fifth without incident, yet encountered one more jam one inning later. With two out in the sixth, he gave up an infield single to Torii Hunter and a double to right by Vladimir Guerrero, putting runners in scoring position.

The stadium crowd, energetic and lively throughout, grew tense when Kendry Morales took three balls from the left-hander.

A two-run lead never looked more fragile.

Pettitte, showing the poise that has made him the most decorated postseason pitcher in baseball history, simply refused to cave in. Reaching deep, he rebounded with a strike, then got the dangerous Morales to hit a fastball back to him. Blocking it, then scrambling to retrieve it, the unflappable hurler threw to first.

Once the out was secured, the whole stadium screamed with Pettitte as he pumped both fists.

"Nine outs away!" I screamed.

I was nine outs away from going to the World Series.

Pettitte pitched to two more batters, and left the game to a standing ovation with one out and one on in the seventh. Doffing his cap to the crowd, he had done his job by giving the Yankees a chance to clinch. Up 3-1, he was on his way to his sixteenth postseason win, a record.

Inheriting a runner on first with one out, Joba Chamberlain

induced two outs; one of which bounced off Derek Jeter's chest and directly to Robinson Cano, who threw on to first for the putout.

Thanks, Babe, I thought.

The Yankee ghosts still loved their new surroundings.

With six outs to go, the Yankees turned to another reliable October arm. Mariano Rivera, normally untouchable in closeout situations, encountered difficulty. Chone Figgins started the eighth inning with a single to left and moved to second when first baseman Mark Teixeira made a nice diving stop on a groundout by Bobby Abreu. After Torii Hunter grounded out for the second out, Vladimir Guerrero ripped an RBI single up the middle.

But just as quickly as the door opened, Rivera slammed it, inducing Kendry Morales to ground out.

Three more outs to go.

By this point, the Legends Suite Club was empty, so I decided to join everyone outside. Standing behind home plate in the concrete moat, I heard a loud voice bragging about the Phillies and what they would do to the Yankees.

Looking up, I saw Charles Barkley and actor/comedian extraordinaire Anthony Anderson.

"C'mon, man, you know your boys are going down," I said.

"Y'all gotta come to Philadelphia," the Round Mound of Rebound announced.

"We're going there to kick your butt, man."

"Oh, really."

"Yes really, Mr. Barkley. You wanna bet on it?"

Cracking a smile, "You're a funny guy," Barkley said. "What's your name?"

Giving him my name, next I made a suggestion. "Why are you sitting up there? You should get a Legends ticket to Game 1 of the series, man."

"I gotta work," he responded, referring to his TNT basketball analyst gig. "Besides, you haven't won this game yet."

He was right...but for a second.

The Angels' defense ended the series the way they started it, by unraveling. Errors by second baseman Howard Kendrick and pitcher Scott Kazmir on bunt plays and a sacrifice fly by Mark Teixeira led to two Yankee insurance runs before Jered Weaver ended the inning by striking out Jorge Posada.

Three outs to go.

Pumping my fists triumphantly, I said goodbye to Charles Barkley and Anthony Anderson and ran back into the Suite Club to check my men's room.

I'm going to the World Series, I kept thinking.

Before I reached the restroom, I ran into Mr. Jolly, the Angels fan I had met the week before. Earlier in the game, I spoke to him, mentioned how sweet the sound of silence would be if his team won, and encouraged him to ignore human obnoxiousness.

"You know, William, as a motivational speaker, I should know that," he said then.

"Mr. Jolly, sometimes we forget things in the heat of battle," I said with a wink.

Lifting me off the ground, "Congratulations, William," he said with a bear hug. "I'm very happy for you."

Seeing the disappointment in his eyes, I muted my celebration.

Now I had to offer comfort.

"Listen, if this is any consolation, Mr. Jolly, I want you to know that I respect your organization more than you'll ever know. Considering the adversity you overcame, you guys had a helluva year, and have nothing to be ashamed of. Hold your head high."

I saw a smile.

"Why are you in a restroom, William?"

Smiling, "The Good Lord moves in some funny ways," I said.

Together, we watched Howie Kendrick ground one to Mark Teixeira for the first out of the ninth.

"Let's go, Yankees!" chants, two-three rhythm strong, filled the brisk night air.

Everything was new, but the joy everyone felt when the New York Yankees won an American League Pennant stayed the same.

The next batter, Juan Rivera, flied to right for the second out.

One out to go.

"You better go enjoy this," Mr. Jolly said as he left the Suite Club. "God bless you, man."

Leaving him, then checking my restroom, I needed to hurry back outside and catch the last out.

I made it just in time to watch left-handed pinch hitter Gary Matthews, Jr. step into the batter's box with two out.

Looking at the scoreboard, I noted the time.

It was one minute after midnight.

Sunday had become a weekday, and the new place on River Avenue was going crazy. Everyone in the place was standing, already cheering in celebration.

As Matthews, Jr. battled to keep the Angels' flicker of hope aflame, I moved into one of the aisles, next to a Yankees fan.

Looking up at the heavens, my emotions got the best of me, and I started to cry.

I felt so thankful that I humbled myself to clean a church; even more grateful of the wonderful blessing that came from my obedience. God does things in ways that we don't always understand, but in the end, we get what we want, His way.

And in my one season in pinstripes, I was getting more than I ever imagined.

This moment also made up for a response to a letter I wrote when I was fourteen. Expressing my love of sports, I sent this note to the

Bronx with the hopes that a kid from the West Brighton Projects on Staten Island might actually be picked as a batboy for the best team in town; only to have my heart broken when the response came in the form of a neatly typed letdown.

This made up for all those times I wished I could afford playoff tickets, and watched the games on television.

As the count on the Angels' batter ran full, I also thought of the famous quote from Leo Durocher about nice guys finishing last.

With joyful tears running down my cheeks, I disagreed.

I have to disagree with you, Leo. Nice guys do finish first, but it takes them years to finish, that's all.

Suddenly, I felt am arm around me.

It was the guy next to me. He had been watching my emotions, and felt so happy for me.

"Your first World Series, huh?" the man said.

"Yes. It most certainly is."

"Congratulations," he said with a hearty embrace.

I wouldn't have expected anything less from Yankee family.

It was right then that Mariano Rivera got Matthews, Jr. to swing at a high fastball for strike three.

The stadium exploded.

Sinatra filled the air in a way he had never before.

Slowly walking toward home plate, into all the joyful noise that screamed AMERICAN LEAGUE CHAMPIONS for the first time in six years; into a familiar moment transferred to this new place across the street, Rivera grinned, pumped a gentle fist in the air and met Jorge Posada.

And like two old warriors leaving a war triumphant, the old Yankee pitcher and catcher hugged for several long moments. A third member of "The Core Four," Andy Pettitte, extended the embrace as a big crowd of pinstripes joined together between short and third, around their captain and repentant son. Manager Joe Girardi, joining in the festivities, found the repentant son, A-Rod, and hugged him as Posada, Rivera, and Pettitte joined in the fun.

It was the New York Yankees fortieth Pennant since Harry Frazee made the mistake of his life.

And I was going to my first World Series.

AN EMPIRE STATE OF MIND: THE WORLD SERIES 14

"So, when are you gonna write that book?" Cheryl asked while clicking on our flat-screen TV.

"I have no clue."

"You're supposed to, you know that, right?"

"I guess."

"So, when the Yankees win, are you going to do it? It's your destiny."

"I write fiction books about men and their feelings."

"Yeah, and your favorite television station is ESPN. William, write the book. It's your destiny."

"I'm thinking about it."

Forgoing our nightly tennis battle on the Wii, we watched Jay Leno's opening monologue together.

Then she left me alone with Leno and that fool Jimmy Rollins.

What the…What's he doing on there?

The shortstop of the Philadelphia Phillies had decided to go Hollywood right before the World Series. Already on my radar because some people thought he should have been the starting shortstop of the 2009 United States World Baseball Classic team over Derek Jeter (baseball's best ambassador and future first ballot Hall of Famer? Give me a break), on this Monday night, he would set it off.

Known for his Nostradamus-like forecasts, before the 2007 season he said that the Philadelphia Phillies, not the New York Mets, were the team to beat in the National League East. He was right. Rollins produced an MVP season and Philadelphia surged in September as the Mets blew a seven-game lead with seventeen games to play.

In 2008, Rollins predicted that the Phillies would win 100 games. They won 103 and the World Series.

And earlier this season—just like I had predicted in May—the Rollins forecast had the Yankees and the Phillies meeting in October for all the marbles.

And there they were, the two best teams in baseball locking horns once more.

And there he was, on the *Jay Leno Show*, telling all of late-night America what would happen once the first pitch was tossed. Not only did he say the defending champions would defeat the Yankees, he indicated that a can of whoop-ass would be opened up in the Bronx by the team that had the best road record in the majors for 2009.

"Of course we're going to win," Rollins told Leno. Then, as if to make sure he had twisted the knife in the back of millions of New Yorkers, Rollins added: "If we're nice, we'll let it go six. But I'm thinking five. Close it out at home."

Biting my lip, I took a deep breath, and changed the channel. Supremely confident, perhaps Rollins was reminding America that the Philadelphia Phillies, not the Yankees, were the defending World Champions. Perhaps he was warning the Big Apple that his Phillies had long ball power—hitting a National League best 224 homers, they had four players: Chase Utley, Ryan Howard, Raul Ibanez and Jayson Werth with thirty or more; tying the Major League record set by the 1977 Los Angeles Dodgers—and that 2008 World Series MVP Cole Hamels that was the *third man in their pitching rotation*; behind Cy Young Award winners Cliff Lee and Pedro Martinez.

Perhaps his prognostication was a calculated motivational tool to light a fire under his teammates.

If that was the case...On Wednesday, October 28, 2009, the ploy worked.

Entering the new Yankee Stadium that afternoon, I went to Legends, then immediately out the exit leading to the box seats behind home plate. Looking around at the grounds crew doing last-minute work on the outfield grass, I peered right, toward the first-base dugout, and saw the makeshift ESPN desk reserved for their pre- and post game analysis. Even closer was a freshly painted insignia that would tell all millions of baseball fans worldwide that yes, you were watching baseball's grandest theater: The Fall Classic.

Also capturing my attention were the production teams. In contrast to a regular-season game, the camera crews, needing to capture every expression from every angle, would multiply by ten. Seeing them work with round-the-clock diligence made me appreciate the television coverage even more.

The media coverage would be intense, especially since our First Lady, Michelle Obama—along with Jill Biden, the vice president's wife—would be throwing out the first pitch; not to mention the security around the stadium being beefed up. Wondering if snipers lurked in the facade—too high up, I concluded—the new ballpark in the Bronx took other precautions by installing metal detectors at the top of all the aisles.

By the eighth inning, long after Michelle and Jill had left, those metal detectors would be gone also.

The FBI or Secret Service should have also taken Philadelphia's Game 1 starter, Cliff Lee, with them, for the job he did in silencing the Yankee bats should have been outlawed.

The starter of the last All-Star game at the old Yankee Stadium, he won the 10-2 home opener at the new stadium as a member of the Cleveland Indians, outpitching his friend and former teammate, C.C. Sabathia, in the process.

Now here he was again, on the mound opening the World Series for the defending champions, trading zeroes for the first two innings with Sabathia once more.

To this point, the Yankees ace had been masterful in the playoffs. Destroying the psyche of American League batters with a devastating fastball and wicked slider, he assumed it would be business as usual when facing the Phillies. And for two innings it was. While not as sharp as he was in previous postseason performances—he threw 10 balls in a 15-pitch stretch in the first inning—Sabathia deceived Phillies batters with his changeup and slider the first time through the Philadelphia batting order.

His fastball, while losing nothing in its velocity, seemed to be missing its usual hop; something I noticed while watching those HDTVs in the men's room.

That missing element would prove to be the undoing of Carsten Charles Sabathia in the Phillies' half of the third. While the big-lefthander didn't break, he bent ever so slightly in his nine-pitch battle with Chase Utley.

Making Sabathia work, the left-handed-hitting second baseman fell behind two strikes, then fought back to work the count full. Fouling off a couple of pitches, he had Sabathia shaking off Jorge Posada several times during the first eight pitches.

The ninth pitch, a 94-miles-per-hour heater, just missed the location both pitcher and catcher wanted.

Utley, making contact, pulled the ball to deep right. Later admitting that he hit the ball off the end of the bat, he had got enough of the pitch to send it over the right-field fence, just beyond the reach of Nick Swisher and beyond the 314-foot sign.

Chase Utley, the first left-handed hitter to homer off Sabathia at the new Yankee Stadium, had given the Phillies a 1-0 lead.

And Phillies fanatics having dinner in the Legends Suite Club sure let me know.

"The champs are here!" one shouted when entering my lounge.

"Were the Yankees thinking they were facing a junior varsity team?" another screamed.

All I could do was smile.

The pre-series buzz surrounding this matchup was real.

In order for us to take the crown off the head of the champions, we would have to knock them the (expletive) out!

But it wouldn't happen in Game 1, because Cliff Lee carved us up. Spellbindingly spectacular, he refused to show a set pattern as he became the first starting pitcher since the very first World Series game to strike out ten batters without issuing a single walk.

I have to say that again.

On October 1, 1903, in the very first World Series game, Pittsburgh Pirate pitcher Deacon Phillippe struck out ten and walked none in a 7-3 victory over the Boston Americans; a feat that was not equaled until Cliff Lee over a century later.

That's how effective the Phillies left-hander was. Masterful yet methodical, he mixed speeds, location, and pitches with pinpoint precision, and completely baffled the Yankee lineup. In total command of his curveballs, cutters and changeups, his fastball was equally confounding as it painted all parts of the strike zone with his excellence. Only Derek Jeter, who had three hits on the night, seemed to have figured him out.

Perhaps the best example of his dominance came in the fourth, when he struck out the side. What made it impressive was that he faced the heart of the Yankee lineup—Mark Teixeira, A-Rod and Posada—and got them out swinging at three different pitches. Teixeira flailed helplessly at a cutter, Rodriguez a changeup, and a curve befuddled Posada.

He never allowed the Yankees to even think they had a chance, and performed so brilliantly that I couldn't even be mad.

His defensive exploits were just as effortless. On a hard hit ball up the middle by Robinson Cano, he made a behind-the-back stab and threw him out. When Johnny Damon hit a soft fly to the mound in the sixth inning, Lee stuck his glove out matter-of-factly, grabbed it, and continued mowing Yankee batters down.

And in the seventh, he fielded a tapper from Posada and planted a tag on his backside to retire the side.

Phillies fans came into the men's room taunting us.

"He tagged him on his ass," one of them announced, drawing laughter from a couple of red-shirted colleagues. And for the first time all season, the Yankee season-ticket holders were completely silent.

When you think about it, the play was symbolic of the gentle, polite ass-kicking administered by the defending champions.

Cliff Lee's performance shined so brightly that it completely overshadowed a workmanlike effort by his left-handed counterpart. Though he didn't own his best stuff, Sabathia kept the Yankees close. After the Utley homer, he retired eight straight batters without incident.

Then in the sixth, he missed the target again with a two-strike pitch.

Again, the batter was Chase Utley.

Validating the George Satayana quote—those who cannot remember the past are condemned to repeat it—Utley made him pay dearly with a more painful result.

Crushing another fastball, this time Swisher never even bothered turning around as the ball ended up in the right-field bleachers above the visitor's bullpen.

That two-run lead the Phillies now owned felt bigger, and the hush that kidnapped a capacity crowd in the Bronx indicated this.

The lead got bigger in the eighth and ninth, as the Phillies tacked on four runs against an assortment of relievers. That the Yankees finally got a run in the ninth—an unearned run, courtesy of a Rollins error—was moot as well.

But what was important was in the statement the defending world champions delivered in a 6-1 victory that was larger than the final score suggested. By way of their ace and a hard-hitting second baseman laying in the cut, their message came through crystal clear: If the Yankees want the World Series crown, they're going to have to knock us the (expletive) out.

Like Kevin Michaels predicted early in the season, the Philadelphia Phillies, Cliff Lee in particular, were a problem.

If we solved the problem, we would have our parade.

If not, there would be no joy in the Yankee Universe.

✪ ✪ ✪

I had to make a trip to my favorite street vendor, and pick up some T-shirts.

You wanna know why?

The self-proclaimed "most influential person to ever perform at Yankee Stadium" had decided to pay us a visit.

To the surprise of many, the Phillies manager decided to start Pedro Martinez in the most important game of the Yankees' season. Martinez, four days past his thirty-eighth birthday, was enjoying a delightful renaissance to a remarkable career, one that has him on the doorstep of Cooperstown…and wearing on the last nerve of the Bronx Bombers.

Through the years, Pedro did any and everything to evoke rage and ire from Yankee fans. Whether it was throwing fireballs at batters in his youth—or threatening to do so; see 2003, when he pointed at his temple in the direction of the New York dugout— outdueling Roger Clemens with a seventeen-strikeout masterpiece on a Friday night in September ten years earlier; or announcing to all at a press conference the day before Game 2 that he was the… ahem… "most influential person to ever perform at Yankee Stadium" (yeah, this is another one of those moments where my face is twisted in disbelief; though I must agree that he goes alongside Reggie Miller and Tom Brady on our modern-day public enemies list), he was always doing or saying something to piss New Yorkers off.

And he always got under our skin when he wore the color red. While his days in blue-and-orange were rather pedestrian—he made one start in the Bronx in his four years in a Mets uniform—what we remember most is those days when he represented our worst nightmare: a dominant Red Sox pitcher.

Now reincarnated in Philadelphia red, here he was again, a notorious villain standing in the way of our championship season.

Well, a certain person working in the Legends Suite Club was about to strike back.

Finding Steve, my favorite River Avenue street vendor, I purchased seven different "Who's Your Daddy?" shirts as giveaways to taunt Martinez with.

"You might see these on TV later," I said.

"I hope so," he responded, "It'll be good for business."

Game 2 of the 2009 World Series was a memorable night for many reasons. Before the contest there was a military flyover (which didn't bother Pedro Martinez whatsoever as he continued his warm-up tosses) as well as a show-stopping tribute to the Big Apple by Jay-Z and Alicia Keys.

Sneaking outside, I had to watch them perform "Empire State of Mind," a song that became the anthem of the 2009 season. As Jay-Z spit rhymes and Alicia sang the riveting chorus, my mind replayed all my 2009 Yankee moments like a big scoreboard. Luis Castillo's drop fly, all those walk-off hits, C.C. and Mariano Rivera's season-long brilliance, Jeter's historic moment and the postseason heroics of Alex Rodriguez—all those moments had me in the Empire State of mind.

Returning to the men's room, I was greeted by Kevin, my Yankee blood brother. He had brought a special visitor with him.

Pointing to me, "Mr. Costas, I thought I was the biggest trivia nut or Yankees fan there was, until I met him," Kevin said.

Smiling, I introduced myself to a man whom I had admired for a very long time. From his studio work to his sports broadcasting, he was, and continues to be, without peer. Combining incredible intelligence and imagery to create illuminating athletic portraits, from Jeter to Jordan, from the Olympics, Super Bowl and the Ryder Cup to a simple baseball game—why he wasn't asked by the Major League Baseball Network to be a major part of the World Series coverage was a glaring omission. While I was fortunate enough to meet him, this is an error that simply cannot be repeated—he took the diversity Brent Musberger capitalized on in his CBS heyday and raised the bar in sports coverage.

My elders had Red Barber, Mel Allen and Ernie Harwell, and we shared Marv Albert, Jack Buck, Vin Scully and Pat Summerall.

But I had Bob Costas in my restroom.

"Do you have that rookie Mickey Mantle card?" I asked.

Smiling, he pulled it from his suit jacket and let me hold it.

"Cool," I said.

I don't know how we drifted to the game, but I mentioned to him that Charlie Manuel's surprise choice of Martinez as a starter reminded me of Game 1 of the 1929 World Series, when Philadelphia Athletics Manager Connie Mack pulled a rabbit out of his hat. Before I could name the starter, I saw Mr. Costas' eyes light up.

"Howard Ehmke," he said.

My eyes lit up too.

We connected.

"He struck out thirteen Cubs that day," I said confidently. "Let's hope Pedro doesn't do the same tonight."

"Who was the Cubs manager that day?" he asked me.

"Joe McCarthy, wasn't it?"

"That's good, William."

"I got that from that four-hour World Series DVD you narrated. Man, how did you do all that?"

The twinkle in his eyes got bigger.

"I think I did it over two days."

"Man, I gotta tell you, it's an honor, Mr. Costas."

As he left, I gave my Yankee blood brother a loving embrace.

This had truly become a special season.

And it would be more special if the Yankees evened up the series.

We needed A.J. Burnett, our starter, to control Game 2, like Cliff Lee did the night before.

And you know what?

He did. Spotting his fastball early, he realized the pitch had terrific movement, and he used this pitch to start the first eleven batters he faced with strikes. Yet Burnett still struggled early, as he needed 61 pitches to complete the first three innings.

The reason for this was because he was trying to locate his curveball. For three innings, he searched for it, and he gave up a run in the process. Phillies outfielder Raul Ibanez led off the second with a slicing ground-rule double, and two outs later, scored when designated hitter Matt Stairs singled under the glove of Alex Rodriguez for the game's first run.

The stadium, rocking to Jay-Z just a while earlier, grew silent as a quiet fear that the Yankees were sliding into a 2-0 series percolated in the stomach of 50,000-plus fans.

Pedro Martinez sure wasn't helping this feeling. Varying the tempo of his pitches from batter-to-batter, for the first three innings, the man who piques New York curiosity in a way no one else does looked to be on his way to another signature performance in Gotham.

The crowd booed him when the lineup was announced and serenaded him with the requisite "Who's Your Daddy?" chants, but our mortal enemy was thriving under his oppression. Throwing junk curveballs and changeups so that his mid-to-high 80s fastball looked faster, he, like Cliff Lee did the night before, had a stretch where he struck out three batters on three different pitches. As the fourth inning started, I went to clean the exits of the Legends Suite Club when I encountered Bob Costas once more.

He was sitting at a table, enjoying the game on the flat-screen monitors we had all over the place.

"The Yankees are in trouble if they don't win this one," I mentioned to him.

"Tell me about it," he agreed.

"You know, so far this series is starting to remind me of the 1966 series, where the Baltimore Orioles' pitching staff really shut down the Dodgers."

Again, I saw that twinkle in his eyes; a look that true sports enthusiasts recognize.

So I continued.

"Jim Palmer pitched a shutout in that series. I think he was the youngest to do it in a Series game, right?"

Costas nodded. "Yes. What people forget is that was Sandy Koufax's last game."

My face brightened once more.

"That's right," I responded enthusiastically. "Didn't Tommy Davis make two errors in the sixth inning to cost the Dodgers the game?"

"It was Willie Davis," Costas corrected.

Smiling as I shook my head, I responded, "Sandy Koufax. Those last five years, Mr. Costas. Imagine if he would have received that advice from Norm Sherry earlier in his career. 'Pitch, don't throw,' he said."

"William, you really know your stuff," he responded.

"So do you, man." I replied. "So do you."

While we admired each other's knowledge of America's Pastime, we both hoped that the Yankees would figure out Pedro Martinez's stuff; going into the last half of the fourth, he had the pinstripes bamboozled.

Leading off the fourth, Mark Teixeira took a ball from Martinez. Having seen Martinez's fastball, cut fastball, curveball and changeup during a five-pitch, first-inning at-bat, he had a sense of what was in his repertoire. So when Martinez threw a 1-0 changeup that stayed in the middle of the plate, Teixeira blasted it deep into the Yankees' bullpen in right-center field.

Not only was the score tied at one and the stadium alive, but the whole complexion of the World Series had changed.

Burnett, finally locating his curveball in the third, used it to strike out Ryan Howard with two runners on base and two outs. And in the top of the fourth, before Teixeira's blast, he got a major break when Jose Molina blocked an 0-2 breaking ball in the dirt and threw a laser to the Yankees first baseman, picking off Phillies runner Jason Werth in the process.

From that point on, Burnett settled into a lights-out rhythm. Firing darts with a high-octane heater one second, moving his curveball up, down and all around the strike zone the next, he got plenty of swings and misses from the potent Phillies lineup as he kept them off balance for the rest of the night. Going seven full innings, he handed the game over to the game's greatest closer after allowing just that one second-inning run on a mere four hits while striking out nine.

Matching his magnificence was Martinez, all the way to the sixth inning. In cruise control after the Teixeira homer, while he didn't possess the blazing speed of his youth, he surpassed all expectations with an arsenal of off-speed pitches that quieted all jeers as he exhibited the competitive will of a future Hall of Famer. Making great theater once more in the Bronx, begrudgingly, the old war-horse was gaining our respect.

His gutsy outing reminded me of Game 2 of the 1938 World Series, when Chicago Cub Hall of Famer Dizzy Dean dueled Yankees pitcher Lefty Gomez. Dean, having lost his blazing fastball after a toe injury the year before affected his throwing motion—he hurt his arm in this process—got through seven innings on sheer heart and guile, and held a slim 3-2 lead going into the eighth inning. But he soon ran out of gas, and late-inning, two-run blasts by Frank Crosetti and Joe DiMaggio gave the Yankees a come-from-behind 6-3 victory.

Sooner or later, the Yankees get 'em all, I thought.

And in the bottom of the sixth, the Yankees finally got to Pedro Martinez. After striking out Teixeira with a curveball and A-Rod on a beautiful changeup, he was one out from getting out of the inning when he got two quick strikes on Hideki Matsui with his fastball. Changing to curveballs, he delivered a 1-2 breaking ball that was beneath the Yankee designated hitter's knees.

Matsui, simply trying to stay alive, reached down and golfed it with his 3-wood disguised as a baseball bat. Hammering it from his knees, the pitch landed five rows over the left-field wall.

The sellout crowd, begging for something to cheer about, erupted.

For the first time in the series, the New York Yankees had a lead.

And the Legends Suite Club went crazy.

At inning's end, I thought Pedro Martinez was through. Having thrown 99 pitches, while he trailed, he kept the defending champions by pitching brilliantly. But I honestly thought he had gone as far as his thirty-eight-year-old body had taken him.

Philadelphia Manager Charlie Manuel, having a heart-to-heart with Martinez in the Phillies' dugout, wanted to know if he had any more guile left in his tank.

Face-to-face with him on national television, "Can you go one more?" he asked him.

Martinez nodded yes.

So Manuel, in a move reminiscent to Grady Little's questionable decision to leave a tiring ace on the mound six years ago—a pitcher by the name of Pedro Martinez—sent his fast-fading hurler out for the bottom of the seventh.

It was a bad move. Leading off the inning, Jerry Hairston, Jr., in the lineup for a slumping Nick Swisher, singled to right. Melky Cabrera followed with a hit-and-run single of his own, putting pinch-runner Brett Gardner on third with no outs.

It was then Manuel removed Martinez.

As the Yankee nemesis left the mound, he pointed at the sky, tapped a fist on his heart and smiled at the stadium crowd as they serenaded him.

"Who's Your Daddy?" 50,000 fans chanted in two-three rhythm. "Who's Your Daddy?"

After Jorge Posada greeted reliever Chan Ho Park with a run-scoring single, the re-energized stadium rocked.

A two-run lead with the Sandman coming in. This one is over, I thought.

Mariano Rivera got his World Series record-setting, fourth six-out save, but not without a little difficulty. Allowing Jimmy Rollins and Shane Victorino to reach base, he induced an inning-ending, double-play ball from Game 1 star Chase Utley. And in the ninth, he ended the game by getting Matt Stairs to chase a cutter for strike three with a runner on second.

The Phillies had an opportunity to put the Yankees in a deep hole and move to within two games of winning a second straight World Series. But in a game they absolutely, positively had to win, the New York Yankees picked themselves off the canvas with a 3-1 victory.

Clenching my fist after that last out, I came out of the men's room and saw Bob Costas for the last time. He was seated at a table right outside the lounge, waiting for someone.

"Man, I want to tell you, it was truly an honor," I said, shaking his hand.

"Likewise," he said.

"We got ourselves a series, Mr. Costas."

"We sure do, William."

"Pedro pitched his heart out, wouldn't you agree?"

His parting words made my eyes widen in amazement.

"But in the end, William, the Yankees always get 'em, don't they?"

"They sure do."

As he walked away, I couldn't help but smile. I may never see that man again, but the fact that we shared a brief connection in time where we shared our love for America's Pastime was an incredible experience that I will cherish for the rest of my days.

Another incredible moment that I would remember is witnessing my first Yankees victory in the Fall Classic.

Three more like that one would be unbelievable, I thought as I returned to my post.

My musings were interrupted by another trash-talking Phillies fan.

"Yeah, the Yankees are coming to the City of Brotherly Love to lose," the well-dressed brother said.

My rebuttal was swift.

"Man, your city had better stick to makin' cheesesteak sandwiches," I replied.

"We're the champs, and we're gonna stay that way."

"You're a very brave man to be talking that mess in here, sir."

Recognizing him from somewhere, I couldn't recall where; that is, until someone else from Philly called him "Mayor."

It was Philadelphia Mayor Michael A. Nutter.

"It's an honor, sir," I said.

"Don't try to be nice to me now, man," he responded. "Your Yankees will lose all three in Philadelphia."

"Hizzoner, you don't really believe that, do you?"

"I have faith in my Phillies, young man. I'll see you at the parade."
As he left, I thought, *he didn't say where the parade would take place.*
Three more Yankee victories would give everyone the destination.

✪ ✪ ✪

I couldn't stand all those white towels they were waving. But the crowd had every right to be fanatical. After all, we were the enemy in their noisy, red-and-white firestorm known as Citizens Bank Park. And the wild inferno that was roaring with every pitch threatened to send the Bronx Bombers title hopes up in smoke.

It was Halloween. And ghost, goblins and all types of monsters were out in Philadelphia, playing tricks with the Yankees' minds. They started their games by causing an eighty-minute rain delay before the start of Game 3. Disrupting the pregame ritual of Game 3 starter Andy Pettitte, when the left-handed master of Octobers past took the mound, I could tell immediately that he wasn't locked in.

He's going to have labor through this one, I said. Watching the game at home for a change, I could see that he was rushing his delivery. Robbing himself of his usual effectiveness, he was forcing his fastball instead of just *pitching it* through the strike zone; and having trouble throwing his curveball for strikes.

He just seemed off-kilter to me, and normally when I sense something amiss with a pitcher, even one with a vast postseason resume like Pettitte, I know that his stay on the mound will be brief.

And for the first two innings it looked like that would be the case for Good Ol' Andy. By the end of the frame, he had thrown 52 pitches.

And the Phillies made him pay for the early, excessive pitch count. Leading off the second, Jayson Werth battled the veteran lefty. Working the count full, the slugging right-fielder was treated a hanging slider and crushed it. The ball parted a red sea of Phillies fanatics, and landed in the left-field stands for a solo shot.

The defending champions, noticing that the normally unflappable Pettitte appeared vulnerable, went on the attack. With one out, Pedro Feliz drove a double off the right-field wall and Carlos Ruiz walked, putting runners on first and second for the Phillies pitcher Cole Hamels. Perfectly executing what he thought would be a sacrifice, Hamels placed down a beautiful bunt between the third-base line and the pitcher's mound that neither Pettitte nor catcher Jorge Posada could make a play on.

The bases were now loaded.

Clearly rattled by the moment, Pettitte walked Jimmy Rollins, forcing in Feliz with the inning's second run, then gave up a sacrifice fly to Shane Victorino to give Philadelphia a 3-0 lead.

The place was going crazy when Chase Utley stepped into the batter's box. A blast at that point would have put the game out of reach, but the Yankee lefty reached into an expansive catalog of post-season moments and remembered who he was. Arguably the best big-time pitcher in baseball history, he found a cut fastball from his past to strike out the Phillies second baseman and end the inning.

Up to that point, his mound counterpart, Hamels, was outstanding. With the partisan Philadelphia crowd roaring on his every pitch, the lanky left-hander was giving the City of Brotherly Love a nice treat with three scoreless innings.

It's amazing how quickly things changed. When it looked like the defending champions might have more scoring opportunities against Pettitte, the left-hander buckled down and showed the resiliency that may one day carry him to Cooperstown. After making 52 pitches in those first two innings, he threw just 52 more over the next four, striking out seven while allowing just one more run—another homer by Werth—and only more two hits.

The Yankees, finally realizing that this was Halloween, had a few tricks of their own up in their bag of goodies, and they would start giving them to Mayor Nutter and the rest of the Philadelphia in the fourth.

After Hamels retired Johnny Damon to start the frame, he walked Mark Teixeira on a 3-and-2 fastball that looked like a strike to all watching at home. The pitch, down and in, appeared to have caught the inside corner of the strike zone, but the home-plate umpire thought otherwise.

Up to the plate stepped Alex Rodriguez. After two outstanding postseason series, he was hitless in his first eight World Series at-bats, with four strikeouts. Reverting back to the A-Rod of seasons past, instead of showing patience in the batter's box he seemed to be pressing; looking for that 600-foot-blast as opposed to just putting the ball in play.

Relax and make contact, I encouraged from my living room. *I have faith in you, A-Rod.*

Two pitches later, A-Rod hit an opposite-field rocket into the right-field corner that struck a hard surface and ricocheted back into the field of play. Cruising into second with an apparent double, A-Rod's first hit had put runners in scoring position.

As Phillies pitching coach Rich Dubee visited Hamels, Joe Girardi came out to protest the call made by right-field umpire Jeff Nelson. The ball, Girardi argued, hit a television camera overhanging onto the field of play and Nelson had mistakenly thought it hit the top of the right-field wall.

Watching the television replays, I smiled.

How appropriate is this? Of all people, A-Rod will be the beneficiary of the first overturned ruling in World Series history.

Nelson convened with the other umpires, and then they all left the field to further examine the play in their replay room. Minutes later, they emerged, with the case of the hard-hit ball solved. It had indeed, struck the lens on the camera.

The first replay reversal in World Series annals had pulled the Yankees within one run, at 3-2.

The next trick for Phillies fans looking for candy at their door would give them the lead. Nick Swisher, back in the lineup after a day to think about his postseason slump (4-for-35; .118 batting average) ripped a curveball down the left-field line for a double. After Hamels struck out Melky Cabrera, many Yankee supporters expected the next batter, Andy Pettitte, to sacrifice Swisher to third and hope that their captain came through with two outs. After all, this was a National League ballpark, so the Yankees had to play by National League rules; meaning the pitcher had to bat.

Pitchers were normally automatic outs, so why should anyone in the ballpark have expected anything different.

Throwing a first-pitch curveball that hung in the strike zone, Hamels shrugged it off as a waste pitch.

Referring to Pettitte, *he's a pitcher, so he'll miss it*, he must have thought.

He'll swing right through it, all of Citizens Bank Park must've thought.

Only Andy Pettitte was determined to help his own cause. Swinging aggressively, the left-handed pitcher became the first Yankees hurler since Jim Bouton in 1964 to knock home a run when his flare dropped in shallow center for an RBI single.

Pettitte's surprise—and trick #2 for the Yankees—was the beginning of a four-pitch sequence that gave the Bombers a 5-3 lead. The very next pitch, to Derek Jeter, was ripped into left for a single, moving Pettitte to second. And two pitches later, Damon laced a double into the right-center field alley, scoring Pettitte and Jeter with the lead runs.

I went crazy. Yelling repeatedly, "Trick or treat," I must have woke up the entire apartment building.

The den of noise that was once Citizens Bank Park grew very quiet. How long did it take?

A New York minute.

We got 'em, I thought.

We had them. In the sixth inning, Swisher, continuing his playoff reawakening, got a hold of a fastball from reliever J.A. Happ and sent it soaring into that red sea in left-field, giving the Yankees more breathing room with his solo blast. The following inning, Jorge Posada drove in Johnny Damon with the Yankees' seventh run of the night with a two-out single to left. And for good measure, Hideki Matsui, coming off the bench as a pinch hitter, drilled yet another homer into the sea of suddenly silent Phillies fans.

The Yankee bullpen, often maligned in the media as a liability to its team's success, was in shutdown mode. After Pettitte's gutsy six innings, Joba Chamberlain came on to pitch a 1-2-3 seventh, and Damaso Marte, firing 95-miles-per-hour darts as well as using an untouchable slider, retired three straight batters in the eighth.

Only Phil Hughes stumbled. With one out in the ninth, he foolishly tried to sneak a fastball by a dead fastball hitter in Carlos Ruiz, and his punishment for the transgression was a homer to left-center; cutting the Yankee lead to 8-5.

Girardi, taking no chances, brought in Rivera, who quickly got the final two outs.

Seizing control of the series with their seventh come-from-behind postseason victory, the New York Yankees, their legion of fans, and a certain restroom attendant were halfway home to a championship.

✪ ✪ ✪

And then, it was one.

Having walked into a tough environment and gutted out a victory with a pitcher that wasn't on his "A" game, the Yankees now approached

Game 4 with a chance to make a major statement. A win in this critical contest would put Citizens Bank Park and the team that played on its field of dreams on life support.

This was one of those statement games with the opposition; in this instance the defending champion Philadelphia Phillies, being stuck in a ditch. The Bronx Bombers needed to turn that ditch into a hole, one that a World Series team hadn't escaped since the 1985 Kansas City Royals came back from two down to take the Series away from the St. Louis Cardinals.

And the prospects for that scenario looked promising: The Phillies Game 4 starter, Joe Blanton, owned a earned run average of over eight against the Bombers.

Immediately, the potent Yankee lineup reminded him of this. On the game's second pitch, Derek Jeter hit a single to shallow center. Following his lead, Johnny Damon—more on his night later— smoked a one-hop shot off the wall in right for a double.

Unnerved, Blanton got Mark Teixeira to groundout to first, but Jeter scored the game's first run while Damon moved to third. After A-Rod got hit by a pitch for the third time in the Series, Jorge Posada brought Damon home with a sacrifice fly.

Armed with a two-run advantage, C.C. Sabathia took the hill. Pitching on three days' rest, he, like Pettitte the night before, didn't have his best stuff, but was effective when he needed to be. Phillies batters Shane Victorino and Chase Utley noticed this as well, for they produced a run on back-to-back doubles.

As the inning ended, I took a calm sip from my Long Island Iced Tea. Simultaneously wanting the total Yankee experience and to be around my Yankee family, I ventured to the Yankee Tavern, the most famous watering hole near the stadium. Once the bar home of the Bambino—who was known to buy a round after a Yankee win— in the twenty-first century the clientele has a broad range. Everyone from courthouse and seasonal Yankee employees to middle-aged fans come there to enjoy their extensive menu. And because there's no cutoff after a certain time, you can drink till your heart's content.

And while you are enjoying the game, you get great service from the wonderful bartenders and support staff. Additionally, one look around the place from your cherry-colored barstool and you'll see that every inch of blue wall space pays homage to Yankee history. Murals of Mantle and both the old and new stadium, photos of Joe DiMaggio and Derek Jeter; you are surrounded by the past, present and future of Pinstriped Power.

The keeper of this treasured flame, bar owner Joe Bastone—a man who's worked there since he was ten years old (!)—wouldn't have it any other way. One of the nicest men around, on game days you'll often find him situated in the tavern's backroom basking in the glow of his renovated, timeless creation.

Throughout the season, the place had become a second home for me. After almost every game, I would treat myself to a Long Island Iced Tea, and drive customers crazy with my Michael Jackson selections in the jukebox before going home.

This Sunday night, however, the greatest entertainer to walk the face of this earth would gladly take a backseat.

The Yankees, playing in Philadelphia on the first day of November, were about to enter into a dogfight.

This is going to be one of those gut-check games, I said to Willie, one of my favorite bartenders.

"It sure is," he said.

"You better keep those Long Island Iced Teas coming all night. I might need them."

By the bottom of the fourth inning, my forecast rang true. Sabathia had settled down and retired eight of his next nine batters before he faced Ryan Howard to start the frame. Howard, who was 1-for-11 at the time, hit a leadoff single to center; then stole second with two out. Pedro Feliz, the Phillies third baseman that would play an important role later in the game, singled to left.

Racing around third, Howard challenged Johnny Damon's throwing arm. The ball arrived at the plate at the same time as Howard, and the Phillies first baseman barreled into Jorge Posada, knocking the ball free.

The game was now tied.

And once again, the Philadelphia Phillies had sent a reminder to the Yankees: If you want to wear the crown, you're going to have to knock us the (expletive) out.

And the Bronx Bombers were sure going to try. Responding in the fifth, the Yankees renewed their assault on Blanton, who to that point had set down eleven batters in a row. Nick Swisher, Blanton's roommate in Oakland, led off the inning with a walk. Melky Cabrera followed with a chopper up the middle that an off-balance Utley gloved, but couldn't complete the force at second.

With runners on first and second and one out—Sabathia whiffed—up stepped the most decorated batter in postseason history. Using the opportunity to reinforce the point, Derek Jeter hit an RBI single to left, and Damon followed that with a Texas Leaguer to right, scoring Cabrera to make the score 4-2.

The Tavern in the Bronx was as noisy as Citizens Bank Park was silent.

And both atmospheres remained the same as the Phillies wasted two more scoring opportunities. With runners on first and second and no one out, Sabathia had the heart of their potent lineup: Utley, Howard and Jayson Werth, staring him in the face.

Relying heavily on his slider, Sabathia induced pop-fly outs from Utley and Howard, and fanned Werth on a changeup.

Sabathia had answered the call; and would do so in the sixth, when he got pinch-hitter Ben Francisco flied out to end the sixth with a runner on second.

"Nine outs away," I said as we cheered the Yankees on. "Just nine more, and we got a stranglehold on this sucker."

If ever there was a time where the heart of a champion was tested, this was one of those moments for the Philadelphia Phillies. Stunned, staggered and stupefied, you wondered if they could get off the canvas like the Yankees did in Game 2.

They tried valiantly.

Sabathia, clearly running on fumes, retired the first two batters in the seventh. Using that faithful slider as his bread-and-butter pitch, he threw many of them to a person that homered twice off him in the Series, Chase Utley.

His 107th and last pitch of the night was another slider; his fifth in a row.

Unfortunately, he left it out over the plate; and Utley, as he did twice before, made him pay.

Launching a rocket blast over the right-field wall for his third home run of the Series, Utley had not only cut the Phillies' deficit to one, but sent the red-and-white fanatics into a towel-waving frenzy.

It was at that time Girardi removed his ace, who received a hearty applause from all of us up the Turnpike. Though he wasn't spectacular, the big left-hander had given us a chance to win. And if this was his last outing of the year, then he gave the New York Yankees their money's worth.

Enter Damaso Marte, who got another dangerous left-handed slugger, Ryan Howard, to fly to center and end the inning.

Joba Chamberlain came to the mound for the eighth, and proceeded to blow away Jayson Werth and Raul Ibanez with a pair of fastballs that registered 97-miles-per-hour on the speed gun.

The Yankee Tavern was rocking. While the crowd was moderately sized, you would have thought you were at the stadium. The place was electric, much like the reliever on the mound.

"Dazzling," I said of Chamberlain. "Just dazzling." Instead of the fourth starter that struggled with his pitches through the regular season, I saw the young man who illuminated all of New York in 2007 when he came out of the bullpen throwing smoke.

The Joba of 2010 got ahead of Pedro Feliz 1-2 with a pair of 96-mph darts, then threw two 87-mph sliders for balls. With the count now full, he turned up the dial on his stove and fired another fastball; this one clocking in at 95 mph.

It never made it to Jorge Posada's glove.

But it made it to the left-field seats.

Feliz had caught up with Joba, and sent a laser into that sea of red.

"One out away, one strike away," I said. "Damn."

Needless to say, the Tavern felt the same way.

All you heard was expletives, as the scoreboard in Citizens Bank Park now read 4-4.

Regrouping, Chamberlain got the last out of the inning and trudged slowly to the dugout.

His inning started great; it couldn't have gotten better for him.

But the ending? It couldn't have been worse.

He needed a quick pick-me-up.

Would the Yankees supply it?

Brad Lidge, the Phillies' closer, took the mound for the ninth. A walking example of what-a-difference-a-year-makes, in the 2008 championship season, he was perfection in cleats; a mind-boggling 48-for-48 in save opportunities. A year later, he lost eight games during a regular season where he posted a 7.21 earned run average, and blew eleven other save opportunities.

All he needed to do was pitch seven perfect days in October and November, and redemption would be his.

He started the inning like he would do just that, as the first two outs came easily.

Then Johnny Damon stepped in the batter's box.

Starting him off with a fastball for a strike, Lidge next threw Damon three straight sliders.

Damon fouled all three off.

Next came four straight fastballs, which Damon took two for balls and fouled the other two off. One of those foul balls was almost caught by catcher Carlos Ruiz. On the ninth pitch of the battle, Lidge threw a fastball.

Damon, looking slider, just reacted and laced a single to left.

Amongst the applause at the Tavern, "Great at-bat!" someone yelled.

Now on first, Damon noticed the Phillies were using an infield shift on Mark Teixeira where the second baseman Chase Utley moved to shallow right-field, shortstop Jimmy Rollins was on the right side of second base, near the outfield grass, and third baseman Pedro Feliz had moved to Rollins' vacated spot.

Taking off for a stolen-base attempt on the first pitch to Teixeira, he slid into second safely and took a quick glance at Feliz and noticed the catcher throw pulled him off and to the right of second base. Instinctively taking advantage of the opportunity before him, he bolted for third; easily winning a footrace between him and the slower Feliz. Lidge had taken a few steps toward third, but never would have made it.

It was a heads-up play that simply couldn't be taught; one of those plays only champions think of making.

Already sitting on their hands, the Philadelphia crowd went into shock as they wondered what in the hell had happened.

At the Tavern, we knew.

"What a play!" I yelled. High-fiving a couple of patrons, boldly I announced, "The Yankees won this game."

It would not be Texeira who would get the attempt to prove me right—rattled by the chain of events, Lidge plunked the Yankees first baseman with a 1-2 fastball—fittingly, it would be Alex Rodriguez.

"This is the biggest at-bat of his career," I said.

After watching a fastball zip by him for a strike, A-Rod must have thought about his three previous encounters with Lidge. There were two hits and three RBIs. One of them, in that May series that unknowingly was a preview of the Fall Classic, was a game-tying home run off a fastball.

He's coming dead red, he figured.

Lidge threw a 94-mph heater.

And with one sweet swing, he sent a curling bullet that sailed past left-fielder Raul Ibanez, and into the corner.

As Damon, the ignition to it all, scored from third, and Teixeira, the antagonist Lidge hit with a pitch, moved to third, you heard nothing; absolutely *nothing* from the Citizens Bank Park crowd. All you saw was A-Rod pointing at Jeter in the dugout, and Teixeira sending a text message by pointing at A-Rod. The only sounds you heard were the sounds of Yankees realizing that all they needed was one more.

That sound roared even louder when Jorge Posada nailed another pitch on the screws, scoring A-Rod and Teixeira with a two-run single.

The score was now 7-4 Yankees.

Immediately after A-Rod's career-redefining hit, FOX television showed the Yankee bullpen.

There was Mariano, ready to turn out the lights.

The electricity was gone from the ballpark, however, for some strange reason the lights were still on.

So we needed Mariano to deliver the final phase of the Yankee victory.

That phrase was: And then, it was one.

Eight pitches later—a Matt Stairs' groundout, Jimmy Rollins' pop-up and Shane Victorino groundout—the message was like Obama in the White House; signed, sealed and delivered to all of Philadelphia.

And then, it was one.

The New York Yankees were on the doorstep of their 27th World Championship.

One more victory would do the trick.

After 103 regular season victories, and ten more in the playoffs, the countdown had reached the number spoken not only by lips, but index fingers as well.

And then, it was one.

✪ ✪ ✪

If you know like I know, the hardest thing for any team to do is to win a close-out playoff game on the road. With desperate fans imploring players they worship to fight to see another day, the adrenaline flow running through the team on the brink of elimination is tremendous.

As the Philadelphia Phillies took the field to play in Game 5, it would have been a perfect occasion to conjure up truisms in tribute to valiant losers who continue to play on with pride and self-respect when all possibilities for victory have vanished. It would have also been true if the defending champions were fueled by the motivation that there would be no passing of the guard, no coronation in their backyard.

Because they won the year before, they knew that there would be plastic sheets over the lockers in the visitors' clubhouse at Citizens Bank Park. They also knew that there were expensive bottles of champagne stored somewhere on the basement-service level.

They could have used all these incentives to fuel their urgency.

But in Game 5, the Philadelphia Phillies used none of them.

They had no pre-game pep talk either. Stepping into the clubhouse, Manager Charlie Manuel thought he needed to say something to his troops as they prepared for battle. When he saw players joking and relaxing, he decided no words were necessary.

He knew that his team, the defending champion Philadelphia Phillies, still believed they could win the Series.

He knew this even after the Yankees took a 1-0 lead in the top of the first; courtesy of an Alex Rodriguez double.

He probably also knew that A.J. Burnett, attempting to close out a series for the second time this postseason, would have that deer-in-headlights look in his eyes again.

For this game, I ventured to Shorty's, a beer and wings place on the corner of Ninth Avenue and Forty-second Street. Invited there by my friend Sandy, a security guard at the stadium who lived nearby, she thought it would be interesting if I watched the game in a place that supported the Phillies.

"A Phillies bar in New York?" I asked her beforehand.

"Yup. And it's an Eagles bar during football season."

An impish smirk found my face.

How could I resist being a villain invading enemy camp, especially on a night when my Yankees could silence Citizens Bank Park with their twenty-seventh baseball championship?

Making sure I wore my Yankees jacket and gray road jersey, you should have seen the dirty looks upon my arrival.

"Get out of here," one person yelled.

A woman approached our pocket of Yankees fans that were in back of the narrow establishment.

"It takes courage to walk in here with that jacket on," she said politely.

But the most part, the Philadelphia fans were cordial. They didn't let me have it...Until the bottom of the first.

The minute Jimmy Rollins ripped a solid single off Burnett, I knew something was wrong.

Tapping Sandy, "This is not going to be our night," I said softly as the bar cheered.

Nodding in agreement, she knew, too.

Our whole Yankee pocket knew.

On this night, we were up against a team that had nothing to lose.

Burnett, pitching on three days' rest, sure helped their cause when he drilled Shane Victorino with a rising fastball.

With two on, Chase Utley made himself comfortable in the batter's box. But he wouldn't stay there long. Burnett's first pitch to him, a 93-miles-per-hour fastball, was supposed to be down and away, but it tailed back over the plate.

Seconds later, Shorty's went crazy.

Lowering my head, I was ready to leave.

The ball was crushed over the right-field fence, and the Phillies had a 3-1 lead.

And those damn towels were waving once more.

With good reason, because after A-Rod's first-inning double, the Yankees were shut down by Cliff Lee—remember him? The next batter who would reach him for a hit would be Derek Jeter four innings later. While not as dominant as he was during Game 1, he did enough to keep the Phillies' championship hopes alive.

He received more help from Utley in the third. Walking to start the third inning, he stole second, and distracted Burnett so much that he walked cleanup-hitter Ryan Howard.

"Burnett has nothing," I said to no one in particular.

A Phillies fan overheard me.

"The Yankees are nothing!" he screamed at me.

Smiling, I bought him a drink, and kept my eyes glued to the carnage on the flat-screen monitor.

Jayson Werth felt the need to back up this man's boast by drilling a single up the middle, scoring Utley to increase the Phillies' lead to 4-1. Seconds later, a Raul Ibanez hit to right made the score 5-1.

Burnett's night was done. In fifty-three pitches, he allowed six runs—Werth would score later on a fielder's choice by Carlos Ruiz—four walks, and failed to record an out in the third inning.

Citizens Bank Park and Shorty's near Times Square were roaring.

So was Cliff Lee. Through seven innings he allowed just two runs. Working quickly, he breezed through the middle innings while his assortment of cutters, curves, changeups and fastballs kept the Yankees off-balance.

In the seventh inning, the Phillies hammered in two more nails to their second win of the Series. Facing reliever Phil Coke, Utley blasted another no-doubter, one that went halfway up the right-field bleachers. In tying Reggie Jackson's record of five homers in single World Series, he joined Willie Aikens in becoming the second person in history to have two multi-homer games in the same Series.

Two batters later, Raul Ibanez hit an even harder blast off Coke; this one hit a billboard hanging off the second deck in right. The sign it hit was from Chrysler, and it read "Drive 'em outta here."

With an 8-2 lead, the defending champs were driving the Yankees out of Citizens Bank Park.

And the Pro-Phillies crowd at Shorty's was trying to drive out of there.

"Nah-nah-nah-nah, nah-nah-nah-nah, hey-hey-hey, goodbye," they sang. By now, our pocket of Yankees fans had given up, leaving Sandy, her son Chris, and myself alone to face the music.

"See you Wednesday," they chanted in two-three rhythm.

Though it was killing me, I remained emotionless. The Phillies had looked their desperation squarely in the face, and played their hearts out.

With six outs to go, they looked to be on their way to New York with a truckload of momentum.

Then a funny thing happened; one that lifted the heads of Yankees fans all over.

Leading of the top of the eighth, Johnny Damon hit a grounder that second baseman Rollins couldn't get out of his glove. Then, Mark Teixeira followed with a double to left. Next A-Rod hit a double past a diving Ibanez that drove in Teixeira and Damon.

Suddenly, it was 8-4.

Charlie Manuel removed Lee, who left to a well-deserved standing ovation. After a crushing Game 4 loss, one that brought an entire city to its knees, he had pitched the Phillies to Wednesday; provided they got six more outs.

Chan Ho Park, the Phillies reliever, did just that, but not without allowing to score on a sacrifice fly.

With their lead trimmed to 8-5, would the Phillies manager again entrust their destiny in the hands of Brad Lidge, who took a psychological beating in the ninth inning the night before?

Nope.

Opting instead to use Ryan Madson, the Yankees kept coming. Leading off the ninth, Jorge Posada greeted him with a ringing double off the right-field wall.

Hearing the collective groans from Shorty's, I refused to bat an eye, even when pinch hitter Hideki Matsui ripped a single to left, moving Posada to third.

With Derek Jeter coming to the plate, the Phillies bar situated in the heart of New York grew silent.

"You think that he'll come through?" Sandy asked me.

"Let's see."

The Yankees captain usually came through in big moments like this; however, the moon was full on this Monday night in November. And while the Bronx Bombers fought back like they were the champions they wanted to become, they weren't there just yet.

After working the count to 2-1, Jeter brought a roar to the bar and all of Philadelphia when he rapped a two-seam fastball on the ground to Jimmy Rollins, who started a 6-4-3 double play.

A run scored, but the heart of the rally was stopped cold.

The Yankees were down to their last out.

But Johnny Damon, refusing to take the 108-mile drive up the Turnpike just yet, hit a single up the middle.

Only when I saw A-Rod in the on deck circle did I crack a smile.

If he gets up, the Yankees are champions, I thought.

One more time, the Yankees had the tying run at the plate.

And one more time, the defending champion Philadelphia Phillies reached deep.

On their 147th and last pitch of the night, Madson got Teixeira to chase a one ball-two strike changeup in the dirt to nail down the 8-6 win.

As a roar of survival surrounded me, I looked at Sandy, and found her looking at me with the same knowing smile.

"We got this, William. The Phillies are finished," Sandy said.

"I know."

Though the Yankees lost, the fact that they battled to within two runs delivered a message to all of Philadelphia that the Series was over once we returned home.

To this day, I wonder if the Phillies fans cheering at the bar that night ever got it.

HOME SWEET HOME!

It's not always reaching the destination; or the end result that matters.

It's in the journey where the lessons are learned.

While the end result can be emotionally exhilarating, the road to accomplishment is what builds character, forges resolve and resiliency, and cultivates respect and appreciation for the task at hand.

The journey to success can often be lonely, painful; full of tremendous sacrifices. The journey to reward can be full of hope one second, yet bring you to your knees the next. Some journeys can be effortless and easy; others amazingly arduous. Sometimes difficult and demanding, sometimes dandy, delightful and delicious, it is the journey that is most important.

The journey consists of you as a participant, but is not about you. Let me explain: the story of your journey; its bright and bitter moments, its ups and downs, the joy and pain of it all always helps another individual. Setting a standard all its own, the journey can be inspiring yet intimidating, can have a muzzling effect on one person's aspirations, or in the alternative, motivate another to reach even higher ground. A story of hope to one person and a cautionary tale to others, the journey can be enlightening, informative and irrelevant all at once.

Behind every noteworthy accomplishment or achievement, there is the story that is the journey. You cannot seek life's greener pastures without embarking on the journey. And no matter the twists and turns along the way, you must stay the course.

I know a little something about journeys. In April 1996, I sat in the living room of my father's Brooklyn apartment with a pen and pad of paper. It is then a journey with a gift that God gave me began. My journey has consisted of sleeping on office floors; losing apartments, friendships and relationships with women I have loved; trips all around this and other countries, interfacing with everyone from prisoners and convicts to some of the greatest intellectual minds God has ever created; receiving rejection letters from agents and editors questioning my gift to winning literary awards; and making bestsellers lists. Making serious mistakes and receiving tremendous blessings along the way, I've also experienced many sleepless nights waffling as to whether I relinquish this gift or keep my dreams alive, no matter what price I may pay.

Through the trials and triumphs, within those blurred crevices of joy and pain is a story; and that story is a journey I thank God for daily.

On October 26, 2000, Yankees centerfielder Bernie Williams went to the deepest part of Shea Stadium to haul in a fly ball hit by Mike Piazza; thus securing the 26th World Championship of the franchise's storied history.

Though few suspected it at the time, a journey, one that saw the Yankees win 44 of 56 postseason games en route to four championship parades in five years, had ended. Winning three of those titles in a row—1998-2000—at a time when professional sports and its constant movement deemed it impossible to do so, many Yankees fans were spoiled by their success, because the team and its core of selfless stars—Paul O' Neill, Scott Brosius, Tino Martinez, Bernie Williams; and the four active holdovers—made the journey look easy. Victims of their own glory as well as many journeys of success throughout the past century, their barometer of success was higher than normal standards and the way they were judged would be different.

When the Yankees won that championship in 2000, Mariano Rivera took care of the last out of a game started by Andy Pettitte, with Jorge Posada behind the plate and Derek Jeter at shortstop.

The stalwarts of that wonderful journey were just entering the prime of their careers and never expected the winning to stop.

But suddenly, in 2001, it did; courtesy of a ninth-inning, broken-bat single by Luis Gonzalez on a Sunday night in Arizona.

That was the beginning of a nine-year journey in the wilderness they subjected many of their opponents to during their championship reign. Frustration settled in as mercenaries from the organization's wild spending sprees—Randy Johnson, Carl Pavano, Gary Sheffield, Kevin Brown and Jason Giambi—came and went, bringing more disappointment with their inability to meet the ultimate Yankee standard; the game-changing ability to produce when the lights shined the brightest.

Soon, the failure to produce in the postseason became the running joke amongst the smaller-market franchises. Four first-round exits—to the Angels in '02 and '05, the Detroit Tigers in '06 and the Cleveland Indians in '07—sandwiched two celebrations in their ballpark: one by a Florida Marlins team in 2003 that shut them down with great pitching; and one by a team that completed the greatest comeback in professional sports.

Every time I think about 2004...those damn Red Sox.

Even one of the linchpins, Petitte, had to take a leave of absence from the growing insanity; as he followed used-to-be-future-Hall of Famer Roger Clemens to the Houston Astros for a three-year sabbatical.

The journey bottomed out in 2008, when for the first time since 1993, the Yankees failed to reach the postseason.

Had the journey reached its conclusion? Would the stories of the trip be of frustration and disappointment, heartbreak and its painful dead-end? Were those four championships from the previous journey the exception as opposed to the rule? Would those "Core Four" from championships past be in pinstripes long enough to see the natural order of the Bronx restored?

Enter 2009, when the journey took a new turn. Landing in a spanking new ballpark, it enjoyed a wonderful transformation; one that included key acquisitions that produced when we needed them the most—A.J. Burnett, Nick Swisher, C.C. Sabathia and Mark Teixeira; had a player rewriting his legacy in going from a magnet of sensationalistic negativity to October hero and true Yankee—Alex Rodriguez; saw a beleaguered manager and front office official on the doorstep of silencing their harshest critics—Joe Girardi and General Manager Brian Cashman; and had a certain restroom attendant in the Legends Suite Club one win away from experiencing a dream that would be shared for years to come.

On the way to the stadium, I reflected on my journey within the Yankees' journey. Feeling blessed that God had prepared me with a three-month crash course on cleaning, what originally looked as if it would be a thankless job had morphed into something I never imagined. Meeting and establishing relationships with people from all races and walks of life, I saw the beauty of love and life on so many different levels. By season's end, everyone felt the love I tried to show daily, and the Legends support staff and management staff treated me as if I was one of their own. And I had gained the respect of the maintenance company, who now called me to work all of the special events the stadium offered the public.

In life, so many of us equate being rich with something tangible, like monetary or materialistic gain. However, this one season in pinstripes had become a dream come true for me, because I was rich from the experience. This was a season that I could share with family members and friends for the rest of my days, and say proudly that I actuality worked an eight-month christening: the inaugural season at the new Yankee Stadium.

However, one final step remained for my journey and the journey of the New York Yankees to be complete.

Twenty-seven outs needed to be recorded in baseball history, and the New York Yankees had to be at least one run ahead of the Philadelphia Phillies.

The first words to everyone that visited me that November evening was "Cherish this moment tonight, for it's something that doesn't happen every day."

Many of the Yankees fans nodded their heads in approval; it had been nine years since our last parade down the Canyon of Heroes, nine years since the most recognized organization in professional sports reached the summit.

A Big Apple too wide awake to sleep on a night like this one was in need of a celebration.

And we needed this moment to come tonight; especially at the expense of Pedro Martinez, our archenemy in red.

(NOTE: *One of the things I also mentioned was that Martinez and Andy Pettitte, the Yankees starter in this matchup, would not only be vying for their team's success, but may have been fighting to see who got into Cooperstown first; for both owned spectacular regular and postseason resumes.)*

The drama of this pairing, one straight out of the Yankee-Red Sox catalog that dominated the middle of the decade, flamed out early. In the bottom of the second inning, Martinez, for years a thorn in the side of Yankees fans, suddenly became the Philadelphia Phillies' sacrificial lamb. Throwing low-eighties fastballs, he halted any momentum he received from an easy first frame by walking A-Rod on four straight pitches.

Next facing designated Hideki Matsui, he got two quick strikes on him, then fell behind after three balls. Two more fastballs were fouled off, and two pickoff throws to first were tossed. The eighth pitch to Matsui was another fastball, one that just missed the spot.

Godzilla crushed it.

Landing in the right-field grandstands, just inside off the foul pole and above a sign for a construction equipment company, it was his second home run in as many at-bats against the former Yankee-killer.

Given a two-run lead, Good Ol' Andy went back to work. A devout Christian, before the game, the reliable left-hander probably went somewhere and prayed for one more championship night from his arm. Once a fresh face of a Yankee championship journey, he now had sprinkles of gray tucked under his cap, a telling sign of twilight on his journey. While his Yankees didn't need a throwback outing, they sure hoped the reliable workhouse could chew up innings and do just enough to help the Yankees become champions.

That's all we needed in the Legends Suite Club. There was a new energy in the establishment, one that was on the precipice of a long-awaited celebration. After we got the game's first two runs, many of the confident patrons were counting the outs.

That count stopped in the third when Phillies catcher Carlos Ruiz tripled and came home on a Jimmy Rollins sacrifice fly.

The two-run Yankee lead was cut in half.

Once again, the Yankees went back to work. After loading the bases against Martinez in the third—Derek Jeter singled, Johnny Damon walked and Mark Teixeira got hit with a pitch—with one batter out, Alex Rodriguez stepped into the batter's box looking to land a knockout blow.

All of Philadelphia held its breath as Martinez battled A-Rod. Knowing that his fastball lacked velocity and his curveball bite, with two strikes the crafty veteran reached back into his past and threw a pretty good slider at the Yankees cleanup hitter. While the pitch appeared to be well off the plate, the home-plate umpire rung A-Rod up for the second out.

The men's room went nuts.

"FOX paid the umpires off so that we'll have a Game 7," one season-ticket holder said.

"They're gonna take it from us," another barked.

One last time, I was reassuring.

"Guys, take it easy. This is our night," I said in a calming tone. "We all earned this."

Little did I realize I had pulled another trick out of my bag of faith; for no sooner than I spoke Yankee victory into the air did Hideki Matsui come up clutch again. Down two strikes in the count, he got a fastball from Pedro and roped it to center, plating two more runs and boosting the Yankee lead to 4-1.

The guys looked at me in amazement.

I smiled.

In my one season in pinstripes, some things were just meant to be.

Martinez would retire the last four batters he faced; then depart the game, and the Yankee rivalry, for the last time. While many New Yorkers loved to hate him, through the years they respected his talents. But we loved to beat him, because to us he still represented the Boston Red Sox. And we always, always had to beat them.

Meanwhile his mound opposite, Pettitte, continued to pitch. Escaping trouble in the fourth, he worked around a pair of two-out walks; then in the fifth he avoided trouble when he got his second inning-ending double play of the night, courtesy of the Phillies' trash-talking prognosticator, Jimmy Rollins.

In the bottom of the fifth, the New York Yankees, picked by Skip Bayless to win the World Series—finally, I shouted when I heard his prediction—put the game away. Reliever Chad Durbin took over in the fifth, and our captain greeted him with a double to right-center. One out later, Teixeira scored Jeter with a single, making the score 5-1.

Clearly rattled, Durbin walked A-Rod, forcing Phillies Manager Charlie Manuel to go to his pen once more.

Out went Durbin, in came rookie J.A. Happ to face the red-hot Yankee designated hitter.

Hideki Matsui, on his way to World Series Most Valuable Player honors, made his last game in a Yankees uniform his greatest. Arriving from Japan seven years, he was a model of professionalism both on and off the field; even taking a reduction in roles—from everyday outfielder to designated hitter, gracefully.

His swan song in a Yankees uniform was beautiful and explosive all at one, for it allowed him to show a worldwide-viewing audience that he could still abuse pitchers on either side of the globe.

In 2003, his first hit at Yankee Stadium was a grand slam.

Six years later, his last hit in the new stadium brought them to the brink of a championship.

After taking thee straight balls from Happ, he boomed a two-run double off the scoreboard in right that not only made the score, 7-1, Yankees, but it broke the competitive will of the defending champions. With his six RBIs, he had garnered a share of a record. Only the Yankees' Bobby Richardson, in 1960, had driven in as many runs in a World Series game as Matsui.

The scene at the new stadium was absolute bedlam. There were twelve outs to go, but they would be more of a victory lap than anything else.

I was like a kid on Christmas. Going outside, I gave the fans in the 100 section hi-fives, and everyone hugs in the Suite Club.

This was a dream come true to me.

Good Ol' Andy, pitching the sixth, gave up a one-out, two-run home run to Ryan Howard, who hit an opposite field homer to left-center, trimming the deficit to 8-3. After another out and double, Joe Girardi, sensing what the entire ballpark knew—that his pitching tank was on "E"—came to get his veteran hurler.

Establishing new decibel levels for the ballpark, the crowd saluted Good Ol' Andy with an ovation like never before.

As Pettitte slowed near the dugout steps, he lifted his cap to reveal his graying scalp. Waving his cap to the crowd, one could sense that his nine-year journey was complete. It would lead him to his eighteenth career postseason victory, far and away the most in baseball history.

Picking up the mantle, relievers Joba Chamberlain and Damaso Marte followed Pettitte with eight outs of scoreless relief, striking out five batters in the process. Producing lights-out efforts throughout the playoffs, the two flamethrowers faced nineteen batters and allowed just two hits.

With one out in the eighth, the manager made his easiest decision of the entire season. Fully cocked and loaded was the greatest reliever the game has ever known.

During the pitching change, many of the regular season-ticket holders came by the men's room to not only use the lower-level restroom, but to say goodbye.

Feeling a little sentimental when they came through, I made my feelings known.

Speaking from my heart, "Well, gentlemen," I said, "We have reached the end of our journey. But I had to say that I never had so much fun, and it's because of so many of you. From the bottom of my heart, I want to say thank you so much."

"Are you trying to make us all cry?" one of them said, bringing laughter from everybody there.

"No. I'm just doing my job."

"You did a dynamite job, man," many of them said.

One of the regular season-ticket holders went as far as to say that I belonged in the front office.

"Your knowledge of the game is outstanding, and your feel of situations is off the charts. You've been calling home runs all year," he continued.

"Just lucky," I responded sheepishly.

Before some of them left, they chanted, "let's go, William" in classic two-three rhythm, then applauded.

When I finally cleared everyone out, I went to a stall and said a prayer of thanks.

Then I went outside for the last three outs.

✪ ✪ ✪

Unlike many of the stories I have written in my past, this journey began with a real-life protagonist, William Fredrick Cooper, at church.

Cleaning a church.

Dreams that come true always start with obedience to the Most High, even when you don't realize it.

But as with everything in life, only God knows the plans He has for all of us.

We're the last to know, what He wants us to know, when He wants us to know.

I didn't know that cleaning a church would lead me to a beautiful experience that I would own forever.

And as I watched Shane Victorino battle Mariano Rivera during that final ten-pitch at-bat —the dying breaths of the Phillies championship reign—I fully identified with Joe DiMaggio when he "thanked the Good Lord for making him a Yankee." The one season I spent as a restroom attendant in the Legends Suite Club, while not glamorous, touched me in a way that I never imagined. Fully breathing in the aura, mystique and tradition of the New York Yankees, I felt as honored as Jeter, as humble as Rivera, and as proud of anyone that ever wore the pinstripes.

When that final out bounced slowly to Robinson Cano, I thought of Jeter, Posada, Pettitte and Rivera, and their nine-year journey back to the mountaintop. The road was rough, but the fact that it didn't come as easy as the first four championships made the end result sweeter.

Finally, the ball reached the second baseman.

As he had done all season, Cano casually flipped it to first. The final out landed softly in Mark Teixeira's glove, and as his teammates rushed the field in ecstasy, the first baseman had to make sure the ball was still there.

It was.

Teixeira erupted, like the 50,000 in attendance for the occasion, and millions more watching in bars and restaurants throughout the city, or in their living rooms.

The bench coaches mobbed their manager; who felt the weight of the world leave his shoulders.

Jeter raised his hands in the air, waving them like he just didn't care. It had been a long time for the Yankees' captain since he'd tasted victory; too long in his book.

The reborn slugger, A-Rod, embraced the manager who never stopped believing in him. Then he would cry like never before.

Some many faces in the stands, young and old, rich and poor, black and white, had tears in their eyes. Others captured the moment on their digital cameras.

The servers, busboys and Legends staff celebrated in the concrete moat while security dressed in blue barely restrained their glee.

After soaking all the euphoria in—and saying goodbye to Mitch Modell and Ross Greenburg, HBO Sports president—I went back inside to work.

Seeing our former mayor along the way, I gave him a huge embrace.

"Thanks for being so special, Mr. Guiliani."

"No, William, thank *you*."

Then he introduced me to his wife.

"You're a lucky woman to be married to a Yankee fan, Ma'am," I joked.

Quickly moving through the required postgame cleaning, I joined the celebration party that had already started in the upper portion of Legends. Along the way, I saw Hal Steinbrenner, the general partner of the best organization in sports.

"Congratulations, Mr. Steinbrenner," I said as we walked up the stairs. "Your father should be really proud of you."

"We all played a part in this, young man. We couldn't have done it without you."

Wow.

Then again, I shouldn't have expected anything less.

After all, in my one season in pinstripes, I was part of a family.

A Yankee family.

And for once in my life, the happy ending was as important as the journey.

Thank you, John Kennedy, for the photo.

Thank you, Alliance Maintenance Company and the New York Yankees, for my one season in pinstripes. God Bless You.

And most importantly, thank you, God, for all that you are doing with me.

And by the way, you can take off that pinstriped jersey now.

JOHN KENNEDY AND WILLIAM FREDRICK COOPER ENJOYING A LEGENDARY SEASON.

Photo courtesy John Kennedy

A TRIBUTE TO
GEORGE M. STEINBRENNER, III
JULY 4, 1930 – JULY 13, 2010

By William Fredrick Cooper

BY GEORGE, YOU HAD ME ALL ALONG

(Dedicated to George M. Steinbrenner III, Principal Owner,
New York Yankees, July 4, 1930–July 13, 2010)

For the past couple of days, the skies opened up, and the tears of Ruth, Gehrig, DiMaggio, and Mantle flowed freely, comforting us all. Colonel Jacob Ruppert has rolled out the red carpet, and Bob Sheppard, the "Voice of Yankee Stadium," arrived just in time to announce his homecoming. Miller Huggins, Joe McCarthy and Casey Stengel, having heard all of Billy Martin's stories, honestly don't know what to expect when he gets there.

I can imagine their collective thought: *Will he fire us, too?*

It's about to get very interesting up there.

But down here, there won't be a man on earth to fill the empty shoes *The Boss* has left behind. How can you actually describe the hurricane of a man that shook up the Bronx thirty-seven years ago and made it his own? Creative and charismatic, was he a cunning, calculating, clever genius who wanted to win at all costs; or in the alternative, a complex, complicated and contradicting character who thrived on constantly capturing the back page? Sometimes cruel, sometimes compassionate but always captivating, whether reviled or revered, George M. Steinbrenner III was truly an original.

And for us New Yorkers, he was all ours.

He was family.

As "The Boss" heads home to a higher calling—as if owning the most successful franchise in the history of American professional sports wasn't big enough—I can't help but think of the relative that simply drives you crazy whenever they're in your presence, yet you realize you're crazier because you miss him whenever they're not around. Recalling the many times I may have talked with envy about an individual that brings life, energy and spirit to a party or gathering from the moment he enters a room, I realized that I always wanted him there for his consistent entertainment and generosity.

I also recalled how I longed to break the car windows of a chorus teacher who always called my mother with behavioral reports, and how years later, I thanked that person for the success and happiness that life now brings because they never gave up on me.

By George, I'm starting to I get it.

George Steinbrenner, the principal owner of the New York Yankees, really cared about us in a way that was all his own. Because of his power, you respected him at *all* times, loathed his methods of madness that confounded you, yet loved him at the end of the day because he never stopped in his efforts to bring you the very best product Major League Baseball had to offer.

On his good days, he was General Douglas McArthur, the fearless leader that produced sixteen divisional championships (tack on two wild-card postseason berths, in 1995 and 2007), eleven American League Pennants and seven Commissioner's trophies. A towering influential presence that represented the courage and will of many New Yorkers, he reached into the rubble of a dull, dark, downtrodden Yankees era (1965-1972) and rebuilt the franchise into a billion-dollar entity.

On his not so good days many labeled him as a bully, an extremely tough man to work for. Difficult and demanding, relentless and ruthless, he could be, in the words of too many (including his own), a gruff son-of-a-bitch. Twenty managerial firings over the first twenty-two years of his regime as well as two suspensions from the game he loved can attest to that. At times a brutal boss who fought with everyone from commissioners and managers to newspaper columnists and elevator walls (broken hand during 1981 World Series), he could be impulsive, irrational and irritating all at once.

But we New Yorkers found him irresistible, because he was all ours. He was family.

And to out-of-towners and others who berate, blast big shots with bad intentions at our Boss, we returned fire in kind. Smaller markets bitched about the money he spent on his ballplayers. What was our response? Don't you want to win at all costs, and leave nothing to chance? Haters, conjuring up memories of the Boss that make us wince—Howard Spira, and feuds with Yogi Berra, Dave Winfield and former Baseball Commissioner Faye Vincent—try to render us mute.

But with all the bombastic bluster of the Boss comes an emphatic rebuttal straight from the heart—Don't hate. Congratulate. And by the way, clean the speck of dirt out of your own eye before looking at mine.

By George, I think I'm getting it.

In realizing that all kings and rulers have messiness in their backyards—Hell, even David had Bathsheba—I focus on the good. Standing by fallen stars Darryl Strawberry and Dwight Gooden, he never gave up on them, even as they continued battling demons. Working at the stadium last year, I heard countless stories of how he saved families from losing homes, paid complete college scholarships and medical bills, and gave millions in charitable assistance to inner-city projects in both New York and his Ohio hometown, and never asked for anything in return.

All he ever wanted was to see people he helped to be successful.

To say that Steinbrenner wanted his *Mona Lisa*, the New York Yankees, to flourish, was grossly understating his objective. A passionate authoritarian who attacked his work with a vengeance, winning here in the Big Apple was second only to breathing. Paying mind-boggling sums of money to his ballplayers, he expected them to exceed even beyond their expectations. From Jackson to Jeter, he counted on their assistance in his commitment to excellence. Demanding production and professionalism from everyone from the players and the front office to the concession people working at the stadium, it didn't make a difference. He expected perfection, and received the resuscitation of the Yankee Way for his efforts.

That determination for the New York Yankees to succeed combined with his deep respect and appreciation for talent and hard work made him not only an icon to baseball, but one of us.

Love him or hate him, he was all ours.

He was family.

Reawakening the ghosts in *The House That Ruth Built*, he was determined never to let them die again. A visionary, he refashioned Yankee tradition with landmark business ventures here and abroad that eventually led to the creation of his own sports network. Like *Casey at the Bat*, there were some big swings and misses, but his major triumphs were Ruthian tape-measure blasts that changed the way business with America's Pastime was done forever.

And at the end of the day, when George M. Steinbrenner III accomplished his goal re-creating not only the greatest organization in baseball, but the greatest sports franchise in history, we New Yorkers understood why he was the way he was. Knowing that tough people lived in this town, he wanted the best for all those pedestrians fighting for taxicabs, trying to get to work to fight for a better way of life. He wanted the best for a make-it-or-break-it town, a city so powerful that even airplanes into skyscrapers killing thousands couldn't stop its movement. He wanted the best for the rich and poor, the young and the old, for black, white, gray, yellow and all colors that inhabited the crazy melting pot of a city that never seemed to sleep.

And most of all, he wanted the best for all those who bleed Yankee blue, like he did. He wanted that winning tradition back, even if it meant teaching us all over again.

The Boss wanted the best for New York, because he loved us.

Because of LOVE, people.

By George, I finally get it.

Because of George M. Steinbrenner, maybe I had it all the time.

Rest in Peace, Boss.

SOMETHING EXTRA:
A TALE OF THREE CITIES...

(NOTE: *Originally, this next segment was supposed to be a part of the Yankee-Red Sox reflective chapter. However, the deeper I went with my recall and research, I came to the realization that this portion of* One Season (in Pinstripes) *deserved its own section. Let's call it a remix section.*)

SOMETHING EXTRA:
A TALE OF THREE CITIES...

I have a confession to make.

While I don't hold a degree in sports psychology, there's nothing more satisfying than watching a long-suffering professional franchise, after years of coming up short in pressure situations, stare down a psychological hurdle, and say, "Enough already." Channeling their frustration as a motivational tool to make themselves better, stronger, and mentally tougher while dispelling unwanted labels placed on tormented teams such as "perennial bridesmaids," "can't win the big one," or more bluntly, being called "chokers," the ability to overcome certain obstacles after years of disappointing adversities only makes the triumphant result that much sweeter.

To fully identify with what the Boston Red Sox may have been feeling going into the 2004 season; I dissected three different teams in sports history—staying away from the obvious baseball analogy of the 1941-1956 New York Yankee-Brooklyn Dodger rivalry; way too predictable—the albatross that encumbered them, and their eventual triumphs of such burdens. Their detailed journeys illustrate the depths of their mental, physical and psychological struggles.

A. The Dallas Cowboys (1965-1971)

In 1965, a young Dallas Cowboy football team, led by defensive tackle Bob Lilly and a young, spectacular defense, was picked to win the NFL's Eastern Division by *Sports Illustrated*. While the defense played up to its lofty expectations, quarterback Don Meredith, 1964 Gold medal sprinter-turned-wide receiver Bob Hayes and the rest of the offense lagged behind in development. Their inconsistency led to a 7-7 record, good for second place in the Eastern Conference.

(NOTE: *In1965, the fourteen-team National Football League was divided into Eastern and Western Conferences. Upon the arrival of two teams—the Atlanta Falcons and New Orleans Saints—in 1967, the conferences were split into four divisions: The Eastern Conference had the Capitol and Century Divisions; the Western Conference owned the Central and Coastal Divisions. From 1967 to 1969 The NFL had a two-tiered playoff system where division winners in the Eastern and Western Divisions faced off, the survivors then meeting in the NFL Championship for the right to face the American Football League Champion in the Super Bowl. After the merger with the American Football League in 1970, the Dallas Cowboys landed a permanent home in the NFC East Division.*)

Finding the balance needed for success on the gridiron in 1966, the following season saw the Cowboys mature into Eastern Division Champions. Behind a potent offense—the running of Don Perkins, the passing of Meredith and the receiving of Hayes, Peter Gent, Buddy Dial and Frank Clarke, Dallas fashioned a 10-3-1 record into a NFL Championship showdown with Vince Lombardi's Green Bay Packers.

Favored by a touchdown over the inexperienced Cowboys, the Packers rode the strength of quarterback Bart Starr's four touchdown passes to a 34-20 fourth-quarter lead. Responding with a long Meredith to Frank Clarke touchdown bomb, Dallas cut the lead to 34-27 and had the ball in the waning minutes. Driving for the game-tying score, a pass interference call on Green Bay left the ball on the Packer two.

A critical offensive penalty and three botched plays left the Cowboys one yard away with time running out. On fourth down, Meredith, rolling out to his right, was pressured by Packer linebacker Dave Robinson into throwing a desperate pass that landed in the arms of Green Bay safety Tom Brown.

From a dejected Cowboy locker room, "The first championship

is the toughest," Cowboy Coach Tom Landry said after the game. "After that, they come easier."

Little did he realize that this game imbedded a negative reflex to big-money moments into the mental psyche of his football team.

A year later, after a 9-5 record earned the Cowboys a Capitol Division title, where they crushed the Cleveland Browns 52-14 for the Eastern Championship. Next traveling to Green Bay for a rematch in the 1967 NFL Championship game, Lone Star state fans, as well the Dallas Cowboys organization, felt as if they possessed the superior team.

Mother Nature must have thought so too.

Conspiring with the Packer gods, December 31, 1967, was the coldest New Year's Eve in the history of Green Bay, Wisconsin. With the game earning the nickname "The Ice Bowl," all thermometers at Lambeau Field were at a game-time temperature of thirteen degrees below zero, and the wind chill made it feel like forty below. The bitter cold overwhelmed the stadium's turf heating system, leaving the playing surface hard as a rock as well as slippery-smooth, much like your local ice skating rink.

A test of intestinal resolve, both teams pushed themselves beyond their limits in this title game. The referees were challenged as well; after the opening kick-off, the officials were unable to use their whistles, and used voice commands and calls to officiate the game.

At first, the frigid conditions of the game helped the Packers to a 14-0 lead halfway through the second quarter. Stripped of its advantages over the Packers in speed, quickness, and multiple formations— deep threat Bob Hayes ran pass patterns with his hands in his pants—the Dallas Cowboys couldn't do anything they had done all season.

They would have to win this game on pure guts.

And they almost pulled it off.

Rallying to a 17-14 fourth-quarter lead, they were four minutes, fifty seconds away from NFL Championship Paradise and a trip to Miami and Super Bowl II opposite the Oakland Raiders. Punting to the Green Bay 32, all they had to do was stop the Packers from going 68 yards to the winning score.

Four minutes and fifty seconds later, head Coach Vince Lombardi and his Green Bay Packers were celebrating an unprecedented third straight NFL title, while the Dallas Cowboys, already hurting physically, were left broken-hearted, shattered spiritually and emotionally with arguably the most devastating loss in franchise history. With the "Doomsday Defense" unfamiliar with the pressure of stopping a team when it mattered most, the Green Bay Packers drove 68 heart-stopping yards, winning the game 21-17 with 16 seconds left on a dramatic one-yard quarterback sneak by Bart Starr.

This loss was so demoralizing that on the long three-hour plane ride home, not a single word was said by any of the Dallas Cowboys.

Not one word.

Rebounding in1968, the Cowboys team produced a 12-2 record; up to that point their finest regular season record ever. Repeating as Capitol Division champions, they went to Cleveland's Municipal Stadium to face the Browns in an Eastern title game rematch. After two consecutive championship game heartbreaks, this was another season where Landry felt his club had everything to go all the way.

The Cleveland Browns, however, thought otherwise.

In a game that wasn't as close as the final score indicated, the Browns avenged their blowout loss from a year earlier by beating Dallas 31-20. Causing much soul searching on the part of Tom Landry and his staff, the process started when he benched Don Meredith when the game was out of reach. This benching effectively ended the career of *Dandy Don*, who retired before training camp in 1969.

With Craig Morton now the Cowboys' quarterback, the 1969 team won their third consecutive Capitol Division title, posting an 11-2-1 regular season record. Once again playing the Browns in the

Eastern Conference Championship game, by halftime, the partisan Texas crowd of 69,321 booed in unison as Cleveland won handily. Led by a stifling defense, running back Leroy Kelly and the quarterback/receiver connection of Bill Nielsen-to-Paul Warfield, the Browns pounded the Cowboys around the Cotton Bowl like a ten-pin in a bowling alley.

The final score of 38-14 could have been worse.

By now, the accumulation of big-game defeats had the media pundits dancing joyfully. Calling the Dallas Cowboys *Next Year's Champions*, the team did itself no favors by living up to the mantra. Week in and week out, the talented Cowboys were the best team in professional football in the regular season.

But in the games that mattered, those for conference or league championships, the Dallas Cowboys were the best team in football at discovering fascinating ways of flushing their season down the toilet.

Simply translated, when the playoff lights burned the brightest, they choked.

After the AFL/NFL merger, the garrote process would happen again in 1970, on an even bigger stage. In winning the NFC East Championship with a 10-4 record, the Cowboys won their first two playoff games versus the Detroit Lions (5-0 in the Divisional Round) and the San Francisco 49ers (17-10 in the NFC Championship), respectively. Ascending to their first Conference Championship, they now competed in Super Bowl V, where they faced off against the Baltimore Colts in Miami's Orange Bowl.

Playing an inferior club, they grasped victory numerous times by way of seven Colt turnovers...numerous times, only to squander it away. Whether it was a fumble, interception or a tipped pass turning into a long touchdown (compliments of Colts tight end John Mackey), this championship contest was a series of big plays, all of which seemed to go against the Cowboys.

Yet with the score tied at 13, it appeared Dallas would have the last chance for victory before the game went into sudden death over-time. With two minutes left to play, and Dallas had the ball and a first down at the Baltimore 48-yard line.

On first down, rookie Duane Thomas lost a yard, then after a holding penalty, the Cowboys were all the way back to their own 27-yard line, facing a second-and-34. Dropping back, Craig Morton threw a high pass that Danny Reeves, the hot receiver on the play, deflected. The ball went off his hands and into the arms of the Baltimore middle linebacker Mike Curtis, who returned the interception 13 yards to the Cowboy 27 with 1:09 to play.

With five seconds left, a thirty-two-yard field goal off the foot of Jim O'Brien drove a stake through the hearts of Dallas fans all over. The Baltimore Colts, another frustrated team battling their own set of demons, had gotten rid of theirs, and were at the top of the world of professional football.

For the Dallas Cowboys, a grim tally of postseason failures had been increased.

They won five division titles over the last five years, and had no championships to show for it.

The proof of the final result still lacking, a lingering question tore at their psyche. Would they ever dispel the notion that they were sunshine soldiers with a hearty appetite of championship aspirations sans the will of commitment to achieve said goal?

Right from the start of training camp, the 1971 season looked like the season where, after years of underachieving, the Dallas Cowboys would finally implode. Running back Duane Thomas, who had gained 800 rushing yards in a sensational rookie campaign, staged a holdout and was traded to the New England Patriots. Five days later, after refusing to complete a physical and defying Patriot coach John Mazur's request to line up in a three-point stance, he was back with the Cowboys by way of Commissioner Pete Rozelle, who negated the trade. Once Thomas returned, he began a season-long silent treatment to teammates and media.

Further complicating matters was the quarterback controversy between incumbent Craig Morton and his twenty-nine-year-old backup and 1963 Heisman Trophy winner, Roger Staubach. Coach Landry, loyal up to this point in the club's history where the position was concerned, was decidedly undecided. Morton, the classic drop-back pocket passer, had more than served his time behind Don Meredith (four years), and had proven the last two years he could play well in the regular season.

His postseason performances, however, were awful.

By contrast, Landry could see he had a wild card in the mobile Staubach. The proud owner of that special elusive dimension, Staubach's scrambling made him more dangerous, for he could create something out of nothing if a play broke down. Additionally, Staubach had incredible pocket presence; possessed the ability to throw with accuracy to his receivers; threw soft touch passes on screens to the running backs; and loved to throw on the run.

Most importantly, the mobile, daring quarterback was an incredible competitor and field general who simply hated to lose. Even if it meant changing the plays ordered from the sidelines—hence, Landry's trepidation—he wanted to win at all costs.

Although it took seven games, a 4-3 record (which included an inexplicable 23-19 loss to the Chicago Bears in a game where coach Landry alternated the quarterbacks on *every* play) and being two games behind the mid-season, division-leading Washington Redskins, he realized that the special intangibles that Staubach owned could possibly save the season. In naming "Roger the Dodger" his starter for the remainder of the campaign, not only did he salvage it, but he altered the history of the Dallas Cowboys in the process.

Focusing on the job ahead as opposed to their troubled beginning, from week eight forward, the team with one star on its helmet was unbeatable. Bringing continuity and chemistry to the offense, Staubach and a resurgent Duane Thomas (two 100-yard rushing games to go with 11 touchdowns in 11 games) infused new blood into the offense. The Doomsday Defense, spearheaded by future Hall of Famers Lilly, Mel Renfro and Herb Adderley, buckled down. In those final seven games, Dallas gave up more than 300 yards of total offense to just one team and forced a total of 24 turnovers.

Running the table with a seven-game win streak (which included a 13-0 blanking of the Redskins in a first-place showdown), the Cowboys surged past Washington, capturing the NFC Eastern Division Title with an 11-3 record. Propelled into the postseason for the sixth consecutive year, rather than celebrate their divisional championship, the burning ember of motivation remained white-hot. They had traveled these roads before, only to meet bitter disappointment at the end of the trail.

Though unspoken, to a man the mission would not be complete unless a new path leading to Vince Lombardi Super Bowl Trophy was blazed.

(NOTE: *The NFL's Super Bowl trophy was renamed the Vince Lombardi Trophy in his honor, after the legendary Packer and Washington Redskin coach passed away in September 1970. It was first awarded under its new name after Super Bowl V.*)

Traveling to Bloomington, Minnesota on Christmas Day for an NFC Divisional Playoff game, the Cowboys shouted, "Bah, humbug," to the NFC Central Champion Minnesota Vikings and their hostile Metropolitan Stadium crowd. Ignoring the derisive chants and anti-Cowboy banners decorating the stadium, Dallas rode the strength of their defense—which forced a fumble and four interceptions—and two late touchdowns to an easy 20-12 victory.

Back at home for an NFC Championship rematch against the 49ers, the defense again played superbly. Limiting quarterback John

Brodie, receiver Gene Washington and the rest of the explosive San Francisco offense to 239 net yards, Doomsday waited patiently for the 49ers' mistakes, and was rewarded with three interceptions in a 14-3 victory.

Still maintaining their focused, steely resolve, one final obstacle stood between the Dallas Cowboys and the long overdue quenching of their championship thirst: the American Football Conference Champion Miami Dolphins.

Arriving in New Orleans to play for pro football's ultimate prize, if anyone wondered whether the Dallas Cowboys were ready to shed themselves of all stigmas associated with a past filled with major disappointments, if any pessimists thought the Cowboys wouldn't close the deal in Super Bowl VI, perhaps a confrontation between two football fans the night before the game epitomized their determination:

In the nearby French Quarter, a Miami fan placed his hands over his neck and gave a Dallas Cowboy fan the universal choke sign.

Standing up, the Cowboy fan calmly walked over to him and decked him.

On Super Sunday, another knockout happened in Tulane Stadium. Before a sold-out crowd of 81,000 (many of whom were Dolphin fans) and interested millions viewing over television, Tom Landry's Cowboys finally won the big game 24-3.

Executing flawlessly, Dallas thoroughly dominated the Dolphins on both sides of the ball. Complementing two touchdown passes by game MVP Roger Staubach was a running game that effectively controlled the clock. Led by the "Silent One," Duane Thomas, the Cowboys rushed the ball for a then-Super Bowl record 252 yards.

Finding the Miami offense predictable, The Doomsday Defense neutralized Dolphin quarterback Bob Griese, shackled running backs Larry Csonka and Jim Kiick, and shut down wide receiver Paul Warfield (a symbol of past Dallas futility, he had been traded from the Cleveland Browns to Miami following the 1969 season) by utilizing double coverage. To this day, Super Bowl VI is the only game in which the losing team failed to score a touchdown.

Finally shedding the "Next Year's Champion" label, the Dallas Cowboys celebrated with an easy smile. Perhaps Bob Lilly's lighting of a cigar said it all: It had taken six long hard years to reach the mountaintop (twelve, if you're counting from the Cowboys' first NFL season in 1960), but the arduous journey made the end result more gratifying.

While the Dallas Cowboys conquered obstacles and circumstances to achieve championship glory, there are other types of psychological burdens in the maturation of a sports champion. History has shown me that rare occasion where a superstar and an entire team had to not only confront a bully kicking sand in their faces, but him/themselves as well.

B. Chicago Bulls vs. Detroit Pistons (1988-1991)

They won six National Basketball Association titles in eight years. And it easily could have been eight.

That bit of information, along with the aerial artistry, competitive desire and unmatched will of the greatest player the game has ever known, is what people remember about the Michael Jordan—led Chicago Bulls. From the image of Jordan crying while holding that initial Lawrence O'Brien trophy in 1991 with father and wife by his side; to his Game 6, era-ending pose in Utah some eight years later, basketball fans all over the world have many reasons why the Windy City franchise became one of sports' enduring dynasties.

While some point to the right collection of players being assembled around Jordan—most notably, his faithful sidekick Scottie Pippen—and others to Zen Master Coach Phil Jackson, long-time assistants John Bach and Tex Winter, and lastly, the implementation of the Triangle Offense, what many people overlook is that Jordan played with the Chicago Bulls for seven seasons before winning his first title.

And to fully appreciate the Bulls run of the '90s, you must realize their toughest obstacle may have been in defeating the team that molded their championship mentality: the Detroit Pistons.

For me, the answer cannot be pinned to a specific reason; ironically, I feel the origin of the Bulls' maturation process started with the Boston Celtics of the 1986-87 season. Having won five Eastern Conference titles and three NBA crowns during the decade, this veteran team taught a hard-charging Detroit Pistons team what it took to win a championship in a spirited Eastern Conference Championship Series.

Normally impervious to big game pressure, with the emergence of the hungry Pistons, the Celtics encountered a serious threat to its conference reign. Coached by Chuck Daly, Detroit played an extremely aggressive game never before seen in the NBA. Rugged front-court men Bill Laimbeer and Rick Mahorn, the chief initiators of this brand of play, were backed up by energetic youngsters John Salley and Dennis Rodman.

While the "Bad Boys," as the Pistons became known, employed physical and often dirty playing tactics to intimidate their opponents and bully their way to victory, they also had a potent trio of backcourt scorers in All-Star guard Isaiah Thomas, Joe Dumars and Vinnie Johnson, as well as a high-scoring, low-post option in forward Adrian Dantley. That a deep, hungry team could add a post-up scoring threat like seven-footer James Edwards (obtained from Phoenix Suns in midseason), the Pistons had all the tools to knock off Boston.

However, victory in this bitter series would go to the Celtics in seven, hotly contested games. In teaching Detroit that the combination of mental toughness and physically intense defense is a lethal, unbeatable one, the lessons proved invaluable the following year as a mature Piston team unseated the Celtics as Eastern Conference Champions.

Along the way to dethroning the aging Celtics in the 1987-88 NBA season, the Pistons encountered another team on the cusp of greatness in the Chicago Bulls in the Eastern Conference Semifinals. While cognizant of the rise of this young basketball team—both teams played in the NBA's Central Division—there was a dismissive feeling amongst the newly crowned conference champions.

To a man, the feelings in the Motor City were that the Chicago Bulls lacked the grit and cerebral know-how to be a legitimate threat for eastern supremacy. Merely a blip on the radar scale of their basketball universe (which comprised of the Pistons, Celtics and NBA Champion Los Angeles Lakers), at the time they never gave them much thought.

Speaking a language only known to them and the other powerhouse teams, when translated to the Chicago Bulls, the message was simple:

Man cannot win an NBA Championship on talent alone, and you're not ready yet to challenge the big dogs. You don't know the process yet, so until you have what it takes, stay in your lane.

The Detroit Pistons

While people around the NBA acknowledged Michael Jordan's greatness—in that 1987-88 season, Jordan won the league's Most Valuable Player and Defensive Player of the Year awards while leading the league in scoring for the second straight season—the Chicago Bulls were still trying to surround him with the right cast. Possessing no other reliable scorers than Jordan, second-year forwards Horace Grant and Scottie Pippen were still finding their way as NBA players and the sole inside offensive presence was rebounding machine Charles Oakley.

In realizing that the younger, more fragile Bulls were the more athletic team, the Pistons also grasped the fact that they were heavily dependent on Jordan's individual exploits, and hadn't developed team cohesiveness. Inducing the Bulls into a psychologically physical battle, one that would shape the course of the rivalry, in that first playoff confrontation, the trap they set worked to perfection.

The Piston strategy for containing Michael Jordan was to challenge him and make every single shot he took a difficult, demanding one. Disguising its defensive schemes, the looks he received varied, throwing him totally off balance. Initially overplaying Jordan to keep the ball from him, sometimes they allowed guard Joe Dumars to play him straight up, or run a double-team at him the minute he touched the ball, forcing him to pass to an ineffective teammate. And whenever he went to the basket, they swarmed to him like bees to honey.

That "help defense" was the beginning of what came to be known as the "Jordan Rules" and would be a staple of the NBA playoffs for the next three seasons.

To get the other Bulls off their game, they literally *beat them up.*

Baiting them into fights, they hit them, pushed and shoved them, knocked them to the floor, then showed the exit to the Eastern Conference playoff door in five games. From there, the Pistons went on to beat the Celtics for the Eastern Conference crown, and lost a tough seven-game series to the Lakers in the NBA Finals.

The Chicago Bulls' trial by fire would continue the following season. As the Pistons fielded the strongest unit in franchise history; their 63-19 record was the NBA's best in 1988-89. The Eastern Conference sixth-seeded Bulls (47-35) had surprising success in the playoffs. After defeating the Cleveland Cavaliers in the first round of the playoffs on a last-second Michael Jordan jumper, next Chicago upset the Atlantic Division Champion New York Knicks in the Conference Semifinals.

For the first time in club history, the Bulls made the Eastern Conference Finals, and waiting for their arrival was a familiar foe, the Detroit Pistons with a new wrinkle to their *Jordan Rules.* Not only was the league's leading scorer followed continuously by Dumars, but a series of defenders—the muscular Vinnie Johnson, the angular John Salley and six-foot-eight-inch defensive wizard Dennis Rodman—took turns harassing him. Placing a bounty above his head, each player guarding Jordan treated him rudely. Pounding on him from the first quarter on, driving shots that normally resulted in scoring plays against other teams never materialized when Jordan faced Detroit; he was hacked, not merely fouled.

Ever the stubborn warrior, Jordan, still determined to show that he was individually dominant, became easy prey as he fell hook, line and sinker into the Piston trap once more. Driving by the defender checking him, he would be met by a big, agile Piston coming from the weak side. With two, sometimes three men confronting him, Jordan would either take the brutal hit and miss the shot; or pass the ball to an open teammate, only to discover that Detroit defenders were quick enough to switch over and harass the other Chicago shooters. The reason why other Bulls, especially Scottie Pippen and Craig Hodges, missed painfully open shots is that Rodman or Salley, usually flying at them as they released the ball, disrupted their concentration.

At first, the Bulls playoff success seemed to continue as they took an early 2-1 lead over the reigning Eastern Conference Champions. But then the mean streak of the ornery Pistons surfaced. Calculating with their attack, every time the Bad Boys knocked Jordan to the floor, they took some steam away from his indomitable will to score. After clamping down on *His Airness*, they next focused their attention on his sidekick, Scottie Pippen. Infuriating him with their aggressive play, the Bulls' second leading scorer felt compelled to match them push for push, elbow for elbow, and menacing glare for menacing glare. When his teammates followed suit, it played into another Piston mental trap: In getting the Chicago Bulls hell-bent on standing up to them physically, their basketball execution went right out the window.

With their intensity ratchet turned up, the Pistons bottled up Michael Jordan with double-teaming in the next three games, holding him—astoundingly—to no points in the second quarter (and 23 overall) in a Game 4 86-80 win, and a measly eight shots (and 18 points) in a 94-85 Game 5 victory in Detroit. In Game 6 in Chicago, the Bulls were still in the game in the fourth period, trailing 81-79 with about eight minutes left, when Detroit guard Joe Dumars pickpocketed Jordan as he drove to the basket. With the steal leading to a fast break and free throw, the Pistons wore down Jordan and finished off the Bulls 103-94, to advance to the NBA Finals and eventually, their first NBA Championship.

Replacing Doug Collins with head Coach Phil Jackson, the 1989-90 campaign brought a change in offensive philosophy. Concentrating on subverting the *Jordan Rules*, Jackson and assistant coach Tex Winter implemented the triangle offense. By focusing on a triple post offense, this philosophy put emphasis on those surrounding Michael Jordan.

Simply translated, it forced the Chicago Bulls to grow up.

By sharing responsibility rather than shouldering it, Jordan led the Bulls to the second best record in the East at 55-27...behind the ever-tough defending champion Pistons, who finished 59-23. In a destined Eastern Conference Finals rematch, the Bulls pushed the Pistons like never before, forcing the series to its seven-game limit.

Would the Bulls finally remove the albatross, one that challenged the core of their fragile psyche?

Their answer came in a disastrous showing. In a cakewalk of a contest, the Pistons showed their dominance by winning a series-deciding Game 7 at home by a score of 93-74. It was in that pivotal game that Scottie Pippen would suffer a migraine headache, confirming many speculations that the Bulls simply weren't mentally strong enough to supplant the Pistons as the best team in the East. The Pistons would go on to win their second consecutive NBA title the following round against the Portland Trail Blazers.

Watching this rivalry unfold in my early twenties, the maturation process of the Chicago Bulls was at times unbearable. Feeling the growing pains along with them, I rooted for Jordan and the Bulls to overcome not only the insurmountable hurdle that was the Detroit Pistons, but the psychological burden of growth they failed to embrace.

It wasn't easy. Recalling that seventh-game blowout in Detroit back in 1990 and understanding the brutality of the lesson that was being inflicted, the viciousness of the Bulls' constant failure was gripping. Seeing Michael Jordan play his heart out against an angry tide of Pistons, the core of me shook after each Detroit basket, and every Chicago turnover.

His heroic thirty-one-point/eight-rebound/nine-assist effort was painful to witness.

"He's all alone," I commented to my girlfriend, Audrey, at the time. "His teammates left him all by himself."

Transcending the Pistons' physical triumph on the basketball court was the mental, emotional and spiritual beating the Bulls were taking. Knowing that they hadn't figured out what was missing in basketball mind, heart and spirit; one of the saddest moments I ever saw watching an NBA game was when Coach Phil Jackson removed Jordan with a minute or so remaining. Sensing the defeat in his soul as he shook his teammates' hands, feeling the frustration that the entire city of Chicago must have felt watching the Pistons emerge victorious as they nursed their wounds yet again, I made a bold statement.

"The Bulls are gonna win the NBA title next year."

"How do you know?" Audrey asked.

"I can feel it."

What I felt was a person and team simply having enough of not being good enough. To this point, the Detroit Pistons were like Sho'nuff, the villainous Shogun of Harlem in that 1980s movie *The*

Last Dragon. Michael Jordan and the Chicago Bulls, perfectly cast as the hero Leroy Green, were a dynasty-in-waiting that lacked self-confidence. Battered, bruised and drowning in a pool of futile frustration, for three straight years Michael Jordan and his teammates lifted their heads out of the water, only to meet more abuse while being dunked repeatedly by the Bad Boys.

"Who is the master?" the Pistons asked in the 1988 Eastern Conference Semifinals.

That the Bulls conceded in five games spoke words they refused to say.

Back into the water the Bulls went.

In the 1989 Eastern Conference Finals, once more, the Pistons again asked, "Who is the master?" while dispatching them in six games.

Swallowing more *H20*, the Bulls, still refusing to acknowledge Detroit's mental superiority had got inside their heads, took their lumps and went home with their heads hung low.

"When I say, who is the master?" the Pistons demanded in the 1990 Conference Finals, "You say the Detroit Pistons."

Pushing them to their championship limit only to be turned away once more, Jordan and the Bulls suffered in silence as they damn near drowned.

Obscured in the immediate disappointment of that narrow, seven-game defeat, however, were the seeds of future triumph being planted. The Chicago Bulls were soon-to-be masters of the NBA, provided they realized what they lacked—belief in themselves—they possessed all the time.

Additionally, there was a sense of urgency for the franchise in 1991. Knowing they were at a crossroads, they matured to a point where they could no longer be recognized as a team on the rise. Sensing how close they were to exorcizing their tormentors in their last defeat, an entire city was at a point where the team's identity would be defined by their success or failure against their nemesis.

Another loss to the Pistons in the playoffs would be devastating.

With a greater concentration on teamwork, the Bulls learned the mental aspect of playing through all adversities, and that bitter failure, when acknowledged and channeled correctly, can produce positive results. In leading his team to the best regular season record in the Eastern Conference with a 61-21 win-loss record, Michael Jordan elevated the play of his supporting cast while regaining league Most Valuable Player status.

Methodically marching to the challenge that awaited them all season, after sweeping the New York Knicks in round one, and eliminating the Philadelphia 76ers in the conference semifinals, their moment of truth arrived in the Eastern Conference Finals. Facing a Detroit Piston squad that finished second to them in the regular season, both teams knew what was at stake. While the Bulls finally had the home-court advantage and were favored this time around, still some maintained that the Pistons' psychological edge and bench strength would loom over the battle.

From the onset of the series, the Bad Boys tried all of their regular mind tricks, but this time around nothing worked. Poised under the Piston pressure, Bulls wouldn't be baited into retaliation. Whenever they were knocked down, Michael Jordan, Scottie Pippen and the others got up immediately, smiled and walked away.

In prior encounters, Detroit's physical play made the Bulls weaker. This time, it was the opposite. With every intimidation tactic, Chicago added more intensity to their counter-attack. Single-minded in its collective focus as they systematically dismantled the Detroit championship reign, perhaps the hunted-to-hunter changing-of-the-guard was best exemplified in a Game One sequence when Jordan found himself isolated on Piston stopper John Salley.

Salley, nicknamed "Spider" because of his defensive prowess, shouted, "You don't go near the Spider's web!"

With that as a cue, Jordan, executing a cross-over, drove by him and slammed the ball home for two.

"Block that, bitch!" he then yelled at Salley.

That move, along with an inspired bench, an energetic, smothering defense and a mental toughness never possessed before, led to Chicago Bull victories in the first three games of the series.

Before Game 4 of the 1991 Eastern Conference Finals, there had been only one time in my life that I had wept when watching a televised sports event. (I'll get to that later.) But after seeing Michael Jordan and his teammates absorb three years of aches and bruises, my spirit told me the only way this rivalry could end was with an emphatic statement symbolizing growth, maturity and long-awaited vindication.

And sure enough, Memorial Day 1991 provided that statement. In vanquishing their three-year Detroit Piston nightmare with a 115-94 blowout victory, I couldn't help but feel their victory was something much deeper than the game itself. Every bully has his day of reckoning, a moment where tricks of intimidation that normally strike fear in those with lesser confidence, wears off. In making up for three long years of pain and suffering at their hands with a four-game sweep, Michael Jordan and the Chicago Bulls finally mastered the learning curve in a way where there was no doubt to anyone watching which of the two teams was better.

Blending their talent with the shrewd knowledge from lessons learned, the Chicago Bulls were like a once-timid schoolboy finally taking control of the Eastern Conference sandbox. Not only displaying that they were stronger physically, but mentally as well, their remarkable exhibition of persistence showed the bewildered Pistons that no matter what they did or tried, they were never going to beat Michael Jordan and the Chicago Bulls anymore.

"Why are you so emotional?" I remember Audrey asking me as we watched those final minutes tick away.

Wiping away the tears, while unable to explain the beauty of sports and its correlation to life, all I could say was "the Bulls are finally moving on." Coming together to exorcise a demon, their triumph over the tremendous obstacle that was the Detroit Pistons allotted the Chicago Bulls a drive that not only inspired the greatness necessary to defeat the Bad Boys, but the greatness necessary to accumulate six NBA Championships in eight years.

That one was as good as it gets...

But we have one more example to analyze, one that runs the closest to the Yankees' dominance over the Red Sox; and provided me with what stands to this day my greatest sense of personal satisfaction when watching sports.

C. Minneapolis/Los Angeles Lakers vs. Boston Celtics (1959-1985)

For two-and-a-half decades, and eight championship battles, there was a fact in the history of the National Basketball Association that was known to all. For a city in Massachusetts, the utter delight that accompanied this fact was nirvana. For two other cities miles away, *the fact* was as annoying as someone making chalk screech against a blackboard.

For the fans in Boston, Minneapolis, then eventually, Los Angeles, euphoria met exasperation with a single fact.

The Lakers have never beaten the Celtics.

Try as they might, the emotions from this fact were startling in their polarization. Exciting and excruciating, simultaneously splendid and spoiling, the power of a single sentence brought joy and pain to legions of basketball fans.

And for twenty-five years, that one sentence screamed an indisputable fact.

The Lakers have never beaten the Celtics.

Whether it was a fluke last-second shot, a gallant penultimate effort that fell short, or the haunting sight of Red Auerbach's victory cigar permeating the stale Boston Garden air, the ghosts that in-habited the psyche of an entire basketball organization were real. From the cold Twin Cities, then the bright lights of the Inglewood Forum to the elevated Orange train line screeching along Causeway Street past the ancient Boston Garden and its parquet floor; from Bill Russell, Bob Cousy, Sam Jones, John Havlicek, and Larry Bird to Elgin Baylor, Jerry West, Wilt Chamberlain and Magic Johnson, the pain of the refrain remained.

The Lakers have never beaten the Celtics.

The championship rivalry began in April 1959, when the Minneapolis Lakers, led by high-scoring, mid-air contortionist Elgin Baylor and veteran Vern Mikkelsen, rallied from a last- place season the year before to upset the favored St. Louis Hawks in the Western Conference Finals. Running into a powerful Celtic team led by Hall of Famers Russell, Cousy and Bill Sharman (one that finished with a 52-20 regular-season record and dispatched the Syracuse Nationals in a tough, seven-game Eastern Conference Finals series), the Lakers managed to keep every game close in the World Championship Series…

(NOTE: *The NBA Finals was called the NBA World Championship Series until 1986.*)

But, couldn't eke out a win.

Boston won the first game in the Garden, 118-115, and then won Game 2, 128-108. Game 3 was in St. Paul, where the Lakers fell, 123-120. And two nights later, Boston finished the first sweep in Championship Series history with a 118-113 victory in Minneapolis.

Unbeknownst to Lakers fans, over the course of two-and-a-half decades, the end result of this series proved to be the least heart-breaking result.

Stretching the NBA's reach beyond the Midwest region, Owner Bob Short moved the financially strapped Lakers to Los Angeles in 1960. Owning the second pick in the league draft that year, the Lakers further lent a more professional look to a league that had been confined to the East Region when they selected All-American guard Jerry West from West Virginia. Coupled with the potent proficiency of Baylor, together they formed the greatest 1-2 scoring tandem in league history. And over the next decade, this prolific, explosive combination would lead the Purple-and-Gold franchise to the precipice of championship glory six more times.

And six more times they encountered a murderous obstacle in the Boston Celtics.

The Los Angeles Lakers were good; really good.

But were they good enough to beat the Boston Celtics?

Though they faced off in the 1959 Championship Series, the spiritual DNA of this storied rivalry was formed in 1962, when the Lakers returned to the stage. By then, their opponent, a three-time defending champion coming off a sixty-win regular season, seemed formidable. A fast-breaking unit that was also a premier defensive power, the Boston Celtics fielded six future Hall of Famers in Cousy, Russell, K.C. Jones, Frank Ramsey, Sam Jones and Tommy Heinsohn.

The Lakers team, coached by Fred Schaus, had one of those golden seasons in which almost everything seemed to go right. Playing before sellout crowds in the Los Angeles Sports Arena (which included celebrity stargazers Doris Day, Danny Thomas, Dinah Shore and Pat Boone; not exactly Jack Nicholson, Arsenio Hall and Dyan Cannon of the *Showtime* era, but their home games became a chic, happening place to be seen by all), they won the Western Division with a 54-26 record, and whipped Detroit in six games in the conference finals.

As if touched by destiny, even their only real setback during the regular season had its advantages. Elgin Baylor, limited to only 48 regular-season games because of reserve duty with the Army, was unstoppable. His scoring average of 38.3 points per game was second only to the 50.2 points a game Wilt Chamberlain put up.

(NOTE: *I have to say this again, so I can actually believe it…Wilt*

Chamberlain averaged 50.2 points a game in the 1961-62 NBA Season. Damn.)

When Baylor wasn't there, Jerry West, averaging 30.8 points a game, shouldered the load, and had help from the likes of "Hot Rod" Hundley, reserve forward Tommy Hawkins, veteran guard Dick Barnett and second-year forward and enforcer Rudy LaRusso. Meshing with their fearless young superstars perfectly, the Lakers seemed ready to supplant the Celtics as league champion.

Splitting the first two games in Boston—the Celtics winning the first game 122-108, and the Lakers bouncing back with a 129-122 road win—another sold-out crowd in Los Angeles was treated to a buzzer-beating finish, compliments of Jerry West. After scoring to tie the game at 115 apiece, West then deflected an inbound pass to Bob Cousy with four seconds remaining on the dead run.

Now in a game of *Beat The Clock*, the future silhouette of the trademark NBA logo raced thirty feet with his dribble, laying the ball through the basket as the buzzer sounded, giving the Lakers a 117-115 victory.

The clutch play sent the City of Angels into a frenzy, but the Celtics promptly killed any thoughts of prolonged jubilation by taking Game 4, 115-103. Heading back to Beantown with the series tied at two apiece and the home court advantage, the defending champions were poised to put the truculent Lakers in their place.

In Game 5, however, the Celtics were ambushed 126-121.

Starring for the Lakers in this movie, in full color, was Elgin Baylor. At the height of his basketball powers, the Boston Garden was the backdrop of one of those nights where the game came effortless to him. Natural ability meeting instinct and court savvy, every move that evening seemed to find Baylor at just the right place on that parquet floor. Grabbing 22 rebounds would have been a memorable achievement itself in this pivotal battle.

But on this night, he had defensive stalwart Tom "Satch" Sanders seriously thinking about another line of work. Conducting a scoring symphony, Baylor lit up the Boston night with 61 points, to this day a record for an NBA Finals game.

To put that feat into perspective, it took Michael Jordan two overtimes to top that playoff total, *by only two points.*

Think about that for a tick…

It took MJ *two extra quarters to score two more points.*

(MEMO: *AN APOLOGY TO MICHAEL JORDAN: Before I start with this missive, please note that instead of the singular "$" I borrowed from Brother Scoop Jackson, Michael Jordan now gets "$$$" of these because he is now the principal owner of the Charlotte Bobcats. Having said that, the letter reads as follows: $$$, I want you to know that I love you more than any other baller that's ever laced up sneakers. Royal Airness, your combination of a tremendous work ethic, uncanny athleticism, un-matched faith and an indomitable competitive will has me calling you my favorite athlete ever. But, with all things being equal, Elgin Baylor's performance twenty-plus years before yours on the parquet floor…*)

Would Baylor's virtuoso in sneakers lead the Los Angeles Lakers to championship-clinching victory at home?

Nope.

The Boston Celtics, showing their trademark resilience, again doused premature elation in Los Angeles by crushing the Lakers 119-105 in Game 6. Knotting the series at three games, Game 7, for all the marbles, was in the Boston Garden.

If ever there was an ancestor to the old "NBA is Fantastic" mantra, then perhaps this thrilling, spine-tingling, roller-coaster ride of a classic game served as a shining example of basketball at its breath-holding best.

Streaking ahead, the Celtics took a 53-47 lead into the halftime locker room. The Lakers, knowing that they would need both Baylor and West to have big nights to pull off the major upset, had been obliged by the two-headed scoring tandem. Bringing their "A" games to the occasion, they were on their way to scoring 41 and 35 points, respectively.

Maintaining their lead through the third quarter, the Celtics were ahead 73-67 heading into the period's final minute. But a mini-explosion by West—who scored seven points in a row—deadlocked the game at 75 apiece as the fourth quarter opened.

From there, and for decades to come, the legacies of two franchises were defined.

Boston quickly rushed to a six-point lead, then fell back into a tie at 88 apiece with only six minutes left. Again, the Celtics went back up, this time by five, 96-91 with about four minutes remaining.

Celtic fans throughout the city breathed easy, as if the game's outcome was secure.

Once again, they were wrong.

First Tom Heinsohn fouled out, joining Sanders and Jim Loscutoff on the bench. All three had fallen trying to stop Elgin Baylor, who was leaving his heart on the parquet floor.

His partner in crime, West, canned a jumper, then Baylor hit one of two free throws to make it 96-94. After two Bill Russell free throws re-established a four-point lead, West quickly answered with another bucket, closing the gap once more to 98-96.

After a missed Celtic jumper, the Lakers had a chance to square things on their next possession when Boston great Sam Jones blocked Frank Selvy's shot, and then hit two free throws at the other end to widen the margin to 100-96.

With a minute remaining, the upstarts from the coast seemed doomed.

But an unlikely hero, Frank Selvy, seemed destined to pick up where Baylor and West left off. Grabbing a rebound and driving the length of the floor for a layup to cut the deficit in half, seconds later he followed up missed West layup with one of his own, squaring the game at 100 apiece.

With their capacity crowd stunned into silence, the Celtics got the ball back with 18 seconds left. Celtic guard Frank Ramsey, driving into heavy traffic, missed a wild running hook shot, and Lakers forward Frank LaRusso grabbed the rebound.

Calling a timeout with five seconds left, the Los Angeles Lakers could have done the improbable...the seemingly impossible...

Carefully diagramming the inbounds play, Lakers Coach Fred Schaus set up Baylor as the first option, West as the second, and whoever else was open as the third. With the ball now in play, Rod Hundley, in the game to handle the ball, dribbled quickly to his right. Suddenly met by Celtic guard Tom Ramsey, in those precious milliseconds, Hundley quickly scanned the floor.

Baylor and West were covered.

But there was Frank Selvy, open along the left baseline. After Hundley rifled the ball past a gambling Bob Cousy (who was frantically rushing back to cover him after double-teaming West), a potential Lakers hero caught the ball in rhythm, then released.

Two seconds were left.

Arching through the air with perfect trajectory, the shot, an eight-foot baseline jumper, was one that Selvy made with regularity through-out his career.

For the Los Angeles Lakers on this particular night, it was a shot that caromed high off the front rim, fell away, and would forever be known as the shot that could have ended the Boston dynasty.

"I would trade all my points for that last basket," Selvy, who once scored 100 points in a college basketball contest for his alma mater Furman, told reporters afterward.

His shot, as well as the Los Angeles Lakers' courageous title effort, fell one inch short.

Celtic great Bill Russell, who finished the game with 30 points and 40 rebounds, wrapped the rebound in his arms to force overtime. And in that extra period the Celtics built a five-point lead and won, 110-

107. Sam Jones scored five of his 27 points in the extra period, Ramsey added 23 of his own, and the Lakers could only watch Bob Cousy run time out on their title hopes with an expert display of right-handed dribbling.

In making the NBA championship something of a birthright, the 1962 title was the fourth of eight consecutive titles for the Boston Celtics, who were in the midst of the greatest dynasty in the history of professional sports. Spanning thirteen years (1957 to 1969), the Celtics were the last basketball team standing an amazing *eleven* times. Always one step ahead of the opposition, they defeated many great teams along the way. The Cincinnati Royals, led by Oscar Robinson and Jerry Lucas, always seemed to be one step short, as were the Wilt Chamberlain-led Philadelphia/San Francisco Warrior ball clubs of the early-to-mid 1960s. Even when Chamberlain was traded back East, to the Philadelphia 76ers in 1965, only once, in 1967, did he and supporting stars Luke Jackson, Hal Greer and Chet Walker experience a championship breakthrough.

However, no team felt the sting of the Boston Celtic juggernaut more than the Los Angeles Lakers. Though the pure talents of West, Baylor and other complementary parts earned them great success in the Western Conference, when confronting the hegemony of those vaunted Celtic teams, they couldn't overcome fate, or their opponent's heroics.

Not that they didn't try. In 1963, 1965, 1966 and 1968, they returned to the brink of the basketball supremacy, only to find the team from Beantown standing in the way of that final step.

Peering down tauntingly from the mountaintop, the Celtics refuted every Lakers challenge. Adjusting their personnel, old standbys Cousy, Sharman, Ramsey and future championship coaches Heinsohn and K.C. Jones were replaced by Bailey Howell, Larry Siegfried, Don Nelson and future all-time great John Havlicek. Joining holdovers Tom "Satch" Sanders and Sam Jones, their dominance over the Lakers never stopped. Even Red Auerbach stepped aside, handing the coaching reins over to linchpin Russell after the 1966 championship.

In six games in 1963, five in 1965, seven in 1966 and six more in 1968, the Celtics cast a shadow over the Los Angeles area with Championship Series victories. Honing in on the Lakers' weaknesses—no post strength to combat Russell and lack of scoring balance—their team play trumped the dual magnificence of Baylor and West, forcing the Lakers to retool.

Still, even after adding Archie Clark and Gail Goodrich to their bench and replacing the docile Fred Schaus with volatile coach Butch Van Breda Kolff, nothing seemed to work. Year after year, everything remained the same: West and Baylor, brilliantly leading the Lakers to the doorstep of success, challenged the Celtics in the most conventional way imaginable, going right at the Celtics full force and having monster games. Yet the end of the script always ended with a close-but-no-cigar finish. Boston, finding five-man answers to brilliant individual efforts, was businesslike, predictable and victorious, and Los Angeles was splendidly talented and second-best.

For the Lakers, in particular "Mr. Inside" (the low-post scorer, Baylor) and "Mr. Outside" (the long-distance shooter, West), the wounds that were imposed on them time and time again were unfair. Like two superheroes experiencing a recurring nightmare, they awakened to the disturbing truth that the bad dream wasn't a dream at all.

It was an excruciatingly agonizing reality, felt over and over again.

And surprisingly, it only got worse.

If there was one moment that simultaneously illustrated complete domination of a rivalry; captured Celtics pride in its finest hour; displayed Lakers frustration in its rawest form, and that moment could be captured in one series, it would be the 1969 NBA Championship Series.

By this time, it became clear to the Lakers that their need for a lost post big-man presence was a mandate. Responding immediately, new Owner Jack Kent Cooke analyzed the availability of centers throughout the league, and found one immensely talented center demanding a trade.

Swiftly acting on this information, Cooke sent center Darrall Imhoff, guards Archie Clark and Jerry Chambers to the 76ers for all-time great Wilt Chamberlain. Blending his game in with fellow greats Baylor and West, the talented triumvirate made short work of the Western Conference during the 1968-69 regular season.

And all three had enjoyed big years. Chamberlain, who led the league in rebounding (21.1) and field-goal percentage (.583), averaged 20.5 points a game to provide an inside scoring threat to complement Baylor's 24.8 points and West's 25.9 points.

Destroying everything in their path while posting a 55-27 record, the Lakers concluded matters by delivering a message to the Eastern Conference in season's final week. On national television, they blasted the Celtics by 35 points in a drubbing so bad it prompted Bill Russell to have a closed-door, twenty-minute meeting with the team. Lashing into them fiercely, he threatened the team with fines if they played so poorly again.

For those aging Celtics, it seemed like the league had finally caught up with them. Battling through injuries, inconsistency and exhaustion, sometimes looking brilliant, other times creaky, the NBA's oldest team made the playoff solely on their undying belief in each other. Limping to a 48-win season and a fourth-place finish—their worst record in the entire Bill Russell era—it wasn't so much whether the Lakers would beat them in the finals; because they wouldn't have the home-court advantage in any playoff series, it was whether the Celtics would even make it there.

Somehow the Celtics found a way. Led by the tenacity of player-coach Russell, they upset the heavily favored 76er team in the Eastern

Conference Semifinals. In the Conference Finals, the up-and-coming New York Knicks were supposed to walk all over their ancient rivals. Six games later, their season was over, for the Celtics ran them out of the playoffs.

In the NBA World Championship Series for the twelfth time in thirteen years, going for their eleventh title in thirteen years, there they were again, one more time.

They were pitted against the Los Angeles Lakers, one more time.

This time, however, the Lakers were the far superior unit, and showed from the series' onset. In Game 1, West, exploiting Russell's coaching decision not to double-team him, scored 53 points and dished out 12 assists as Los Angeles took the opener 120-118, then came back with 41 more in Game 2. Along with 26 points from fellow guard Johnny Egan and 31 points of Elgin Baylor (among them the team's last dozen points), the Lakers won 118-112.

Going back to Boston down 0-2, the Celtics seemed on the verge of a three-game series deficit after team scoring leader John Havlicek was accidentally poked in the eye during the third quarter of Game Three. Returning in the final period to hit several clutch free throws, the Celtics, urged on by capacity Boston Garden crowd as well as Havlicek's return, regrouped for a 111-105 triumph.

If the Lakers had missed a good opportunity in Game 3, they squandered an even bigger one a few days later. In a turnover-marred Game 4, the Lakers held an 88-87 lead with 15 seconds left to play, and had the ball out of bounds. All they had to do was hold on to the ball, and a commanding 3-1 series would be theirs.

But Boston's Emmett Bryant stole the inbounds pass, and after a missed jump shot and follow-up rebound, the Celtics called timeout with seven seconds left. Deploying four shooters on the floor, Bryant inbounded the ball to Havlicek, who found Sam Jones behind a Bailey Howell screen. Off-balance when in receipt of the pass, Jones rose off the wrong foot while lofting an off-balance 18-footer with three seconds left. Rattling on the front part of the rim, the ball hit the back iron and then fell through the net.

Boston had escaped with an 89-88 win and the series was tied.

Responding in Game Five, the Lakers, playing ferociously, ran circles around the old Celtics, winning 117-104; and holding serve in kind, the slower Celtics won an ugly Game 6 in Boston 99-90.

For the third time in eight years, a Boston-Los Angeles Championship series would go to its limit.

But this time, all signals pointed to a Lakers' championship.

For starters, Jerry West was having the series of a lifetime. Despite playing with a pulled hamstring, he was averaging over 40 points a game. Baylor was playing well, and Chamberlain had completely neutralized Russell. Even more important was the fact that the Lakers, playing in their newly constructed Forum, had the home court advantage.

For the first time, it seemed there would be no ghosts to help the Celtics win.

In anticipation of a Lakers' victory, Lakers Owner Jack Kent Cooke was so confident that he placed thousands of balloons into the ceiling of the arena, and meticulously planned the victory celebrations. Stocking the home team locker room with iced champagne, he hired the University of Southern California marching band to play "Happy Days Are Here Again" and worked out details on paper as to how the Lakers should be interviewed after the big win.

Jerry West, when looking up in the rafters at the balloons, was livid. Famed Lakers announcer Chick Hearn, equally miffed when Celtic counterpart Johnny Most read a flyer explaining the celebration particulars, said, "It's dumb. I can only imagine what Bill Russell is telling his Celtics."

Russell, about to play/coach in his final game and given the perfect motivational theme on a silver platter, simply told his team: "One thing that cannot happen, one thing that will not happen, is the

Lakers beating us. It's something that cannot happen. But I'll tell you this: It will be fun watching the home team take those balloons from the ceiling one at a time."

Inspired one last time, the old men from Boston came out flying. Surprising the Lakers with their fast-break offense, they hit eight of their first ten shots and raced to a 24-12 lead. By halftime, however, the Lakers had battled to within three points. West, on his way to playoff Most Valuable Player honors, was halfway to a spectacular 42-point/13-rebound/12-assist performance. Elgin Baylor was complementing him with 20 points. But Wilt Chamberlain, long thought to be the missing piece of the championship puzzle, was in foul trouble. When he picked up his fifth foul in the third quarter, he found a seat on the Lakers bench and watched the aging, aching Celtics stretch out to a fifteen-point lead, 91-76, by quarter's end.

Fighting back yet again, the Lakers whittled the lead down to single digits. Then it was Boston's turn to run into foul trouble. Sam Jones, also playing in his last professional game, fouled out, and Russell and the indefatigable Havlicek picked up their fifth fouls.

Could the Lakers make it all the way back?

With about six minutes left, Chamberlain twisted his knee while grabbing a rebound and asked Coach Bill Van Breda Kolff to take him out. Still, the Lakers comeback roared on, and with three minutes left in the 1969 Finals, the Celtic lead was down to one, 103-102.

With the game very much in the balance, a championship and the legacy of two historic franchises on the line, the tension on the court was thick.

At this point, Chamberlain indicated that he was ready to return to the fray.

"Put me back in," he said.

"Wait," Van Breda Kolff said, "Wait."

Signaling to his coach repeatedly, when the coach did nothing, he finally approached him.

"Put me back in," he pleaded.

But Van Breda Kolff, for reasons only known to him, refused to put him back in. Like Red Sox Manager Grady Little some thirty-four years later, this move proved to be the most questionable call in the rivalry's history.

Chamberlain, utterly humiliated, returned to the end of the bench and sat down.

It was then those lucky Celtic leprechauns finally arrived from Boston. With no time to check into a hotel, they unpacked their bags of tricks in the Inglewood Forum, perched themselves on top of the Celtics basket with about two minutes to go, and operated its magic once more.

After scooping up a loose ball by the foul line, Celtic forward Don Nelson tossed up a short awkward jumper that hit the back rim and bounced up vertically, about three feet in the air. Then, as if guided by a lucky four-leaf clover, the ball dropped straight through the net.

The Forum crowd, once raucous in preparation for a long-awaited party, suddenly grew quiet.

Shoulders on the Lakers bench slumped.

The knees of Elgin Baylor, West and the other Los Angeles players on the hardwood buckled as their bodies, once filled with supreme confidence, sighed in resignation as their title hopes disintegrated.

The men in green had done it to them again.

Moments later, the Celtics had their eleventh championship with a heart-stopping 108-106 victory.

"What are they going to do with those goddamned balloons up there?" victorious GM Red Auerbach asked ABC sportscaster Jack Twyman. Before Tyman could answer, "They'll eat them!" he shouted, then burst into giddy laughter.

The Lakers locker room ran the gamut of emotions.

Like tragic Greek figures again deprived of the one thing they truly wanted, West and Baylor, fighting off tears, were both inconsolable. Wilt Chamberlain, bewildered, befuddled and now having to ward off an unwanted "choker" stigma, called his coach "a liar, the dumbest coach he had ever seen." Van Breda Kolff in turn, called the player the Lakers gave a king's ransom to acquire for moments like this, a "quitter," because he left a championship game when his team needed him most.

The two men had to be physically restrained from going after each other.

And Lakers Owner Jack Kent Cooke, eating the most expensive piece of humble pie in NBA annals, was left with an interesting dilemma:

What do you do with thousands of inflated balloons?

✪ ✪ ✪

One of my favorite basketball memories is of a Friday night in May 1974, when just before my eighth birthday I watched Kareem Abdul-Jabbar drop in a seventeen-foot sky-hook to end a double overtime Championship Series classic in the Boston Garden. While Jabbar's team, the Milwaukee Bucks, would lose the deciding championship game two days later, Kareem would become one of my first sports heroes.

After being traded to the Los Angeles Lakers in 1976, he lifted the franchise from the doldrums of mediocrity. Returning to its position of championship contender, over the next few seasons, the Lakers, building around Jabbar, forward Jamaal Wilkes and guards Norm Nixon and Michael Cooper, were like a well-running vehicle that was missing a very important piece.

That piece would arrive by way of a coin toss just before the 1979-

80 season. In possession of the top overall draft pick in the Western Conference, the Lakers flipped against the Eastern Conference representative Chicago Bulls via conference call. With team and league officials from New York listening intently, Chicago's then-General Manager Rod Thorn called heads.

It landed on tails, and that stroke of fortune helped change the NBA forever.

The toss of fate brought an ignition system to Los Angeles, one that infused intensity, the seriousness of winning and the love of life into the Lakers' basketball engine. The basketball wizardry, unparalleled enthusiasm, commanding leadership qualities and sparkling smile of Michigan State All-American Earvin "Magic" Johnson was coming to the City of Angels, and "Showtime" was born.

Meanwhile, in Boston, after years of dominance, it looked as if the Celtics were finally becoming victims to the substandard play that thwarted so many opposing teams for so many years. In 1978, following a 32-50 season which saw old standby John Havlicek retire after sixteen seasons, the Celtics owned two of the top eight first-round draft picks. Taking advantage of a soon-to-be change rule, General Manager Red Auerbach selected Indiana State junior Larry Bird of Indiana State with the sixth pick, knowing that Bird would remain in college for his senior year. Retaining his draft rights for one year, it was a huge, unprecedented risk, but Auerbach, believing that Bird's potential made him worth the wait, had a feeling the gamble would have handsome returns.

It would. In his rookie campaign (the 1979-80 season), he inspired a city, and more importantly *a team*, to excel beyond their limitations. A confident player with a tremendous worth ethic and high basketball IQ, like his league-changing counterpart across the great states, he possessed a pass-first hardwood mentality and the ability to make his teammates better. Leading the team in scoring and rebounding while blending his talents perfectly with teammates

Chris Ford, Nate "Tiny" Archibald, Gerald Henderson, M.L. Carr and Cedric "Cornbread" Maxwell, the Celtics, improving on a 29-53 record the year before, made what was then the greatest single-season turnaround in NBA history. In winning sixty-one games, they were back amongst the NBA's elite.

Though they lost to the Philadelphia 76ers in the Eastern Conference Finals, for his accomplishments Larry Bird won the NBA Rookie of the Year Award. A season later, after trading for Robert Parish and drafting rugged Minnesota forward Kevin McHale, they were league champions once more.

The Celtics' swift climb to the top was an impressive feat by all standards.

All standards, that is, except one.

In that same rookie year Bird introduced himself to professional basketball, an incredible magic act was taking place 3,000 miles away. Succeeding where Bird had failed, the Los Angeles Lakers, led by a Game 6 42-point/15-rebound/7-assist Magic Johnson masterpiece, won the NBA championship over the Philadelphia 76ers.

By 1984, the stage was set for a Celtic-Lakers reunion in the NBA World Championship Series. Headlining the marquee were the two greatest players of that generation at the height of their powers. Bird, twenty-seven years old at the time, and Magic, twenty-four, both with five NBA regular seasons behind them, had established themselves as the unquestioned leaders of their teams. Also on the bill were future Hall of Famers everywhere. From teammates (Boston's Kevin McHale, Robert Parish; L.A.'s Kareem Abdul-Jabbar and James Worthy), to coaches (Boston's K.C. Jones and L.A.'s Pat Riley) and general managers (Boston's Red Auerbach and L.A.'s Jerry West), even team play-by-play announcers Johnny Most and Chick Hearn were bringing their "A" games.

An exciting ensemble of basketball talent had gathered to give the world a classic series; a historic showcase that was the most-watched basketball championship of its era, and now is recognized as arguably the greatest finals series ever. Like an Academy Award-winning movie, the flair, drama, twists and turns of this series had a country transfixed.

And a certain seventeen-year-old high school junior from Staten Island's West Brighton Projects was hoping for a Lakers victory. Known throughout the hallways of my high school for my passionate sports debates before class, an entire community knew about my obsession with the "Purple and Gold."

Wearing my love for *Showtime* on my sleeve proudly, I talked major shit.

Cursing the words of Philadelphia Sixer fans; ones still celebrating their 1983 sweep of an injured Lakers team, yet were on the playoff sidelines early in 1984, "Shut up," I taunted with all the voice I could muster.

"Y'all lost to the Nets in the first round!"

"The New Jersey Nets! THE NETS!"

To the fans of the Milwaukee Bucks and San Antonio Spurs, I showed a mock compassion. Embracing those perennial bridesmaids left at the brink of a Championship Series appearance, during the sportsman's hug, I said, "Your time is coming soon."

After the embrace?

Yeah, right, I thought, sarcastically cutting my eyes to the sky.

The Spurs' day came when Duncan rolled with "The Admiral" in '99; and Tony Parker and Manu Ginobili thereafter.

The Bucks?

They never should have traded Kareem.

They haven't been to the finals since.

Marques and Moncrief and Big Dog, *Oh my...*

And Brandon Jennings ain't gonna get you there now.

Oops. Old habits die hard.

Seriously, in that groundbreaking, trendsetting era of Prince, Run-

DMC and Madonna, the place where I came from, one of the rules in the "Wild, Wild West" was this: If you weren't playin' ball for real, then you had better pledge allegiance to a winner in professional sports.

And you had better know your stuff.

With the latter prerequisite, I had no problem. Possessing encyclopedic knowledge of sports dates, facts, scores and statistics, a cool residue of aura surrounded me. Reinforcing this intimidation factor with every opportunity, you couldn't step to me talking smack about any sport with no clue.

And if you did, it was akin to those saloon days in the west when you walked into a strange bar.

If no respect was shown, an ominous chord from one of those Clint Eastwood spaghetti westerns played. Then you were ushered back out, and made to choose a weapon. Walking fifty paces, we waited until the long hand struck twelve.

Then, we both fired away.

Victory was always *good* for me, *bad* for you, and if I were with fellow Lakers enthusiasts, the taunting got very *ugly*.

But with my Dallas Cowboys losing three straight NFC Conference Championship games in the early eighties (*I still hadn't accepted the Yankees as my favorite baseball team*), I had yet to be voted onto "Silence Island," a resting place that brings a peace in knowing that your favorite sports team defeated all comers.

But if ever there was anything that drew me close, my Lakers were that sure thing.

Two league titles and four conference championships in five years told me so.

However, something negative lingered in my subconscious; a disturbing bit of information that kept me from the space where haters had no place, and trash-talkers were forever muted. As much as I wanted to, I couldn't shout from the mountaintop the words of MC Hammer: *You can't touch this.*

Do you want to know why?

The Lakers had never beaten the Celtics.

Celtic fans all over, well-versed and rehearsed, left their sounds of silence like ghosts eager to torment an old friend. Invading my protective place, one that allows complete faith, they screamed an awful, uncomfortable fact into my senses.

The Lakers had never beaten the Celtics.

Reading through research, of which included seven finals losses in twenty-four years, all the stories of balloons being left in rafters, back-rimmed jumpers and seventh-game devastation were acknowledged and ignored. Finding solace that all of the past Celtic victories were ancient history, I felt secure in the legacy of Pat Riley and his fast-breaking Lakers. This meeting at the NBA summit, I surmised, would produce a different outcome.

Still, that one indisputable fact tortured me.

The Lakers had never beaten the Celtics.

A scab to my soul itched.

Scratching it foolishly, I reopened the wounds of Baylor, West and Chamberlain and made them my own.

And a horrific nightmare was about to come true.

Things didn't start that way, however. Entering the Boston Garden with force, the Lakers overwhelmed the Celtics in Game One. Racing to a fifteen-point lead seven minutes into the contest, they were two steps quicker than the Eastern Conference champions. Magic Johnson, a six-nine freak of nature at the point guard position, completely dominated Gerald Henderson, his six-two Boston counterpart. Blitzing Boston with 18 points, 10 assists and 6 rebounds, he set up a thirty-year-old center, Abdul-Jabbar, for numerous skyhooks, leading to Kareem's 12-for-17 shooting, 32-point performance.

Meanwhile, Celtic center Robert Parish, who finished with only 13 points, eventually fouled out with seven minutes left in the game. The Celtics never got within four points of the Lakers, as L.A. finished Game 1 with a 115-109 victory.

With about twenty seconds left in Game 2, I was in a happy purple haze. My Lakers, successful in fighting through Boston momentum, (a 10-point, first-quarter deficit and a constant slim lead) had stayed within striking range throughout the contest, and finally took a 113-111 lead on two Magic Johnson free throws. After forward Kevin McHale missed a pair for Boston, I was overjoyed at the silence coming from the Boston Garden during their final timeout.

Two wins down, two to go. Halfway home to a championship, I assumed.

Little did I know, assumptions are the mother of all screw-ups.

From the Lakers' end of the floor, James Worthy inbounded the ball to Magic Johnson. At the same time, a sudden anxiety disrupted my bliss, causing me to suck in air at an alarming rate. Stifling my capacity to breathe normally, the next few seconds left me stunned and shuddering as my exhale ability was stunted. Finally releasing air in harsh spurts and pants, my eyes widened in horror.

Trespassing without warning, the Celtic mystique had penetrated my kingdom.

With a swarming full-court press, Boston forced Johnson to pass off to Worthy and then overplayed Magic, denying him a return pass. Under double-team pressure, Worthy attempted a foolish cross-court pass. The ball was picked off by Celtic guard Henderson, who scored the tying hoop with 13 ticks left.

The Boston Garden crowd went bonkers.

Time out, Lakers.

Frozen in a mortified stupor, my place of peace and tranquility came crashing down, while the team from Los Angeles also became catatonic.

With ample time for a game-winning shot, the Lakers isolated

Kareem Abdul-Jabbar and Magic on the left side. Receiving another inbound pass from half-court, Magic Johnson started his dribble as the seconds ticked away.

Twelve…Eleven…Ten…Nine…

Celtic forward Cedric Maxwell, applying pressure up high, stayed with him while Robert Parish was overplaying Kareem down low. Obstinately looking for that perfect pass to the low post, Johnson just kept dribbling away.

Eight…Seven…Six…

By now, my senses were returned.

"Pass the ball!" I screamed from my Staten Island bedroom.

Some 500 miles north, the Lakers point guard refused to hear my pleas.

Five…Four…Three…

My mother, trying desperately to help in the reconstruction of my happy place, rushed into the room.

"Pass the damn ball, Magic!" she screamed.

Two…One…

Magic, by now clearly rattled, finally passed the ball as the buzzer sounded.

Overtime.

The Celtic fans, smelling purple blood in the water, began its derisive chant.

BEAT L.A.… BEAT L.A.… BEAT L.A.

By now, the whole Lakers team was unnerved. Handing the game to its bitter rivals on a silver platter, the extra session proved a formality to the Boston faithful. Overcoming a three-point deficit with a spirited rally, the Celtics evened the series with a thrilling 124-121 victory.

I couldn't believe it. The two-games-to-none lead that I envisioned now a distant memory, the governor removed the blindfolds from the eyes of those green leprechauns, snatched the cigarettes from their mouths, and gave the Celtics a reprieve from the gas chamber.

The dynamics of the series had been dramatically altered.

What I encountered the next day only reinforced my agony. Taunting and teasing me in the hallways of Susan Wagner High School the next day, the ridicule I received from classmates, teachers and students I didn't even know, was merciless. Filling me with a distasteful feeling I never knew before, I possessed a hatred for a certain type green.

Celtic green sucked, big time.

And I was pissed.

So were my Lakers. Mad as hell, from the outset of Game three days later in the Fabulous Forum, they were determined to regain control of the series. Burying the Celtics with an assortment of jumpers and high-flying jams, the Lakers had their place rocking as they ran to an early 14-point lead.

After the Celtics weathered the early game storm with a spurt of their own, they owned a 40-35 second-quarter lead when the Lakers turned on their afterburners. Kicking matters into high gear, the fast-break baskets came in waves. Eighteen consecutive Los Angeles points led to a 57-46 lead, and after hitting their first seven shots on their way to a championship series third-quarter, record 47 points, the Lakers were on their way to a decisive rout. If this basketball game were a prizefight, the Celtics were on the ropes, absorbing body blows and staggering right crosses.

Showtime basketball was never better.

Gleefully, I viewed that game on a Sunday with Gerald, another one of my younger brothers. Ten years old at the time, he was just starting to love the Lakers.

Exchanging hi-fives with him, "The series is over," I boasted. The convincing 137-104 blowout told me this, despite the fact we needed two more wins.

"Yeah, it's all over," Gerald agreed.

Meanwhile, in the visiting locker room, a furious Larry Bird called his teammates "sissies." Looking for a release from their created chaos, to a man the Celtics decided the only way to beat the Lakers was to turn the series into a knock-down, drag-out alley fight. Triggering a newfound physicality with his stinging analysis, the play of Bird's running mates would immediately reflect the power of his words...

And, by his actions.

Changing the tenor of the rivalry during Game 4, in the second quarter Bird pushed Lakers defensive stalwart Michael Cooper into the baseline crowd following a basket during the second quarter, then took on Jabbar in a late-game skirmish for a rebound. Exchanging elbows while battling for a loose ball, the two future Hall of Famers then went face-to-face, jawing at each other in competitive fury.

However, nothing marked the scenery transformation more than what occurred early in the third quarter. With Boston trailing 76-70 in the third quarter, Magic Johnson was again leading a fast break. Hitting forward Kurt Rambis on the dead run, the Lakers were on their way to another layup when Kevin McHale lassoed him with a clothesline and slammed him to the hardwood floor.

As both benches emptied, I screamed at my television.

"What the fuck is going on here?!?"

I was ready to jump through the screen and fight the Celtics myself.

Unfortunately, my mother heard my expletive, and ordered me to turn off the game.

What I missed was another Lakers meltdown. Leading by five with less than a minute to play, they made several execution errors, including Magic Johnson's bad pass to Robert Parish late in the fourth quarter as the Celtics tied the game. In overtime, after forward Cedric Maxwell further antagonized the Lakers by putting his hands around his neck (symbolizing that Los Angeles was wilting under pressure), Boston took control of the contest with a Bird jumper with a minute left. Cementing the victory was towel-waving reserve guard M.L. Carr, who stole another errant Worthy pass and dunked in the game-clinching points.

With the series tied once more at two, the trash-talking at school became more intense. The Celtics fans had gotten inside my head, and started banging things around.

"You should have swept us," I kept hearing. "Now, we're going to take it!"

And my tormentors were right. With the Lakers squandering a stranglehold, the series should have been over, and what was once total confidence in my sure thing was evolving into my worst fear. Covered and completely confused by this nightmare turned reality, puzzled and panicked all at once, a growing feeling of doom gripped me. Bravely I tried to discard my negative thoughts, but my classmates refused to give me the peace I so desperately needed.

Every time I tried to get away from this dreadful premonition, a fact haunted me, pulling me toward a black hole.

The Lakers have never beaten the Celtics.

As I watched Game 5 two days later, I could see the Celtics' confidence building by leaps and bounds. Knowing that they could be outplayed yet still win the game, they didn't have to worry about stealing this contest. Strutting their swagger around the Boston Garden, they gave literal meaning to the phrase "home-court cooking." Playing in a ninety-seven-degree arena without that newfangled thing called air conditioning, while players on both teams struggled with oppressive, stifling conditions and dehydration, Larry Bird let fly.

In a brilliant display of long-range beauty, Bird bombed the Lakers for 34 points on 15-of-20 shooting. Moving without the ball, muscling the opposition and inspiring his teammates with his tenacity, he was so unstoppable that his teammates fanned him with towels not to cool him off from the sauna that was the Garden, but in tribute for him finding his element.

On defense, the Celtics forced Los Angeles into bad shot collection in its half-court offense, and completely shut down *Showtime*. Scoring just 15 fast-break points, the Lakers depended on Kareem Abdul-Jabbar to rescue them. He couldn't. Shooting 7-for-25 from the floor, he ended the game on the bench, sucking air from an oxygen mask.

The Celtic crowd, celebrating the absurd conditions as opposed to bemoaning the heat, added to the intensity as well. Cheering their storied franchise on, they contributed to Boston taking control of the series with a 121-103 victory.

This trouncing, which occurred on a Friday night, had given me a reprieve from whatever abuse I may have faced at school, but it failed to do my psyche and spirit any favors. Refusing to quell itself, the thunder that was the storm in my stomach raged furiously. As they had done to Baylor, West, Chamberlain, Goodrich and others, those damn Celtics were driving me crazy. Coming at me once more were the sounds of harps not yet tuned playing an appalling melody; a tormented tune unpleasant to the ears.

The Lakers had never beaten the Celtics.

Over and over the band played that awful song, destroying whatever confidence I had left in spite of the fact that we had the better team on paper. None of that mattered anymore.

The Lakers had never beaten the Celtics.

Would I hear it even louder that Sunday, if the Forum grew silent with another Celtic championship celebration?

Unlike fifteen years earlier, there were no balloons in the rafters for Game Six. In its place were 17,500 fans holding their breath as the Celtics attempted to deliver its knockout punch.

The tension in the Forum traveled 3,000 miles east, where two more Lakers fans were watching the game.

"Are they gonna win?" Gerald asked me.

"I don't know," I responded tersely.

Sitting on our hands, we watched the first three quarters of the game like frozen statues. Unable to offer any hope to my younger sibling, the words unable to come, I couldn't breathe as I watched Boston hold an advantage after each period (33-29 after one, 65-59 at halftime, and 87-83 after three quarters). Turning numerous Lakers' mistakes into easy baskets, the Celtics were in command.

Struggling to save the season, time was running out on my Lakers. We needed someone to step up.

Enter rookie Byron Scott. A gunner acquired in a deal for guard Norm Nixon, Scott was the catalyst of a comeback. Drilling a 16-foot jumper, he then fed James Worthy on a breakaway layup, dunked on another fast break, and, after a timely steal, scored on an acrobatic drive to the basket.

Injecting life into all of Los Angeles, the Lakers rose from their abyss and were off to the races.

With 6:41 left in the game and the score tied at 93, Scott buried a three-pointer, giving the Lakers the lead for good.

"We're going to win!" Gerald screamed. His youthful exuberance sent a jolt of happiness through me, and a renewed confidence in my sure thing returned quickly.

Just in time to watch Kareem Abdul-Jabbar finish the Celtics off. Plagued by another painful migraine headache, for almost three quarters, he and the rest of his Lakers teammates were taking Excedrin, Tylenol and smelling salts, trying desperately to ward off a Boston Tea Party on their home floor. Playing with a renewed passion, Abdul-Jabbar scored a game-high 30 points, grabbed a team-high 10 rebounds, and watched his Lakers out-score Boston 36-21 in the final stanza. Emerging with a 119-108 win, the Los Angeles Lakers had given historians and fans all over something that professional basketball sorely missed: a seventh and deciding game between the Lakers and Celtics in the ancient Boston Garden.

This one I would not read about.

I would watch it for my very eyes.

And feel the gamut of deep emotions in my heart.

Would the Boston Celtics get the bounces, as they did in three previous Game 7 showdowns? Or would the Los Angeles Lakers win their third championship of the 1980s and make history by ending the Celtic hex?

Watching the game on June 12, 1984 with Gerald, the tension was so thick in my bedroom you could cut it with a knife. From the player introductions, a juiced-up Celtic crowd, along with an entire city and ghosts from Celtic past, spewed venom at the Lakers. Then the television announcers calling the game for CBS—Dick Stockton and Boston "homer" Tom Heinsohn—reminded the millions viewing the game from their living rooms that the Celtics never lost a deciding Championship Series game at home.

"The Lakers have never beaten the Celtics," Stockton added.

There it was; that odious refrain again. Driving me to the doorway of insanity, the fact hammered my senses once more.

Somehow the phrase injected fear into a whole franchise; for the Lakers came out of the gate extremely tight. Playing cautious, points that usually came in clusters never came. Every trip down the floor seemed stiff and guarded; instead of playing to win, they were playing not to lose.

No one seemed to embody the jangled nerves more than Magic Johnson. Normally confident, carefree and creative, the leader of *Showtime* was clearly affected by the big moment. Playing as if the burden of a team's entire history was upon his shoulders, the infectious trademark smile that accompanied his wizardry was not there. As opposed to directing the lively fast-breaking tempo song he loved so much, on this night he would conduct a tense waltz. The mirth-filled musical he and his Lakers teammates sorely needed, a merry joyride filled with speed and easy baskets, had been stripped away.

Making a definitive stand from the onset, however, were the Celtics. Forward Cedric Maxwell, a Finals MVP three years earlier, put on his hard hat, placed a lunch pail in his hands, and told his teammates to climb aboard his back; he alone would carry the team home to its fifteenth championship.

Demoralizing the Lakers on the offensive boards, he confounded Los Angeles by drawing fouls as he collected eight rebounds. The unsolvable low-post puzzle the Lakers never expected, he scored 17 of his game-high 24 points by halftime. And when the opposition finally caught on to him and double-teamed him, he passed for eight assists.

Feeding off his energy, Larry Bird (20 points, 12 rebounds) and Robert Parish (14 points, 16 rebounds) concentrated their efforts on controlling the glass, while guards Dennis Johnson (22 points) and Gerald Henderson (nine third-quarter points) were accurate marksmen as Boston moved the ball effortlessly along the perimeter to find the open man.

Watching the game in complete silence, my face was contorted in pain throughout. Every time Celtic guard/cheerleader extraordinaire M.L. Carr waved that damn towel over his head, the words that plagued Baylor, West and Chamberlain, ones that had spooked the team on the floor that night, rang in my head like gongs going off at the most inopportune time.

The Lakers have never beaten the Celtics.

After a 30-all deadlock in the first quarter, the Celtics, showing more will than at any point during the series, slowly pulled away. Ahead by as many as nine points in the second period, by halftime, their lead was six, at 58-52.

Thinking about the abuse I would face the next morning at school, bravely I hoped for a patented cluster of Lakers points from one of their trademark rallies.

What I received instead was another Celtic push. Clearly dominating Los Angeles on both ends of the floor, by the end of the third quarter, not only had they maintained their advantage, but they stretched the lead to thirteen points, 91-78, entering the final frame.

By now, I wondered aloud if anyone in Purple and Gold would show up and help Kareem Abdul-Jabbar, who would finish the game with 28 points and 10 rebounds. Standing tall alone against a rebounding barrage (the Celtics finished with 52 boards, while the Lakers had 33), he needed help from somewhere.

Trembling nervously while fidgeting, the veins rose in my neck as a somber sadness enveloped me.

My sure thing was being snatched away.

But not without one last ditch effort by my Lakers to turn my impending pain into unbridled joy. Down by 14 with a little less than eight minutes left, the Lakers finally began climbing the mountain. Tailoring their game to the urgent moment, point by point, they chipped away at what seemed insurmountable. The Celtic lead went from 14…to nine…to eight…to five…to three, at 105-102, with 1:15 left in the game.

After a Celtic miss, the Lakers quickly moved across the timeline with a chance to close the gap to a single point, or with a three-point play, even the score. At the top of the key, Magic Johnson looked to make a pass, but had the ball stripped away by Celtic guard Dennis Johnson.

As my head lowered in defeat, the Celtic ghosts twisted the knife they plunged in my back. Lakers guard Michael Cooper made a highlight-reel block of an attempted layup, and again my sure thing raced up court with another opportunity to tie.

Moving across the timeline, Magic dribbled behind his back at the top of the key, and then jumped in the air to make another pass.

Seeing James Worthy alone underneath the basket, "Pass it there!" I screamed at my television.

Cedric Maxwell must have heard me give the play away, for before Magic could complete the pass, he knocked the ball away again, and the Celtics recovered. At the other end, Dennis Johnson drew a foul and made free throws to give his team much needed breathing room.

As the Boston Garden crowd cheered and the soon-to-be crowned champion Celtic players saluted each other, I stared blankly at my TV for two minutes. Filled with the dejection of a heartbroken soul, I looked to my right and saw the agony of defeat in my little brother Gerald by way of his tears.

Seeing his young pain and understanding how unbearable it must have felt to him to watch the Lakers lose was more devastating than anything I was feeling.

Taking his hand, then wrapping him in a protective, brotherly embrace, "It's going to be okay," I comforted.

Seconds later, the final horn sounded, and the jubilant Celtic crowd rushed the parquet floor. The final score 111-102, Boston, was irrelevant. So was CBS announcer Tommy Heinsohn, who crowed how painful the loss would be for the Lakers, especially knowing they had a better team and still came up short. Also unimportant was the "Tragic Johnson" label inherited by L.A.'s superstar point guard for his inability to perform when the lights burned the brightest; those moments the media referred to as "clutch."

In fact, I was even numb to the unrelenting abuse I endured the next day at school, because my sure thing failed to win a championship.

What bothered me most was that annoying little fact, one whose truth assaulted my core. Eight times over the course of twenty-five years, two teams faced off for basketball's most coveted prize; and eight times the result, and unchanging fact, remained par for the course.

The Lakers had never beaten the Celtics.

This fact, an annoying, persistent leech sucking the joy from my love of sports, needed to be removed soon.

✪ ✪ ✪

At what point does the misery of failure become a mission for redemption? For the Los Angeles Lakers, that task of exorcising demons began the night of their heartbreaking seventh-game loss to Boston. Spending one more sleepless night in the city that took away their championship dreams for the eighth straight time, this was a team that never received any bounces, had postponed many title celebrations, and was constantly left with finding new ways to console the hearts of fans all over the country.

The sight of Red Auerbach lighting a victory cigar re-opening wounds from yesteryear, dark cloud of reality hung over the head of everyone bleeding purple blood. The burden of beating those hated Celtics the franchise carried was now the size of a humongous gorilla.

Perhaps no one shouldered the weight of this burden more than three people: Kareem Abdul-Jabbar, Magic Johnson, and a passionate Lakers fan some three-thousand miles away, William Fredrick Cooper.

For the Lakers point guard in particular, the spirit-damaging loss so thoroughly engulfed him that the pain of it would remain for months. Acutely sensitive to what people thought of him and his game, his reputation as a great player was in such disrepair it seemed like everywhere he turned, he was being called derisive nicknames. From the "Tragic Johnson" moniker given to him by Boston's Kevin McHale to "Apple Turnover" by Celtic fans, he heard it all not only from victors…

But the newspapers and sports magazines as well. Questioning his ability to perform in pressure situations—this in spite of the fact he owned two championship rings and Finals MVP awards—the pundits said he was unreliable in crunch-time. One periodical bluntly said he detested pressure situations.

However, the worst dig at his psyche came from his arch-nemesis. When asked about the 1984-85 season, Larry Bird said this regarding the Lakers, "I'd like to give them the opportunity to redeem themselves. I'm sure they have guys who feel they didn't play up to their capabilities."

It didn't take rocket science to know who he meant.

Kareem Abdul-Jabbar would turn thirty-eight years old in April of that season. The NBA's all-time leading scorer, he had been contemplating retirement, but felt the need to accomplish the only thing he hadn't in all his years of playing. In 1974 with the Milwaukee Bucks, he had taken his team to the seventh game of the NBA Finals against the Boston Celtics, and came away empty; a loss that stuck in his craw.

Ten years later, history repeated itself.

Like an impressive portfolio missing its most important piece, his legacy as one of the greatest basketball players who ever lived would be incomplete if he didn't help remove a twenty-five-year albatross from around the neck of the Lakers fans all over.

For me personally, the 1984 Championship Series loss was, to that point, the single most humiliating sports experience I've ever known. Owning a deep compassion for the Lakers organization and wanting them to overcome their psychological hurdle, when they fell short, I struggled with the Lakers stigma and felt the rawness of their pain as if it were my own.

Cutting me deeply, with cosmetic sutures, other sports to talk about, my wounds would heal.

But the tenderness of that heartbreaking memory remained; through trash-talking kids in the West Brighton Projects and Markham Homes (housing developments in that northern section on Staten Island) who constantly reminded me of Magic Johnson's late-game meltdowns, as well as through my high school classmates, most of whom had Boston green bloodstreams. Quieting my Lakers roar with their Celtics championship apparel and notes on my desk about the recent past, people that were once in awe of my sure thing carved me up in a way that I never imagined.

After a while, I became immune to the ribbing. But something else tore at my soul. Replaying the bad dream of the series loss repeatedly, every time I heard the most odious phrase in all of sports, I was defenseless in my silence.

The Lakers had never beaten the Celtics.

Sometimes *the facts* can be broadcasted silently, yet so loudly that the echo of its reality looms large in one's soul. Sometimes facts are saved to fit the needs of a particular moment in time. Stored away in some mental journal, we choose *what* facts we disclose, *when and where* we disclose the facts, and *how and why* we disclose the facts.

Having control over *the facts* is akin to having the keys to a kingdom. Possessing the power of truth and ultimate knowledge, *the facts* are often indisputable, not open for revisions or embellishment, and can either bring a person to heights unknown or, in the alternative, to their knees.

For twenty-five years, the Boston Celtics faced the Minneapolis/Los Angeles Lakers franchise on basketball's biggest stage, and brought them to their knees with one disturbing fact: In eight tries, they had never lost to the Lakers. No matter how successful the Lakers were, the Boston Celtics, that one thorn in their side, were always there to remind them of their mortality.

It was time for the Lakers, and one particular fan in New York, to get up.

But before this could happen, we would have to wait a long year, and endure the worst embarrassment of all along the way.

During that long year, which included the 1984-85 regular season, Boston Celtic fans crowed about their championship victory, an NBA-best 63-19 regular-season record, and, after dispatching the Cleveland Cavaliers (four games), Detroit Pistons (six games) and Philadelphia 76ers (five games) in postseason action, a great opportunity to reclaim the championship glory they already possessed.

Awaiting them in the finals, however, was a team that was afforded the opportunity to banish that horrible fact once and for all, or alternatively, be consumed by it.

I supported the former theory, for I felt that the Lakers, still burning inside from their traumatic disappointment, were on a mission. Driven by failure and humiliation, they played the season as if they owed their entire history a championship victory over the Celtics and finished with sixty-two victories.

Winning the Pacific Division by a whopping twenty games meant nothing to them. Nor did a first-round playoff sweep of the Portland Trail Blazers (three games), or five-game triumphs over the Portland Trail Blazers and Denver Nuggets in the Western Semifinals and Conference Championship, respectively. Vengeance and fierce determination fueling this unit and its unassuming, deliberate march, they were giving every ounce within themselves to purge a fact that haunted an entire organization.

They had to beat the Boston Celtics.

For Elgin Baylor.

For Jerry West.

For Wilt Chamberlain.

For all those that tried and failed over the course of two-and-a-half decades.

And unknowingly, for William Fredrick Cooper.

With my confidence in what was once my sure thing reduced to a modest cheer, I packed a bag and went on this mission with my Lakers. Whenever bold Celtic arrogance screamed its superiority though taunting, teasing and...GET THIS...mail from other schools (my passion for the Purple and Gold was so well known that neighborhood friends attending other high schools on Staten Island passed along Lakers hate letters from Celtic fans at *their* schools), I stayed unusually quiet while my intensity burned white-hot on the inside. Accepting regular season and Western Conference championship success with no celebration whatsoever, hoping and praying for a championship series rematch, all I saw was the removal of a misery that stayed with me way too long.

And when my humble request for a championship rematch was fulfilled, the fire that the Lakers owned for redemption blazed through me like a five-alarm fire. Instead of walking around my high school hallways happy that I was graduating in a matter of weeks, I was focused, much like the basketball team from the left side headed back to war in Boston.

I wanted peace.

So did my Lakers.

The mission for this peace would not be complete until the most odious phrase in the English language was permanently muted.

And on Memorial Day, May 27, 1985, the quest to eradication and celebration would begin...

In a way that I had never envisioned.

Only one team showed up to play Game 1 of the NBA Championship Series, and that team wasn't the Los Angeles Lakers. Playing wobbly, the weight of a troublesome past collapsed upon them, and the damage that it left to their collective psyche was exposed to a capacity crowd of Celtic fans in the Boston Garden, as well as the millions of viewers watching from their living rooms.

To say that they were intimidated into embarrassment is a gross understatement. What occurred in the hallowed hallway was a complete destruction; a total rout that boggled the minds of most rational-thinking basketball fans.

All that is, except one.

I watched this debacle away from home, after getting my ass whipped in a basketball game by the older brother of my senior prom date. John Roseborough, a lifelong Celtic fan, had challenged me to a one-on-one duel, and in an attempt at defending the honor of my Lakers, I readily accepted.

Playing him in his Port Richmond neighborhood, it was akin to the Lakers invading Boston Garden. Feeling as if I had something to prove, yet too terrified to move, I opened the game tight and nervous. As opposed to utilizing the skills honed through many West Brighton Project battles, I played awful basketball. Frightened, fretting and fearful, I blew easy layups and made turnovers all over the place.

The final score, 25-12, in favor of my prom date Monica's brother, was a humiliating experience. To this day, I felt I was the far superior player, but experienced a bad case of stage fright.

Little did I know, my horrendous showing was a portent of things to come.

What I saw later that afternoon in the Boston Garden was my game, on a larger scale. Reliving the horrors of the previous year, the Los Angeles Lakers came out tentative in the opening minutes. Hoisting bricks at the basket, James Worthy and Byron Scott missed shots they normally drained throughout the Western Conference playoffs. And further complicating matters was the fact that the Lakers got demolished on the boards.

Meanwhile, the Celtics, running on all cylinders, conducted a systematic dismantling of a proud franchise. While their counterparts concentrated on double-teaming their massive front line, Boston countered by making extra passes around the perimeter, staying one step ahead of the Lakers' defensive rotation.

Moving the ball with briskness, thus resulting in open jumpers from 15 to 20 feet for Celtic distance shooters Danny Ainge, Dennis Johnson and, of course, Larry Bird, Boston blissfully bombed away from long-range.

And bombed away.

And bombed away.

And bombed away.

Futilely, the Lakers hoped that the Celtic squad would miss shots they made all season. What they received was a strong dose of Danny Ainge in the first quarter. Drilling six straight jumpers on his way to a 15-point first quarter, he had tons of help. Dennis Johnson, leading a poised, intelligent Boston offense while spearheading a brilliant defensive effort, slowed the Lakers' *Showtime* by disrupting their passing lanes. Alert to every opportunity to run themselves, with each Los Angeles miss, they were off and flying; much like the Lakers did most of the time.

Succumbing to the Celtic dominance, Los Angeles did themselves no favors by playing listless defense. Broken down by the Celtics making fourth and fifth passes in their half-court offense, the speed and athleticism of their break was nullified by the Celtics outstanding shooting. Soon, everything fell apart as they became victims of sensational backdoor passes and the inside play of Kevin McHale, who scored 13 of his 26 points in a third-quarter blitz that blew the game wide open.

There were two final indignities in Game One of the 1985 NBA World Championship Series that left me mortified. With the Lakers' running game stopped cold, they desperately funneled the ball inside to a foul-plagued Kareem Abdul-Jabbar.

Aided by Boston wingmen, center Robert Parish smothered him and held him to 12 points and 3 rebounds. Completely frustrated by everything green and lugging slowly up and down the court, a dispirited Abdul-Jabbar was made to look his age (thirty-eight) by

Parish, who motored from baseline to baseline. That the Boston pivot man beat him repeatedly up the court resulted in more easy buckets for the Celtics.

As the Boston lead grew out of control (from a 38-24 advantage after one period to 79-49 at halftime), Celtic reserve swingman Scott Wedman entered the fray. Noted for his long-range exploits, he launched his first shot from long distance.

Good.

And another.

Good.

One from twenty feet.

Good.

"Someone gave Scott Wedman a hot foot, because he's on fire!" John announced. Prouder than the NBC peacock, his day was on its way to perfection.

Anguish, angst and agony rising within me like the summer heat of this Memorial Day, a gracious smile concealed the sting of this massacre.

Silently watching Wedman's moment in time, all I could do was smile the pain away as he continued tormenting me with his accuracy.

A three-pointer.

Good.

Another three.

Good.

Each shot he made was like a slap in my face.

The second half was more of the same: inside-out Celtic brilliance, long distance bombing (Boston, led by Wedman's 11-for-11 shooting performance, shot 60 percent from the floor), back picks leading to easy baskets, and the Lakers ineptitude and frustration (Abdul-Jabbar being whipped from pillar to post by Parish, Magic Johnson leading a slow, semi-walk of an offense); all of which led to a detailed demolition job that should have been taped and distributed globally to every basketball coach yearning to dissect a powerful defense.

And all I could do was sit back and smile.

Smile away the hurt.

Smile away the pain.

Smile to keep the tears from racing down my cheeks and meeting at my chin.

Smile and endure one of the most brutal sports days of my life.

I get my ass kicked, 25-12, by a Celtic fan on the hardwood.

And hours later, I watched helplessly as my Lakers suffered the most lopsided loss in championship game history, a 148-114 ass-whipping on the parquet floor.

And all I could do was smile.

Smile, and take it.

The Lakers had to take this gruesome medicine as well; most notably, Kareem Abdul-Jabbar. In the film session the next morning, instead of finding a seat near the back of the room, Abdul-Jabbar moved to the front row, and watched Lakers Coach Pat Riley show his disgust. Zeroing in on the future Hall of Fame center's terrible performance, Kareem didn't blink when Riley ran and reran evidence of his showing. Profoundly humiliated, the captain later went to each of his teammates individually and personally apologized for his effort.

The next day, during a frantic two-hour practice, Abdul-Jabbar whipped himself mercilessly up and down the court.

Seeing his effort after thirty minutes, "Take a break," Riley said.

"No," Kareem responded.

Another half-hour passed.

"Mitch, go in for him," Riley said, referring to reserve center Mitch Kupchak.

Again Kareem refused to come out.

After an hour and a half of straight sprinting on transition drills, Coach ordered him to sit down.

A third time, Abdul-Jabbar declined.

Thursday night, before Game 2, Kareem quietly told his teammates, "Let's make it worthy of us."

As the CBS telecast hit the air, I was a nervous wreck. Knowing this was the biggest game of the Lakers' season, I wondered how they would respond.

Another slow start and the mission would be doomed.

What I saw in the first six minutes was a determined, desperate unit that looked far better than at any point in Game 1. Dominating the boards early on, they took the Boston Garden crowd out of the contest with an early 15-6 advantage. Like bees to honey, Los Angeles swarmed their opposition with tough defense, pressuring them into poor perimeter play. The Celtic marksmen, producing a merry parade of jump shots just seventy-two hours earlier, now were missing their mark.

And those misses ignited *Showtime*.

Pacing the game with their overwhelming quickness advantage, the Celtics were unable to slow down the Lakers' transition game. Quicker, sharper and more physical, the Lakers played with reckless abandon. Sacrificing their bodies for every rebound and loose ball, they completely turned the tables on Boston.

Perhaps no one best exemplified the Lakers' transformation more than Kareem Abdul-Jabbar. Looming large on the defensive end, he looked nothing like the aging man witnessed in Game 1. Spry and spectacular, the re-energized wonder was at the top of his game.

He rebounded.

He blocked shots.

And when *Showtime* slowed to a half-court waltz, he bailed the Lakers out repeatedly with his offensive arsenal.

Sky-hooks.

Drop-step dunks.

Perfect passes when double-teamed.

If the Lakers were desperate swashbucklers, then Kareem played the role of *Blackbeard*, a passionate pirate king determined to prove that all eulogy reports given by the sports media were premature. Reasserting his playoff power with a 30-point/17-rebound/eight-assist/three-block effort, he led Los Angeles to a 64-46 halftime lead.

Yet while my Lakers were dominant, I sat on my bed, worried and waiting for a Celtic run.

It came in the fourth period. Entering the fourth quarter down twelve, 87-75, Boston began fighting back. Playing crisper, harder and faster, they staged a furious rally. Led by Larry Bird, they chipped away at the Lakers' lead, eventually cutting the deficit to 100-96, with two minutes left.

Nervous as all Lakers fans were throughout the country, *how they weather this storm might determine the whole series*, I thought.

As the Celtic crowd roared during a timeout, I knew someone had to step up and help Kareem.

It seemed fitting that the last name of the Lakers' hero would be named Cooper.

Michael Cooper, normally a defensive stalwart assigned to Bird, had a career night. En route to 8-of-9 shooting display that produced 22 points, perhaps no shot was bigger than the one he took with 1:48 remaining. With the 24-second shot clock down to one, he diffused the Celtic comeback with a back-breaking jumper just before the buzzer.

Hitting nothing but net, his clutch shot pulled the plug on an electric Celtic crowd trying to will its team to victory. Hushing the Garden, the Lakers silenced the intense scrutiny heaped upon them with their 109-102 triumph.

Evening the series at one game apiece, they had stolen a game in the Garden and now, because of a new championship series format, returned home to the Forum for three straight games.

By the skin of their teeth, their mission was still alive.

✪ ✪ ✪

Do you want to know when I knew the Lakers would win Game 3 of the 1985 NBA World Championship Series?

About five minutes into the game.

With the score tied at eight, Larry Bird missed a perimeter shot, then Celtic center Robert Parish tossed up an errant turnaround jumper. With the rebound bouncing through a sea of hands, the basketball was recovered on the dribble by Kareem Abdul-Jabbar.

With Magic Johnson on his left, James Worthy, Kurt Rambis and Byron Scott to his right, did the thirty-eight-year-old center give up the "rock"?

Nope.

Leading the *Showtime* fast break for the only time in his career, "the Begoggled One" drove into the length of the floor, backed Dennis Johnson down from the key, and tossed in a sky-hook.

Leaping up from my bed, I went crazy.

My brother Gerald, watching the game with me, went crazy.

The sold-out Forum also went crazy.

A minute later, I saw him dive into the stands to deflect a loose ball.

With a little more than forty minutes left in this pivotal contest, my thoughts went the way of famed Lakers announcer Chick Hearn: The game was in the refrigerator, the door was closed, the lights were out, and the gelatin was jiggling. Sure, the Celtics would go on to hold a 10-point, second-quarter lead. Sure the Lakers would have to ward off Kevin McHale, who put on a 16-point, low-post scoring clinic in the first half. Sure, it would take the Los Angeles deep into the second quarter to take the lead for good; which they did at the 2:30 mark en route to a six-point halftime lead.

After I saw Kareem hustle for that loose ball, somehow I knew the game was over.

Pulling away in the second half, the Lakers made me look like a seer. On defense, they flew around the perimeter, creating havoc when the ball was swung. Boston's starting guards, Dennis Johnson and Danny Ainge, clanged the rims to the tune of 23 percent shooting (5 for 22). And it didn't hurt that their most potent weapon, Larry Bird, had picked the worst time to be mired in a shooting slump. Like a great closer without his lights-out fastball, the Celtic great missed 13 of 21 shots while scoring twenty inconsequential points.

And on defense, James Worthy torched him. Leaving him slow footed, the sharp-shooting Lakers forward exploded for 14 third-quarter points as his team pulled away to a 15-point spread.

Like the whole franchise, they were sharper, quicker and mentally tougher than their Eastern counterparts.

And to the surprise of everyone, they were more physical.

Unlike the previous year's epic battle, the Western Conference champions were beating the defending champions at their own game. Matching them body-for-body and bang-for-bang, there were several altercations throughout the contest, including a fourth-quarter tussle between Lakers forward Kurt Rambis and Celtic reserve Ray Williams which resulted in William's ejection from the contest.

Between the spectacular speed of *Showtime*, the elegant skyhooks of Kareem Abdul-Jabbar and a newfound aggression on defense, the bullies from Boston, ones who had repeatedly robbed the Los Angeles Lakers of their lunch money, had finally got whacked over the head with their own medicine.

And after the decisive 136-11 blowout victory, you knew that an entire city was praying for them to banish a disturbing fact that tormented their collective souls. Abdul-Jabbar, for one, remained focused on the job at hand. After throwing in a third-quarter skyhook which made him the NBA's all-time playoff scoring leader with 4,458 points, "the record," he said, "was not the thing I was after."

What he, Magic Johnson, the Los Angeles Lakers organization, and a high school senior on Staten Island, sought was closure. We sought closure from the wounds of yesteryear; piercings that looked healed on the surface, yet remained fresh in our minds because of the mission. We sought closure for Frank Selvy, who came oh-so-close to glory in 1962, yet some twenty-three years after the fact, remained still far away. We sought closure for Jerry West and Elgin Baylor, the gallant warriors who lost seven times in uniform; eight times for West if you counted the 1984 heartbreak, for he was the Lakers' GM. We wanted closure for the many spirits that had been damaged by fluke occurrences, disappointing finishes, painful Game 7 losses, and the vision of Red Auerbach lighting up that damn victory cigar.

A person, team and franchise could only take but so much. And while we were halfway to the permanent removal of a fact, it still remained.

The Lakers had never beaten the Celtics.

Two more wins and we would never hear from the ghosts of Boston's past again.

Alas, the exorcising process would not be easy, for the Celtics were conceding nothing. Realizing the work they had cut out for them, feeling embarrassed by their Game 3 showing, the defending-champions—in particular, Larry Bird—vowed to play better when the two teams met again.

In Game Four three days later, Boston buckled down and played spirited basketball. Led by Bird, whose shooting touch returned to the tune of 26 points, the Celtics played extremely smart half-court basketball in the first half. Making sure there was room for their varied methods of attack, the Celtics were careful to keep the floor spread. Unveiling dribble-drive penetration, Dennis Johnson scored baskets and drew fouls on the Lakers by taking the ball to the basket. By halftime, he had 14 points and nine assists. But more importantly, he forced Los Angeles out of its double-team tactics on Kevin McHale. McHale, responding to the challenge of this vital game, helped carry the Celtics offensively with 23 of his 28 points in the first three quarters, almost all of them coming on unstoppable post-ups.

But as good as the Celtics were playing, the Lakers kept it close. Through flawless execution of their own half-court offense, they went to their halftime locker room down by only one, 59-58.

Bombarding Boston with suffocating defense and the blinding speed of *Showtime*, with a sudden spurt, they raced to an eight-point, third-quarter advantage.

Just as quickly as the Lakers broke it open, the Celtics, led by Bird, McHale and Johnson, responded with a burst of its own to forge ahead early in the fourth quarter.

From there, the game ebbed and flowed, with both teams exchanging baskets, especially in the final 1:40 of what Lakers Coach Pat Riley called "the most competitive game of the series." After Kareem Abdul-Jabbar's soft hook with 2:02 left gave the Lakers a 102-99 lead, Danny Ainge quickly answered with a 20-foot baseline jumper that cut the lead to one, 102-101, with 1:42 left.

A minute later, after Lakers reserve Bob McAdoo missed a jumper, Ainge drilled another rainbow with one second on the shot clock that put Boston ahead 105-103.

Lakers' ball.

Thirty-three seconds were left.

Watching the game with my mother in her bedroom, she asked me who I thought was going to win.

Instead of giving her a victor, "We're headed to overtime. Watch," I replied.

When Magic Johnson evened the score with a follow-up after an Abdul-Jabbar miss, pandemonium found its place in the Forum.

Seventeen seconds were left.

"You might be right, son," my mother agreed.

Other people were listening to my forecast, as I would soon find out.

Inbounding the ball from underneath their basket, Celtic guard Dennis Johnson brought the ball over the timeline and had the ball out top of the key for what seemed like an eternity. Then, with five seconds, left he found Bird on his right, and swung the ball over to him. Bird tried to work something, but couldn't shoot or feed inside.

Instinctively, Magic Johnson rushed over to double-team him, and just as instinctively, Bird shoveled the ball back over to DJ.

With two seconds left on the clock, Johnson, who was having the game of his life, launched a shot from nineteen feet.

As I watched the ball spin through the climate-controlled air, the Celtic leprechauns again traveled from Boston to stop a party in the Fabulous Forum. Guiding the ball through the net as the buzzer sounded, they took great joy in seeing Lakers fans walk out of the building with that dumbstruck feeling that, after a quarter century, continued to fracture their emotions.

"Well, son, I guess you can't be right all the time," my mother said as we watched the guys in green celebrate as if they'd won the title.

Sighing with a resignation that was deeper than the game we had just witnessed, somehow I knew all along how the Lakers would have to accomplish their mission. Seeing Larry Bird dancing up and down, and hearing the same song that played in my head with every Celtic victory over my Lakers; no, those weren't issues on this night. Nor was cheerleading reserve M.L. Carr, who was whirly-birding that damn towel again. I didn't even have a problem with the derisive "Sweet Sixteen" serenade I heard the next day from hopeful Boston fans at school.

What bothered me was that I was still a prisoner of one single fact. *The Lakers had never beaten the Celtics.*

And in order to clean out all the skeletons in the closet concerning the Celtics and their domination, we would need one or two victories in our own haunted mansion: a dark, dingy, dirty place on Causeway Street complete with parquet hardwood, leprechauns on each rim, and fifteen championship banners; eight of them at the expense of a Lakers organization.

The Boston Garden, and twenty-five years of heartbreaking agonies awaited us.

That it would come to that bit of uncertainty ...

Now *that* bothered me.

But as much as the necessary trip to Boston rankled my core, I also knew that this year was different for one reason: Because of the new 2-3-2 championship series format—meaning the team with the better regular-season record played the first and last pair of games on their home floor, and the other team had the three middle games—the Lakers still had an advantage:

On Friday night, the all-important Game 5 would be played at home.

CBS announcers Dick Stockton and Tom Heinsohn, stressing the psychological difference during pregame warm-ups and perhaps taking a stab at the Purple and Gold for giving a title away the year before, also mentioned that the Lakers' record in games decided by three points or less was decidedly worse.

Seeing the focused expressions of both teams, I knew this would be a test of wills. In the first four games, I witnessed a battle of contrasts, and chameleon-like changes. For stretches on end, the Celtics ran like the Lakers, and the Lakers banged bodies aggressively like the Celtics. When both teams returned to their strengths, Boston dissected the Lakers' defense with precision passing, and *Showtime* was on the move like a runaway freight train. For four games they battled, and were even in total points, rebounds, field-goal percentage and games won.

Someone would have to blink first.

And for nearly a quarter and a half of free-flowing, aggressive basketball, neither team budged. When the teams were in their half-court offenses, Kevin McHale and Kareem Abdul-Jabbar staged a duel for the ages. Reaching into his bag of tricks for an assortment of low-post moves, the Celtic forward invited forwards Kurt Rambis and Bob McAdoo into his personal torture chamber. Out-leaping, out-spinning and out-maneuvering both players into total embarrassment, the Lakers soon ran out of defensive options.

"Who would check him?" Riley wondered aloud, after McHale blitzed his squad for 18 first-half points.

Meanwhile, Abdul-Jabbar continued to sip from his fountain of youth. Digging deep within to play the most intense basketball of his illustrious career, against the meanest, toughest team in basketball, and under the harshest scrutiny of his life, Kareem was finding what he needed to excel. In actuality, all he needed was his dependable, unstoppable weapon to keep falling. And his skyhook did; by the end of the second quarter, he turned, hopped and flicked his way to twenty points.

Both offensive forces had help. Dennis Johnson, fresh off of his game-winner, continued his red-hot shooting for Boston. And a resolute Magic Johnson, desperate to live down the turnovers and bad passes of a year earlier, was on his way to a brilliant all-around floor game.

They key in the first half, was again the play of Larry Bird and James Worthy. Though the Celtics were close, Larry Legend was nowhere to be found. Sticking to him like glue was Michael Cooper, who held him to five shots and two points before intermission.

His counterpart, Worthy ignited a 15-3 second-quarter ending spurt by scoring 11 of his 19 first-half points. Spearheading *Showtime* with his speed, the unique ability to score with either hand and play above the rim, the last four minutes of the first half was a clinic in his trademark Statue of Liberty dunks, swooping finger rolls and quick spin moves.

The efforts of Worthy led the streaking Lakers to a 64-51 halftime lead.

Once again I watched this game with my mother, who moved the only color television in our apartment into our living room. A history buff and basketball fan in her own right, in spite of the fact that Julius "Dr. J" Erving was her favorite player—*that man is fine, and intelligent too,* I remember her constantly gushing—her allegiance, albeit temporarily, was rooted in the color purple .

For deeper reasons than I ever imagined. Having first-hand knowledge that Boston was a racially troubled city in the '60s, during the break she told me stories about the unfair treatment of Bill Russell, the greatest winner in Boston's long history of professional sports, in the city newspapers.

If I wasn't stunned by that revelation, my mother, Ethel Cooper-Meyers, supplied the *coup de grace* with what came next. Confounding my senses, she spoke of watching the seventh game of the 1969 NBA Championship Series, and how Jerry West, determined to end the Celtics' hex, had given everything he had on one leg.

"He played that game with a pulled hamstring," she said.

My eyes widened as she recalled how she cried at the end of it for the Lakers; in particular, for Jerry West.

Sighing, she completed her memory by reciting his box score.

"Forty-two points, thirteen rebounds and twelve assists, and he came up two points short. He's the only player ever to be named the Most Valuable Player of a series from a losing team," she lamented.

With that story, the unwavering focus I owned for the mission became more personal than ever.

But would the team in the gold uniforms respond to my sense of urgency?

They sure started the second half as if they would. When it appeared the Lakers had exhausted their options in defending McHale, coach Riley turned the assignment over to the oldest man on the court, Kareem Abdul-Jabbar. Accepting the additional responsibility with vigor, the Lakers captain limited McHale to six points in the final two quarters.

Doing whatever it took to stem his tide, an example of his determination came in an instance when McHale attempted a fourth-quarter baseline move. Shoving him out of bounds, Abdul-Jabbar took the personal foul, and McHale went to the line and sank both free throws. But Kareem had made his point, which basically was, "McHale is to be stopped inside, by any means necessary."

Feeding fuel to his teammates, the Lakers extended their halftime lead to 18 points, 70-52. They had the Celtics reeling and seemed ready to land a knockout punch; especially when Boston Coach K. C. Jones received two technical fouls and was ejected from the game some four and-a-half minutes into the third quarter.

Up by seventeen at the time, 76-59, the game appeared to have been salted away.

Only someone forgot to tell the Celtics. Battling back with grit and urgency, the defending champions quickly shaved the deficit to eight, 78-70, by the five-minute mark. Larry Bird, awakened from hibernation, led the charge by scoring 10 points.

Just as quickly as they charged, the Lakers answered even quicker. With an 11-2 spurt of their own, in less than two minutes, they repelled the first Celtic surge and reopened the lead to 17, at 89-72.

Another quick rush by Boston closed the gap to 91-81, but the Lakers closed the third quarter with a 14-point advantage when they scored the period's last two points.

I knew the game was far from over. Displaying their championship grit, the Celtics proved me correct. Rallying once more as the Lakers missed their first seven shots of the fourth quarter, they showed patience in their offensive sets while trimming the lead to six, at 95-89.

As they made their run, I looked at my mother. Worry and insecurity etched all over her face, I knew that the series, and the burden that an entire franchise carried to beat Boston, had been placed upon her back as well.

A small fear rose inside of me as I watched her nervousness.

And on the floor, the Los Angeles Lakers were again feeling the full weight of their past failures. With *Showtime* stalled, they now depended on a half-court offense that previously stopped working in pressure-packed moments. Tension gripped the Forum, and knowing that a Game 6 loomed in Boston, Lakers fans all over braced themselves for the worst by saying, "It's happening to us again."

Under siege, the mission reached a crisis point as the Celtics delivered mind-crumbling headshots to the collective psyche of an entire organization. Following the mental assault with brutal body blows, Bird, McHale, DJ, Danny Ainge, Robert Parish and gremlin ghosts of a quarter century landed haymakers that in the past destroyed destinies and produced eight titles against the Lakers.

Bird hit a beautiful rainbow over Magic, and the Lakers' advantage, once at 18, was reduced to a measly four points, 99-95, with less than seven minutes left in the game.

Reaching into an untapped reservoir of character, this Lakers team did something it had never done before.

They stared the Celtics down.

A jumper by Michael Cooper opened the cushion back to six, at 101-95.

Robert Parish hit two free throws, cutting it back to four, 101-97.

Answering immediately, Magic Johnson launched a teardrop in the lane that rattled home.

103-97, Lakers.

A banker by DJ in the lane, and the Celtics were again within four, 103-99 with 5:20 remaining.

Kareem responded with a 14-foot baseline skyhook.

105-99, Lakers.

Applying more pressure, Bird followed up a DJ miss with two more.

Again the lead was four, 105-101, with 4:35 to go in the game.

Magic again responded, with a jumper from 19 feet.

107-101, Lakers.

Two Bird free throws made it 107-103, Lakers, with 3:53 to play.

After another Kareem skyhook returned the lead to six, the collective will of the Celtics did not break, but it bent. After rebounding a Celtic miss, Lakers power forward Kurt Rambis stepped up. First hitting two free throws, he then stole a pass intended for Parish, and fed Magic, who was flying down court, for a breakaway layup. Another skyhook swish and dunk by Kareem Abdul-Jabbar later, and the Lakers had weathered the storm.

In reviewing the statistics from the Lakers' hard-earned 120-111 victory, you'll see a collective effort. Magic Johnson led *Showtime* with 26 points and 17 assists; Kurt Rambis, hitting the boards with abandon, had a team-high nine rebounds while embodying an aggressive unselfishness; and "Big Game James" Worthy illuminated the Los Angeles evening with 33 points.

But the focal point in eliminating the theory that the Lakers couldn't win the close game was in a 36 point/seven rebound/seven assist/three block shot effort by its leader, Kareem Abdul-Jabbar. Still burning inside from the premature "heart failure" reports given by cynical sportswriters, he was determined to give reporters nothing to say. With the stuff of legends, he was an all-time great doing a Hall of Fame job.

My mother, cheering loudly, noticed my very subdued, serious demeanor.

Thinking something was wrong, "Aren't you happy?" she asked.

Looking at her, "We need one more, and the mission will be complete," I responded calmly.

She didn't know it, but I was speaking not only for myself, but for all the stories I read over the years; the ones about Lakers stars that endured so much pain at the hands of the Boston Celtics, the ones that always came up short. No, I couldn't celebrate, for the pain of that 1984 series still lingered. No, I could not celebrate until the mountain was climbed and a flag was placed at its apex.

I admit: The victory felt good, but the ultimate task had not yet been completed, and the NBA fact that was spoken for twenty-five years still hung about.

The Lakers have never beaten the Celtics.

Apparently, the players on the Lakers shared my sentiment. When the CBS cameras showed them filing into the dressing room one-by-one, you saw no smiles, no grins; no emotion whatsoever. Appearing restrained and determined, they knew that one last step remained.

That step would be this: On Sunday, June 9, 1985, the Los Angeles Lakers would enter the Boston Garden, a hot arena with its stuffy air, beer-stained aisles and dangling green-and-white banners filled with championships and retired numbers; and with the noise coming from overhanging balconies where every sound would be against them, attempt to do what no team in the history of professional basketball had ever done before...

Win an NBA title on the parquet floor.

In addition to that herculean task, they would open the door to painful championship memories, walk into their personal room of horrors, and try to slay the demons that came with a simple fact.

The Lakers had never beaten the Celtics.

If *the fact* had to be expelled forever, it had to happen this way.

✪ ✪ ✪

Once upon a time, long ago, there was an index finger. Before the birth of the hi-five, slick handshake, chest or fist bump, there was the index finger. Long before trash-talk and taunting became the anthem for an ESPN "look at me" generation, even longer before the word "hater" became slang for jealousy, a simple index finger extended overhead screamed an emphatic meaning even the strongest words couldn't define. An index finger overhead was a signal to your opponent that the ultimate goal of success was realized. The gesture, rooted in sportsmanship yet indicating decisive victory, let it be known that you were the best, and the others took a backseat along with the rest.

You, or your team, were number one.

The index finger told us so.

The first time it told me so was when I saw highlights of Super Bowl III. Playing in Miami's Orange Bowl, the New York Jets were decided underdogs against the Baltimore Colts; but you couldn't tell Joe Namath that. Changing the competitive landscape in pro football, he led his team to the greatest upset in sports history.

How did he celebrate his landmark triumph?

By running off the field with his index finger raised high.

Another fond memory of the number one salute is when, after decades of futility, the Pittsburgh Steelers finally won an NFL championship in 1974. When the team presented beloved Owner Art Rooney with a game ball, he held it aloft, as it were his index finger.

When then Commissioner Pete Rozelle presented him with the Vince Lombardi trophy, his bifocal glasses seemed to get foggy. Visibly moved from knowing that a long journey had reached its destination, you could see him, in a humble state, struggling to maintain his composure.

There wasn't a dry eye in the locker room.

On a sunny Sunday in June 1985, I could relate to the feelings of "Broadway Joe," Art Rooney and the Pittsburgh Steelers.

Instead of watching Game 6 of the 1985 NBA Championship Series with my family in color, I turned on the old black-and-white in my bedroom.

Me and the Lakers, alone, against *the fact*.

In hindsight, my decision seemed fitting, for there were many grainy, colorless films I saw over the years which showed the Boston Garden as a graveyard for opponents with championship aspirations. Haunted by images of Bob Cousy dribbling out Lakers title hopes, Red Auerbach lighting a victory cigar, then John Havlicek deflecting a pass over to Sam Jones, the next thing I saw in this recurring nightmare was a color clip showing a partisan crowd from 1984 storming the parquet floor in utter delirium.

As if on cue, CBS announcer Dick Stockton made sure everyone in the world knew that no team had ever won an NBA championship against the Celtics in the Boston Garden. Even Jerry West, the Lakers' general manager and enduring symbol of anyone who was a part of the Lakers' organization in the last twenty-six years, elected not to make the trip back to Boston, for fear of spooking the proceedings.

A little after one o' clock in the afternoon, old Lakers players and fans all over the country held their breath and watched the tube. Transfixed to the tip-off in silence, I listened to the raucous "Beat L.A," chant.

On that day, it sounded louder than ever before.

I think our time has come to silence the place, and those damn ghosts, I thought and hoped.

Anxious, tense and fatigued from a cross-country flight and their epic struggle a mere thirty-eight hours earlier, both teams began the game blowing easy layup opportunities. While playing great defense, Boston forced five first-quarter turnovers, but couldn't build any momentum lead because of horrendous perimeter shooting. Guards Danny Ainge and Dennis Johnson, deadeye marksmen in Los Angeles, came home to Beantown and took up masonry. Bricking 25 or their

31 shots, one might say they were building a championship for the Lakers.

Only the team from Los Angeles was their own worst enemy. Fighting nerves and history while playing in spurts of scattered brilliance, every time they tried to pull away, they allowed the Celtics to reel them back in. A seven-point advantage, 21-14, with 3:20 left in the first period, quickly evaporated with a 12-4 Celtic run. By quarter's end, the Lakers regrouped in time to take a 28-26 lead.

The second quarter was a nip-and-tuck struggle as the two NBA superpowers stood in the middle of the ring of basketball supremacy and went toe-to-toe. Trading baskets throughout the period, there were 18 ties or lead changes. With the pressure of forcing a deciding seventh game upon them, Boston once again relied heavily on Kevin McHale to carry them. The 6-10 Celtic forward, the one player whom the Lakers were never able to contain, scored 21 points in the first half.

Riding shotgun was Larry Bird. Though the league's Most Valuable Player would shoot 12-for-28 from the floor this game, his all-around presence (playing with nagging injuries, Boston's super-star forward averaged 23.8 points/8.8 rebounds/six assists per game in the six-game series) kept the defending champions afloat.

Even as the Celtics stayed close, something seemed different about this game than what I ever read about pertaining to this rivalry; or ever witnessed. About halfway through the second quarter, Kareem Abdul-Jabbar got whistled for his third personal foul. Going to the bench for the rest of the first half, about a minute later, he was joined by Magic Johnson, who also picked up his third foul.

With their kingpins on the bench in foul trouble and forward James Worthy the lone-scoring option for the final five minutes of the half, the Lakers received inspired play from reserves Mitch Kupchak, Michael Cooper and Bob McAdoo. Together they compensated for the absence of two future Hall of Famers with hunger, hustle and heart.

"Big Game James" took care of the offense. By scoring fifteen of his 28 points in the first half, Worthy and the Lakers' bench kept the Celtics at bay; thus turning the foul trouble into a blessing in disguise.

The score was tied at 55 at halftime, and Kareem and Magic were rested and ready for the second half. Meanwhile, the Celtics, rotating only seven players in the first half, were slowly showing signs of fatigue.

Keep the pressure on, and don't look back, I thought during intermission. *Keep the pressure on, and they'll crack.*

This time has to be different.

It just has to be.

The third quarter began with Magic Johnson moving across the midcourt stripe. Veering to the right baseline with his dribble, he spotted Kareem cutting to the Celtic basket. With pinpoint precision, he fired a pass between Larry Bird and Robert Parish.

Kareem slammed the ball home.

And with that dunk came an unfamiliar level of intensity from the Lakers; one that was higher than at any point in its nine championship battles with Boston. Picking the Celtics apart like surgeons with *their* half-court offense, they had the Boston Garden crowd sitting on their hands as they bombarded the home team with its versatility.

Kareem, playing with a youthful zest, hit skyhooks. Worthy continued to balance the scoring load, Byron Scott knocked down jump shots, and Magic Johnson, at times running a controlled break, threaded the needle with his laser passes. And all of them played suffocating defense. Forcing the Celtics into horrendous shooting—they began the series by shooting a record 60.8 percent from the field in Game 2. They ended it with a miserable 38.5 percent effort in Game 6—their united front had the whole apartment cheering as the Lakers took an 82-73 lead into the final quarter.

Rushing into my bedroom all excited was my younger brother Gerald, now eleven years old.

"We're going to do it!" he screamed twice.

Remembering championships in the past seemingly won only to be lost while refusing his hopeful ladle, I chose not to sip the juice from the wells of victory just yet.

Meeting his energy with a controlled tone, he could see that I was struggling when I said, "Twelve more minutes."

Twelve more minutes were all that remained, and an enduring sensation of pain for millions would be washed away by sweet redemption. Twelve minutes before the ghosts of Celtics past and those relentless nightmares of Cousy, Hondo, Russell and Bird would be replaced by the dawning of a new day; one filled with the peace of knowing *the fact* would be gone forever, and those damn ghosts would go on with their lives.

"Twelve more minutes," I repeated quietly.

At the doorway watching this exchange was my mother. Watching my reaction carefully, seeing me lower my head in an effort to conceal deep emotions, "Let him watch the game alone," she said to Gerald.

Mothers know their children.

Closing the door to my room, everyone in the house left me alone again.

Twelve more minutes of fighting those demons of defeat with my Lakers.

Continuing their execution in their personal lion's den, the Lakers had the Garden in an uproar. Desperately chanting, "Larry! Larry! Larry!" they pleaded to their green-sneakered god, Larry Bird, for a lifeline to a seventh game.

"Larry Legend," the savior who thrived in moments like this, was slumping, so the ghosts of Celtics continued supplying Kevin McHale in his place. In an indomitable, indefatigable performance—42 minutes, 32 points, 16 rebounds—he was devastatingly efficient. In many other years, he would have been the most valuable player in the playoff finals; especially since his excellence helped the Celtics cut the Lakers lead to four, 86-82, with 8:45 to go.

Again, the will of the Lakers' franchise was being tested.

And again they responded, opening the lead immediately to ten, 92-82.

Soon, with five minutes and twenty seconds left, the Celtics again closed the deficit to six, 94-88.

The Celtic crowd, sensing another charge, began cheering wildly as the Lakers brought the ball across midcourt. Overhead, the banners of Celtic greats recited a familiar mantra with the greatest urgency of their dominance. Desperately trying to avoid the unusual sight of the visiting team celebrating on the parquet floor, *the Lakers have never beaten the Celtics*, they chanted, hoping to accomplish what they had done so many times before.

The chant from those ghosts was silenced when McHale clipped Kurt Rambis as the Lakers' lunch-pail forward went up for a shot.

"He fouled out!" I yelled.

Those were the first words I uttered during the entire game.

The foul was McHale's sixth, which meant he would be an unwilling spectator the rest of the way.

For the first time in over a year, I cracked a smile when watching NBA basketball.

The ghosts of Celtics past had been harpooned.

The Minneapolis/Los Angeles Lakers, a franchise that had enough of the Celtic Mystique, saw the green blood on the parquet floor and went for the kill.

After a Bird drive reduced the Lakers' lead to five, 95-90 with 4:54 showing, Michael Cooper hit two free throws to extend the bulge to seven. Then Bird missed a three-pointer, and Magic Johnson scored on a drive to make it 99-90 with 4:23 left.

Robert Parish interrupted the Lakers' flow with a basket, and after Bird missed another three-pointer, Byron Scott hit two free throws, and Magic, a stronger person than a year earlier, finally converted another Celtic miss into two more.

It was 103-92, Lakers, with three minutes to play.

The CBS cameras scanned the Boston Celtic bench, and the look on their faces told a story words couldn't capture.

They knew what I knew.

The Boston Garden crowd knew as well. The same crowd that had mocked, jostled and disrespected the Lakers the year before, as well as so many others since 1959, was so quiet that you could actually hear the squeak of players' sneakers against the hardwood floor.

"Oh yeah!" someone yelled into the silence.

Clenching a fist, I punched the air.

"Yes!" I screamed.

It was a scream for Elgin Baylor, who never beat those damned Celtics.

It was a scream for Jerry West, who endured so much pain at the hands of Boston that he gained the sympathy of Bill Russell and John Havlicek.

It was a scream for Wilt Chamberlain, who had been called a "selfish quitter" by cynics who romanticized about Celtics pride.

And it was a scream for Doc Kerlan, the Lakers' team physician since they'd come to Los Angeles in 1960; as well as Chick Hearn, the broadcaster who had the misfortune of calling all those Boston victories.

The Los Angeles Lakers had pride too, but one fact had blinded everyone.

The Lakers had never beaten the Celtics.

Until now.

Fittingly, Kareem Abdul-Jabbar, their captain and the man most humiliated by his performance in L.A.'s 148-114 Game 1 loss, closed the door once and for all over a fact that tortured, tormented and terrorized an entire organization for a quarter-century. Scoring 18 of his team-high 29 points in the second half, the final six from the 1985 NBA Championship Series Most Valuable Player were like nails being hammered in a coffin.

A skyhook at the 2:30 mark made it 105-94, Lakers.

Catching a Magic Johnson pass at the two-minute mark, he slammed home two more.

107-97, Lakers.

Byron Scott, in his second year, raised his fists in the air in salute to a king as Abdul-Jabbar passed him by. After another Celtic miss, with a minute left, he took another skyhook from 20 feet out.

Cutting through the quiet Garden air, the shot hit nothing but net.

Seeing Abdul-Jabbar running up the court with fists in the air in victory got to me. Unable to control the tears streaming down my teenage cheeks, I thought of the past year. Like the Lakers, I was humiliated and had been redeemed. The pain of former hurts, things I read over the years about my favorite basketball team, and the abuse I took when sharing my passion for them, had been washed away by the joy of sweet victory.

Agony now transformed into ecstasy, I never felt more satisfied.

Then after fouling out with 14 seconds left, Kareem Abdul-Jabbar had a similar display of emotion. Knowing that the Lakers were assured of winning the title, Abdul-Jabbar raised his right index finger in the air and screamed.

In an instant, he was swarmed by teammates.

In that same instant, my mother came into my bedroom, and saw my joyful sobbing.

Fourteen seconds later, the scoreboard clock read zero.

On June 9, 1985, at precisely 3:34 p.m., Sunday Eastern Standard Time (12:34 p.m., L.A. time) in an antique sweatbox of an arena, a new history was created. The Los Angeles Lakers ended more than a quarter-century of frustration by defeating the Boston Celtics, 111-100.

Now I said at the beginning of this confession that I wouldn't refer to the old Yankee-Dodger analogy of the 1940s and '50s. I won't elaborate on all those heartbreaking Brooklyn losses in the World Series, or how the Dodgers finally won in 1955. But I will say this: I identify totally with legendary broadcaster Vin Scully. Scully, only twenty-eight at the time, had simple news to give to the long-suffering fans of Brooklyn at the conclusion of the 1955 World Series:

"Ladies and gentlemen, the Brooklyn Dodgers are champions of the world."

When asked why he couldn't say anything more dramatic, his response was "I couldn't. I was too overcome with emotion."

Fast-forward thirty years later, to the moment my mother came into the bedroom of our Staten Island project apartment to celebrate the greatest moment in the history of the Lakers' organization, and the banishment of *the fact* that was a psychological ape on the back of millions of fans all over.

Seeing my tears that day, she didn't say a word as she hugged me. But I did.

"Mission accomplished," I said through happy sniffles.

Mission accomplished. Call this weird motivation, but whenever I have herculean tasks before me, whenever I need to channel in and focus on an assignment from God, whenever I have to reach deep within for self-motivation, I think of the determination, drive, and then deliverance of those 1985 Lakers. There was no celebrating till the deed is performed, and on that journey to fulfillment you may go through trials and tribulation, as that team encountered trying to do what no team did before. Their walk through fire produced a gold trophy that washed away twenty years of ridicule, frustration and heartbreaking disappointment.

My trophy will be of a divine plan; as I long to hear God say, "Well done."

In his arms, I'll breathe easily, and in a humble tone, say… Mission accomplished.

ONE SEASON (IN PINSTRIPES):
THE REFERENCES

One of things I found compelling about writing *One Season (in Pinstripes)* is the fact that it rekindled my passion and love for sports. As a room full of sports magazines, videos and books kept me company throughout this journey, I realized that the sports story is some of the best writing out there. Dramatically dancing to a melody of metaphors, a reporter's command for history and current events was combined with convincing storytelling to produce something more than a simple reciting of the facts.

I truly believe that there are no coincidences in life. The reason why I ended up in the Legends Suite Club in the inaugural season of the new Yankee Stadium was that I was supposed to challenge myself as a writer. Creating fictional stories—telling lies, some have called it—can be an enjoyable journey. Witty dialogue, flowery words and carefully placed narrative can be fun. However, in my personal opinion, it pales in comparison to the incredible imagery captured by a writer's thrilling account of a moment in time that may have produced victory, defeat, or an unforgettable landmark in history.

The thing that makes fiction writing enjoyable is the fact that many readers want their stories to scream reality; something they can relate to. Writing sports is *real*. Providing me with a vehicle to connect with a world beyond fiction, sports writing took me inside myself in a whole different way. Over the years, I learned that sports allowed me to discover my body, and the emotions that it brought. As you have read, sports made me laugh, tore my heart in two, forced me to confront my enemies, and introduced me to friends and people that I never thought I'd meet in a million years. Sports showed me what I could and could not do, and expanded my limitations in a way that I never imagined.

Writing about sports presented a unique challenge for me, as it gave me an opportunity to better everything I do in terms of the craft. Because I had read so many sports writers throughout the years, I found it to be demanding or intimidating to live up to the intelligence of David Halberstam (summer of '49, October '64, *Playing For Keeps: Michael Jordan, and the World He Made*), William C. Rhoden (*Forty Million Dollar Slaves; Third and a Mile: The Trials and Triumphs of the Black Quarterback*) or David Maraniss (*When Pride Still Mattered: A Life Of Vince Lombardi*); the opinionated cleverness of Mike Lupica and Bill Madden; the articulate wit of Peter Vescey; and maintain a sense of self. I honestly don't think that any form of writing I take on will be as difficult as composing this real story. Sure, because I merely presented the facts as they played out was a tremendous advantage. But this one question—how do you keep reality fresh?—presented an imposing challenge. As a writer, the death knell to your creativity is having a reader get bored with the way you tell a story. I only hope and pray that readers, sportswriters and Yankees fans all don't get bored with this composition.

I had plenty of help telling this about the 2009 World Championship season of the New York Yankees, and through countless hours of research I've gotten acquainted with some of the best sports writing around through internet blogs, sports magazines and newspaper columns. So from the bottom of my heart I'd like to thank the following: Jack Curry and Tyler Kepner (*New York Times*); Mark Feinsand, Tim Smith, Bill Madden, Anthony McCarron and Mike Lupica (*New York Daily News*); Joel Sherman, Kevin Kernan and Mike Vaccaro (*New York Post*); Jerry Crasnick (ESPN.com); Bryan Hoch, Mike Bauman, Anthony Castrovince, Anthony DiComo,

Kelly Thesier, Lyle Spencer, Todd Zolecki and Ian Browne (MLB. com); Bob Ryan and Dan Shaugnessy (*Boston Globe*); the late Tex Maule, Joe Sheehan, Joe Popnanski, Lee Jenkins, Tom Verducci, Frank Deford, David Sabino and Ben Reiter (*Sports Illustrated*); Alex Sachare (NBA.com); Drew Sharp (*Detroit Free Press*) and Bob St. John (*Dallas Morning News*); and NFL FILMS.

I have to also thank all those who put up some fantastic videos on YouTube. You guys rekindled so many memories. Steve Sabol and NFL Films: God, I miss John Facenda, Harry Kalas and the old NFC Central. READJACK.COM—your site is amazing. I also want to thank anyone who writes about sports. I never knew it would be so much fun.

ACKNOWLEDGMENTS

SEPTEMBER 30, 2010

Faith is the substance of things hoped for, and the evidence in things not yet seen. —HEBREWS 11:1

A couple of times during the 2009 championship season of the New York Yankees, film director Spike Lee came into the men's restroom of the Legends Suite Club to ask me about that scripture. A Morehouse Man like my pastor, perhaps he too was a messenger from above. God Bless Him.

When reviewing my entire literary journey, I thank God for doing what He needs to do to bring out the very best in me. When composing my first novel, *Six Days In January*, I think of the many nights I spent sleeping on a cold office floor, daring to dream. Most of novel two, *There's Always A Reason*, was written while I was unemployed, trying to keep from losing everything I owned, something which eventually happened when I toured with the book. And the final months of research and writing *One Season (in Pinstripes)* were spent in a period of tremendous transition, one that I fought with My Father about until He made me look at the focus needed to complete the assignment at hand. And because I'm hard-headed, sometimes God has to kick over that glass I hold on to dearly to fill it up with Him.

Throughout all my struggles in pursuit of my endeavors, all the mistakes I made along the way because I felt unworthy of the gift He gave me, all those tears I have shed fighting His will for me when no one was around, the one thing I refuse to relinquish is my faith in God and His most precious gift to His children on Earth:

Love. He has, and always will, provide for me all that I need to glorify His name. And I only hope *One Season* reflects a blessing you receive when you are obedient to His will for you.

Heavenly Father, continue to use me with this gift I have yet to understand completely. I know at times you took things away when I became obsessed with accomplishment as opposed to the real author of my words, You. I will never make those mistakes again. You are my rock, my redeemer, my righteousness, and I only pray that I give you glory and honor in all that I do. Thank you so much, for blessing me with this gift to tell stories, both real and imagined.

Father, You have provided me with so many people that have supported and helped me along the way. (Please forgive me if it gets a little long-winded here, but that's how the God in me operates.)

To my Pastor, the Reverend Michael A. Walrond, Jr: I can't begin to thank you enough for what you did for me when you asked me to take care of FCBC (First Corinthian Baptist Church) for those three months. Not only did it bring me closer to God, it was the catalyst behind a dream come true. You are an amazing man, one who does it all with grace, humility, and love. May God continue to use you, so that I might learn more from His anointed on earth.

To our Executive Pastor, Reverend LaKeesha Walrond: The love that you share with Pastor is so beautiful. But more importantly, I love the cohesiveness/teamwork between you both, as well as your powerful sermons from God's heart. Bless you.

To our Youth Pastor, Tory Liferidge: Yes, I want to be a solution! Thank you so much for the tireless work you do with our youth, as well as your love for God.

Cheryl Faye Smith: To watch your transformation and love for God from both near and far has been an absolute blessing. At this time, we don't know whether we finish this journey together as one, or God will grant you a man that gives you the things I cannot supply at this present time. But one thing I am certain of is that only

God fully understands the depth of our bond, even when we, and others on the outside looking in, don't always understand His ways.

While my heart hurts because of what I don't understand—the pain that bubbled to the surface while completing this book made the task unbearable at times—know that I want nothing but the best for you. No matter where life takes us, know that I have never loved anyone the way I do you. No matter the proximity, know that you have meant everything to me here on earth.

To my family: Stephanie, Adrian, Jeffrey, Gerald and Janessa: Another one is on the bookshelves. Thank you guys for staying on this roller-coaster ride with me. Ma: No one said this journey of life would be easy, but I love it. However, I love you more for creating me. Grandma and Rufus: I love you guys so much. Pop: You know how we do.

Maranda: With all my heart, I apologize for all that I missed in pursuit of my passion. I know the disappointment you have often felt. But the lesson Daddy is teaching you is to never give up on your dreams, no matter how long and hard the struggles may be, no matter how lonely the road gets. Lean on God, and seek His wisdom before all others, and you'll avoid some of the mistakes I have made in my travels. You have made me so proud of you with all that you have accomplished.

Audrey Cooper: At times, I know it hasn't been easy on you doing the job alone. I never meant to put so much on you; I never knew how much sacrifice it took to make this writing thing come true. We both have paid some tremendous prices. But God couldn't have blessed our daughter with a more amazing mother. I thank you for all that you are doing.

Uncle Charles: It took me years to understand how Our Father is using you in the lives of others. Now, through my own connection with Christ, I get it. Thank you for always being there for me. I will obey.

To the Smith Family: Jackie, Mamie and Stephanie: I have loved each of you as if you were my own sisters. Douglas and Michael: You are the sons I never had, and I am so proud of your accomplishments. James Edward Smith, Jr: Thank you so much for your tough love. Growing up late in life is difficult, but feeding off of a man with your strength has been a great starting point. Thanks, man.

To my writing mentor, David McGoy: Did you ever think it would turn into all of this? I know I never did. Thank you for always being there for me with love, and never judging me when I fell. To the families of Allen Brown, Askia Farrell, Bobby Moore, Al Harrison, Daniel Marks and Melody Hawkins: I knew no other way to follow my dreams, and it has strained our relationships at times because I'm never around. But know that my love for each of you has never changed. I appreciate the village from afar and all that you've done for my daughter. Josephine Tucker: Thank you for fully understanding the depths of my journey.

To my brothers at FCBC: Lord knows, I haven't always been good at returning phone calls (I love you, Steve Clampton, Donovan Smith and Wynn Adams), but know that my heart is with you all. Keith Collins, Charles Powell, Rashii Moorehead, Jason Lumpkin, Roy Bernard, Steven Jones, Brother Bernard Greene, Gregory Spence, Douglas Adams, Todd Rivero, Adler Merveille, Darnell McLaurin, Jermaine Small and Melvin Pleasant: I love you brothers so much.

There are so many of you at FCBC whose names escape me—The Deacons, Trustees and Security Team comes to mind—who God has used to provide words of encouragement to my soul, know that all the love in my heart is in my Sunday embrace. I love all the brothers and sisters of our wonderful family.

To Arlene Shuler and Inez Simmons: I can't begin to tell you how much I appreciated you sisters during that maintenance stretch. Your selflessness and love for God shined through, and always gave me strength whenever I grew weary. I miss our group prayers.

Bishop Ronald Hobson: Thank you so much for reaching out and just talking to me, as well as teaching me to give honor and glory while in the fires life often brings. Continue to glorify God with your love and kindness.

To Margaret Ann Quinlan, General Manager of Legends Hospitality LLC: You are an amazing woman. It was really an honor keeping the Legends Suite Club clean for that magical year. From the bottom of my heart, I thank you for the experience of a lifetime. To Jim, Chris, Jeannie, Stephanie and Willie: It was an honor working with all of you. "Mugsy" has an excellent team behind her. To all the talented chefs, cooks, bussers, servers and order takers of Legends Hospitality LLC: So many of you kept my spirits up during those rare moments I thought of my responsibilities as thankless, and that meant more to me than you'll ever know. I love you guys so much. Elton Ottley, Michael McPartland, Josh Velez and Jeff Esteban: Continue to cherish the Stadium experience, and don't forget to share it with your grandkids years from now. You guys are the best. Spencer Sally and Torin Cotten: You guys are like family to me.

Kevin Michaels: Don't ever let that love for the Yankees die. I miss you, blood brother.

To Hank and Hal Steinbrenner, Brian Cashman, and many of the Yankees ownership I interacted with throughout the glorious 2009 campaign: I bought completely into the tradition that came with wearing the Yankee pinstripes, and had one of the most incredible experiences of my life. Thank you so much for making my dreams of being a "Yankee Batboy" come true. To Jennifer Reilly, Senior Director, Client Relations of the New York Yankees: It was truly an honor meeting you during that wonderful season. I appreciate your kindness through professionalism. To so many employees at the Stadium: security, merchants, vendors and fellow maintenance team: I love all of you so much!!! You guys were an important part of my dreams.

To Gary Green, Michael Rodriguez, Paula Collins, Isaac Del Rio and the Alliance/First Quality Maintenance Team: You guys gave me an opportunity at the Stadium, and for that, I'm so thankful. I had a lot of fun!!! To Angel Chavez, Sandy Perez, Patrick Paris, Chris Soto, Danny, Muhammad, and Reverend Tony: I miss the lunchtime walks to McDonald's, the drinks at the Yankee Tavern, and our crazy time together. Know that you guys will be in my heart always. Angel, remember your name. That's what you are. That's who you are. Sandy Hazeltine: Thank you for being there for me. I needed a special friend to help me through. God Bless you. Ed Healy: You are the greatest!!!

Throughout the 2009 season, so many Yankees season-ticket holders and guests touched my soul, and it would take another book to thank you all. But I couldn't let this opportunity go by without expressing my appreciation for the following: Harry Belafonte (you see, I didn't settle; I love you, man), Former New York City Mayor Rudy Giuliani (you're the best, man), Keith Olbermann, Mitch Modell, CEO of Modell's Sporting Goods (I used all those gift cards—smile), Bob Costas, Paul Simon, Brian Williams, HBO's Ross Greenburg, Jay-Z, Fat Joe, Taye Diggs, Christopher Gardner, the family of Barry "Rock Of Ages" Habib (Barry, I miss my big hugs), Roy and James Judelson (James, remember what I said about cherishing that magical 2009 season. What you experienced doesn't happen every year. Roy...Thanks, man) Michael and Danny Weinberger (I miss you guys so much), Joel "Super Joe" Oks (say hi to "Super Irv" for me), Tiernan Kundla, Anthony Rhodes, William F. Ramonas (I must come down to see Villanova play), Mitchell S. Kaneff, Dr. Thomas M. Haveron, Edward (Smiley) Echavarria, Richard Goldstein, Harold Peguero and Jeffrey R. Wallner. There are so many others who showed me so much love: students and families that shared birthdays and school stories; CEOs and their important business triumphs. You can't possibly imagine how much your trust and support meant to me. God Bless You All. Rick: What you did for me was incredible. I'll never forget your kindness.

To Skip Bayless: Don't hate on the Pinstripes, dude. Congratulate. Can't wait to do a First and 10 segment with you. You'd lose, Skip. To the blog/sports columnists/beat writers for MLB.com, *Sports Illustrated*, ESPN.com, *The New York Daily News*, *New York Post*, *The Boston Globe*, *Dallas Morning News* and many periodicals throughout the United States: Thank you for helping me tell my story. Your articles provided me with so much research material that I only hope I did you all proud with the way I intertwined sports history with everyday life.

To Joe Bastone, owner of the Yankee Tavern: You are the best. I had so much fun in your establishment. To John, Willie and so many of my favorite bartenders, Phil Dussek and all my fellow "Tavernites" who watched me dance and have good clean fun letting off steam: God Bless You All.

Brandon Fay and the Trattoria Dell'arte staff: Thank you so much for making my 2009 Holiday Season a very special experience.

To the usual suspects: Steven McGoy, Christian Davis, Tad and Stacey Spencer, Darren McCalla, Matthew Fudge, Alvin Alexander Lloyd, S.B. Redd, Theodosia Barriero, Brian (B.K.) Simpson, Hector and Martha Gonzalez, John Fleming, Dennis Farrell, Marc Piovanetti (I told you Seyfarth would hire you), Anthony Lopez, Michael "R.D." Cooper, Nashaun Pass, Carlton Watler, Icsom Jones, James Bethea, Jesus Hernandez, Belinda Ramos, Bergie Pietro, Ana Marrero, Gail and Lisa Carr: Thank you so much for your never-ending support.

To my screenwriting partner, James Patterson: You mean the world to me. The mistake I made in referring to you as the author of the Alex Cross series was one of the best errors of my life, for God introduced me to another big brother. We have so much work to do, and we will get it done. God told me so.

To Stuart Williams, Frederick Izzard, Michael Bryant Garland and Jewel Steambridge: When I came to the Academy Hotel to live during my transition, there were times I needed a hug, words of encouragement, or even a meal when I had no money. I will never forget how each of you placed me in your hearts in your own unique ways. God bless all of you.

To the many readers and bookclubs that have supported my fiction novels: Tee C. Royal and RAWSISTAZ, The United Sisters Bookclub (Brooklyn, N.Y.), Judi Belle Raines and the Sugar and Spice Bookclub (Jamaica, N.Y.), Michelle Carswell and the Turning Pages Book Club (Upper Marlboro, Maryland), Peace in Pages Bookclub (Upper Marlboro, Maryland), Carolyn Towles and The Buy The Book Club (New Haven, Connecticut) and Adrienne Dortche and the Black Women Who Read Book Club (New Haven, Connecticut): May God continue to bless you ladies with the continued joy of reading. I am so grateful that so many of you have enjoyed my books. If you're not a sports fan, please give the men in your lives a copy of this book.

Knowledge Bookstore (Brampton, Ontario): I hope you enjoy this one as much as my fiction novels. Your love from up north means more than you'll ever know. Sean and Michelle Liburd, know that I love you guys so much! Neil Armstrong: I miss your kind insight more than you'll ever know.

Kimberly Floyd: In hindsight, I appreciate what you tried to show me; things I wasn't ready for in my growth as a man until God forced me to look at myself. Thank you for being there and loving me in spite of my confusion. Jan Forney and Alicia Clarke: Thanks so much for forgiving me for my growing pains. Tracy Grant and Vincent Alexandria: Thank you, guys, for just loving me for me. It means so much. Mrs. Audra Wooten: Did you ever think that you were at the origin of my writing madness? I appreciate you, after all these years.

Zane and Charmaine: I am here, because you are there. Jessica Tilles: The word "friend" doesn't adequately describe what you mean to me, as I am so glad that God has placed you in my life for so many incredible reasons that I can't count them all. You are an amazing spirit, a righteous queen that deserves the best in life and love. Elissa Gabrielle: We have yet to meet, but I know you through your giving heart. It's truly an honor. Thank you. Nathasha Brooks-Harris: You were a vehicle used to bring me closer to Him. I can't thank you enough for your shelter and friendship during some grinding times. Donna Hill and Bernice L. McFadden: You ladies were so right when you preached "change" to me. Robin L. Anderson: You mean the world to me. That long talk in the park meant more than you can ever imagine, as well your loving spirit of strength. Thank you much for nursing me to health with your love. God Bless You. Dr. Tracy G. Brown: When the storm clouds gathered once more, you provided comfort, wisdom and a listening ear. I love you so much for your patience, wisdom, understanding, blunt honesty, and…(smile). God Bless you for our unique relationship.

A 3,100-word acknowledgment section. As usual, I thought it would be brief, but so many have touched my life on this journey through life and the written word. And while I haven't listed every-one, please know that those I may have forgotten are near in my soul.

Before I go, I want to make reference to Vince Lombardi and his reasoning behind his unforgettable accomplishments with the Green Bay Packers; something that brings the meaning behind this sports book, the trials of real life that we encounter daily during these social, emotional and economically grinding times, and God's most precious gift to us altogether. He indicated that in order for him and his team to go through the mental anguish that comes with playing football, in order for them to endure the emotionalism and give everything of themselves to each other sans expectation or remuneration, there has to be LOVE for that person or teammate within the confines of the sport.

LOVE.

LOVE, people.

As with everything in life, all you need is LOVE.

A little LOVE is all it takes.

Still.

A little LOVE for each other is all we need.

Still.

When we show LOVE, then we connect with the God that's in all of us.

For God is LOVE, and if we are created in his likeness, we are LOVE as well.

May God be with all of you on your journey through this amazing thing called life.

And His most precious gift to us all, LOVE, follow closely behind.

Peace.

William Fredrick Cooper

ABOUT THE AUTHOR

William Fredrick Cooper was born in Brooklyn, reared on Staten Island, and presently resides in Jersey City, New Jersey. The proud father of a lovely daughter named Maranda, Mr. Cooper is an active member of First Corinthian Baptist Church in Harlem, New York, and the acting secretary of Brother 2 Brother Symposium, Inc., a program that encourages black men and young adults to read fiction literature. (http://www.b2bls.com)

Not only is Mr. Cooper known for his enlightening radio interviews throughout the United States and Canada, he has served as host, executive producer, guest speaker and moderator/facilitator of numerous literary events, which includes an annual appearance at the University of Maryland, College Park African-American Literary Conference; the 2004 Harlem Book Fair; the 2004 Disilgold Unity Literary Awards Show; the 2004 Bring Your Book To Life Seminar/ Music concert in Philadelphia, Pennsylvania; and the 2006 Erotica Lounge and Lingerie show in conjunction with the African American Literary and Media Group Seminar, held in Reno, Nevada.

His first novel, *Six Days In January*, was published in February 2004 by Strebor Books, an imprint of Simon and Schuster. A ground-breaking piece of literature that explores the heart of an African-American man damaged by love, the novel received rave reviews in major periodicals in the United States, Canada, Bermuda and the United Kingdom.

In July 2006, Mr. Cooper appeared in a feature article in the July issue of *Ebony* magazine, "After The Breakup: Get Over it and Get On With Your Life."

His second novel, *There's Always A Reason*, was featured in the March

2007 issue of *Ebony* magazine and was chosen as a Main Selection for the Black Expressions Book Club in April 2007. Positioned on the Black Expressions Book Club best-seller list in August 2007, the *Essence* magazine best-seller in April 2008 and described by many in the African-American community as a message-delivering emotional masterpiece, *There's Always A Reason* was nominated for an African-American Literary Award in September 2007, a finalist for a 2008 NAACP Image Award Nomination in the Outstanding Literary Work Fiction category, and the recipient of four 2008 Infini Literary Awards, including Book of the Year.

Mr. Cooper is a contributing author to several anthologies. "Legal Days, Lonely Nights" appeared in Zane's *Sistergirls.com;* "Watering Cherry's Garden" was written for *Twilight Moods—African American Erotica;* "Snowy Moonlit Evenings" was composed for *Journey to Timbooktu*, a collection of poetry and prose as compiled by Memphis Vaughn; and "More and More" and "Sweet Dreams" were included in *Morning, Noon and Night: Can't Get Enough*, a collection of erotic fiction. "Te Deseo" was a contribution to Zane's *New York Times* bestselling anthology *Caramel Flava*, published by Simon and Schuster in August 2006. "Dear Zane: A Lust Letter From A Fan" appeared as an extra piece in the Zane non-fiction book, *Dear G-Spot: Straight Talk about Sex And Love*, released by Atria Books in July 2007. "No One Has To Know," an erotic duet with Jessica Tilles, appeared in *Erogenous Zone: A Sexual Voyage* in August 2007. "No Regrets," a candid story about Mr. Cooper's literary journey, appears in the African American Literary Award winning anthology, *Soul Of A Man: Triumph Of My Soul*, published by Peace In The Storm Publishing in June 2009.

He is working on his next novel, *Love Is All You Need*.

Mr. Cooper can be reached at www.myspace.com/wfcooper, www.facebook.com/wfcooper, as well as his email address: areason006@yahoo.com.